The Exotic Pla

Happy Xmas 2007
And a Merry New Year 2098!

love
Mark x.

The Exotic Plant

A History of
the Moravian Church in Britain,
1742–2000

Geoffrey Stead

Margaret Stead

EPWORTH PRESS

Copyright © Geoffrey Stead and Margaret Stead 2003

British Library Cataloguing in Publication data

A catalogue record for this book is available
from the British Library

0 7162 0573 4

First published 2003
by Epworth Press
4 John Wesley Road
Werrington
Peterborough PE4 6ZP

Typeset by Regent Typesetting, London
Printed and bound by
Biddles Ltd, www.biddles.co.uk

For Chrissie and Janet
and in memory of Sr Dorothy Swithenbank, a true Moravian

Contents

Foreword

It is a double pleasure to have the opportunity to commend Dr Geoffrey and Dr Margaret Stead's *Exotic Plant*. Twenty years ago in the dark days of the DDR when I was working in the Archives at Herrnhut, local people, discovering who I was would say, 'English Methodist, eh! John Wesley was a friend of the Moravians'; to which I could only reply, 'Well, sometimes he was!' But now a Methodist press has made it possible for this history of British Moravianism to appear as part of the celebrations of the tercentenary of Wesley's birth, a small token of acknowledgement of the endless kindnesses which the Steads and I and other British scholars have received from Moravians here and in Germany. More to the point, they have made available for everyone a work of scholarship which has no competitors in its field, and which successfully elucidates from British and exotic history what was peculiar to the Moravian Church in Great Britain. It is a bold work, venturing upon social history, theology, liturgy, hymnody and schools, but in all of them the Steads have findings to report which are of interest not just to Moravians, but to anyone with an interest in policy in the field of religion. They lay a huge range of library and archival work under contribution in lucid prose, modestly concealing their learning. I wish the book every success.

W. R. Ward

Preface

To Moravians and those outside the church who know it well, the title of our book may come as a surprise, since present congregations of the British Province of the Moravian Church appear to function in much the same way as those of other Nonconformist denominations. There is little outward difference in religious belief: although the Moravians have usages which include lovefeasts and the Easter morning graveyard service, these tend to be regarded by outsiders as minor variations from current Nonconformist practice. Yet appearances are deceptive; in reality they are surviving remnants of an elegant and elaborate eighteenth-century religious style emanating from a dominant German centre in Central Europe towards which the earliest British Moravians were drawn, and as such recall for present-day members the period of intense spirituality which saw the beginning of their church in its present form.

The eighteenth-century Moravian Church, otherwise known as the Unity of the Brethren, originated at Herrnhut in Saxony in 1722, as a result of the enthusiasm of a small group of Protestant religious exiles with a strong sense of identity and an urge to recreate the pre-Reformation Unity of the Brethren from which they were descended. Under the leadership and patronage of Count Zinzendorf, this community developed as an exceptionally vigorous and expansive lay evangelistic branch of contemporary Lutheranism. Later, using an episcopal succession derived from its fifteenth-century Bohemian predecessor, it took its place as a separate, centralized and primarily German-speaking denomination with the same name and a tradition of continuity. It spread rapidly in Central Europe, forming a number of congregations and an extensive network, or diaspora, of associated religious societies with a passion for evangelism and the establishment of missions.

Britain, geographically on the periphery of this area of activity, was included in its sphere of influence by the 1740s, but the British Province, though originally like its continental parent, developed differently, becoming a less fervent, Anglo-German organization more akin to the indigenous Nonconformist denominations. Despite these changes there have always been strong cultural and personal bonds between the British and Continental provinces, so that this close relationship and its progressive development are central to an understanding of the history of the British Province. On the other hand, the experience of being an English-speaking national institution within the German-centred Unity has led to recurrent crises of loyalty. These have been most severe in response to wider political and social developments in Europe, particularly those occurring during the first half of the twentieth century, the 'German century', when tremendous violence was meted out by and visited upon that country.

Present-day Moravian worship and the wider activity of the church thus retain features which can be understood only by examining their original forms, the appeal of these to early converts, and the spiritual dynamic which led the eighteenth-century Unity to establish and nurture its British mission. For this reason, in addition to our survey of the history of the province and its characteristic institutions, we have analysed in some detail the distinctively German religious and cultural elements in the original tradition, which we define as 'Moravianism', particularly its musical and linguistic forms, its educational principles, and the intricate network by which its members kept in touch across the globe. Without a study of these aspects of the church as a whole, it would be difficult to appreciate the survivals of the eighteenth-century tradition which still draw its members together.

Moravian theology as expressed by Zinzendorf has been presented here in a simplified form as his personal interpretation of Protestantism. This is because his views, expressed at length and with an intricacy for which he has become famous, have already generated a vast amount of scholarship, continue to do so, and are outside the scope of this book. One recent distinguished contribution has been made by the Moravian Bishop, Arthur J. Freeman, in *An Ecumenical Theology of the Heart: The Theology of Count Nicholas Ludwig von Zinzendorf* (Bethlehem, Pa., 1998). Similarly, we have not been able to include more than a passing reference to the influence of the Brotherhood on such outstanding German thinkers as Friedrich Schleiermacher. For this we must refer the reader to the helpful study of James D. Nelson, in his Chicago University 1963 doctoral thesis, 'Herrnhut: Friedrich Schleiermacher's Spiritual Home'.

Since a single-volume history must be selective, we have emphasized context, continuity and change as keys to an understanding of the origins and subsequent development of the British Province. This means that some aspects of provincial life have been unavoidably under-represented, especially those which were not central to the original German model, with its emphasis on the spiritual rebirth of adults and their formation into like-minded groups for the support of existing denominations. As a result, the development of the province's Sunday and day schools, and youth work in Britain, though still largely unresearched, are not explored here in depth, since they were a feature of all denominational provisions at about the same time, and were much the same wherever they were carried on. This is true, also, of Moravian boarding schools, which have already been studied by other historians. They had an important role in the nineteenth century, but do not appear to have differed in any fundamental sense from those run by the Anglicans, as well as the Methodists, Quakers and other Nonconformists, which were equally committed to providing private Christian education for the children of fee-paying non-members. Two establishments survive and remain well-known to the wider public – Fulneck School, in Yorkshire, now coeducational, and the girls' school at Ockbrook in Derbyshire.

Missions are referred to very briefly. This is mainly because the British contribution to them in manpower was small until immediately after the First World War, when continental provincial missionaries, mostly German, were debarred from many areas where they had formerly been active. Consequently it was only then that a relatively large proportion of British ordained men began to be called to the mission fields. Further research into the post-1919 British provincial contribution to foreign missions is clearly needed, but a separate volume would be necessary to do justice to this important subject.

It would have been impracticable in a history covering two and a half centuries to write a comprehensive account of individual congregations and the highlights of their achievements, or, with some notable exceptions, to describe the important contribution to provincial life of outstanding members, particularly those in senior positions in the church. We have resisted the temptation to explore many fascinating by-ways, such as the story of the ministerial dynasties to which the British Province has owed and continues to owe so much. All these subjects remain as a rich field for future exploration, particularly at the local level. Ours is a more limited study of provincial evolution as a whole, which we hope will go some way towards explaining why and how such a distinctive denomination originated and survived, and will show that present members of its British province can be proud to regard themselves as guardians of this exotic plant.

Acknowledgements

This book is in every sense a joint enterprise on the part of its two authors. Geoffrey's work on the history of the Moravian Church began as an M.A. dissertation and was continued as a Ph.D. thesis, the regional aspects of which were published by the Thoresby Society in 1998 under the title *The Moravian Settlement at Fulneck 1742–1790*. Although our academic interests followed different paths for a number of years, we were both fascinated by the Moravian Church and Moravianism and discussed its every aspect; when the opportunity arose it seemed inevitable that we should collaborate on this book.

We are grateful to the Provincial Board of the Moravian Church for inviting Geoffrey to write a history of the British Province and later agreeing to accept Margaret as co-author. We have enjoyed their unstinting support during the five years of research and writing, and have particularly appreciated the freedom to stay in the Mission flat at Church House, with open access to the provincial library and archive there. Without the support of Bishop John McOwat, Bishop Geoffrey Birtill, Sr Jackie Morten and other members of the Board in this respect the research would have been much more arduous. We also thank Revd Fred Linyard and Bishop Joe Cooper, who read and commented on the text on behalf of the Board.

Many other Moravian ministers and church members have been most helpful and generous in providing access to local archives and hospitality in their homes. We particularly thank Revd David Dickinson for making the rich resource of the Fulneck congregational archive equally freely available, similarly Revd Hilary Smith at Ockbrook, Revd David Newman and Sr Margaret Geddes at Fairfield and Revd Victor and Sr Sylvia Launder at Gracehill, where Sr Edna Cooper and Sr Roberta Thompson also provided valuable guidance and information concerning local material. Our thanks go, too, to the members of Hornsey Moravian Church and its minister, Revd Joachim Kreuzel. The Men's Fellowship, in particular, made us very welcome and spoke freely of their experiences on coming to Britain from the West Indies and settling in London, giving us valuable insights into the problems of coming as strangers to a new country. We appreciate the help given by Sr Olive Linyard in augmenting the archival records of the Moravian Women's Association by providing access to papers written for their fiftieth anniversary celebrations. Thanks are due, also, to other serving and retired ministers who have shared their memories of ministerial training, and to members of the non-stipendiary ministry who have contributed helpfully to our understanding of their congregational role.

It would have been impossible to write this book without extensive reading in university libraries, with their substantial resources of scholarship relevant to our subject. We are indebted to librarians and archivists who have welcomed our special enquiries in the course of research, in the Brotherton Library of Leeds University, in Cambridge University Library, particularly the Rare Books Room, in the John Rylands Library, Manchester, and in the British Library. We are grateful to Revd Tom Minor, former Librarian of Moravian College, Bethlehem, Pennsylvania, who introduced us to American scholars and helped us to locate several seminal studies; thanks are due, also, to Dr Vernon Nelson, archivist of the Provincial Archive in Bethlehem. Our early research in the Unity archive at Herrnhut was facilitated by Sr Ingeborg Baldauf, the former archivist there, who was generous with her time on our behalf and later sent us photocopies of important documents.

Throughout the project we have received valuable support from Dr David Steele, whose enthusiasm for the Moravian Church was awakened when, as a senior tutor in the History Department of Leeds University, he supervised Geoffrey's thesis. His comments on the text have provided a salutary perspective on some of our idiosyncrasies. We are particularly grateful to Professor W. Reginald Ward, Emeritus Professor of Modern History at the University of Durham, who agreed to read our work in progress, and the final text, and has written the Foreword. He has been generous in his advice concerning the wider European context of Moravian study and has made helpful comments on the work as a whole. We have profited immensely from the expertise of both these scholars and from the encouragement they have given us on the way.

Revd Gerald Burt, Editorial Secretary of Epworth Press, has guided us through the preparatory work for publication with kindness and consideration, giving us a real sense of participation in the process. Dr Anna Hardman of SCM-Canterbury Press has provided welcome practical advice, and we have appreciated the care and thoroughness with which

David Sanders, our copy-editor, has assisted us in the final preparation of the manuscript.

Our greatest debt is to each other, for the joy of working together and the sense of adventure and fulfilment which this shared endeavour has brought.

Abbreviations

Add. MSS	British Library Additional Manuscripts
BL	British Library
CUL	Cambridge University Library
FA	Archive of Fulneck Moravian Church, West Yorkshire
FCD	Fulneck Congregation Diary
FLCD	Congregational Diary of Fetter Lane Church, London
GA	Archive of Gracehill Moravian Church, Northern Ireland
JRUL	John Rylands University Library, Manchester
MCH	Archive and Library of Moravian Church House, Muswell Hill, London
MPB	Minutes of the Provincial Board
MPC	Minutes of the Provincial Conference
MWA	Moravian Women's Auxiliary/ Moravian Women's Association
OCA	Ockbrook Church Archive
OCD	Ockbrook Congregation Diary
OCCT	*Oxford Companion to Christian Thought*, ed. A. Hastings, et al.
PB	Provincial Board of the Moravian Church
PC	Place Congregation
PEC	Provincial Elders' Conference
PHD	Pilgrim House Diary – account of daily activities of Zinzendorf and his colleagues when in Britain
TC	Town Congregation
UAH	Unity Archive, Herrnhut

Introduction

Since the late nineteenth century the British Province of the Moravian Church has been aware of the need for a provincial history highlighting its own development while retaining a due acknowledgement of its position in the Unity as a whole. This is a difficult undertaking for several reasons, not the least of which is the uneven quantity and quality of original source material. The province was defined, its avowed objectives and methods laid down, and its congregational network instituted in this country, during the middle decades of the eighteenth century in a short-lived flurry of evangelistic activity, providing an exceptionally rich archive which has engaged the interest of historians and church members alike as a remarkable illustration of the power of organized artisans under aristocratic leadership. Later, from the 1780s onwards throughout the nineteenth and early twentieth centuries, the initial dynamic having been irretrievably lost, any changes were not only slow, but seriously under-recorded. In contrast, the province has undergone rapid and better-recorded changes since the Second World War, so that the events of the last sixty years provide the historian with the new challenge of making appropriate selections and a balanced interpretation in the context of a continuing decline in communicant membership.

The underlying pattern of provincial history is relatively simple. A powerful spirituality, conveyed in the 1740s by the German founders and their early converts, gave way to something which, while not tepid, operated at a much lower spiritual temperature with little appeal to outsiders. This is well illustrated by the accompanying statistical table which is a stark reminder that, despite the brief early Moravian successes, it was to the followers of Wesley that most of the religiously inclined English turned to find an alternative to the Anglicans.

Although in this context the congregational numbers of the Moravians are statistically irrelevant, they are associated with a religious tradition which, having gained a foothold from Germany, has survived despite the difficulty of retaining its unique identity while adapting to the pressures of British religious conventions. This in itself is no mean achievement, but its struggle for survival has been exacerbated in recent times by the problem which it shares with all the mainstream denominations, that of diminishing support for organized religion, so that at the beginning of the twenty-first century it does not have sufficient numbers to absorb the loss of its older members, and function, without gaining substantially more support from succeeding generations. With a membership, including those already worshipping with the United Reformed Church, perilously close to 2,000 and still falling, the British Province is already facing increasingly difficult decisions about its future.

Table 1. Communicant Membership of the British Province of the Moravian Church in comparison with the Anglicans and Methodists from the mid-eighteenth century to the end of the twentieth century.

Date	Anglican	Methodist*	Moravian
1750+		(1767) 25,911	(1753) c.1,000
1800	577,000	115,860	2,596
1850	953,000	534,212	2,865
1900	2,089,000	798,151	3,364
1950	2,077,000	776,748	3,040
1975	2,297,571	596,406	2,660
1992	1,808,174	458,773	(1998) 2,073

*The figures include Wesleyan Methodists, Primitive Methodists, Methodist New Connection, Wesleyan Methodist Association and United Methodist Free Churches as appropriate.

Sources: Anglican and Methodist. The estimates for 1800, 1850 and 1900 are from R. Currie, A. Gilbert and L. Horsley, *Churches and Churchgoers: Patterns of Church Growth in the British Isles since 1700* (Oxford: Clarendon Press, 1977), pp. 25 and 139–44 respectively. The Anglican figures from Currie et al. are based on the number of Easter Day communicants of the Church of England, the Church in Wales and the Episcopal Church in Scotland. The figures for 1975 and 1992 are from G. Davie, *Religion in Britain since 1945* (Oxford: Blackwell, 1997), p. 46.
Moravian figures are from Synodal statistical tables, with the exception of the 1753 estimate, which is from C. Podmore, *The Moravian Church in England, 1728–1760* (Oxford: Oxford University Press, 1998), p. 120.

Two other problems must be addressed in writing a provincial history. The first is that most previous English Moravian historians have written from inside the Church. They have subsumed provincial considerations within those of the Unity as a whole, giving disproportionate attention to one particular interpretation of its past which originated and was propagated in its early years for reasons which were important at the time, emphasizing the Czech element in its origins. This book does not deny the factual basis used to justify such an interpretation, but rather suggests that the emphasis placed on it in successive studies has narrowed the perspective from which the Church's achievements should rightly have been evaluated, and has undervalued major aspects of its rich inheritance. The book offers a different interpretation by presenting a wider view of events, giving greater weight to the eighteenth-century Brotherhood as an international movement in the almost exclusive context of German history. This enables the nature of the British Province and the significance of what has happened in it during the last two and a half centuries to be better understood, for it has continued to value those German elements which distinguish it from other religious bodies with a broadly similar evangelical tradition, but by coming to resemble them in many other respects, it has made a valuable contribution to the rich variety of British Nonconformity.

The second problem is a consequence of the first. By concentrating on the Unity as a whole, these writers have unintentionally fostered widespread misunderstanding of the role of the British Province within it by implying that Unity and provincial achievement are synonymous. Grounds for this view certainly existed during Zinzendorf's lifetime, but afterwards became progressively remote from reality. In drawing attention to this disparity the intention here is not to denigrate provincial achievement, but to reassess it in accordance with archival evidence rather than sentiment.

Use of the terms 'Moravian', 'German' and 'Renewed Unity of the Brethren'

The exclusive use of the name 'Moravian' instead of 'Unity of the Brethren', or 'Brethren' to define the British Province of the Church was decided upon as late as 1908 at the Dukinfield Synod, a change illustrated by the renaming of the provincial hymnal. The 1902 edition, like its predecessors since the eighteenth century, had referred to 'The Unity of the Brethren'; the 1912 edition referred to 'The Moravian Church'. Such a change implied historic religious connections with the Czech geographical entity of Moravia; but early twentieth-century Czechs living in Moravia gave their allegiance to Rome as they had done for centuries, regarding themselves as members of the international Roman Catholic Church.

In fact, reasons for the change were those of usage. The term

'Moravian' as used within the Unity was based on an original practice of Count Zinzendorf appropriate to the circumstances and needs of the 1720s, and was an alternative name used in the province by Brethren and others from the early years. As leader of the original community at Herrnhut in Saxony, which included Moravian descendants of the old Bohemian Unity who were conscious of their past traditions, Zinzendorf adopted the term to describe the group collectively and to use their valid credentials as descendants of an ancient episcopal Church,[1] particularly in official correspondence. An example of his use of the term occurs in a letter written from Marienborn in December 1746 to an unnamed ordained British correspondent, where Zinzendorf confirmed that the Brethren did not intend to proselytize. He claimed, 'The Moravian Brethren shall never receive any member of the Church of England in their Body . . . because it would favour schism,' but suggested that it would be ideal, 'that our Brethren may have a Place of public worship in London known to be a Moravian Episcopal Chappel'.[2]

Eighteenth-century outsiders such as Whitefield and others who knew the work of these evangelists sometimes referred to them as 'Moravians' along with the more usual term 'Brethren'. On one occasion Whitefield had been incensed by having heard that Zinzendorf had claimed him as a confirmed member. He wrote to his friend James Hutton, 'I am not a Son of the Moravian Church, tho' I love the members of it . . . But I would not have the Brethren for their own sakes and the Gospel abuse my love of them.'[3]

British members did not usually refer to themselves as 'Moravians' during the eighteenth century, and it is doubtful whether they did for most of the nineteenth. Archival evidence confirms that, while using the term 'Moravian' in some contexts, leaders and congregations still thought and wrote of themselves primarily as 'United Brethren', or 'Brethren', in unity with their fellow members in the Continental Province. There, from the 1720s to the present time, the name 'Moravian', though known, has had only marginal significance, because Unity organization and practice have remained much closer to the original model, so that the more precise German name, *Brüdergemeine*, i.e. 'Brethren's Congregation', has been retained, with the word 'congregation' taken to mean the entire membership. Though it might have been simpler in this book, as an English-language text, to use 'Moravian' throughout – and there are precedents for doing so, particularly among recent historians – the term has connotations which disguise the authentic continental style established in the eighteenth century. For this reason the older descriptive terms emphasizing brotherhood and unity will mainly be used here when describing events of the eighteenth and nineteenth centuries, after which 'Moravian' is adopted in accordance with later usage in Britain.

The use of the term 'German' requires some clarification. Germany as a unified political entity came into existence in 1871. Before then, German-speaking people had for centuries been dispersed throughout continental Europe in the loosely structured and largely independent regions of the Holy Roman Empire of the German Peoples, and after 1806 in a German Confederation of substantially fewer member states. The original Moravian settlers at Herrnhut, for example, were German-speakers whose ancestors had been members of the German-speaking minority rather than the Czech majority of the old Unity. In general, they thought of themselves as members of their own state, as Bavarians, Saxons and so on, retaining a strong sense of regional identity and using dialect forms of the language. Zinzendorf's own dialect was that of Upper Lusatia, but as far as English-speaking Brethren were concerned, he addressed their congregations either in German or in English, and, from the eighteenth century onwards, the continental leaders of the Unity were regarded and spoken of as 'the Germans'. Since it is now conventional among twentieth-century historians to refer to these mid-European peoples as Germans, and the lands they occupied as Germany when interpreting their convoluted history,[4] the same strategy is adopted here.

The fact that people of different nationalities perceive others as belonging to a different culture, and value their own way of doing things, is a formative element in the evolving relationship between them. This was the case in the interaction between the continental brethren, leaders of the missionary outreach into Britain, and the converts whom they influenced. A marked distinction was perceived by both groups between the local people and Zinzendorf and his 'pilgrims', whose organization was centred in Herrnhut and later in Herrnhaag and other continental establishments. Zinzendorf himself, and his colleagues such as Spangenberg and Nitschmann, preserved this distinction and, as we shall see, were firmly of the belief that the 'English' were different in temperament and inclinations. As the Brethren set up congregations, and leading British enthusiasts took up positions of responsibility, there was never any doubt that the 'German' leaders were in charge, and they took every opportunity to introduce their British followers and colleagues to the continental centres with their distinctive way of life. Since these people were perceived by their contemporaries and referred to as 'the Germans', this term is used here to refer to the continental Brethren themselves and the unique organization and philosophy which they brought into Britain and from which British congregational practices eventually diverged. The term 'British', as applied to eighteenth-century society, is the subject of current historical debate.[5] It is used here because congregations were established by the Brethren in Ireland, Scotland and Wales, and it is necessary to distinguish between English congregations and British provincial establishments as a whole.

The idea of renewal adopted by Moravian members of the Unity of Brethren in eighteenth-century Herrnhut, which became important in subsequent Unity tradition, looked back to an institutional predecessor of the same name of which they claimed to be the continuation. They were proud of their vision of a distant Bohemian past, reinforced by stories inherited by some early members from previous generations of their families. Service books of the old Bohemian Unity were brought to Herrnhut by its original settlers: Anna Nitschmann, later Zinzendorf's second wife, described in her memoir how as a child she sang the old Moravian Brethren's hymns in the fields as she looked after her father's sheep.[6] Despite such anecdotal evidence, and the crucial episcopal succession from the Old Unity used to authenticate the Church and its ministry in eighteenth-century Europe and beyond, the concept of continuity, and from what, must be used with caution. It was not from the misleadingly named 'Hussite' Utraquist Church of which Hus was not the founder, but the best-known member. This 'reformed' church did not regard itself as a new creation, but as a direct continuation of the medieval Roman Catholic Church. Continuity, as far as the Unity was concerned, was with the small, devout Czech Taborite sect, enthusiastic supporters of the radical reformist teaching of John Wyclif which was wholly opposed to the moderate Utraquistic model. Instead, it provided a workable programme for a genuine Bohemian Reformation and, although this did not materialize, both the Taborites and the old Unity can be regarded as proto-Protestant, part of the limited local and essentially Bohemian defection from Roman Catholicism.[7] The 'renewed' religious organization which came into being at Herrnhut was primarily a product of late seventeenth- and eighteenth-century German Protestant spirituality; in its institutions and usages it was a new and radically different body.

Outline of this provincial history

The book is divided into four parts. Part One provides the essential background to a reappraisal of the history of the British Province. Initially it reviews the existing historiography of the Unity and its British province. It goes on to summarize the nature and purpose of the organization which decided to establish a presence in eighteenth-century England.

Parts Two and Three deal with the history of the British Province and its current activities. Four historical periods are identified, each with distinctive characteristics, and Part Two concerns the first three. It charts the development of the Church in two ways: it is broadly chronological, but at the same time identifies and explores themes which dominated provincial thinking and practice. By so doing it describes the gradual changes of outlook and practice which characterized the first two hundred years of the work of the Unity in Britain, while analysing its problems and achievements.

The first and shortest period, lasting about forty years (1742–*c.*1780), is regarded as the period of German religious and cultural ascendancy. The primary concerns then were evangelical outreach and pastoral oversight of converted adults. These developments were accompanied by rising tension between German leaders who, following Zinzendorf's vision, wished to concentrate primarily on the formation of ecumenical religious societies on continental lines to support existing denominations, despite early evidence of the failure of this approach, and English colleagues who increasingly favoured settlement-building and congregational development as a means of denominational expansion.

A second period began in the 1780s and occupied most of the next hundred years. It was characterized by congregational languor, accompanied by continuing divergence of views between those who wished to break away from their continental cultural heritage and those conservatives who wished to preserve it. Concurrently, provincial leaders took advantage of a widespread demand for education, common to all denominations, and a network of boarding schools was gradually established, along with an institution for the training of ministers and teachers. The schools became an important element in the evolution of the province and, for the British religious public, the Brotherhood in Britain became known as providers of education and missionaries to the heathen, and hardly at all as a separate religious denomination.

A third historical period, occupying the last two decades of the nineteenth century and the twentieth century up to the end of the Second World War, was a period of uneasy adaptation, firstly to changes in

British society, including national educational policies which led to the virtual collapse of the Brethren's boarding school network, and secondly to the emergence of Germany as a rival great power in Europe. Although the province had by then largely freed itself from outward signs of German influence, the dilemmas of the eighteenth century returned, and it tried to redefine its own style and clarify its position in relation to influences from the continent. The catastrophe of the First World War and a general weakening of the European missionary endeavour made this particularly difficult. After 1918, the British Province, still ill at ease with the German aspects of its identity in some respects, nevertheless clung to its heritage and worked to rebuild and maintain its relationship with the wider Unity. At the same time it participated as an independent British denomination in interdenominational activities and ecumenical discussions, which were stimulated by the determination of all denominations in Britain to build a better society. When the Second World War intervened, the province was again separated from its continental roots.

The fourth and final provincial historical period from 1945 to 2000, which provides the main subject matter for Part Three, may be thought of as a period of renewed creativity in a living, though contracting Church. It has been marked by a number of distinctive features. Women have been ordained, the principle of a non-stipendiary ministry has been successfully adopted and lay leadership has continued to grow in importance. Out of a total ministerial staff of twenty-five in 1998, seven are women, two being non-stipendiary, and a further five men also fall into this category. Twenty-one members are on the official roll of lay preachers. Congregations, especially in London and the Midlands, have been stimulated by the inclusion of immigrant West Indian Moravians, but even so in the year 2000 total only about 2,000 communicant members (2,073 in 1998). There has also been some amalgamation of congregations, particularly between Moravian and United Reformed Churches, as a result of the increasing expense and falling congregational rolls which all Protestant Churches have experienced. Representatives of the Church have been involved in ecumenical discussions since their inception, and continue to work towards a closer relationship with other denominations. Despite a narrowing of provincial responsibility, congregational interest in missions has grown, encouraged by the supportive work of the Moravian Women's Auxiliary. Church leaders and individual members have maintained a strong connection with other members of the Unity, particularly with the American provinces, and have worked tirelessly to rebuild the British link with the Continental

Province. Since the collapse of the GDR made visits to Herrnhut and other Eastern European centres easier than they have been since the 1930s, a warm relationship with the German Province has emerged.

Part Three, therefore, since it is less concerned with slow evolution, places more emphasis on themes than on chronology, setting developments in the British Province since the Second World War in their wider context of time and place, viewing retrospectively where necessary those aspects of church history, such as the training and deployment of ministers, which have become increasingly significant during the last sixty years of the twentieth century, and assessing their importance for the future of the province.

Part Four attempts an explanation in depth of Moravianism and its distinctive features, those spiritual resources which have enabled the Church to endure in Britain as a community with a strong sense of identity and tradition, despite its numerical smallness and the pressures which it shares with all Christian denominations as a result of cultural changes in European society. This is the most ambitious part of the joint authors' work, since it seeks to analyse and clarify the Unity's contribution to European Protestantism.

Sources

The most important primary sources for this study have been the Minute Books and Reports of Provincial Conferences and Synods, which provide an unequalled interpretation of the thoughts of the provincial clergy, all of whom were usually present, and the congregational deputies who also took part. Because these gatherings were a microcosm of the province as a whole, the essence of their recorded deliberations reveals the distinctive features of each successive period. The reports of various organizations and committees to Synod have been valuable guides to the activities of groups within the Church and as accounts of its missionary and ecumenical representation, particularly since the 1940s. Extensive use has been made, also, of manuscript collections in Moravian Church House library and archive, and in various congregational archives, especially Minutes of Elders' Conferences, and Congregation Diaries. The latter were kept in meticulous detail during the eighteenth century and chronicle movements of personnel and the devotional background to the Brethren's life and missionary enterprise. Since the early nineteenth century, when the German leaders gradually withdrew and these records no longer served to encourage the congregations and confirm for Unity leaders the success of the British mission, they have been restricted to brief general comment, with the result that the nineteenth and twentieth centuries are under-recorded. This deficiency coincided initially with a period when the British Province became much less sure of its identity and direction, and repeatedly looked back to what it perceived as a period of intense spirituality, since lost. In the absence of more detailed official records *The Messenger* has been a valuable printed primary source, particularly in the early years when it was a substantial magazine. Articulate, intelligent and comprehensive, it accurately reflected the erudition of its contributors and the serious interests of readers, giving insights into provincial thinking and a contemporary commentary on events within the Unity as well as in the province itself. The smaller, post-war editions have continued the earlier tradition. Though always primarily an expression of contemporary opinion, this publication has served as an official record of decision-making in areas where other material has been in short supply, being used by the Provincial Board as a means of informing the church membership of significant changes of policy.

The published texts referred to in the historiography have made an invaluable contribution to the knowledge of provincial history, particularly that of the eighteenth century. Since material is scarce, there has been no equivalent detailed study of the nineteenth century, a period in which changes were protracted and often comparatively slight. For the twentieth century, especially the period after the Second World War, this book has no predecessors. So far there have been no major studies of post-war developments in the province as a whole, and available written records consist mainly of formal reports to Synod from the Provincial Board and various church organizations. In writing about this most recent period, the research has been enriched by hearing of the experiences of ordained and lay brethren and sisters with a lifetime of service in the ministry and as members of congregations. Their individual contributions are acknowledged elsewhere.

Part One

Historical Background

The Historiography of the British Province of the Unity of the Brethren

The Unity has had congregations in Britain since the first one was founded in London in 1742, mainly to function as an administrative base for a provincial network of religious societies in support of Anglicanism. Since then, historians, mostly drawn from its ordained ministry, have chronicled provincial development, rightly setting it within the history of the Unity as a whole, usually along lines laid down by the first official historian of the Brethren, David Cranz, whose seminal work, *Alte und Neue Brüder-Historie* (1771), became available in London in English translation during 1780 as *The Ancient and Modern History of the Brethren*. In this, the first in a series of English-language texts on the subject, he endorsed the politically influential and agreed belief of contemporary continental leaders that their religious organization was essentially a continuation of the formerly well-known Bohemian Unity of the Brethren.

Cranz described for late eighteenth-century Unity members and others unfamiliar with the tumultuous history of Central Europe how the original Czech-speaking Unity had been influential from medieval times within a relatively small geographical area comprising Bohemia, Moravia and a few isolated areas of Poland, but had been virtually annihilated in its homeland during the Thirty Years War (1618–48). A minute remnant had reappeared as its renewed form, originating at Herrnhut (Saxony) in 1722, and had become active over extensive regions of Protestant Europe, including Britain, setting up religious settlements and affiliated networks of religious societies, which were to be closely associated with one another, with frequent changes of leading personnel, and subject to detailed centralized direction from Unity headquarters in Herrnhut. In addition, the Renewed Unity had developed far beyond its medieval antecedent by being involved in transatlantic missionary outreach among the heathen. The eighteenth-century Unity as Cranz presented it was, in short, an ancient foundation in a new form with a very much wider field of operation.

The role of Count Zinzendorf and that of other contemporary religious thinkers, particularly the Pietists, as inspirers of this diffusion of spiritual energy, was minimized, because at the time of writing in the late 1760s it was important for this emergent religious body to reinforce its conservative Bohemian credentials and credibility. After a meteoric career as leader, Zinzendorf was already regarded by some as having been a liability as well as a benefactor, having died in 1760 leaving the Unity with enormous debts and a questionable reputation among the religious public on the continent and in Britain. Following Cranz's lead, this concept of a Renewed Unity, smoothly evolving with very little modification directly from the old and acquiring a lengthy and illustrious Bohemian religious pedigree in the process, has been repeated by most British provincial historians, and its pleasing implications generally accepted by lay and ordained members ever since.

Fifty-four years later, the next history was written by John Holmes, also an ordained minister of the British Province, who used the same method and made the same assumptions as Cranz, updating the history of the province within the context of the Unity as a whole to 1822, the hundredth anniversary of the founding of Herrnhut. His two-volume *History of the Protestant Church of the United Brethren* (published in 1825 and 1830) was effectively 'Cranz continued', since it reinforced what were by now traditional perceptions of Unity identity deriving from the difficult period which followed Zinzendorf's death. In the preface to volume 1 he stated that he had been invited to compile a history by many of the religious public in Britain who, although they had heard about Unity overseas missionary activities, were unfamiliar with it as a regularly constituted European Church, a deficiency suggesting that Cranz's work had had only a limited circulation.

Holmes's history was followed by Daniel Benham's edited *Memoirs of James Hutton* published in 1856. This made an exceptional and more restricted approach to the historiography of the British Province, concentrating on the period 1737–95 and using the voluminous memoirs of one man as its primary source. James Hutton had lived and worked in London for most of his life, having set up business as a religious publisher/bookseller in 1737 at 'The Bible and Sun' near Temple Bar, and having become associated with the Brethren there. Though not an ordained member of the church, he soon became closely involved at the highest level with their provincial administration, naturally centred on the metropolis, and visited some of their continental settlements. He was also on familiar terms with other prominent figures in the Evangelical Revival, including George Whitefield, many of whose writings he subsequently printed. The two men were close friends: Whitefield lodged for a while in the Hutton family home at the time when James was leaving his parents' house to set up his printing business. He published Whitefield's journals and religious writings until the latter felt that Hutton's increasing spiritual affinities and involvement with the Brethren were beginning to prejudice their professional relationship on account of doctrinal differences which Whitefield could not tolerate.[1] For some years Hutton contributed regularly to worship in the London Unity congregation and published its early hymnals which were mainly translations from the original German.

From the point of view of the mid-nineteenth-century religious public, and congregational members in particular, Benham's work on Hutton mainly served to highlight and amplify important material which had already been dealt with in principle by Cranz and Holmes. It added an appealing intimate and detailed personal element in revealing Hutton's contribution to the work of the Brethren during the early years of their activity in the British Province. Yet, valuable and detailed as it was, Benham's study functioned essentially as an appendix to earlier published histories.

It was not until 1901 that the first contribution from the academic world appeared, in the form of an English translation of a German Ph.D. dissertation by G. A. Wauer,[2] entitled 'The Beginnings of the Brethren's Church in England: A Chapter of the Commerce of Thought between Germany and England', in which the history of the British Province was largely detached from that of the Unity as a whole. Wauer sketched the ecclesiastical condition of England in the mid-eighteenth century and described the Brethren's expansion from 1728 onwards, after which he gave an account of the passing of the unprecedented 1749 Act of Parliament which recognized the Brotherhood as an Ancient Protestant Church, granting it freedom to build itself up in England as it wished.[3]

These topics had already been referred to in detail by previous historians, and Wauer had little significant to add, but as the view of an outsider his introduction drew attention to the complexity and paradoxical nature of the evolution of the British province of the Unity. He commented that, of all the religious bodies in England, the Brethren's Church was an exception to the rule that the English rigidly shut out foreign

ways,[4] and that this must be regarded as remarkable. He was aware
that its membership in 1901 consisted with few exceptions of people of
English descent; yet consciousness of its foreign roots was kept alive by
its traditions and practices. The name Moravian, which by then was
widely used, he regarded as a misleading geographical association;
indeed, far from bearing the characteristics of anything peculiar to
Moravia, as had usually been implied, the Unity was, in Wauer's view,
the offspring of German spirituality, a view which eminent non-
Moravian academic historians including Professors W. R. Ward and D.
J. Bosch have now taken up.[5] They question the traditional presentation
of an apparently inexorable transition from the older to the Renewed
Unity, arguing that it is an over-simplification not warranted by the
available evidence; and for Professor Bosch and others, the Herrnhuter
Brotherhood under Zinzendorf was the nucleus of a new religious body
with fascinating local roots.

Further, for Wauer, it was still more remarkable that the Unity had
gained a foothold in England, when its first appearance coincided with
the rise of Methodism, a complementary English religious movement
(with 798,151 members in 1900[6]), and that it had gained the early
advantage of recognition by Parliament. This could only imply that the
secret of its taking root in England had been its unique characteristics
which, for a time, had supplied religious needs as widely felt in England
as in Germany, and that subsequently the religious societies (diaspora)
founded in the eighteenth century had grown into settled congregations
on a scale which was unexpected and different from the original intention. In the course of time these congregations had acquired 'a firm foot-
ing in their surroundings', while being compelled to rethink their relation
to the Mother Church on the continent, which retained its society-
forming style, a process involving gradual changes in both sentiment and
organization.

The comprehensive recapitulation of well-known elements from previous histories by the Moravian minister, Joseph E. Hutton, entitled *A
History of the Moravian Church*, was published in 1909 as an enlarged
and updated version of his *A Short History of the Moravian Church* of
1895. Hutton's book loyally followed the pattern of Cranz and Holmes,
outlining the history of the Unity as a whole from a Bohemian origin. He
ignored the doubts on this relationship raised in Wauer's recent book,
subsuming the history of the British Province within the whole and failing to distinguish between Unity and provincial achievement. Even
though 129 years had elapsed since the appearance of Cranz's book in

London, his interpretation still had considerable emotional significance for Hutton and fellow British Moravians, because it enshrined principles which they cherished as the pleasing foundation of current philosophy and practice; for example, the link with the Old Bohemian Unity was valued because it enhanced the church's continuing claim to distinction in education, perceived by its members as the legacy of Comenius. The book also expressed pride in Unity missionary activity, in which the British Province was regarded incorrectly as having an important role, despite ample evidence that the provincial contribution was being criticized by Unity Synods as inadequate. Further, Hutton's sketchy treatment of nineteenth-century provincial history, which in 1909 accounted for two-thirds of the time the province had existed, suggests that he had no clear idea of its overall direction in relation to other denominations and the wider concerns of contemporary society. For these reasons his history of the church was inadequate as a basis for understanding British provincial development.

In 1932, a non-Moravian, William George Addison, abandoned the stance of Cranz and Holmes, and in his Ph.D. study *The Renewed Church of the United Brethren, 1722–1930*, he wrote very little about the medieval Unity. Like Wauer, his interest was mainly in the eighteenth and subsequent centuries, with the Renewed Unity alone identified as the basis of institutional activity in the British Province. This enabled him to focus more attention on British affairs, an important and substantial part of his work, although, like his predecessors, he recognized that no single province could be dealt with in complete isolation from the evolution of the Unity as a whole.

In 1937 the Provincial Board attempted to ensure that the history of the church was brought up to date by a revision of J. E. Hutton's 1909 history,[7] preferably by the author. Unfortunately he died at the end of September, the same month in which the proposal was discussed. As the Bedford Synod had authorized the preparation of such a revised or new History of the Moravian Church, steps were taken to find someone to replace Hutton. George W. MacLeavy agreed to carry out the revision and was reported to be working on it in July 1938. At that stage he was nearing the end of his time as Principal of the Moravian Theological College at Fairfield, Manchester, and was due to take over the Bristol congregation. In June 1939 he reported that he found the responsibilities of a manse and congregation such that he could not continue his revision of Hutton's work, but expressed the hope that it might be completed in two or three years if he could find the necessary time. He was evidently unable to do so, but the idea remained in the background during the war years and was brought up again in 1948, when the Quincentenary Preparation Committee recommended such a project to Synod, with a specific brief that it should be prepared in three sections. Parts 1 and 2 were to deal respectively with the Ancient Unity and the Renewed Church, the latter dealing mostly with the Continental Province, and were to be written by MacLeavy. Part 3 would deal with the British Province and would be written by Arthur J. Lewis. Although this project fell through, on 24 July 1956 the Provincial Board recorded that A. J. Lewis had written a new history. At that time no publisher had been found who would take it on without a substantial subsidy,[8] but a few years later, although SCM Press agreed to publish it, no further action was taken.

In the slim volume *History of the Moravian Church*, published in 1956, a non-Moravian, Edward Langton, returned once again to the study of the early period of church history. His main interest and the bulk of his text concentrated on developments occurring in the eighteenth century during the limited period of Zinzendorf's lifetime. Langton appeared only marginally interested in events after the Count's death in 1760, which were discussed briefly at the end of his book.

Although no text of his 1956 study has been found for comparison, Arthur J. Lewis's *Zinzendorf the Ecumenical Pioneer: A Study in the Moravian Contribution to Christian Mission and Unity* was published in 1962. Like Langton, Lewis made brief reference to the old Bohemian Unity, but his main preoccupation, also, was with the evolutionary developments of the Renewed Unity during Zinzendorf's lifetime. He, too, was only marginally concerned with the post-1760 period, which was dispatched briefly as an epilogue of seven pages covering the period 1760–1961.

In 1967 the American sociologist Gillian Gollin published *Moravians in Two Worlds: A Study of Changing Communities* based on her doctoral thesis, 'Communal Pietism and Secular Drift: A Comparative Study of Social Change in the Moravian Communities of Bethlehem and Herrnhut'. In it she showed how, despite residual similarities of religious and occupational structure, during the first century of their existence both communities underwent a gradual process of secularization at a rate in direct proportion to the presence of an aristocratic elite. At Bethlehem,

Pennsylvania, where there was no elite and the entrepreneurial spirit was strong, the community evolved as a base for the Bethlehem Steel Corporation. In German Herrnhut, where the elite was dominant and the entrepreneurial spirit weak, craft industry was perpetuated in a cosy economic backwater. Bethlehem and Herrnhut represented the extremes; the other settlements, including those in the British Province, showed the same tendencies, but to a variable and lesser extent.

Another Unity history published in 1967 followed Addison's lead, dealing solely with the Renewed Unity. Written by two ordained Americans, John T. and Kenneth G. Hamilton, father and son, and published as *The History of the Moravian Church: The Renewed Unitas Fratrum 1722– 1957*, this substantial volume emphasized and described the congregational and missionary extension of the Church in North America. Several chapters were devoted to the evolution of the British Province in the context of the development of the Unity as a whole, but, like the rest of the book, they treated the subject in such minute detail as to obscure the main issues. Essentially, the Hamiltons accepted the well-established interpretations fostered by Hutton.

A few years later, in 1975, *Christian Spirituality: Essays in Honour of Gordon Rupp* included 'The Cambridge Methodists', by J. Walsh,[9] which made an important contribution to provincial historiography. He listed the five 'Cambridge Methodists', Okely, Delamotte, Hammond, Batty and Rogers, 'who came to rest among the Brethren', and then provided arresting insights into the seductive appeal of the Brethren's spirituality. 'Though luscious, gruesome and sensuous, this intense passion-piety seemed to provide some seekers with an ingredient missing from their spiritual lives.' His analysis, presented with a brevity and clarity which had largely eluded previous writers, also had a seminal influence on subsequent research, particularly into the role of the Brethren's religious settlements as places of refuge for those who, in the early years, yearned for a religion of feeling rather than rational understanding.

The most recent contribution, also by a non-Moravian historian, is Colin Podmore's 1998 study, *The Moravian Church in England, 1728–1760*,[10] based on his 1994 Oxford doctoral thesis.[11] It provides an incisive analysis of British provincial development during the early period of rapid expansion, turbulent experience of doctrinal eccentricities and progressive financial embarrassment. Podmore also suggests reasons for the appeal of the Brethren's style to their eighteenth-century contemporaries and analyses in detail their relationship with the Church of England, culminating in the 1749 Act of Parliament. Because of the limited period involved, however, his work must be regarded, with Daniel Benham's *Memoirs of James Hutton*, as a rich, invaluable, but inevitably restricted contribution to the historiography of the British Province over its 260-year life-span.

Although these historians varied in their degree of interest in the Bohemian Unity, all dealt in detail with the eighteenth-century Unity, and were agreed that, on the continent, it had originally aspired to be a small, centrally directed brotherhood based on a number of religious settlements such as Herrnhut, the first of a series of so-called Place Congregations. They showed that, under Zinzendorf's leadership, members served as itinerant, society-forming evangelists, working where they could help established clergy of Protestant denominations to strengthen the faith of congregations and encourage greater application of Christian principles in everyday life.

The original model, in practice, involved preaching in homes or local rented premises in order to foster small, informal, religious societies for mutual support. When several societies were established close to one another they were grouped under central control and referred to as a 'connexion' of societies. They were visited from time to time to maintain the momentum of spiritual renewal already set in motion, but were not regarded as the nuclei of new Unity congregations which might be tempted to engage in competition with the Established church. On the contrary, society membership was usually conditional upon remaining fully committed to its ministrations, and on regular attendance at its local parish services. As soon as evangelists were convinced that the societies in a particular area no longer needed their services they were expected to move on, because they were merely representatives of an 'outside' religious Brotherhood with a permanent non-denominational stance, looking only to evangelize and not proselytize. In principle they were temporary residents in various places over a wide area.

That was the early model on the continent, and few of the published histories referred to here show convincingly how it exemplified a form of Lutheran activity already familiar to devotees of the late seventeenth- and early eighteenth-century Pietist movement, so that, even after it was recognized as a separate denomination, no fundamental change in its evangelizing and society-forming objectives was necessary. Further, not all historians have demonstrated that, because of the exceptional energy, original spiritual insights, literary creativity and aristocratic style of Zinzendorf and his principal colleagues, this body rapidly acquired a corpus of religious literature, hymnody and liturgical style, firmly based within orthodox Christian belief and practice, yet unique to itself; nor have they made clear that most of its European members have tended to be Germans, and that it was always fundamentally German in spirit, arguably most at home and most successful among people who spoke that language.

Some of these historians showed that Germans predominated in overseas missions to the heathen, and successes in this field brought the Unity to the attention of the British religious public, many of whom had little idea of its domestic history. In subsequent decades of the eighteenth century and the whole of the nineteenth, the Continental Province of the Unity made major investments of money and personnel in foreign missions, and it was for this international aspect of its evangelistic endeavour that the Unity became most widely known.

As this survey of Unity historiography has demonstrated, historical writing involves both selection and interpretation. No written history can be definitive, since historians, like the rest of society, are products of the generation in which they live. They look again at the evidence and present it in ways consistent with their own insights and the historical thinking of their time. From the perspective of the year 2000 it seems that, by subsuming the evolution of the British Province in the development of the Unity as a whole, most English-speaking historians who have written formerly about a lengthy period of provincial development have tended to gloss over the full implications and far-reaching consequences of an institutional change of direction which developed gradually in the province during the nineteenth century. With the exception of Podmore, they have neither made explicit, nor perhaps been prepared to admit, that as early as the latter part of the eighteenth century, this change from the powerful spirituality of the mid-eighteenth century to something very different was well advanced in Britain and continued to strengthen. Institutionally the Church evolved from an interdenominational organization to one which was denominational in outlook. In contrast, the Continental Province, the definitive ecumenical prototype, remained largely as it had been established in Zinzendorf's time, firmly and successfully rooted in contemporary German thinking and practice. With few exceptions, these historians have failed to recognize the increasing difference between the religion of the first Brotherhood in Britain and its late nineteenth- and twentieth-century manifestations. The British

Province developed progressively on the basis of a paradox, aspiring to be and in many ways acting the role of an independent denomination, yet still clinging to its place in the general Unity scheme of things. Inevitably this led to and sustained a state of uncertainty about its identity, and is one reason why it has remained very small.

This book, while following the mainstream of historical thinking in some areas, suggests a new overall interpretation of events in the British Province. It presents a view of provincial history which accepts the continuing influence of this paradox, and concentrates on the gradual and uncertain emergence of a very idiosyncratic British denominational style, dogged by a persistent problem of identity in relation to the conservative Continental Province, which was always more assured of its historical continuity. It looks at this uncomfortable evolutionary process as a whole, aiming to present an account of provincial development which re-examines the significance of its emergent character within the Unity, particularly in contrast to the Continental Province, and does not aspire to be an encyclopaedic study of the changing fortunes of individual districts and congregations, no matter how important these may have been locally. In short, the book describes how, in Britain, a German evangelizing agency with an alien social and cultural ethos, designed for temporary service in support of spiritual renewal among members of established denominations, abandoned its original intention because it failed to appeal, and struggled instead to set up and maintain a network of fixed congregations, as if it were in reality a new denomination.

2

The Eighteenth-Century Continental Brotherhood: Its Sources and Character

As already indicated in the Introduction, from the Middle Ages to the latter part of the nineteenth century much of Central Europe was a loosely structured collection of the virtually independent principalities, duchies and free cities which constituted the Holy Roman Empire of the German Peoples.[1] Yet, despite this political fragmentation, which in some respects proved culturally stimulating,[2] the inhabitants shared a common language, German, and a characteristic culture to which they clung tenaciously.

From the Middle Ages, too, the movement of German-speaking people across the eastern borders of their empire to form enclaves in foreign countries was the norm rather than the exception.[3] The motives for each migration were always complex, although economic and social problems were usually decisive in promoting mass movements of small family groups to areas of greater opportunity. An early example of this occurred in the twelfth century when some of these people from the Rhine and Mosel areas settled in the Kingdom of Hungary. There they founded seven urban settlements subsequently referred to by German historians as *Die Siebenburgen*, whose residents were *Die Siebenburgen Sachsen*, 'The Saxons of the Seven Towns'.[4] Other areas beyond the eastern frontier of the empire into which large numbers migrated included the Baltic States, Latvia, Lithuania and Estonia, Poland and parts of Russia, particularly the lower Volga region, and in these territories they were often granted special economic, legal and cultural privileges because they tended to be perceived as law-abiding and exceptionally industrious. In this way, over centuries, the German-speakers accumulated a considerable number of ethnic enclaves which collectively formed a truly international community, the members of which preserved and treasured their common language and characteristic culture. They usually learned the language of the host region and became fellow citizens, but proved resistant to complete assimilation, experiencing all the problems of being a separatist, alien minority in a fundamentally foreign environment.[5]

The sixteenth-century Protestant Reformation was rooted in the Holy Roman Empire and radiated its doctrines and practices outwards from this centre into neighbouring foreign regions to the north and east, soon becoming an international institution with, amongst others, Danish, Swedish, Baltic, Russian, Polish and Hungarian branches. The long-established German-speaking enclaves in these regions, with their strong cultural ties with the imperial heartland, were important agencies in this process, and so the spread of Protestantism was related to the existence of a sympathetic international community.

During the seventeenth century the Lutheran Pietist movement sought to reform and re-enliven the Protestant Church. This movement, also, originated in the Holy Roman Empire. Its influence spread across the borders into established Protestant Churches, for example, in Sweden, and infiltrated the German-speaking foreign enclaves, particularly those in the Baltic States, which became the bastions of this truly international movement.[6]

In the eighteenth century emigration across the eastern borders continued; for example, groups subsequently known as Banater and Sathmarer-Schwaben formed additional enclaves in Slavonic south-eastern Europe. Despite this, the focus of attention for potential migrants was gradually changing to the west, and from the early part of the century a steadily increasing number crossed the Atlantic to settle in the North American colonies. In contrast to the earlier mass movements to the east, this westward flow included groups leaving primarily for religious reasons. They, too, resolutely preserved their distinctive identity and, as part of this exodus, the international German-speaking community extended geographically to include a flourishing transatlantic dimension. Because the port of London was often the point of departure from Europe and the terminus of return sailings, it became vital for agents from the continent to be located there, to handle the flow of their own people as well as the commercial traffic bound for America.

Sooner or later, therefore, any significant cultural or religious movements originating in the centre of the German-speaking international domain had repercussions on the other parts, including the foreign enclaves which had been established for centuries. As in the case of the dissemination of Protestantism during the sixteenth century and the spread of Pietism during the seventeenth and early eighteenth centuries, the emergent Unity of the Brethren from 1722 onwards inevitably became international, and its leaders soon found it necessary to establish a base in London for the dispatch of members to North America. From the beginning, therefore, the Unity was international in both outlook and membership, not primarily because of a deliberate act of policy, but as an unavoidable consequence of long-established precedents in the history of the German-speaking people among whom it originated, and the circumstances in which its members were living at the time.

The emergence of the eighteenth-century Unity

Just as the medieval Hussite Protestant movement originated in one specific place, Prague, and the Protestant Reformation of the sixteenth century in Wittenberg, so the Unity had its birthplace at Herrnhut in Saxony on the eastern periphery of the Holy Roman Empire. This location, close to the border separating the Empire from foreign Slavonic peoples whose territories extended from there far to the east, was an area which had been characterized for centuries by a clash of cultures. Here, then, the distinctive features of the Renewed Unity were formed, as a result of the conjunction of German-speaking people from different parts of Central Europe, who had strongly-held but different religious and cultural aspirations which they were unwilling to modify or relinquish.

In his article 'The Renewed Unity of the Brethren: Ancient Church, New Sect or Interconfessional Movement?',[7] W. R. Ward looked at this conjunction in detail and argued that in Herrnhut during the 1720s there coexisted determined people with varied and overlapping, but fundamentally different objectives which they resolutely pursued, and that the so-called Renewed Unity which emerged was both spiritually and institutionally a compromise to enable these differing objectives to be reconciled. The first element consisted of a few German-speaking Protestant emigrants from Bohemia and Moravia seeking to resurrect an ancient Church. Secondly, there was a much larger number of religious refugees of other sects seeking to find a new home, who were attracted by the tolerant atmosphere of the settlement. Thirdly, there was Zinzendorf himself, whose ambition was to create an interdenominational movement in support of existing Protestant Churches. Ward maintains that all three made a significant contribution to the final outcome. Furthermore, they achieved what they wanted.

The origins and ambitions of the early Moravian contingent at Herrnhut

The religious immigrants from Bohemia and Moravia in the 1720s were German-speakers, whose ancestors, not they themselves, had belonged to the weaker German branch of the mainly Czech Unity of the Brethren.[8] This body had originated from within the Taborite sect, a radical group dissatisfied with the institutional achievements of the so-called Hussite[9] or Bohemian Reformation, which had succeeded in establishing a moderately reformed and generally popular Czech national church. This was usually described as Utraquist,[10] because of its contributions to Eucharistic understanding and practice. The Taborites had called for a return to the assumed simplicities of the primitive Church of Apostolic times, without a priestly caste. They had emphasized faith as the primary Christian virtue, demanding greater freedom to read the Bible, and the use of Czech or German instead of Latin in all forms of liturgical and general Christian literature, so that the laity could have direct access to religious sources. At the same time, Utraquism had become influential throughout Bohemia and Moravia, and its doctrines had spread with increasing vigour after the invention of printing, so that, from about 1472, most books published there were no longer in Latin but in Czech or German, the majority being Bibles or other religious works.

The original Unity of the Brethren[11] founded its own priesthood, and thus its own Church, in 1457,[12] by creating an episcopate based on ambiguous apostolic succession from the separatist Waldensians,[13] as well as appointment by individual congregations.[14] In the early sixteenth century, Unity leaders made contact with the Lutheran and Reformed Churches during the German Reformation, in which Europe's peoples learned to choose and develop the forms of religious piety which suited them best,[15] but insisted that the Unity would always retain its independence, despite having much in common with these other churches. Most Czech Protestants belonged to the Utraquist Church, and it is generally accepted that the Unity appealed to a minority only, in spite of its widespread intellectual impact.[16] Thus, by the beginning of the seventeenth century, the Czech-speaking lands were unique in Europe in having four legitimate denominations working side by side – the Utraquists, the Unity of the Brethren, the Lutheran Church and the Roman Catholic Church.[17] Most people, certainly most nobles and town-dwellers,[18] were either Utraquist or Unity members, whereas the German-speaking enclave on the western Czech border were Lutheran; Roman Catholics were a minority.

The destruction of the original Unity in 1648 was associated with an unfortunate development affecting all Protestants living in Bohemia. This occurred as a result of the vigorous revival of Roman Catholicism[19] in parts of Central Europe in the early seventeenth century, culminating in the Thirty Years War (1618–48).[20] During this conflict Bohemia and Moravia were forcibly re-Catholicized from 1620 onwards[21] after the decisive Battle of the White Mountain. Many Protestants immediately fled the country, emigrating to German-speaking Lutheran areas and to Poland. The post-war settlement of 1648 effectively marked the end of the Unity as an institutional church in its homeland, though not in Poland. By then, most of those who still valued its teaching had already emigrated, and later, throughout the rest of the seventeenth and early eighteenth centuries, others followed. This led to recurrent tension between the governments of German-speaking Protestant states such as Saxony[22] to the west, and Czech-speaking Catholic Bohemia, where there was resentment at the granting of asylum to Protestant refugees.

Refugees of this type were the original settlers of Herrnhut in 1722. Most had come from Moravia as opposed to Bohemia, and had brought with them 'what they believed to be their traditions, imperfectly understood and remembered as they were',[23] as a hidden seed of continuity from the old Unity. The significance of this 'hidden seed' tradition in creating an impressive pedigree for the Renewed Unity was stressed by Cranz to strengthen the argument for continuity which was important for leaders of opinion when he was writing, although its influence on Zinzendorf's thinking was probably slight at first. After he finally, and most reluctantly, gave way to persistent Moravian demands for an institutional renewal of the old Unity because it was confirmed by lot on 7 January 1731, Zinzendorf realized that the Moravians had something to offer him which could be of inestimable value in the advancement of his own interests. Not only would the religious pedigree of the old Unity be a useful acquisition in itself, but it included Unity Bishop Comenius (1592–1670) as its outstanding figure. He had been compelled to emigrate from Moravia during the Thirty Years War, going first to Poland, where he had joined other Brethren who had gone there to find peace, and subsequently he had travelled extensively throughout Protestant Western Europe. It was on the basis of a link with this man that the 'Moravian' Herrnhuters made their most valuable contribution to the compromise referred to by Ward. The other bishops and ministers of the original Unity had all been essentially local men, and their church, although known and respected among the Protestant religious public abroad, was imperfectly understood. Comenius, on the other hand, had an outstanding international reputation as an intellectual and was recognized as the greatest figure of seventeenth-century Czech culture.[24] He had been famous, not primarily because of his work as a Unity bishop, but because he had propagated a philosophy concerning the social and political advancement of society everywhere in Europe. This, he believed, could be achieved by the civilizing influence of a mystical religious faith[25] combined with learning, a vital precondition of which was an enlightened and spiritually-based system of education.[26] His world view and visionary style had been presented so authoritatively in his writings and personal practice that he had made a deep impression on social elites, and in 1722 his fame remained undiminished.

At this time his grandson, Daniel Ernest Jablonsky, who had also been consecrated as a Unity bishop, was living in Berlin, and Zinzendorf realized that Jablonsky could legitimize an ordained ministry in a Renewed Unity of Brethren which would satisfy the deeply felt aspirations of the Moravians. It could also provide the tactical advantage of a valuable religious pedigree, including the illustrious Comenius and stretching back to Hussite times, which he could use in any future negotiations with foreign ecclesiastical authorities concerning the legal status of his movement. The count therefore arranged for Jablonsky to consecrate the Herrnhuter layman David Nitschmann on 13 March 1735. Nitschmann could then legitimately ordain other laymen in the settlement, so that from then onwards a Renewed Unity came into institutional but unofficial existence as an independent religious body with the Moravian component forming its dedicated core of evangelists. This body was then used by Zinzendorf to advance his primary aim of creating an interdenominational movement in support of the main Protestant Churches.

The supportive role of the religious separatists at Herrnhut

Most of the early settlers in Herrnhut were German-speaking religious separatists of various strongly held persuasions who were attracted by the tolerance for which the settlement soon became locally well known. This meant that from the beginning the inhabitants suffered divisions of their own in addition to the grinding poverty of a new start. These divisions were partly social: a sizeable proportion of these people were peasants who had lost everything by leaving their original rural homes in which at least they had land to cultivate; others were artisans, including weavers, shoemakers and potters who, because of their expertise, could more easily find employment in a new area. The divisions were also partly religious, in that some were unwilling to accept membership of the Lutheran Church, preferring the doctrines of the Reformed with its emphasis on predestination, while others were supporters of the sixteenth-century mystic and separatist, Caspar Schwenkfeld. Even the refugees from Moravia were not united in the aim of renewing the original Unity, some preferring a closer association with the Lutherans, while others were strongly opposed to this.

Fearful of the adverse publicity that this communal dissension and religious controversy was generating, and uneasily aware of the possibility of intervention by the Saxon government to close the settlement and expel its members, Zinzendorf came back from Dresden to live on the estate. There he quelled the dissidents, and in 1727 imposed a civil and religious constitution on them which effectively fixed them into the prevailing legal and religious system of the state. From then onwards the members of this group of former religious separatists accepted Zinzendorf's leadership and paid lip-service to the principle that they belonged to a body which was a renewal of an ancient church. It was obvious to them that its organization and practices, whatever the name, were substantially different from anything they had previously experienced; so they, too, achieved their objective of participation in a new religious body in an atmosphere of tolerance, and became dedicated supporters of Zinzendorf's ambitious and unchanging objective of creating an interdenominational movement.

Count Zinzendorf's vision of a Renewed Unity

Zinzendorf was, naturally, a man of his time, and his objective was the result of his background and upbringing in a distinguished family with an influential role in the contemporary Pietist movement for the promotion of practical divinity,[27] which had already spread throughout the international German community. Consequently, his personal interpretation of pietistic spirituality and practices had a fundamental and formative influence on Unity spirituality, institutions and activities, so much so that a detailed analysis of Pietism is justified at this stage.

Pietism was part of the greatest, most diversified,[28] widely spread[29] movement for religious renewal in Protestantism since the Reformation.[30] It has also been claimed as the most intense and thoroughgoing attempt in the history of the Christian Church to revive the power of early Christianity, and has, in consequence, never ceased to inspire. It was a phenomenon found in different countries and confessions during the sixteenth, seventeenth and eighteenth centuries – the Puritans and

Methodists in Anglican England, the Jansenists in Catholic France and
Belgium, the Lutheran and Reformed in Protestant Germany. What
bound all Pietists together was a particular personal experience of a
divine presence, which they believed resulted in spiritual rebirth and
conversion and consequent commitment and growth in holiness. Thus
Pietism was a reform movement within various confessions, and at the
same time an interconfessional development. In a scriptural context it
was a consequence of the conflict between the doctrine of salvation and
the divine requirement to grow in personal holiness.[31] As the offspring of
German orthodoxy, it had late sixteenth-century origins among those
Lutheran and Reformed clergy who were concerned at a widespread and
serious decline in congregational spirituality. This, in their view, was
linked to lack of knowledge of the Bible and general ignorance of Christ's
teaching, made worse by excessive clerical emphasis on purity of doctrine
and intellectual speculation, as opposed to a more emotionally appealing
religion of the heart. The seriousness with which this state of affairs was
regarded led to the publication of helpful spiritual guides emphasizing
heart religion, such as those by Johann Arndt (1525–1621), whose *True
Christianity* (1606) and *Little Paradise Garden* (1612) were an influential protest at declining spirituality and a programme for its enrichment.[32]
Arndt's programme included the propagation of what was for him a
more authentic Lutheranism enriched by pre-Reformation mystical
sources. In his books, therefore, he looked back to and quoted extensively from long-established literature of this type, such as the world-famous
Imitation of Christ, by Thomas à Kempis, (1380–1471),[33] because he had
been unable to find comparable material in Protestant devotional literature. Arndt also recommended that congregational members should
form networks of house-groups (religious societies) for mutual edification and sharing of religious experiences. Overall he looked to conversion and the joy of a personal experience of union with Christ, so that the
promptings of the Holy Spirit would then direct the spiritually reborn to
a life of virtue and Christian service. This became among the laity the
basis of a self-consciously cultured movement for social and spiritual
renewal within the Established church, backed up by intensive clerical
pastoral oversight.

Arndt's two books, more especially the first, though intended originally for his parishioners at Brunswick and Celle, soon became more widely known and immensely popular. *True Christianity* was reprinted ninety
times in German between 1606 and 1740, as well as three times each in
Dutch and Swedish, opening up a major channel for the spread, amongst
Germans in particular, of elements of the great medieval Roman Catholic

devotional tradition of the heart,[34] i.e. a distinctively emotional form of piety. Because of this, Arndt has been recognized as the father of German Pietism,[35] and Zinzendorf was the third in chronological order of the three major Pietist leaders to retain Arndt's programme, develop it, and direct it towards religious and social renewal in Central Europe.[36] The first two were Philip Jakob Spener (1635–1705)[37] and August Hermann Francke (1663–1727), who were both known personally to Zinzendorf, and what they had already achieved largely determined the direction which he took after he established his leadership at Herrnhut in 1727.

Pietism appealed to only a minority of the laity, but it was well represented and influential among educational and social elites in urban areas such as Berlin, Dresden, Halle and Frankfurt-am-Main, where between 1666 and 1686 Spener was head of the Lutheran clergy, and where Pietism developed as an identifiable religious movement. These areas were experiencing rapid population growth during the latter half of the seventeenth century as a result of natural increase, as well as absorbing a continuing influx of immigrants of Dutch and French Huguenot origin, the former arriving mainly as a result of trade, the latter because of religious persecution. Many of these newcomers were well educated and tended to be drawn to Pietist congregations. There they joined the newly formed pietistic religious societies of educated Germans[38] who met regularly to read the Bible, particularly the writings of St Paul,[39] to study devotional literature such as Arndt's *True Christianity* and Spener's *Pious Desires*, and to pray and sing hymns together.[40] These groups, which gave the Pietist movement its distinctive character, inevitably tended to consist of the more zealous lay members of each congregation, and were often referred to as 'churches within a church', because participants aspired to personal spiritual advancement and practice which would benefit the congregation as a whole. Such lay-led religious societies of the Established churches were the bedrock on which early pietistic organization rested and the prototype for the forthcoming Unity diaspora.

Pietism also proved attractive to noble families[41] dominant in many of the principalities, duchies and kingdoms of the mid-eighteenth-century Holy Roman Empire, who were on the whole a working social class with a comparatively modest lifestyle, since management of rural estates allowed for neither luxury nor laziness,[42] and it was as the founder of scientific genealogy and heraldry in Germany that Spener initially gained direct access to them. These families tended to be linked by intermarriage and remarriage,[43] forming networks of potentially influential sympathizers, some of whom knew Spener and Francke and shared their religious aspirations. Spener's association with Zinzendorf's family, residents of Dresden, was so close that, after being senior court chaplain there from 1686 to 1691, he was invited in 1700 by Baroness Gersdorf,[44] Zinzendorf's maternal grandmother, to be the newly born count's god-father. Indeed Spener and Francke became so influential largely because they gained access to many sophisticated, spiritually inclined and related groups of noble families.[45] Their success among this social class was such that, by 1720, a network of pietistic noble and princely families stretched eastward from Frankfurt to southern Saxony, Silesia and Poland, extending by 1730 to include the area north from Halle to the Baltic States and the Danish court at Copenhagen.[46]

Francke extended Arndt's and Spener's programmes from a fixed base at Halle, and was one of the few men of his day in the Lutheran Church whose interests and compassion were not confined to Germany or even just to Europe, but, as in the Roman Catholic Church, included the whole world. He declared that a principal objective of the Pietist movement was to be 'the concrete improvement of all walks of life everywhere'.[47] With regard to the means to be employed for this purpose Francke went beyond Spener, who had hoped that religious and social renewal could be accomplished solely within the framework of the existing Protestant denominations, and as a result had worked entirely in this field. While accepting that much spiritual enrichment could be achieved within individual congregations and society in general by a core of devout laity, he became convinced that an enlightened and spiritually sensitive education in both schools and universities also had a vital role. As a practical application of this very important principle, he developed in Halle from 1695 a novel educational and philanthropical residential community embodying pietistic principles and financed largely by generous donations from wealthy noble supporters, which worked in close co-operation with Halle University (opened in 1694). This purpose-built educational and religious settlement did not have a fixed congregational base; yet its institutions were in some ways similar to the first specially constructed settlement at Herrnhaag (1738–50) and subsequent establishments set up by the Unity.

Though not architecturally distinguished, the Halle complex, which comprised several separate four-storey wings, was regarded by contemporaries as a milestone in planned building.[48] It included four kinds of school, three for fee-payers, the other free. Stoeffler lists them as follows:

1. A Paedagogium in which the sons of nobles were educated. Zinzendorf was a pupil there from 1710 to 1716, thus being nurtured in pietistic circles under Spener's and Francke's influence from an early age.[49]
2. A Latin school, adjusted specially to the needs of the sons of the professional and merchant classes, to supply future members of these groups.
3. A so-called 'German' school for the children of ordinary citizens, which would fit them to earn their livelihood as artisans.
4. A school for the poor, allied to the Orphan House, in which board and tuition were free; a practical experiment aiming at the betterment of the most deprived in society. Included in the Orphan House was a children's clinic in which treatment was provided by the Halle University Medical School students. This medical institution gradually became the base for a commercial company which exported medicaments all over Europe.

In 1707 a specially built seminary was founded for the training of both ministers and teachers, because it was believed that true godliness would best be implanted in a child's mind by teachers who were also preparing for service in the ordained ministry, a method which later became a characteristic feature of the staffing of Unity boarding schools. Residential accommodation in the complex was combined with workshops, as in the subsequent Single Brethren's and Single Sisters' Choir Houses, so that in addition to their traditional academic studies, pupils could learn practical skills such as tailoring, shoemaking and gardening.

A Halle printing press was established for the publication of Bibles and theological and devotional subjects, later extended to include books on other subjects. This press rapidly became one of the most important in Germany, publishing in German, Greek and a wide range of Slavonic languages.[50] Much of it was directed to nominal Christians in central and eastern parts of northern Europe where German-speaking people were settled. The characteristic insights of Hallesian Pietism entered Sweden, for example, via Swedish civil servants and army families who had experienced an unusual form of deprivation. Some thirty thousand of them returned from Russia in 1721 after being captured and imprisoned in Siberia after the Battle of Poltava. According to Hope, material and spiritual adversity in these harsh landscapes had been softened for these people by devotional and pastoral literature sent to them from Halle.[51] Other prisoners had originated in the Baltic States, and they had been similarly sustained, so that on returning home they, too, had spread pietistic ideas among fellow Lutherans. By the early eighteenth century, also, a new generation of Hallesian clergy were working in the Baltic States, Sweden and Finland, where orthodox Lutheranism had previously been dominant and where Pietism rapidly became influential.[52] By the time of Francke's death in 1727 Halle was famous as the focal point of a wide range of new enterprises involving about three thousand people and generating, by trade within the context of state privilege, an enormous annual income which contributed to the material and spiritual improvement of people of all walks of life within the area and much further afield.

Francke's influence was not confined to Central Europe: against considerable resistance he pioneered initiatives in foreign mission to the heathen, regarded in Lutheran circles before 1700 as unnecessary on a number of grounds, though mainly that the Christian Church had already been planted everywhere that mattered, and that if God wished to convert more of the heathen he would do so without human effort.[53] This point of view seemed defeatist to Francke in the light of the long-established and successful overseas missionary enterprise of the Roman Catholic Church which, during the second half of the sixteenth century, established numerous Jesuit, Dominican, Carmelite, Capuchin and other missions in regions as far apart as India, the East Indies, Japan, America, the Congo Basin, Madagascar and the coastal regions of North Africa.[54] These were still operational and included schools and colleges for converts. Thus Francke recognized the importance of Roman Catholic missionary agencies in Europe and the wider world,[55] and was aware that they had established the principles and practice which any subsequent mission work outside Europe would be likely to follow. Pietism thus became the driving force in the missionary movement within the Protestant Churches. Mission was a sign that the world was being changed.[56]

Francke's personal contribution to missionary activity was inevitably small-scale and experimental in comparison with the Roman Catholic model,[57] but it pointed the way for Protestants generally and for Zinzendorf and the Unity in particular.[58] Like the Brethren, somewhat later, Francke found support for his ideas in Copenhagen, where the Protestant Danish royal family were interested in the conversion of the heathen, allowing the city to become a centre for Hallesian foreign mission. In 1706, with royal permission, two pietistic Lutheran missionaries were sent to work at the Danish trading post at Tranquebar, south of Madras. When it soon became apparent that more men were needed, a state-sponsored mission college was established in Copenhagen in 1714 to supply missionaries for service in other peripheral Lutheran fields where Christianity was not always deep-rooted, such as Lappland, and in 1721 a distinguished Norwegian pietistic Lutheran minister, Hans Egede, was sent to work among the Eskimos in the Danish colony of Greenland.[59]

An ecumenical perspective was another important outcome of the basic principles of Pietism. Since its focus was on spiritual rebirth and the new life of individual communion with the Saviour, particular church institutions, the sacraments and doctrinal differences were less important; what mattered was this common experience spanning all confessional divisions. Pietism was thus the first major ecumenical impulse within Protestantism,[60] though efforts to repair ecclesiastical breaches go back at least to the Reformation.

In addition to establishing a spiritual and institutional exemplar for Zinzendorf and the Brethren, as demonstrated by the above account of their interests and achievements, Spener and Francke wrote letters which, like those of St Paul, were meant to convey information and, more importantly, to function as devotional aids to raise the spirits of leaders and assure them of continuing support. Other letters, designed to meet the special needs of society members, were normally read to them collectively, so that the number of readers or hearers would often be considerable. It is estimated that Francke had about five thousand correspondents to whom he wrote occasionally, and between three and four hundred to whom he wrote regularly.[61] Bearing in mind contemporary hazards in the postal service and the general practice of sending two copies at different times in case one was lost, this working method was inevitably time-consuming, yet clearly central to their work.

Spener and Francke, more particularly the latter, also arranged for the widespread distribution from Halle of quite lengthy handwritten or printed news reports among groups of sympathizers. This was necessary because their movement had its greatest appeal to a devout and sophisticated minority and was never taken seriously in the majority of German congregations.[62] Because its groups of adherents tended to be widely scattered, the circulation of letters and regular news-sheets describing the activities of similar groups had a cohesive influence on society members, encouraging them to exert a beneficial influence on the nominal Christians among whom they lived. The principles involved were not new; they had been used with great skill and sophistication by the Jesuits[63] and by Jewish leaders of the Diaspora to keep in touch with their scattered congregations. The value of this method of communication was appreciated by Zinzendorf and it was adopted in the Renewed Unity.

The Continental Brotherhood's interpretation of Pietism

When, in 1727, Zinzendorf took control at Herrnhut, his fundamentally feudal outlook[64] and social expertise were used with consummate skill to inaugurate there a more idiosyncratic and emotional[65] form of Pietism appealing to an educated urban and aristocratic laity and a selected group of artisans engaged in society formation and missionary activity over an increasingly wide area. Artisans, in particular, already belonged to a culture of mobility and soon became the characteristic messengers of the Unity.[66] This initially small but evolving group exemplified his interpretation of Pietism, even after his break with the contemporary Pietist leaders a few years later over the precise methodology of conversion. The characteristic Pietist argument was that conversion was the result of an intense sense of unworthiness and long agonizing, whereas Zinzendorf's concept, an amalgam of Lutheranism, Spenerism and mysticism,[67] was that it was an undeserved gift of God following the sinner's acknowledgement of unworthiness. This philosophy encompassed conversion, spiritual rebirth, a joyful sense of salvation and the cultivation of a personal, intensely loving relationship with the Saviour, all of which would generate self-sacrificing good works.[68] The values and activities which these experiences engendered, comparable with the endeavours undertaken by some who in previous centuries had taken monastic vows, were now in Zinzendorf's view to be shouldered by laymen.[69] Their central aim was to act as an interdenominational (interconfessional) movement.

When the earliest Unity network of pietistic-style societies, the Diaspora, was being established in the 1720s, most members were Lutherans or Reformed, who were expected to remain committed to their original heritage in their own congregations and to cultivate a richer personal spiritual life. In Zinzendorf's view Christians who had experienced conversion and the spiritual rebirth which enabled them to sustain a loving personal relationship with the Saviour had nothing to gain from switching denominations, being already united in spirit, no matter to which denomination they belonged. Indeed he was hostile to any attempt by the Brethren to gain proselytes from any other Church, including the Roman Catholics.[70]

Zinzendorf recognized that to be a member of a pietistic-type religious society was difficult compared with being an overseas missionary to the heathen. In a nominally Christian community, members would always be liable to misrepresentation and criticism, even assuming that the parochial clergy sympathized with their declared aims. Unity networks required a dedicated body of volunteer stewards capable of organizing and caring for each society, and such leaders were expected to offer themselves voluntarily. Married couples were usually preferred, since meetings were held in the stewards' homes, and it was an advantage if both husband and wife shared a commitment to this type of religious organization. They were required to decide on the size of each group in accordance with the accommodation available and provide a programme for each meeting because, no matter how informal and varied the proceedings, some kind of preparation was necessary. Stewards were also expected to exercise pastoral care over society members, particularly where they were widely dispersed, a responsibility which was facilitated by the practice of circulating Unity devotional literature and correspondence. Finally, they were expected to work with clergymen and local Unity representatives to ensure as far as possible that society members remained loyal to the Established church.

It is clear, therefore, that the early model established by Zinzendorf and his leading colleagues on the continent needed only a few Unity members to supervise the stewards and societies over a wide area, visiting them from time to time, ideally with the agreement of the local clergy. The model was versatile and could readily adapt to variations in local circumstances such as the influx of immigrants or changes in the economy. No capital investment was needed for the building of new premises, and the running costs of society networks run by volunteers were very small. Provided that widespread zeal for religious experience continued and society members were content to remain members of their original denominations, the model could be expanded or contracted at will with only marginal need for an increase in Unity membership.

Since it was Zinzendorf's hope that the Unity society network would be large yet the Brotherhood itself remain small, an arduous procedure for admission into the Unity itself was established. Over the years, a carefully selected and trusted group was received into membership and encouraged to live in Place Congregations to prepare for continental or overseas missionary service. These communities offered accommodation and varied activity similar to that which Zinzendorf had admired at Halle, although the immediate prototype for Herrnhut seems to have been the ecumenical community at Ebersdorf Castle in Thuringia on the estate of Zinzendorf's parents-in-law, a branch of the Reuss family. Zinzendorf visited the community there in 1721, before embarking on his religious career, and was impressed by the way Christians of varying denominational persuasions lived together in close fellowship. He also perceived that, in a rural or semi-rural setting, impressive buildings had a considerable visual and psychological impact on outsiders, suggesting the prestigious nature of the Christian witness which was taking place within. This principle did not apply so much to Herrnhut, which grew organically without prior overall planning, but it did at Herrnhaag, which was purpose-built and architecturally magnificent. Fulneck, on a smaller scale, followed the Herrnhaag example, as did the settlements established in Pennsylvania and North Carolina in the 1740s.

Zinzendorf's spirituality was also in part a reflection of his experience of Roman Catholicism, probably beginning with his study of Arndt's thesis that lay and clerical devotional practice could be enriched by drawing on medieval Roman Catholic spirituality. Such enrichment, by returning to the simpler tried and tested ways of the past, 'Reform by Retrogression' as opposed to the less durable 'Reform by Advances',[71] was a principle close to Zinzendorf's heart in any case, and it was part of the special devotional appeal of Pietism evident by Zinzendorf's time. A further consideration was that Protestantism had not generated enough spiritual literature to meet the demand, and so Pietists continued to use the main pre-Reformation mystical tradition. The influence of Roman Catholicism on Zinzendorf gained a personal dimension while he was living in Paris as part of his Grand Tour, from late September 1719 to the end of March 1720. There he was welcomed by and became closely acquainted with the Roman Catholic hierarchy, including Cardinal de Noailles, Primate of Paris, with whom he developed a close and permanent friendship. With their assistance he looked deeply into Protestant mythology about Roman Catholicism and considered afresh the appeal of pre-Reformation Catholicism. He soon realized that it had achieved much more than the growth of papalism and the commercialization of penance.[72] He also found that leading French ecclesiastics were more tolerant of Reformation doctrine and Protestant schism than he had expected,[73] seldom using arguments attributed to them in books, but advancing others which were new to him. Some of these appealed to him very much, particularly the notion of the unfathomable ocean of the suffering of Jesus Christ, and the grace he had obtained for believers.[74]

Largely as a result of these emphases, Christ's atonement became the central theme of Zinzendorf's theology, associated with the grand principle of Protestantism as expounded by Luther, that all who had been washed and sanctified by the blood of Christ belonged to the true Church. Furthermore, they were members of Christ's body, and brethren, whether they belonged to Rome or to the Protestant denominations.[75] This evidence that Archbishop Noailles was thus privy to what he believed to be the essentials of true Christianity[76] strengthened still further Zinzendorf's conviction that existing denominations should continue their traditional rites and practices and not seek to attract proselytes from each other.

Further continental cultural and religious influences on the early Renewed Unity

Zinzendorf shared the aesthetic interests of Europe's cultured upper classes among whom musical performance was valued highly as a routine feature of the good life, and he regarded it as appropriate to the needs of the Unity.[77] Indeed, in addition to architecture, music was one of the fine arts in which Germany could claim real distinction, especially after 1700.[78] Dresden, Zinzendorf's native city, was outstanding in this respect, with a rich tradition carried on in the Saxon court at great expense, augmented by a loyal city council which, among other acts of generosity, had provided a splendid city opera house holding two thousand spectators, complete with its own orchestra and resident opera company.

Similarly, the writing of poetry was a prized form of literary expression among the cultured classes,[79] and Zinzendorf himself, true to his background, wrote a large amount of religious poetry, mostly in the form of hymns, which dominated Unity hymnody for generations. Other authors and composers also made their contribution, and the Brethren's early hymnals drew lavishly on the rich traditions of the German Protestant Church, based on the characteristic hymnal chorale, typified by Luther's hymn, 'A Safe Stronghold Our God Is Still'. Another part of this poetic tradition linked to music was the widespread use of cantata, a form of composition containing choruses, solo arias, recitatives and instrumental interludes from which the oratorio, a longer and more elaborate version of the cantata, was derived. As a more detailed survey of the Brethren's hymnody, liturgical and musical style is given in Part Four of this book, it is only necessary here to note that by the time the Brethren formed their first English congregation they already had a mature musical and poetical style into which more localized forms, such as the hymns of Methodism, could easily be incorporated.

Frequent reference to the lot for making decisions, a practice used by other Christian groups since apostolic times, characterized Unity organization both at provincial and congregational level. It was held that Jesus Christ used this device to guide the various Elders' Conferences which sometimes felt it necessary to consult him. In such circumstances a question was put, and various alternative answers were written down on separate sheets of paper. Another sheet was left blank. Each was then rolled up to form identical items and after prayer one was chosen at random, that is, in theory, as directed by the Saviour, and what was written on it was taken to be his will. If the blank turned up it was assumed that he was not at that stage prepared to decide on the particular issue, and the Elders were either to postpone their request or rephrase it and try again.

Recourse to the lot in this way facilitated what believers regarded as divine intervention in everyday life, another principle as old as Christianity, alluded to by Luther, who declared repeatedly, 'Here I was driven by God, here I was hurled from the beginning to the outcome.'[80] He, too, drew upon the medieval mystical tradition that individual life could be directed by the intervention of a present, all-powerful God.[81] For Luther, man's destiny was not in his own hands, but was divinely guided, a principle which he argued was fundamental to Christian living.

The Brethren went further than this. For them, the use of the lot was closely connected with their supposition that Jesus Christ had agreed to lead the Unity personally. On 16 September 1741, at a provincial conference in London and not on the continent where it might perhaps have been expected, he accepted by lot the appointment of Chief Elder, that is, executive head of the Unity. News of this was announced simultaneously in all congregations on 13 November 1741, confirming the illustrious nature of the Unity over and above all other denominations, and as a result they enjoyed the corporate sense of superiority of an elite. The extent to which this was taken seriously can be gauged by this summary of a sermon preached by Bishop Johannes von Watteville in Fulneck, England, on 9 April 1755:

> He kept the Evening Meeting, wherein was an extraordinary happy Feeling. Text. 'I am with you always, nobody does supply thy Place.' He spoke of the Character of the Unity which is quite different from all other Denominations since they have not got our Lord and Lamb for their Elder as we have and daily experience in a blessed Manner to our Comfort.[82]

Zinzendorf persistently defended the decision-making role of the lot. 'For me,' he said, 'the Lot and the Will of the Saviour will be one and the same until I gain more Wisdom.'[83] At the 1754 London Synod he argued that the Saviour was bodily present in the Brethren's Halls and Synods. He claimed, 'the Man Jesus of Nazareth is present in this our Oeconomy[84] not only as the omnipresent God . . . He frequently visits us, and is as a Man so bodily amongst us that He, at that Time, cannot be said to be anywhere else.'[85]

In practical terms, one important consequence was that those called upon to serve the religious societies and the overseas missions could do so with the utmost confidence and without fear, because they had been chosen by lot, i.e. by the Saviour in person. In the words of Bosch, 'ordinary men and women, many of them simple artisans, went literally to the ends of the earth, devoting themselves for life to people often living in the most degrading circumstances, identifying with them and living the gospel in their midst'.[86] Surely, he argues, 'this was Protestantism's "answer" to the very best there was in the Roman Catholic Jesuit and monastic orders'. In this way the Renewed Unity were following the earlier work of Halle in the expansion of Protestant missions.

The motives of the Brethren in this connection were initially not quite as altruistic as might be thought. By 1731 their continental base at Herrnhut was under threat of closure by the Saxon authorities on the grounds that its inhabitants were tempting away citizens of Catholic Bohemia and were an unauthorized Protestant body. This was no idle threat; during the following year thousands of Protestants were expelled from the archbishopric of Salzburg, causing outrage in Protestant Europe, and in 1733 the Protestant Schwenkfelders who had sought refuge on Zinzendorf's estates at Herrnhut were similarly expelled, many emigrating to North America. He, too, was banished. As a result, fearful in case Herrnhut should become untenable and its residents dispersed, Zinzendorf began negotiations to transfer some of them to bases abroad, first in Denmark, then in Georgia, showing, according to Ward,[87] that in such uncertain times the Renewed Unity had no option but to become a missionary body. Lutheran pietistic missionary activity was religious mission pure and simple, whereas that of the Unity began in part as organized migration.

The white-hot spirituality of Herrnhaag (1740–1750)

Unity re-absorption of pre-Reformation devotional and liturgical practices in the medieval mystical tradition, combined with contemporary aristocratic interest in music and poetry, had sensational consequences in the new settlement at Herrnhaag, near Frankfurt-am-Main. This began as a colony of Herrnhut, but evolved into the first really substantial alternative to it, two other settlements planned for Heerendyk in Holland and Pilgerruh in Denmark having failed to develop as hoped. During the 1740s Herrnhaag became a 'super-charged space',[88] attracting hundreds of young exuberant religious revivalists, including some of noble birth from all over the German Empire, and the non-Lutherans from Herrnhut, whom Zinzendorf needed to place elsewhere for security from the Bohemian authorities. Within a few years the new establishment had totally eclipsed Herrnhut in both influence and numbers. It soon became the source of an extraordinary explosion of spiritual power, one aspect of which was a self-sacrificing worldwide 'offensive' of missionary expansion.[89] The successful expansion of the Unity into Britain and other areas during the 1740s and 1750s was part of this offensive with its remarkable outpouring of spiritual, literary, musical and artistic energy.

Love, the dominant emotional force of Herrnhaag, was associated with deep gratitude to the Saviour for undeserved redemption and expressed in terms of 'blood and wounds' theology. Yet it should be emphasized that the spirit of Herrnhaag was a reiteration and practical application of well-established traditions of pre-Reformation mystical writing, as exemplified in *The Imitation of Christ* (*c*.1413), where Thomas à Kempis wrote,

> If you cannot contemplate high and heavenly things take refuge in the Passion of Christ and love to dwell within his sacred wounds. For if you devoutly seek the wounds of Jesus and the precious marks of his passion you will find great strength in all troubles.[90]

This mystical approach to worship, which brought to ardent aspirants the fulfilment of their highest desires,[91] was familiar, also, from the works of the Erfurt Augustinian monk, Johannes von Paltz. His *Heavenly Treasure Trove*, published in 1490, which was very widely read as a guide to meditation, saw nearly twenty editions in thirty years. The writer argued that one should submerge oneself in the five sacred wounds and school oneself in this way to overcome the world, kill off the flesh, and drive away evil thoughts. Meditating devoutly on Christ's passion would inspire such intense love of God that the meditator would become capable of true contrition for his sins.[92]

By 1745, prominence given to love imagery in Herrnhaag's spirituality led to the spontaneous emergence of a literary movement specializing in the production of emotive poetry in which the 'bloody' crucifixion was the central motif.[93] Christ's side wound in particular, variously referred to as the Side Shrine, Crevice, Hole or Cavern, became an object of intense devotional meditation, using a new, esoteric and excessively metaphorical religious language which was developed and systematically inculcated in special courses on religious poetry.

Further, the combination of intense love and gratitude to the Saviour was linked to sexual love, following another well-known feature of medieval mysticism, typified in the writings of Ramon Lull (1232–1315), which were characterized by repeated erotic imagery.[94] Luther, too, was influenced by these pre-Reformation sources, asserting that human sexual drives were a divine force, or evidence of God's vital presence, finding the scriptural basis for this view in Genesis 2.18, 'It is not good that man should be alone; I will make a helpmeet for him.' In Luther's view, since God's power was already present in the sexual instinct, marriage was simply the right way to use it, the genuinely spiritual and divinely ordained way to live one's sexuality.[95] Zinzendorf was profoundly influenced by these pre-Reformation and Lutheran views relating divine love with human sexuality, and, despite several prolonged absences, he had a leading role in the spiritual renaissance in the Herrnhaag community.[96] In 1746 he introduced his version of 'Marriage Religion'. The divine marriage in this view was between God the father and the Holy Spirit the mother. Jesus Christ was the son and he was the Bridegroom of the Church.[97] This relationship was deemed to parallel the union of a married couple in that the husband was head over his wife as Christ was head of the Church, a notion found in early seventeenth-century Anglicanism. It followed that their physical union was a sacrament.

There were other ramifications, including the exaltation of childish simplicity, again with a genuinely scriptural derivation, which inspired a newly created 'Order of Little Fools', and trusting childish sentiments were expressed in an appropriately symbolic language. 'Playing' became important: colourful and extravagant festivals were organized with all kinds of special robes, gowns, ornamental decoration and illuminations reminiscent of the opulent entertainment provided in the palaces of some of the aristocracy. Musical festivals with specially composed items, where the emphasis was wholly on feeling and atmosphere, became commonplace.[98] Unfortunately, but probably inevitably, this communal psychic liberation expressed in such an ardent aesthetic culture became so intense that by 1750 it cracked. By then, the younger generation of Brethren were beginning to use the special Herrnhaag spiritual language to such an extent that it became absurd and could only be understood by an exclusive body of insiders. Many of these enthusiasts joined the great missionary offensive, but other older and more conservative elements in the Unity, particularly in Herrnhut, were outraged; outsiders, hearing wildly exaggerated accounts of the Brethren's marriage religion, were scandalized. The result was a split between radicals and conservatives, a sifting process. At the eleventh hour Zinzendorf returned from England and tried to intervene to restore a sense of balance, but it was too late. In February 1750 Herrnhaag was closed by the Count of Büdingen on the grounds of its notoriety throughout Protestant Europe, and its residents were dispersed, many going to the Rhineland to build a new settlement at Neuwied. From then onwards, in the Unity as a whole, the more ortho-dox struggled to restrict the influence of colleagues who had been intensely stirred by the esoteric spirituality of Herrnhaag. This was not easy, because it undoubtedly met the deepest religious needs of many in contemporary society, not only for the limited period during which it flowered, but for several decades afterwards while its acolytes were still alive.[99] The language of Herrnhaag is explored in more detail in Part Four as an important expression of Unity identity during the 1740s, essential to an understanding of evolving Moravianism and its initial impact on the British Province.

Diaspora Societies and Place Congregations

It was intended from the beginning that the Brotherhood itself should remain numerically small, a principle which accorded with Zinzendorf's original aim of building a devout and dedicated elite with spiritual qualities which ensured that they would become respected among fellow Germans. In the early years, this formation of networks of religious societies in a diaspora was the primary activity and the authentic style of the Renewed Unity as understood by its founders, and among German-speakers it was successful. Its itinerant evangelists benefited from intellectual and cultural contact with enthusiastic members of other denominations in the intimate atmosphere of society meetings. Travel in itself was believed to be spiritually rewarding, particularly so when the traveller could carry the message of revival as far afield as Switzerland and Holland, through the whole of the German Empire to the Baltic regions, and into Britain. From 1732, when the second phase of Unity activity was initiated among the heathen abroad, especially in the Americas and Greenland, Germans provided the bulk of the resources and personnel; Zinzendorf himself used his fortune and credit to ensure that finance was available to support his vision.

As the Brethren's area of influence extended during the 1740s, more evangelists were required. This spiritual elite was recruited partly from the diaspora societies, but mainly from a small number of fixed congregational bases built originally for this specific purpose. These strictly organized and exclusive religious settlements,[100] derivatives of the Herrnhut prototype though later typified by Herrnhaag, Niesky and Gnadenfrei, were similar in style. Private houses and apartments were provided for families, but the unmarried majority lived in collegiate-style Single Brethren's or Single Sisters' Houses, which were usually substantial buildings incorporating a full range of residential facilities including a meeting hall (chapel), dining hall and dormitory. In addition, and owing something to Francke's establishment at Halle, these premises included various types of workshop so that residents could earn a living and pay for their upkeep. Widowers and widows usually shared this accommodation unless there were premises expressly built for them. Children lived with their parents until they were old enough to move into either the Single Brethren's or Single Sisters' Houses.

All residents were subdivided administratively into groups of the same sex and similar age range, called choirs; for example, there was a Single Brethren's Choir, and a Single Sisters' Choir, older boys' and girls' choirs, and a joint choir for all married people. Residence in settlements was partly intended to promote a recommended type of choir loyalty, encouraging behaviour worthy of the choir, in practice an education in forbearance and the discipline of living and working together in harmony. Choirs were subdivided into educational groups known as classes, which met regularly, and smaller more informal bands, which were intended to encourage intimate mutual discussion of secular and spiritual matters. The graveyard was similarly subdivided; the deceased were interred in their choir area, a further example for the living of the principle of group identity.

An elaborate administrative structure was established to ensure that settlement life proceeded smoothly for the residents, who typically numbered several hundred members. At the head was the Congregational Helper, who was the president and spiritual leader, assisted by the Congregational Servant, who specialized in the practical business and quartermastering aspect of settlement life. Each choir house was led by its own Helper and Servant and functioned as a largely autonomous corporate body within the settlement as a whole. Inevitably, regulations pervaded most aspects of settlement life, but were intended to provide a great deal of support for every congregational member. Administrators and all full-time Unity employees, whether ordained or not, were defined as 'Labourers', and it was these men and women who introduced this well-organized and smooth-running continental model into Britain during the early 1740s.

This was not all. There were two underlying objectives in Place Congregational construction and internal organization, which were far more subtle than these administrative details might suggest. One was spiritual; the other social. It was Unity dogma that their geographical locations were chosen by the Saviour and that he was personally interested in their subsequent development, a theme which will be dealt with more fully later. The social aspect was partly related to this, but perhaps more to Zinzendorf's aristocratic background, because in scale and architectural style these purpose-built premises surrounded by their landscaped gardens could be matched only by the most prestigious Roman Catholic continental monasteries. Thus, for the purposes for which they were built, Place Congregations were far more impressive than the multitude of buildings erected on behalf of the Lutheran, Reformed or Methodist Churches. The fact that this was done under Zinzendorf's direction confirmed his instinctive recognition of the respect which attended property, a characteristic feature of the eighteenth-century mentality.[101] His concern with ground and place typified the aristocratic, propertied mind, which identified possession of land with power.[102] When augmented by imposing buildings and landscaped gardens, there was an even greater demonstration of authority and wealth. Power was thus made visible in stone;[103] but all too often it went along with an accumulation of debt. The aristocratic predilection for heavy borrowing had been a matter for contemporary comment down the centuries, and Zinzendorf, too, fell victim to its temptation. Place Congregations, therefore, as well as being an expression of Unity spirituality, were intended to impress a propertied society, but in Britain were not destined to last for long in their original form.[104] Paradoxically, despite Zinzendorf's desire for the fervour and simplicity of the New Testament Church, the style of building which he affected had little of the spirit of earlier times when the Church had no special holy places, times or persons;[105] but then, in the first century AD, it was not serving a propertied society. Zinzendorf was an eighteenth-century aristocrat, and the Unity which he established reflected his taste.

Part Two

Evolution of the British Provincial Character and Congregational Network

3

German Religious and Cultural Ascendancy, 1742–c.1780

The establishment of the Brethren as part of the Evangelical Revival in Britain

The Renewed Unity, authorized by the lot, became officially involved in Britain among non-Germans in 1742. It was very successful for a time, and a British province came into being, headed by Bishop August Gottlieb Spangenberg and characterized by German religious and cultural dominance. The brief period of enthusiasm and rapid expansion which followed, lasting until about 1780, is arguably the most interesting in the history of the British Province, and has received the greatest attention from scholars. The most recent contribution by Colin Podmore covers the years 1728–60 in detail, though he had to admit that 'the lack of an adequate narrative and the volume of available source material'[1] made it impossible for him to offer a comprehensive history of the province in this, its initial period. As a result, though analysing its style and suggesting reasons for its initial appeal, he concentrated mainly on its external relations within the Evangelical Revival, particularly with the Church of England and Parliament, and on public opinion. While acknowledging valuable insights from his research, the aim in this chapter is to look at the British Province as a whole during the period from 1742 to c.1780, dealing primarily with general principles and overall patterns of development rather than merely repeating what has been described in Podmore's and previous publications.

The starting point, central to the argument of this book, is that the eighteenth-century Unity was fundamentally German in spirit and style. Consequently, when its influence radiated abroad from its Central European heartland where it was most at home, it achieved the greatest success and remained truest to its original intentions in German-speaking enclaves, particularly those in Eastern European countries. Further, there was a greater likelihood of a favourable response from those people if they had already been influenced by the Pietist wing of the Lutheran Church. Thus, throughout the German international community, there was a frequent correlation between pietistic and Unity spheres of influence, in which the latter tended to reap where it had not sown. This is not to suggest that its members progressed from pietistic Lutheran into Unity institutions, but a substantial number did so, because the interpretation of Pietism which they found there met their deepest religious needs. In practice, on the continent, as Zinzendorf intended, most Christians who came under the influence of Unity evangelists retained their original confessional allegiance while taking up membership of Unity religious societies.

Considering their preferred link with pietistic communities the Unity incursion into Britain was exceptional, although there was a minute German Pietist enclave at court, some of whom were sympathetic and even helpful. It included Johanna Sophia, Countess of Schaumburg-Lippe, who had a potentially influential role as one of the Queen's ladies-in-waiting, and Friedrich Michael Ziegenhagen, the Lutheran court chaplain. Because they had heard with interest of recent events in Herrnhut and were aware of the leading role of Count Zinzendorf, they took the initiative of writing to the count to enquire further. As a result, in July 1728, three Brethren came to London to visit them, but the visit did not leave, among the Pietists at court, the nucleus of a new religious society. Other Germans living in London do not appear to have come under Unity influence.

One significant element in British religious life during the 1730s was a loosely organized network of societies, led primarily by enthusiastic laymen, which had been established as a result of a similar pietistic impulse to that which had originated on the continent during the late seventeenth century. Since these were totally English and Anglican, Zinzendorf and his German-speaking colleagues had no reason at that time to think of Britain as a likely area of evangelistic activity. For them, deep in Central Europe, Britain was important primarily because of the transatlantic shipping facilities available in London for emigrants to join the huge number of Germans already settled in the American colonies,[2] for the spiritual oversight provided for those going out by the German chaplains at the London Court, and for the dispersal of the beleaguered inhabitants of Herrnhut should this become necessary.

Contact with London was resumed six years later, still mainly connected with the Unity programme of dispersal from Herrnhut. It involved a visit to London by Bishop August Gottlieb Spangenberg in December 1734 to negotiate with the Georgia Trustees for a settlement as distinct from a mission there. In January 1735 land was made available for this purpose, and the first group of Brethren under Spangenberg's leadership sailed from London shortly afterwards. Others sailed in October of the same year, and it was by coincidence that, on this voyage and subsequently in Georgia, the Wesley brothers, Benjamin Ingham and Charles Delamotte, key figures in the future development of the British province of the Unity, first came into close contact with the Brethren and became familiar with their style; yet even at this stage, in 1735, Unity leaders in Germany still did not see any potential in Britain in the absence of the all-important sizeable and sympathetic German enclave.

Early in 1737 Count Zinzendorf came to London to negotiate still further with the Georgia Trustees about the dispersal of Unity members, aiming also to make personal contact with leading members of the Anglican Church, particularly the Archbishop of Canterbury. As a typical aristocrat accustomed to making easy social contact with significant members of the international religious hierarchy to whom he was indebted, such as Cardinal Noailles and other leading Roman Catholics in Paris, Zinzendorf appreciated that it might be valuable to ascertain Archbishop Potter's view of Unity ordination and of the potentialities for an interdenominational movement in support of existing Protestant denominations. While in London, almost incidentally, he founded a religious society for German-speakers, which attracted very few members and which subsequently maintained a precarious existence with no perceptible influence on Unity activity.

In early February 1738 four more Brethren, Peter Böhler, Georg Schulius, Friedrich Wenzel Neisser and Abraham Ehrenfried Richter, arrived in London.[3] The first three were on their way to America, and Richter had been detailed to care for the tiny German society organized by the Count the previous year. By this time John Wesley had returned from Georgia; so the stage was set for his close relationship with the Brethren in London. This was possible because Germans who could not proceed immediately to America remained in the capital for several months, being drawn into the group of religious activists associated with James Hutton, particularly the pietistic-style Anglican religious society formed by him in 1736, which met at his home. The consequent Anglo-German mix formed the nucleus of what was to be a permanent Unity presence in Britain when Peter Böhler drew off a select group from Hutton's society on 1 May 1738 to form a derivative more in line with Unity thinking. This group was not then an official Unity society, but its foundation was momentous, for on 1 January 1739 its members, who included the Wesley brothers, George Whitefield and Benjamin Ingham (not Peter Böhler, who was by then in America), experienced a moving effusion of the Holy Spirit at their meeting. The events which followed, according to Podmore, justify the claim that 'it was from the Fetter Lane Society which Böhler founded that the Revival burst out in 1739 to spread throughout England'.[4] Podmore follows Hutton's 1909 history in maintaining that 'the Fetter Lane Society was nothing less than the head-quarters of the growing Evangelical Revival'.[5] Thus the Brethren were an important conduit through which continental traditions of spirituality passed into English evangelicalism.[6]

In the autumn a new stage in Unity involvement in Britain began when Ingham applied to the continental leadership for assistance, naming especially John Töltschig, with whom he had worked previously in Georgia. Ingham argued that this man would be of great assistance in converting English people touched by the Evangelical Revival, and on these urgent grounds the request was granted. As a result, Töltschig arrived in London in October 1739, preceded by Philipp Heinrich Molther who, though nominally destined for America, remained in Britain for several months. In November Richard Viney arrived from Zeist, and for a time these men were the spearhead of Unity activity. With their help the Fetter Lane Society, which still included the Wesleys, maintained its seminal role in the general revival until July 1740, when a serious breach occurred as a result of internal tension, and John Wesley and his supporters left to form another society.[7] Details of the events and mis-understandings leading to this schism have been researched and well recorded[8] and need no repetition here; suffice it to say that from July 1740 onwards the Methodists and the Brethren followed separate courses within the continuing Evangelical Revival. Remaining members of the Fetter Lane Society were organized more characteristically on Unity lines until, on 30 October 1742, this group was constituted the first Unity Congregation in Britain and became the core of all subsequent provincial development.

During the brief and turbulent lifetime of the original Fetter Lane Society, effectively 1 May 1738 to 30 October 1742, the Revival had been spreading in various parts of the country under local leaders, most of whom ultimately declared their allegiance to John Wesley, George Whitefield or the Brethren, and in this state of flux the Brethren were exceptionally fortunate. As had happened so often on the continent, they reaped where they had not sown, acquiring spheres of influence in wide-ly scattered areas, not of their own choosing, where several prestigious Anglican predecessors had been active independently for some time. These individuals succumbed to the seductive appeal of the Brethren and enthusiastically handed over the networks of independent societies which they had laboriously created, and their members augmented the existing Unity society network.[9]

The key exponents of revival who united with the Brethren in this way, and their respective spheres of influence, were Benjamin Ingham,[10] active in West Yorkshire; David Taylor, active in Cheshire and Derbyshire; and Francis Okely[11] and Jacob Rogers, working in the Bedford area and equally successful in Bristol and other places in the West of England such as Tytherton and Malmesbury. John Cennick was active initially in Wiltshire and later with outstanding success in Ireland. These were the areas, demarcated early and vigorously maintained, in which most Unity congregations were later located and where the great majority of British members have always lived.

Although the extent to which evangelists adhered to precise territories is unknown, there is some evidence that the boundaries of their spheres of influence were jealously guarded; for example, in November 1745 Cennick staked his claim 'in the name of the Lord'[12] to the areas of the West Country where he had societies, forbidding other evangelists, particularly Whitefield's supporters, to trespass. In March 1746 Whitefield's Association of Preachers wrote from Bristol requesting permission to preach in Wiltshire near established Unity societies, 'at the request of old friends'. Two months later, Unity leaders in London received a complaint that Unity evangelists were 'trespassing' in an area where Whitefield's people were active. Even John Wesley was noted to have been very circumspect in this matter when preaching in Dublin in January 1748.

The willingness of Ingham and the others to contribute to Unity influence did not necessarily imply that they took no further personal interest in the work they had started. When Richard Viney went to work in Yorkshire in 1743 he found that Benjamin Ingham still influenced decision-making in his former network. His diary recorded:

> I find matters are so ordered now that nothing great or small is done in ye Yorkshire societys by ye Brethren but what Mr. Ingham is first consulted with and his approbation obtained. He visits and speaks with each Soul in ye Societys this month and Br Teltshig and wife follows him and Br Holland is to follow them and do the same.[13]

A brief outline of the career of John Cennick (1718–1755)[14] typifies the role of these benefactors and illustrates how the Unity was able to take advantage of their successful labours. Born in Reading to an Anglican family and stirred by the Evangelical Revival, he was attracted to the Methodists as a young adult, but soon abandoned them in favour of

Whitefield's movement.[15] In June 1739 he accepted Whitefield's offer of a position as schoolmaster for the children of colliers at Kingswood (Bristol). There he felt called to evangelize not only in Kingswood but much further afield in Wiltshire and Somerset, forming numerous religious societies on Whitefield's behalf, and becoming regarded as one of his most important colleagues. From 1741 he also became active in London, where he was attracted to the Brethren to such an extent that in 1745 he left Whitefield's movement and joined the Unity. The societies he had formed in the West of England then wrote to the Brethren asking to be accepted as Unity religious societies, a request which was granted.

Like many other converts, Cennick travelled to the continent to visit some Unity congregations, and in 1746 began on the Brethren's behalf what became an outstandingly successful mission to Ireland, where he was mainly instrumental in laying the foundations for most of their later congregations. He began his labours in the capital, Dublin, and soon became famous in that city. In June 1746 he formed a society comprising people of various denominations, and also attracted Benjamin LaTrobe into membership, thus beginning the important LaTrobe ministerial dynasty. In August 1748 he was invited to meet the Anglican Primate of Ireland.[16] Even leaders of the Irish Roman Catholic Church showed interest in Cennick's preaching, noting its beneficent influence, and in the following October the Bishop of Down and Connor invited him to go to the west of Ireland and preach to the Catholics there. The extent to which he influenced practising Catholics or made converts to Protestantism is uncertain and a subject for further research.

John Töltschig was sent to assist Cennick for a time towards the end of 1747, and Bishop Peter Böhler in June 1750, during which month he settled the Dublin society as a Town Congregation, declaring its members to be received into the Unity forthwith and accepting that they had now left their former denominations. This example illustrates the beginning of a progressive abandonment of the expressed intention of the Unity that members should remain loyal to their original congregations, a development which was soon to become the norm in Britain.

Using the Dublin congregation as his base, Cennick campaigned further afield in the counties of Down, Antrim, Derry and Armagh. There he was received enthusiastically and formed numerous Unity societies, a few of which were soon promoted to congregational status, including Ballinderry (1755) and Drumargan (1757), both of which became Country Congregations in an area where Presbyterians were the chief source of recruitment. Cennick's work was hindered to some extent by local difficulties of communication, but in this area of poverty and privation many people were responsive to his evangelistic initiative. Although he received considerable help from colleagues from England, the stress of unremitting work damaged his health, so that he died on 4 July 1755 after only nine years' labour in London and Ireland. He had contributed significantly to provincial development, having made the work of the Unity extensively known in Dublin and the northern counties.

During the next few years, colleagues built further on this foundation by establishing the Place Congregation of Gracehill on land between Ballymena and Gloonen in 1765. Two years later the Brethren leased land near Lough Neagh, County Derry, and founded another smaller Place Congregation which they named Gracefield.

A further significant factor which subsequently influenced the British Province's sense of identity, was that most of the areas where they were established initially were undergoing industrialization and the social changes associated with migration from rural to developing urban areas.[17] Here religious pluralism was the norm, particularly in West Yorkshire and Lancashire, where pressure was soon applied to change the original society-forming rationale of all the eighteenth-century Protestant revivalist networks in favour of the establishment of congregations.

Neither the Unity hierarchy in Germany nor the provincial leaders in England had experience of coping with this type of pressure, and were fortunate that the pace of change was relatively slow, though it soon became nationwide. For a time, therefore, they consolidated the networks of religious societies so unexpectedly bestowed upon them and, with the addition of a few others gained entirely by their efforts, they set up the familiar continental model, focusing first on Fulneck, near Leeds. This settlement and its related societies, some of which later advanced to congregational status, was the nearest that the British Province came to the authentic continental model, which had been conceived in very different circumstances. It has been the subject of a book by one of the present authors, *The Moravian Settlement at Fulneck, 1742–1790*.[18] In West Yorkshire, as well as in the other widely separated areas of the evolving British Province, so long as the Brethren used their continental model they were doing so in competition with the Methodists, who had more resources to develop an indigenous movement and whose appeal was far greater.

The early development of Methodism, with its thoroughly conservative and staunchly Anglican high church leadership,[19] and the incursion of the

Brethren into Britain, both began during the late 1730s. At that stage their objectives and methods had much in common, since both bodies saw the enthusiasm for spiritual revival as an opportunity to reinvigorate the Established church,[20] believing that this could be achieved by organizing those 'newly awakened' by their itinerant preachers into home-based societies grouped in circuits or connexions for ease of administration.

In the case of the Methodists, who soon became a large-scale evangelizing agency,[21] this society- and circuit-forming movement developed from many focal points in different parts of the country, being especially popular in newly industrializing and mining areas where established religion had little hold on the working population. Roy Porter[22] argues that the Anglican Church, the nation's largest and wealthiest religious institution, did not appeal to plebeian parishioners, and that many attended services as a reluctant captive audience, while some of the more spiritually inclined joined tolerated dissenting groups. This uniquely British compromise was particularly prevalent in northern industrializing areas, where Anglicanism was relatively weak and dissenting groups correspondingly influential. Methodism was particularly strong in rural parishes, despite the expectation that people employed on landed estates would worship in the Anglican Church alongside their employers. In such areas those who became 'religious' in the Methodist sense were often regarded with suspicion. The movement developed naturally and organically and, where it was appreciated, many joined Methodist societies without withdrawing from the active church life of their parishes.[23] Despite the fact that many of the numerous enthusiasts who joined the movement soon withdrew or were dismissed,[24] circuits were sufficiently vigorous and flexible to cope with rapid changes in fortune and fluctuating local interest. Once a particular circuit had been established it could usually survive, even if the number of participating societies varied considerably, provided that the itinerant preacher and his stewards were dedicated and well organized. In this way the early Methodist organization, like that of the Unity in Britain, functioned as a centrally controlled, evangelizing, society-forming agency to complement the ministrations of the established clergy in what throughout the late eighteenth century was still the fashionable Church.[25] Although this supportive rationale was never accepted by all its members, while John Wesley remained alive they were held to his off-beat Anglican stance, in effect for the rest of the century,[26] in contrast to the Brethren, who changed direction much earlier.

Because the original focal points from which the Brethren's influence subsequently radiated were relatively remote and few in number, unlike the Methodists, their potential for development was restricted, a limitation which contributed to the difficulties faced by the Church during the nineteenth century in administering and extending the work of the province, and one which effectively prevented it from becoming well known in the country as a whole.

The period of enthusiasm and rapid expansion illustrated from Unity archives

The Fetter Lane Congregational Diary for the period July 1743–February 1744 records in detail the daily comings and goings of the leading Germans and prominent Labourers (Unity officials)[27] within the British network and between London and other Unity establishments. It gives a vivid impression of the international organization of which the London congregation was at that time a focal point. This congregation functioned as a spiritual centre for those in transit between the continent and the Americas, and its members were sensitive to this pivotal role in the Unity. On 1 August 1743, having previously recorded the final preparations of a contingent of Brethren and their departure for America at 5 a.m., the diary continues simply:

> The Prayer Day began at near 7. Br. Hutton sang a Hymn, then pray'd for a Blessing and read some sweet Accts [Accounts] from divers Parts of the World, then Marshall spoke on the Lamb's Losung[28] and Word of the Day and concluded with Prayer.

From the very early years German and British members and adherents of the Fetter Lane community were drawn together into the work of the Unity in Britain and abroad through the correspondence which circulated from all areas of involvement, and the diary reveals how the whole enterprise was bound up with daily worship:

> Monday Oct 3d. 1743
> 3–4 the General Meeting began, Br. Hutton for a Blessing then read many Letters from different Parts of England, Prycelcius' and Bitners Journalls, also the Greenland Do.[ditto] and we trust with many Blessings, afterwards Br. Schlicht spoke on the Word of the Day and Holland concluded with a Prayer and the Blessing. We collected £5.16.5½, then the Society met by themselves, Br. Spang's [Spangenberg's] Letter was read, wherein he desired that our Br. George Neisser

might be furthered in his Journey to Silesia by reason he should be there the Beginning of next month . . . His Journal of the Sea Congregation Affairs commencing from the time the Ship sailed from Helvoet-Sluys [?] to her arrival off Plymouth was read also with a Sweet Inward Stillness, and Br. Hutton concluded with a Prayer.

On an administrative level there were frequent policy meetings between members of the 'Pilgrim Congregation' – the German leaders – and their British colleagues, at which the married couples involved in decision-making discussed current issues. One such meeting was recorded in the diary on 22 August 1743, and the close fellowship which had been established between the German Brethren and their English colleagues is very evident.

Schlicht and She [his wife], Holland and She and Clagget went to Blackheath where they together with Neissor and She, Hutton and She and Teltchig had a sweet Conference concerning plans in General as well as many Matters and Persons in Particular, twas observed that the London Congregation stood in the same Relation with the Pilgrim Congregation[29] as the Body did to the Soul.

These records illustrate the practicalities of daily decision-making in a developing organization which was attracting enquirers in various parts of the country. The evolving method of providing financial support for Brethren who went to a new place was recorded on 7 August 1743 in connection with a request from Mr How in Nottingham for a Labourer to work in the area. He had asked Br Holland how such a Brother was maintained, and had been told that Labourers sent out in answer to such requests were usually cared for by those among whom they worked. Labourers recruited from English members were not necessarily without resources and obviously expected to bring their occupational skills to the community in which they worked. It is difficult to ascertain how typical was a man called Pearson. He was expecting to work in Yorkshire for the Brethren, who were then at Smith House near Halifax. Obviously of some means and standing as a successful businessman, he asked Br Holland, 'whether he should now give Warning for his House and Quit Business &c., and also how he should live in Yorkshire, whether follow any Business &c., for he was not willing to live upon the Bren., that he had 400£ of his Own'.[30]

Another aspect of the work of the Brethren, in line with their expressed intention of supporting the Anglican Church, was that of advising members of the clergy who approached them for counsel. At this time of revival and enthusiasm there were those who were aware of their short-comings as ministers. One such who had asked the Brethren for help had expressed his high regard for their work: 'Tuesday, Augt. 16th 1743. Mr. Dove . . . also told one of our Bren. that he had lately spoke with a Clergyman who esteem'd the Bren. and desired their acquaintance for he confess'd his Ignorance of guiding Souls.'

The overwhelming impression given by the diarist, possibly Br Schlicht, is of a lively and flexible community in England at the hub of an organization whose German leaders and prominent British members came and went freely among the Brethren's bases in continental Europe, some visiting America. It was an establishment in which from time to time visitors from other areas were entertained. The diary for 28 August 1743 records that, 'a Swedish Minister [Arvid Gradin, who had met Wesley at Herrnhut] dined with Schlicht who was intimately acquainted with the Brethren in that Nation'. He stayed for some weeks and there are various references to shared fellowship and hospitality. The church in Fetter Lane accommodated German- and English-speaking members, often in separate worship, partly because of the language problem and partly on account of the distinction made between German leaders with their English colleagues and ordinary congregation members.

Its members' constant awareness of the wider pattern of communication within the Unity is illustrated by an account of an informal after-supper meeting on 11 September 1743 between the wife of Br Holland, who was then on his way to Portsmouth with a pilgrim group, and Br Schlicht and his wife. They remembered the work of the Brethren in various parts of the country and the wider world by opening Losungen (Watchwords) of different dates, while bearing in mind the Brethren's establishments and the people for whom they sought a scriptural message. These included Mr Holland, Br Töltschig, Herrnhut, 'Smith in the Cape', 'the Savage Church' and 'Lamb's Inn'. The latter was the first school for boys and girls established by the Brethren in 1742 at Broadoaks in Kent and named by Zinzendorf. Later, the boys' section was transferred briefly to Wiltshire in 1745, established at Smith House, near Halifax in Yorkshire in 1748 and moved to Fulneck in 1753, the girls following in 1755. At this stage, however, it featured regularly in the accounts of visits made by leading German and English brethren.

German and English leaders co-operated over the production of suitable material for congregational use. James Hutton, whose business as a printer and bookseller was so crucial to the production of the early hymns, participated actively in this process, and the German style of creating material for immediate use was an important part of the developing pattern of worship in the English societies. On 6 October 1743 it was recorded that, 'Schlicht was busy in setting to Musick a Hymn composed by Br Hutton. . . . In the evening the Anthem was sung with Musick and Old Mrs Hutton said it was very Heavenly.' She was not alone. Many others came to listen to the music used at Unity services, often showing more interest in that than in the evangelistic preaching, which they accepted in a spirit of tolerance. Although the Labourers viewed this with some dismay, there was little they could do about it without radical changes in the normal acts of worship, and, during the 1740s, particularly in London, it was an on-going problem.[31] Yet here was one clue to the appeal of the Brotherhood: it had an exceptionally rich musical repertoire in comparison with the style of other contemporary evangelistic bodies.

In the early years of the Brethren's incursion into Britain, the factors which were to create a distinctive British provincial style were not yet evident. The first British converts were caught up in the enthusiasm and optimism which accompanied the rapid establishment of societies, accepting the leading role of the German Brethren. The latter faced a problem without parallel on the continent, namely, that these converts had not been drawn from the ranks of a substantial and well-established German community. With few exceptions they had never visited Germany, nor were they familiar with the language. To make up for this deficiency as many converts as possible, not just prominent British members, were encouraged to visit the continental settlements. There they could be indoctrinated with the ideals of international and interdenominational brotherhood, share the vibrant communal life and religious observances of show-places, particularly Herrnhaag, and come closer to the authentic style of the Unity than was possible in, say, Yorkshire or Wiltshire. There were frequent references to such visits during the 1740s in the Fetter Lane and London Pilgrim House Diaries. Sometimes the groups who undertook these 'pilgrimages' were small; occasionally they were quite large. It was noted, for example, in the Pilgrim House Diary on 22 November 1746 that Hintz, Okeley (*sic*), Cennick, Hammond, Hunt and Ills were to go to Germany. On 23 January 1747 a party of twenty-three was being arranged, including two unnamed participants from Chesterfield and one from Newcastle.[32] Although no documentary evidence has been found of these people's responses to visiting their new spiritual homeland, the experience would encourage personal friendships and strengthen a sense of belonging to what was then unmistakably a German organization. When they returned to their own societies or congregations, the regular newsletters from Unity headquarters with accounts of German congregational life would have far more significance for them.

First signs of disparity: the Viney affair

Once it became policy to establish residential settlements outside London, Fulneck being the prime example, there was more potential for a conflict of cultures than had been experienced in the capital. German leaders who went to work in Yorkshire soon found evidence in the English temperament of that undesirable tendency towards independent thinking which was destined to have far-reaching consequences in the long-term history of the province. More immediately, it threatened the very existence of the Unity mission.

The case of Richard Viney provides a revealing example of how, as early as 1743, the authoritarian style of the Germans clashed with the assumptions of one British Labourer who did not show the deference and unquestioning obedience which Zinzendorf and his senior colleagues expected. Viney was a prominent and respected English member of the Brethren's Church,[33] and served Peter Böhler as translator.[34] He had been one of a party who visited Germany in 1736, and in 1738 he and James Hutton were the first two Englishmen whose names were entered on the Moravian register at Fetter Lane. On 14 June 1738 he went to Holland and Germany with Töltschig, Ingham and others including John Wesley; in May 1739 he was again at Heerendyke in Holland, and in the spring of 1740 he was working in Oxford. In October 1741 he was made president of the London Moravians, with James Hutton and William Holland as stewards. In 1742 he and his wife moved to Broad Oaks, Essex, to superintend the Unity boarding school which had been established there for the children of missionaries. On 17 June 1743 he went to Yorkshire as preacher and warden of the Brethren's societies at Smith House and in the neighbourhood. Unfortunately, he soon dared to question some of Zinzendorf's policies, in particular his use of the lot, and gained sympathy and support among like-minded Brethren in Yorkshire and even in London. From his point of view, as a leading British member of the Brotherhood, he was offering constructive criticism for consideration by Zinzendorf and his German colleagues, and obviously expected that his views would be received seriously; but this state of affairs could not be permitted by the Germans.

Spangenberg, who adopted a domineering and authoritarian stance over this dispute, visited Yorkshire and took immediate steps to limit the

damage and bring the Labourers back into line. On 22 October 1743 the
Fetter Lane diarist recorded:

> Br. Spangenberg and She and Weisser found that some of the
> Labourers in London were infected with the same [argumentative
> spirit] as Br. Viney tho' not in an equal degree, and that they thought
> they could do without the Assistance of their Old Labourers &c all
> proceeding from Pride and Self-Conceit.

The diary records the message of Spangenberg received on 7 November
1743 by the London congregation during his visit to Yorkshire to
investigate this aberration. It left none of the members in doubt about the
seriousness of questioning German authority and the Saviour's will. 'Br.
Sp. writ from Yorkshire yt he had declared V. by ye X [Cross] an Enemy
of the good order of God in his Church & a Satan, which hath made a
great Stirring among the Labourers.'

A week later, on 14 November news was received in a letter to
Spangenberg's wife that Viney had requested that the matter should be
decided by lot, an ironical choice in view of his expressed opinion. This
process took place on 20 November in the presence of witnesses nominated by Viney, and is described in the diary. The result confirmed the
language in which Spangenberg had denounced him.

> Several Lots, made and written by Ingham, were drawn by Br.
> Toltschig, and by them Viney was declared to be an Enemy of God's
> Order in the church, and a Satan, which caused great fear and induced
> Viney to ask the Prayers of the Brethren. One Lot, however, had been
> drawn against himself (Sp.) from which he understood that he had
> given Viney cause for his bitterness.

The distress which this declaration caused Viney was recorded. He had
requested the prayers of the Brethren, because 'it was so much to him as
if our Saviour was come down from Heaven and had declared him'.
When this account was delivered to the Fetter Lane congregation, they
were exhorted to 'see whether there was not such Seed in them and to
humble themselves before their Saviour'. They prayed for Viney and for
all their circumstances. The diarist recorded: 'This Quarter Hour hath
been very awfull and blessed to many.'

A letter from Spangenberg in Yorkshire to his wife in London, written
on 18 November, was more outspoken about the clashes of temperament
behind the Viney affair. It reveals differences of expectation, even at this

early stage in Unity activity, between the Yorkshire brethren and the German leaders.

> [Letters came] also from Br. Sp. to his wife, reporting that the Devil is using great cunning in Yorkshire. He leads the English Labourers astray to think it a shame to be ruled by Germans, . . . that almost all the Labourers are infected with this Plague; that he (Sp.) had written a sharp letter to Viney, and told him his mind plainly. On the 13th Nov. all the Labourers, 40 in number, came together, when he read them Viney's Letter, and his Answer to it, and declared Viney . . . to be an enemy of God's Order in the Church, and a Satan, whereupon a great Commotion arose, many declaring themselves for Viney, while others remained doubtful.

The conformist message was reinforced for the Fetter Lane congregation over the following weeks in addresses concerning issues such as the Lamb's care to cleanse his sheep, and the nature of the lot as a way by which the Saviour made his love known. The process of rehabilitation culminated in an address by Spangenberg on 31 December 1743 to the Congregational Lovefeast at Fetter Lane, attended by both German and English brethren and sisters. Its main theme was the interdependence of members and their duty to pray for the government which allowed them to work as a small church within a larger organization. Having given thanks for the blessings and peace which the community had enjoyed during the past year, he emphasized the duty owed by the Children of God to those with authority over them, observing that in the past, where matters of conscience were involved, the Brethren had 'left the Country or Place' rather than defy the will of 'the Magistrate in the Place'. The parallel between the ideal of submission to authority and Viney's insubordination was addressed obliquely in significant comments on the character of the English which followed.

> He testify'd his Love to the English Brn & Srs and beg'd leave to speak freely unto them: He had observ'd the English Nation was a rebellious nation, and an old English man had once told him, that since the English had kill'd their [king] ev'ry thing were in Confusion. The women wanted to be Heads &c. and among the Brn. it was very often so that no one wanted to be Master.

These words reveal at this early stage in the Brethren's activity in Britain how fundamentally the attitudes of Britons as perceived by the German leaders differed from those they were accustomed to in the German-speaking Brotherhood as a whole, and even more ominously shows a fundamental lack of willingness on the part of the German hierarchy to accept any criticism of the established leadership. Although he expressed nominal responsibility for contributing to Viney's 'bitterness', Spangenberg could not tolerate potential independence of thinking, and reacted with draconian measures ensuring that Viney was excommunicated from the Brethren. In such differences lay the seeds of the independent development of denominationalism in the British province of the Unity.

Viney's account of the distress in which he left the Brotherhood is recorded in his 1744 diary,[35] which presents a different, though only a limited, description of his confrontation with the authoritarian style of Zinzendorf's inner circle. It is clear that he wrote an apology and asked to be forgiven, but the leaders did not regard an apology alone as adequate. He wrote:

> My thoughts about it are that Spangenberg has done very unjustly by me in excluding me when I declar'd my Sorrow for what I had done and said and promised not to meddle with them Things any more. Yet because I believe my Objections to be true, they have excluded me. This appears to me like Popery, it being expected that I shall implicitly believe all what ye Count does as right and make no Question in Faith or Obedience to Anything he or ye Pilgrim Church does or says. This, not being likely to come to pass in me, in as much as I firmly believe they are in some things wrong.[36]

Viney's unprecedented challenge to the authority of Zinzendorf stirred up considerable hostility among leaders. In May 1744 the Count wrote to the British Labourers and threatened to withdraw all Germans from the province, effectively terminating the mission if they did not completely dissociate themselves from Viney's criticisms. Fear of abandonment caused consternation in London and a hasty withdrawal of support from him,[37] which nevertheless did not amount to a fundamental change of attitude, but merely represented a desire to keep the peace.

Unity leaders had been deeply disturbed, and some subsequently recorded their criticism of the English mentality as they saw it. Bishop Martin Dober arrived in London on 30 July 1744 to take charge of the province in place of Bishop Spangenberg, and commented that the English were not child-like enough, so that many blessings were withheld.[38] In November of the same year he expressed his dissatisfaction with the English way of taking objection to what was the Saviour's will, and said he believed they would have to be converted from the English habit of reasoning as much as from English fornication, robbery and murder. He also complained that, 'they think themselves so wise and understand everything better than the labourers who have tried it out already and have risked their lives and goods for the Saviour's sake'.[39]

The extent to which these and other related criticisms became common knowledge among ordinary members is uncertain, but they were undoubtedly known in detail to local leaders, who presumably acted upon them as far as possible. The resulting wariness with which the German hierarchy subsequently treated the British Province during the period of their religious and cultural ascendancy ultimately failed to restrain the drift towards a more distinctive and less conformist provincial style. The trend was slow to develop because in many ways the mission was successful throughout the eighteenth century; but in the longer term a more easy-going and flexible style appealed much more to the English mind, though this in turn had its limitations, as the history of the British Province in the nineteenth century reveals.

The 1749 Act of Parliament: Acta Fratrum Unitatis

This Act, unique in parliamentary history, granted official recognition to another episcopal church within Britain and the colonies, members of which would no longer be classified as Protestant Dissenters, a designation which Zinzendorf had previously refused to accept. Its easy passage through both Houses was achieved because of an influential coalition of supporters, many of whom had been beguiled by the persuasive arguments and impressive aristocratic style of Zinzendorf and his entourage, and were appreciative of the genuine achievements of Unity members both at home and overseas as loyal and hard-working citizens. The colonial proprietors were the most important, either being owners of or bearing responsibility for land in the American colonies. They were eager to attract diligent Protestants to their estates, an economic advantage which Zinzendorf had been careful to stress. One of the proprietors, James Oglethorpe, Governor of Georgia, acted as the Brethren's main adviser, introduced the bill in the Commons and chaired its committee stages. Thomas Penn, another supporter, was familiar with Unity settlements near Philadelphia in Pennsylvania, and he lobbied influential government ministers such as the President of the Board of Trade on the Brethren's behalf. In the House of Lords most bishops were in favour of acceptance, with the bishops of Lincoln and Worcester being particularly enthusiastic. The Scottish peers offered support, eager for hard-working settlers on their estates, and an influential group of peers associated with the Prince and Princess of Wales also concurred because Zinzendorf had charmed them too. Thus, in 1749, the Unity enclave in England was making its presence felt at the highest levels and achieving the objective of the first Moravians who, at Herrnhut, had looked to resurrect an ancient Protestant Church, even if they had not anticipated that the first governmental step in this direction would occur in London.

Shortly before its passage through Parliament, Zinzendorf was active in London organizing a suitable public relations campaign and speaking to the Fetter Lane congregation about the continual need for vigilance to ensure that the Unity remained numerically small. A case in point is his address to the Synodal Conference on 6 January 1749 shortly after his arrival in London. The Fetter Lane diarist[40] recorded a synopsis of this address, the theme of which was his conviction that the Unity should remain a select body, distinct from the converts who might be attracted by its preaching:

> January. Friday 6 was the first Synodal Conference at which the Ordinary [i.e. Zinzendorf], in a long Discourse, showed that the Design of our Saviour with the Moravian Church was, that she should build herself, and maintain her Rights in Stillness, and with small Numbers, avoiding all odious Embarrassments [*sic*] with Nations; but that if large Multitudes are brought together by the Preaching of the Gospel, it must always be charged upon the private Zeal of those Men, who are the Instruments of it, and those Multitudes must afterwards not be Moravian Brethren, even though they may have conversed with and benefited by that Church, but must take upon them some religious Profession most agreeing with their Convictions, which in the case now supposed will be the Lutheran preferable to all others.

The enthusiasm with which he and the Brethren anticipated the official acceptance of the Unity was recorded in the report of a meeting held shortly before the celebration of the Church Festival, due on 12 May 1749. Zinzendorf addressed those present in German concerning the naming of the Church and its secure establishment in England, and his words were repeated in English. His address illustrates the skill with which he integrated the establishment of the Church in London with the organization and doctrines of the Brotherhood as a whole. The final reading of the bill would coincide with a significant date in Unity history,

the very Day and Hour when 25 years ago the first 5 Brethren of the
Moravian Stock came to Herrnhut, and the Foundation-Stone there
was laid . . . That what pleases him (the Ord) is particularly this, that
by the English Nation and Government, which he has a particular
regard for, the simple Appellation of Brethren, without any addition,
is allowed us, that being the most amiable and proper Name of all our
Saviour's Members. . . . He had also . . . express'd his Satisfaction at
the pretty Name of our Chapel 'Brethren's-Chapel', and thought it a
happy Place, in that amidst this great City we could have there such
Liberty and Quietness. That it did not appear at first, why the Saviour
led matters on in such an Apostolic manner at Herrnhut . . . when there
were but few Souls; the First Moravian Brethren were but 5, one of
whom soon went Home, suffering Martyrdom like Huss, 3 were still in
our Saviour's Work in different Places, one now in Holland, John
Teltshig [*sic*], had been a long time in England, and one here present,
Syndicus Nitschman: but now the Intention and Fruit was manifest.

The Act was read at the lovefeast the day after it had received the
Royal Assent (26 May 1749). Zinzendorf took the opportunity to
observe that his first intention had been to procure a public hearing to
remove prejudice. Now the Act had resulted in many advantages, of
particular significance being that they had been named 'Unitas Fratrum'
(Unity of the Brethren) and their adherence to the Augsburg Confession
and Synod of Bern had been established. The Unity had also become
more familiar to the bishops of the Anglican Church, many of whom
were 'surprisingly hearty' and supportive in consequence of its impressive pedigree.[41]

Even before 1749 there had been tactical use of the pedigree. In con-
nection with settlement of Unity members in Georgia the governor,
General Oglethorpe, declared in 1735 that the Unity was linked with the
English reformer John Wyclif, through the Bohemian reformer John
Hus, and so had special claims on English help.[42] In 1737 the Earl of
Egmont noted that Zinzendorf, his social equal, was 'a Prince of Empire'
and 'of the only Protestant Sect in Germany that has regular ordained
Bishops'.[43] A third example refers to the loyal address delivered to the
king on 8 May 1744, in which the point was made that the eighteenth-
century Unity was 'in union with the ancient Protestant Episcopalian
Bohemian Mission Church, one of the earliest witnesses and sufferers by
the papists, a sister of the Church of England whose doctrines also in
fundamental points are the same'.[44]

The authentication in Britain of his family's association with earlier

reformers, and the Unity pedigree, was of prime importance to Zinzendorf during the late 1740s and early 1750s, when he was spending a great
deal of time in the province. He was particularly active in preaching to
the Fetter Lane congregation, addressing the Brethren and Sisters in
both German and English as appropriate. On 1 May 1750 the diarist
recorded: 'Countess Zinzendorf, the young Countesses Benigna and
Elizabeth, Count Reuss (Henry the 28th) and his Lady, coming just then
from Ingalstone, were present at the Lovefeast.' Zinzendorf spoke at
length in English on the connections between his family and earlier
religious leaders, referring to the occasion as a

> manifold commemorative Festival; this being the Day of the Arrival of
> the first 5 of the old Brethren in Herrnhut, of the first Intercourse
> between the Congregation and the Souls in England 12 years ago by
> means of Boehler; and of the acknowledging our Congregation under
> the name of Brethren by this Nation a year ago. [Anniversaries were
> recapitulated.] It is the Day now of the Arrival of beloved Guests, and
> of a race very remarkable among us; because the Family which hath
> the Happiness to see now the English Congregation before it, are the
> Descendants both of the Lutheran and Reformed Branches at the same
> time. My wife and her Family descend from the first Patrons of the
> Brethren, who have built the first City, the first Villages of their
> Communion 300 years ago: They also descend from the Reformed
> Branch of the Dukes of Silesia. My [. . . ?] is an immediate Descendant
> from Duke Henry of Saxony, who was the first Reformer in Saxony,
> and was deprived of his Dutchy [sic] by Duke George, that great
> Enemy; who died, and not only left him his Dominions, but the Family
> of Henry subsists to this Day, there being (as I said) some here of a
> Posterity of that first Reformer, who had lost all his Possessions for the
> Gospel's sake.

This example of the assiduous cultivation of a personal and family mys-
tique and its careful association with the ancient Church is characteristic
of many of Zinzendorf's speeches during these early years of the mission,
and occurs also in some of his correspondence.

The 1749 Act effectively institutionalized the religious pedigree and
enabled Unity missionaries to work in Britain and British colonies on the
same terms as their Anglican and Lutheran colleagues. Previously, most
Unity missionaries had not been educated for the ministry at a university
and had not been qualified for legitimate mission work in English
Protestant colonies; their lay status had precluded them from administer-

ing any sacraments of the Protestant Churches, especially baptism, among their overseas converts. The alternative of leaving the Unity and training for the Anglican or Lutheran ministry in order to work in their overseas missions was neither acceptable to Unity leaders nor desired by its members. Under the terms of this 1749 Act the Unity had finally achieved official recognition as an orthodox Protestant denomination with a legitimate ordained ministry free to work in English-speaking colonies. Technically the Act's provisions were not applicable in Britain itself, but in practice such a legalistic distinction was ignored and Unity Labourers became free to regard themselves as acceptable representatives of a fourth Protestant denomination. In licensing their premises for public worship it was no longer necessary to apply as Protestant Dissenters, a regulation reluctantly accepted before 1749 in order to comply with English law,[45] in spite of the rejection of the term by Zinzendorf and other leaders. At the same time it introduced a paradox into Unity ideology, which still maintained that its primary objective in Europe was that of an interdenominational movement. The paradox was deepened when, in September of the same year, the Saxon government officially recognized the Unity as a legitimate Protestant denomination subscribing, as did the Lutherans, to the Augsburg Confession. Thus the Unity was simultaneously an interdenominational body which ostensibly did not proselytize and continued to regard itself as a supporter of other denominations; yet at the same time it was now a recognized Protestant denomination with the right to operate as such entirely independently of them.

Despite the tactical advantages gained by official recognition of the Unity as an additional Protestant denomination in its own right, the paradox remained at the heart of Zinzendorf's own thinking. He never abandoned his vision of the Unity as a Brotherhood at the centre of evangelistic outreach with networks of societies for the converted of any denomination, for whom they were to be responsible. Only two years before his death he preached to a gathering of about six hundred society (diaspora) adherents at Herrnhut,[46] and argued:

> I would rather be a Diaspora peasant than a Messenger [missionary] to the Heathen. A true Brother and Sister among the scattered ones, a Heart of Jesus in the midst of the World is the greatest Martyr . . . He must deny himself much; he dare not live free and lax . . . If with Grace of Heart, accuracy, punctuality and purification of the Vessel from the outside is necessary, it is in the Diaspora. Many Eyes look upon the Diaspora Brethren, every Step which they take, every Expression which they make is noticed.

Thus, while admitting the difficulties involved in setting an example of living everyday life in accordance with Christian principles, the Count still had no doubt that the Unity as then constituted was uniquely suited to carry out this task. By so doing, its exponents would meet the religious needs of many people in existing Protestant denominations. It is significant that he was addressing these thoughts about the influence of disciplined diaspora living to German-speaking people who, after his death in 1760, exemplified above all others the continuity of this model, and justified Zinzendorf's related conviction that a scattered diaspora membership was more effective in Christian influence than a concentrated membership in a few localities,[47] excluding Place Congregations, which were essential recruiting agencies for Labourers. There is ample evidence of the success of this policy.[48]

The closure of Herrnhaag and the threat of bankruptcy during the 1750s

1749 was a prestigious year for the British Province, since it marked the start of a six-year period during which Unity Headquarters was centred at Lindsey House in Chelsea. Ambitious plans were made to develop the site as a major settlement to be called Sharon, but these were never implemented,[49] since a series of setbacks for the Unity intervened, initially centred on revelations about congregational activities in the large and influential Unity settlement of Herrnhaag. In Chapter 2 it was shown how, inspired by intense spirituality with deeply emotional, cultural and erotic overtones, a vigorous missionary movement spread from this place to many parts of the world, including Britain. This was too explosive to last, and in the early 1750s, after its closure by the local authorities following scandalous revelations of its literary and cultural style, several books were published on the continent and subsequently in London which criticized most of what Herrnhaag stood for and drew attention to error and deviancy in the thinking of the Unity as a whole and Zinzendorf in particular. This was nothing new; he had been the target of a major literary industry throughout the 1740s.

The writings of John Roche (1751), Henry Rimius (three volumes 1753, 1754, 1755), George Livington (1755) and T. Green (1755) were uniformly hostile; for example, they collectively expressed doubt as to whether the Renewed Unity was really an institutional successor of the old Bohemian brotherhood, Rimius arguing that Zinzendorf had craftily 'borrowed' a denomination to serve his own purposes.[50] The declared religious pedigree already used so successfully in Britain and on the continent to further Unity interests was rejected as totally invalid. In their view this religious body, originating in Herrnhut and evolving with alarming notoriety in Herrnhaag before its closure, was totally new; furthermore it was being led by a man who not only aspired to papal authority, but was being granted it by his followers. He and his principal colleagues claimed that they were being directed by Jesus Christ in person in a unique relationship shared by no other Protestant denomination, and appeared contemptuous of the work of other Protestant divines. This led to widespread dissension among devout members of other denominations who were in contact with the Brethren, since they resented the suggestion of inferiority and error. The authors argued further that, by propagating a doctrine which valued emotion and intuition rather than reasoning and book-learning, well-meaning laymen had been deluded into adventurous and frequently dangerous missions overseas without adequate education and training, whilst under the impression that they were doing the will of the Saviour. In short, the whole Unity was arguably not really Protestant, but a dictatorship in the guise of a renewal of an illustrious predecessor, enabling Zinzendorf to exercise secular and spiritual authority on a worldwide scale. A recent study of the Countess of Huntingdon by B. S. Schlenther, which describes the crisis of faith and society in Britain during the eighteenth century, describes how, in 1755, the Brethren's reputation in London was at rock bottom and they were ridiculed for looking upon Zinzendorf as, 'the true Apostle, the Pope, the Perfect Pattern, the Paragon'.[51]

The nature of the Herrnhaag period and its repercussions in Britain are discussed further in Part Four of this book. There it is argued that, as one eminent German historian has already described it, the Herrnhaag period was simultaneously a high point and a low point in Unity history.[52] Despite the fact that these critical publications had a wide circulation among the religious public, seriously damaging the Unity's reputation, the activities of the Brethren in Britain continued unabated and with the utmost vigour among those for whom these strictures had little significance. Indeed, the Brethren had their own supporters in this propaganda war. Francis Okely, one of five Cambridge graduates who joined the Brotherhood, attracted by the mystical aspects of their faith, published in 1775 a book of letters between Brethren written in the early 1740s.[53] Its explicit intention was to counterbalance the work of their detractors, and to this end he wrote a substantial invocation and a preface setting out his intentions.

The seven-page 'Supplicant Invocation Dedicatory' is a long prayer to Jesus, towards the end of which comes this extract:

Thou ELDER and FIRST-BORN among many Brethren! Thou only good SHEPHERD of the Sheep, pardon all the SINS and MISTAKES of a CHOSEN, a long and a much exercised FLOCK; and my own heartily acknowledged ones, together with theirs. Perfect us more and more every Day, and still help us to go on courageously, wisely, and successfully, thro' all the difficulties of our Warfare: Till having, thro' the Blood of the LAMB, and the WORD of our TESTIMONY, over-come the ACCUSER of the BRETHREN; we may not love our very Lives unto the Death.[54]

In the preface he paid tribute to the influence of the Brethren on his own life. When he met them he discovered, 'fervent witnesses of Jesus. . . . Among this PEOPLE, HEART and CONSCIENCE, and the true Blessing thereof by the BLOOD of the LAMB was the perpetual THEME, and the sole OBJECT of their incessant LABOURS, both *public* and *private*, at HOME and ABROAD.' He had received guidance from the letters, written to himself or friends, and he wished to share this with his readers; but another reason for publishing them was to help restore the Brethren's good name, since their sincerity would be obvious to an unbiased reader.

For just as an honest SAMPLE of Corn is the very best compendious Evidence of the true Quality of the Heap it is taken from; so it must be easy for every Person of common Sense and Candour to discern and be assured from *hence*, that it is not *possible* for the PEOPLE, called the BRETHREN, to have been either *then* or *since*, those 'flagitious MISCREANTS' they have been by some represented, and by others *too willingly* believed to be.

Some of these letters are discussed in Part Four, since they refer to voyages undertaken by the Brethren and illustrate the support given by the leaders to less-experienced Labourers.

Further, and equally seriously for the public image of the Unity in Britain, the development of the Brethren's establishments was constrained in the early 1750s by shortage of money to sustain the momentum of its ambitious and enthusiastic worldwide mission. During the 1730s, when the activities of the Unity were largely confined to Herrnhut and groups of self-supporting religious societies in easily accessible parts of Central Europe, Zinzendorf's family and friends, who had large estates and were wealthy, paid all expenses.[55] This sufficed until the Unity expanded, requiring ever larger subsidies for lavish development; Herrnhaag, for example, was a spacious, elegant financial disaster. Since Zinzendorf was not prepared to see the Unity collapse, he began to borrow large sums of money on the security of his family estates, a method familiar to many aristocratic families, before and since.[56] For this reason it was a hazard that an aristocrat, as opposed to someone who was merely rich, should lead the Unity. Zinzendorf exemplified an aristocratic concern with visible pre-eminence in the community, using buildings such as the settlement at Herrnhaag as expressions of power in stone.[57]

This perilous expedient of borrowing increasing amounts of money was adopted well before 1750, and by the beginning of 1753 the Unity was in debt by about £135,000.[58] A major crisis was narrowly averted in March of that year by the arrival of funds from Holland borrowed on the strength of Unity assets and property in Britain and abroad, which were still considerable and acceptable as security. The chief creditors agreed a settlement with Zinzendorf on 29 March, and thereafter he kept up the necessary instalments to repay what had been borrowed. Although the legal agreement was settled within three months, the fact that it had been necessary was public knowledge, and regarded as further evidence of the unstable circumstances of this body. After Zinzendorf's death in 1760, the Unity owed the daunting sum of £150,000 and was on the brink of bankruptcy. The Unity, not the Zinzendorf family, shouldered this debt, adopting protracted and ultimately successful methods of meeting it, but for the rest of the eighteenth century struggled to survive a chronic shortage of money. Economies were made and resources conserved, the remarkable achievement being that evangelistic activity continued, though with diminished intensity and with marked changes in religious temper introduced by Spangenberg. This legacy of financial problems dogged the British Province throughout the nineteenth and early twentieth centuries.

During the period of German religious and cultural ascendancy there were practical problems resulting from the employment in Britain of the Brethren's continental model, which was primarily concerned to refine the spiritual qualities of a minority who fulfilled its stringent require-ments, in order to strengthen existing congregations. Because Unity organization in Britain was directed from the continental centre as part of the larger whole, with day-to-day business controlled by Germans, it was expected that only extra-parochial spiritual ministration would be offered by the Brethren. Leading British members, therefore, were not allowed the kind of open preaching which their Methodist counterparts enjoyed, being ordered instead to have dealings only with groups who took the initiative of requesting them to do so.

Admission to full membership of the Brotherhood itself, which required the abandonment of previous denominational allegiance, was severely restricted, those accepted being encouraged to leave home to live in Unity communal establishments. When the evangelistic zeal of the Germans and the enthusiastic response of their British converts led to unexpectedly numerous demands for admission, the pressure was sufficiently strong to force local leaders to modify their official position and preferred role as a society-forming body. Most British members wanting closer association with the Brotherhood, particularly those appointed as stewards, were not satisfied with society membership alone, and demanded to be integrated into the whole religious and social system set up at Herrnhut during the 1730s and elaborated at Herrnhaag during the 1740s. In the heady atmosphere of recent conversion it was not obvious that this ideal would be virtually impossible to sustain in the longer term.

Thus, by a series of compromises, including the validation of 1749, the British Province began to evolve into a denominational, congregation-forming agency, attracting members from other persuasions. This unforeseen, unintended and irresistible development was a turning-point in the history of the province, which began to deviate from its continental source. There the original model was retained and the Unity remained a supportive, non-denominational, society-forming organization based on a few religious settlements from which itinerant evangelists and missionaries were dispatched on a worldwide mission.

In the 1760s and '70s, two factors in particular influenced the future direction of the Brethren's work in Britain. On the one hand the initial evangelistic zeal engendered by Zinzendorf's energy and charisma was beginning to weaken, and at the same time the province was called upon to take its share of Unity debt. As a result of the first factor, the provincial network of societies became aware of a diminishing response from local people and a consequent failure to expand, a problem exacerbated by lack of resources resulting from the second. Although the Brethren still retained most of the original societal structure, parts were beginning to collapse. There was increasing awareness of competition from others, particularly the congenial Methodists, by then a nationwide community with a strong sense of self-awareness,[59] who sustained vigorous evangelism in Britain so successfully that large numbers of adherents flocked to them. In 1767, for example, the total number of Methodist members was in the order of 26,000, of whom about 20,000 were English.[60]

Provincial changes from the 1760s onwards

Manuscript records of provincial conferences, composed of British and German members, provide an invaluable record of provincial thinking from the 1760s onwards, and reflect the concerns and problems which were to dominate the province and direct its administrative decisions. They reveal tensions and difficulties implicit in the varying objectives and inclinations of members, showing how and why these shaped future policies and limited provincial growth and achievement.

One dominant theme was the direction which the provincial organization should take. In the earliest available minutes, those of the Provincial Conference held at Lindsey House, Chelsea, in 1765,[61] there was already a dilemma posed by differences of outlook between those who believed in the original society-forming rationale of the Brotherhood and vigorously reaffirmed the Brethren's strong support for the Anglican Church, and those who sought to separate from their old denomination. The conference pledged to do all in its power to bring these misguided separatists back, since they were undermining established principles.[62] Even so, it was admitted that society members in most areas wished to be granted congregational membership and complete separation from their original denomination. Despite these problems, other aspects of provincial development were a source of satisfaction because they reflected consolidation of Unity principles. The Place Congregation at Fulneck was already providing members with a welcome opportunity to have their children appropriately educated, and hope was expressed that, after the founding near Belfast of Gracehill, a second Place Congregation might soon be possible in Northern Ireland.

Six years later, in 1771, when the Provincial Conference met again in London,[63] doubts were expressed more strongly about the usefulness of the continental model in Britain. There were early signs of what were to be long-term differences of opinion separating conservatives, some of whom were British wishing to preserve the original German style, from others who wanted modifications along denominational lines more suited to late eighteenth-century British society as they saw it. All the Labourers present agreed that the fervour of the Evangelical Revival had ended, and accepted reluctantly that the provincial network of societies was weakening, both spiritually and numerically. It was becoming increasingly difficult to find suitable people to act as society stewards and some of those already in office were resigning because they no longer aspired to live inordinately holy lives and act as disciplinarians of their society members.[64] Another complicating factor was the rapid spread of

Methodism as a competing agency, whereas in the Continental Province
there was loyal enthusiasm for maintaining the original rationale; there
stewards could be recruited with ease and the popularity of the
Brethren's society networks in support of the Lutheran and Reformed
Churches showed no signs of diminishing.

Conference records of the 1770s show that even within the Place
Congregations there was pressure for change from the original model.
The validity of Choir House living was being questioned, particularly its
suitability for young men. Commercial activity being pursued there was
being complicated by attempts to trade 'morally'. As early as 1762 it had
been noted in the minutes of a special conference to consider general
Unity organization, held between May and September that,

> concerning commerce, a great deal has been said at Synods for and
> against it. The middle part therein is very difficult to hit. It is for a con-
> gregation one of the most dangerous and ensnaring things. One may
> very easily, under the pretext that one does it for the congregation,
> cloak many indirect and wrong inclinations. The first view with com-
> merce in a congregation must always be, 'I serve'.[65]

Nevertheless, these Place Congregations, Fulneck and Gracehill (settled 1765), still had considerable appeal for the devout, and they were
evidently drawing off too many of the spiritual elite from local societies,
diminishing their vitality even further and prejudicing their survival. This
attraction may reflect the lamented change in the spirituality of society
members, since in these organizations some traditions, such as the subdivision of the membership into informal Bands sharing close fellowship
and providing opportunities for mutual edification, were becoming less
popular.

A further problem influencing the viability of all the establishments
was that it had been more difficult than church leaders had expected to
persuade children of the first generation of young adult converts to join
the Brotherhood. All these misgivings pointed to a new emphasis on the
needs of each establishment, implying a distinct change of role for both
Place Congregations and societies.

Another cause of unease, a foretaste of an obstacle which was to
dominate provincial concerns into the next century and beyond, was the
shortage of money which was increasingly restricting British provincial
development. At the 1771 conference, while the Labourers acknowledged that the province had a duty to accept a proportionate share of the
debts which the Unity as a whole was struggling to pay off, they con-

demned the parsimony of many congregational members, since most of them were better off than they had been twenty or thirty years previously because of the increased volume of industrial and trading activity in the province.[66]

By 1782 the main pattern of provincial settlement was already established, but the growth of the province was slowing. Twenty-two congregations had been settled, mostly as town or country congregations, but this had been possible largely because of the exceptional zeal which had characterized the mid-century evangelical revival, and most dated from the early period. They were as follows:[67]

Bedfordshire: Bedford 1745; Riseley 1759
London: Fetter Lane 1742
Northern Ireland: Ballinderry 1755; Dublin 1750; Gracefield 1759; Gracehill 1765; Kilwarlin 1755
Scotland: Ayr 1778
Wales: Haverfordwest 1763
West of England: Bath 1765; Bristol 1755; Kingswood 1757; Leominster 1759; Malmesbury 1770; Tytherton 1743
Yorkshire, Lancashire and Derbyshire: Dukinfield 1755; Fulneck 1755; Gomersal 1755; Mirfield[68] 1755; Ockbrook 1750; Wyke 1755

These congregations were established because local members had applied increasing pressure to bring the imported continental model more in line with a traditional British denominational style, with the establishment of fixed congregations as the principal objective of future provincial outreach. The province, therefore, began to take the form of a cultural hybrid, combining an uneasy mix of German and British expectations and institutions. Though more of its practices were to adapt during the next century to the nonconformist style of the society in which it operated, a strong awareness of its origins and unique traditions survived among its leaders and congregational members as a symbol of its distinctiveness as a denomination, and provided a rationale by which it justified remaining self-consciously small, a situation forced upon it by long-term financial constraints.

4

British Educational Expansion and Congregational Stability, *c.*1780–*c.*1883

From the historian's point of view, local congregational and society activity during the late eighteenth and nineteenth centuries was under-recorded. The voluminous diaries and other manuscripts which chronicled daily events so assiduously in the mid-eighteenth century, because of a conviction that they were evidence of the way God was operating in history,[1] became briefer and increasingly devoid of comment as enthusiasm and growth gave way to routine management of established congregations and societies. Fortunately, provincial changes were recorded in considerable detail in Conference and Synodal Minutes. Later, *The Messenger*, the official provincial journal founded in 1864, served both to convey provincial policy to the membership and as a vehicle for the personal opinions of ministers and prominent laity, as well as providing articles of general congregational interest. These minutes and articles, therefore, provide the only significant records of provincial thinking and experience as a whole during this period.

Since the pace of change was extremely slow, a survey of this lengthy historical period shows step-by-step adjustments to the original model, and reveals how the underlying aims and thinking of the province responded to changing circumstances, even while superficially it appeared to settle into a relatively unchanging system of administration and practice. Several practical issues shaped the pattern of provincial development over the period as a whole, the most insidious of which was its shortage of money for investment and consequent failure to grow, a situation which was alleviated to some extent by investment in educational expansion. As it became less dependent on the Continental Province for leadership, its thinking and practice deviated increasingly from Unity tradition. Finally, as a result of these two trends, the province evolved a new hybrid provincial character which remained self-consciously distinct from other Nonconformist denominations. These three themes are the key to a closer understanding of the hundred years of British provincial development which followed the early period of enthusiasm, and are analysed initially in this chapter to provide a context for the subsequent chronology, which uses Conference and Synodal Minutes as landmarks.

Chronic shortage of money: small number of communicant members

During the nineteenth century there was a slow increase in the number of British congregations – no mean achievement, though mostly in rural or semi-rural areas with limited numbers of potential new members. Despite this, what the Brethren had to offer appealed to a very small number of people; there were probably about 2,000 communicant members in the entire province in 1800, rising to 2,698 in 1835,[2] and 3,176 in 1885.[3] Had a significant number of these been drawn from the professions, they would have been capable of raising the funds necessary to sustain their congregations without undue difficulty. This was the case among the Unitarians and the Quakers, both relatively small bodies, which nevertheless contained the largest proportion of wealthy families of all the Dissenting denominations; they were also the best educated and the most socially exclusive.[4] All the evidence suggests that, with rare exceptions, there were few affluent people in the British Province, the majority of members being families of artisans with limited means. Despite this, by the end of the eighteenth century, having contributed to the paying off of Zinzendorf's debts, they were being called upon to raise money to maintain a disproportionately large infrastructure, consisting of eighteen – mostly small – town and country congregations, each with its own resident married Labourer, together with four substantial Place Congregations. Even though several of these institutions generated part of their income by commercial activity, the province as a whole was so short of money that regular, long-term, substantial subsidies from external sources were essential for its survival. This persistent state of dependence on financial support from outside its congregations lies at the root of the nineteenth-century history of the province. It was alleviated to some extent in the twentieth century by an increase in the income level of most members, who could then support provincial activities on a scale denied to their nineteenth-century predecessors; but even so the province remained dependent on additional income to maintain its viability.

Sources of subsidy

These vital nineteenth-century subsidies came from a number of sources, the first and most important of which was the provincial boarding school network. This was set up in the last decade of the eighteenth and the first decade of the nineteenth centuries, in line with similar initiatives taking place in Germany. There, also, by the 1780s, Unity recognition of the need for more public educational provision on social grounds was motivated partly by its fund-raising potentiality. As a result, at the 1782 General Synod, the provision of boarding school education for fee-paying children of members and non-members was recognized officially as a branch of church work, and the twenty-year period from 1790 onwards was distinguished throughout the Unity by the building and opening of new boarding schools. In the British Province, fourteen schools, five for boys and nine for girls, were established in existing congregational premises and, except for Bedford, Gracehill and Tytherton, were located in the Manchester–Leeds–Derby triangle.[5] These schools were expressly designed for fee-paying children of non-members and were never intended to cater primarily for the children of members; apart from the children of Labourers, very few of these attended. The overt motive for opening them was to exert a wider spiritual influence among the young, an objective shared by other denominations,[6] but the urgent need for cash subsidies was openly admitted by the province, and it was hoped that profits from boarding schools would provide them. In fact, they did.

By 1859, when the network was well established, the Synodal Report referred to the 'important moral and spiritual benefit' which the boarding schools were providing, but also commented realistically that,

> It would be wrong to pass over without notice the material advantage which the Province derives from these institutions in the way of pecuniary contribution. Indeed, under present circumstances it is hard to see how our provincial establishments could be maintained without them. Besides large payments towards the congregations where they have been established and towards the salaries of their Labourers, the schools render liberal aid towards the general expenses of the province. Thus, in the last three years they have contributed £515-3s-0d to the Labourers' Children's Fund alone.[7]

This comment shows that, quite apart from contributing to Labourers' salaries and other general expenses, virtually the full cost of educating

Labourers' children at Fulneck was being met from fees paid by non-members. Theoretically, congregations were supposed to raise money for this purpose in addition to all their other commitments, but occasional references show that very little was contributed by them despite recurrent complaints from Labourers.[8]

Although most of the boarding schools were small and there is no evidence that they recruited many congregational members, they were a commercial success for about eighty years. The boys' and girls' schools at Fulneck usually had the most pupils because they met provincial as well as local needs: in 1859, for example, they had 80 boys and 50 girls. Most of the others had places for fewer than 40 boarders, with a few, including Tytherton, being half that size. Despite this, their successful and profitable 'golden age' continued until the 1880s, when the first ominous signs of collapse were announced by the 1883 Synod, which disclosed that the girls' school at Wyke (20 residential places) and the boys' school at Gracehill (21 residential places) 'were not flourishing'.[9] These two schools, the smallest in the provincial network, became the first victims of changes in Victorian society's perceptions of the desired amenities of boarding school education, in particular, the need for higher academic qualifications for staff, more comfortable facilities, and a wider range of subjects, including sciences which required expensive laboratory space. As these amenities were increasingly provided by local authorities and other private sources, parents who had been satisfied by Unity provision now began to look elsewhere, so that 1883 can be regarded as a turning-point, beginning the decline of the 14-school establishment which had seemed so secure in 1859.

A second major subsidy, alleviating another burden which would otherwise have fallen on the communicant members, came from the London Association in Aid of the Missions of the United Brethren. This was established in the capital in 1817, by non-members, and has provided regular, substantial subsidies ever since. Originally it comprised approximately four hundred fund-raising societies located throughout Britain, primarily in urban areas, being well represented in Edinburgh and Glasgow. As far as England was concerned, most participants were Anglican; in Scotland they tended to be members of the Scottish Episcopal Church. A useful guide to the amount of money raised is that in 1903 it was officially stated that several hundred thousand pounds had been contributed since 1817.[10] This money was sent to the Unity Mission Board in Germany, from where it was administered to needy areas in the worldwide Unity network, and was a substantial contributor to the total sum available from all Unity sources. Thus, although the mission contribution from Britain as a whole was enormous in proportion to the size of the Brethren's provincial congregations, communicant members subscribed very little for this purpose, a source of recurrent criticism; for example, the admonitory pastoral letter of 1847, issued on the authority of that year's provincial Synod, noted that from the earliest times the Unity had been a missionary church, and requested greater support for missions. Later, in 1874, Synod admitted: 'There has for some time been a growing conviction among our missionary Brethren that the interest of the British Province in our mission work is rapidly declining.'[11] Pressure was experienced again in the 1883 Synod, where it was suggested by the Unity representative that more men from the province should be encouraged to offer to serve in overseas missions, since members of British provincial congregations were still not contributing the money and personnel which it was their duty to provide.[12] Clearly, without the support of the London Association there would have been even stronger complaint from Unity headquarters.

Another long-term source of funding contributed to the viability of the British Province in the nineteenth century and beyond. The Bates Trust was set up in 1813 by a provincial family owning residential property in London. Since then, the income generated by this trust has regularly provided substantial resources to sustain provincial activity. A detailed study of this trust is outside the scope of this book, but the subject would repay research as an example of the decisive influence which one property-owning benefactor can have on the survival of a small denomination.

In the shorter term there have been occasional payments which have made a big difference to provincial resources in particular circumstances. In 1857, for example, when the General Synod announced complete separation of British and continental provincial funding, Unity funds were used to pay off £15,000 of outstanding debts, mainly connected with the British settlements, particularly their commercial activities. It was made clear at the 1863 Synod that, as a consequence of separation, the British members would be called upon to bear the full cost of maintaining provincial properties. In context, the synodal notes implied that subsidies for this purpose had been provided by the Continental Province for some time.[13]

These alternative sources of income kept the province viable during the nineteenth century in a way which its small congregations could never have hoped to sustain without assistance. Many people, most of whom had no direct connection with and probably little knowledge of the individual churches in the British Province, enabled the congregational network to meet its obligations and so were crucial to its survival. Some of these appreciated the Christian emphasis which education in the denominational schools provided; others had an interest in the well-being of the Unity as a whole and supported its missionary activities. They were all instrumental in preserving the original eighteenth-century congregational network, even ensuring a modest increase in its sphere of influence; but in spite of this support the desired expansion remained stubbornly out of reach because of the small communicant membership and the marginal viability of remoter congregations.

Progressive deviation from traditional continental thinking and practice

The decline of the diaspora societies

Everything new which the Brethren had to say about religious belief and related social organization was said in the 1740s, and the spiritual context was emphatically Pietism as interpreted by Count Zinzendorf. Since their original institutional structure was controlled primarily by Germans no matter where it was located, German religious practice and cultural dominance were assured throughout the entire Unity during the early years, being sustained by the strict spiritual discipline imposed by its early leaders. In Britain, although diaspora societies and congregations were established as in the Continental Province, the system could not be maintained for long because of the culture and religious practices of the host community. Here, the dominant Protestant Churches were traditionally denominational and pluralistic, and the growing influence of British converts during the 1760s and 1770s introduced a trend into the Brethren's congregations which gradually weakened the prestige and effectiveness of the initial Germanic structure. This had been rooted primarily in the diaspora societies, which continued to flourish in accordance with Zinzendorf's intention in the non-pluralistic Continental Province, being boosted still further as the nineteenth century progressed by changes in society which will be described shortly. In the very different conditions prevailing in Britain, however, the collapse of the diaspora societies was probably inevitable.

The characteristic pluralism of British society, with its toleration of dissent and emerging new persuasions such as Methodism, had for many years been familiar to continental observers, who frequently commented

on it. Johann Wilhelm von Archenholz[14] reported with enthusiasm
on, 'the prodigious number of dissenters; and the liberty with which
mankind are there allowed to think and act as they please', arguing that
this was the result of a legislative power which had raised the principles
of toleration to the highest degree of perfection. He quoted Voltaire:

> If there was only one religion in England, despotism would infallibly
> ensue; if there were two they would cut each other's throats, but as
> such a number of sects are there tolerated who worship the Supreme
> Being in so many different manners, a holy enthusiasm never troubles
> their minds and they live in quiet and tranquillity.

Archenholz concluded that, 'The various sects that prevail in that island
weaken the interest of religion in general and inspire but little esteem for
those [Anglican] ecclesiastics, who live for the most part, according to
their own caprice.'

In this mental climate British diaspora society members who had
temporarily experienced 'a holy enthusiasm' became increasingly reluctant to accept the mid-eighteenth-century orthodoxy that they should
maintain their original denominational allegiance – in most cases to the
Anglican Church – while regarding association with the Brethren as
ancillary to it. Many requested to be made members of the Brotherhood
in the fullest sense and, if rejected for any reason such as by reference to
the lot, they drifted out of the diaspora network to join an alternative
group. In practice, the Methodists probably benefited the most, though
the number of people involved was very small compared with total
Methodist membership. There is ample evidence that, because of this
trend, the decline in the British diaspora was well under way by the
1780s despite the efforts of the Labourers to prevent it. Inevitably, this
province, where a minority of the original congregations were accepted
Unity members and a majority especially in the diaspora were not,
gradually progressed towards an alternative in which the majority of
those in regular association with the Brotherhood were also members of
it, being in effect a separate, self-contained denomination.

By the time of the 1848 General Synod this fundamental change was
being openly recognized. It was noted in the report that, on the continent,
diaspora work in the form of labour among those who were not members
of the Brotherhood continued along lines laid down by Zinzendorf, but
differences between the British and German provinces were admitted: on
the continent, any who wanted communion with the Brethren joined a
diaspora society, but did not renounce membership of their national

church. 'In Britain there is no provision for this. Those from outside who want communion with the Brethren's Church join it.' The report concluded that, as a result, in Britain, 'There are no such things as societies in the German sense of the word.'[15]

This was a more serious loss than could be imagined by most British members. On the continent 105 Unity Labourers served the diaspora societies, which were widely distributed over Protestant Western Europe. The 1848 Synodal Report recognized that, on the continent, these societies were enriching the whole Church by extending the range of acquaintances beyond the narrow circle of local congregations, thereby counteracting 'that one-sidedness and that stagnation of spiritual life to which every small community is exposed', reflecting that, 'the affectionate respect which they entertain for our church has been a call upon us to value our union more highly than we might otherwise have done'.[16]

There were other important and far-reaching developments in continental German-speaking areas which helped to strengthen Unity diaspora societies, and these were evident as early as the 1830s, when the traditional dividing line between a Protestant north and a Roman Catholic south began to crumble under the pressures of industrialization, urbanization and migration. As populations became less homogeneous, strenuous efforts were made by both Protestant and Roman Catholic churches to minister to co-religionists in their respective diasporas. A Protestant organization for this purpose, the Gustavus Adolphus Association, was set up in 1832; its Catholic equivalent, the Boniface Association, was established in 1849.[17] It followed that Unity work to deepen the spirituality of the 70,000 or so Lutherans in their mainly Lutheran diaspora societies[18] was increasingly appreciated, and was strongly supported throughout the nineteenth and into the early twentieth centuries.

In Britain, however, rapid decline of the diaspora society network was a sign that further deviations from continental practice would inevitably follow, since the original diaspora expansion had been regarded as a frontier ministry in conditions where the Brethren were competing with evangelists of other persuasions. Success or failure in this endeavour was easy to assess, because it could be related directly both to the number who remained loyal to their own denominations and to the number of outsiders who were converted and requested congregational membership. When the early enthusiasm waned, this did not cause an administrative problem; it was easy to scale down or abandon this form of local evangelism in order to concentrate on conserving the membership already acquired, and this is what occurred. Every effort was made to maintain the existing congregational network, and deviations from continental practice took place in a protracted period of institutional stability where congregational members felt little change from year to year and were not tempted to join other congregations.

This stability could be achieved only by deviating gradually from the imposed continental practice in a way which accorded with evolving congregational and ministerial expectations, a delicate and complex process because of the Anglo-German ethos of the province and the varying strength of individual attachment to what was, or what was thought to be, the original style. Opinion included at one extreme members, usually ordained, who were German or had been educated in Germany and had an unshakeable conviction that the Unity's continental practices still had a powerful attraction; at the other extreme were those who regarded the original style as outdated and hoped to create a more independent British style free from the continental domination which they now saw as an impediment.

Diminishing use of the lot

One measure of the relative influence in the province of these opposing points of view is its progressive deviation from continental practice in recourse to the lot. Synodal decisions over the lot chart the controversy, showing how scepticism on the part of ordinary members led to protracted disagreement and gradual reduction in its use in the real world of congregational and personal decision-making.

Official use of the lot was not merely a relatively esoteric element in an otherwise familiar evangelical interpretation of Christian belief. Because it had been accepted since 1741 as a manifestation of the unique authority of Christ as Chief Elder and was central to members' belief that the Unity was uniquely blessed and guided by the Saviour, its consultation on general policy and contentious issues at congregational and personal level was perceived as an exclusive privilege, essential to the Brethren's faith and practice. The fact that discussion about its place in decision-making featured prominently at the 1795 Fulneck Conference indicates that, as early as the end of the eighteenth century, thinking in the British Province was beginning to move away from the German model, although objections were not yet sufficient to bring about a change of policy. Although it was still respected by most brethren and sisters, a significant minority were pressing for a reduction in its influence. The process by which it was gradually superseded during the nineteenth century by a discursive form of decision-making is an indicator of the gradual transformation of the inherited German organization into a more indigenous administrative system.

All the ordained brethren assembled at Fairfield in 1824 appeared to feel it expedient to preserve the principle that the Saviour continued to govern through the lot. In practice, however, its use was becoming increasingly dependent on the views of individual Labourers, which were open to considerable variation. Where they doubted its value, reference to the lot in their congregations was being quietly abandoned. Conference decisions showed some weakening in the official position; it was no longer deemed necessary to authenticate the marriages of congregational members by lot, and it was agreed by only a narrow majority to continue the practice in the case of ordained brethren. In 1847, the Fairfield Conference acknowledged that the rejection of calls to Church service based on it was widespread: as many calls were being rejected as accepted.

The final demise of decision by lot as an official expression of the will of Christ came when the British Province separated from the continent in 1856. There was detailed discussion at the Fulneck Conference as a result of which it was unanimously decided that, while accepting the memorial day of 13 November 1741, the reason for it should be that, 'Our Saviour being the Chief Shepherd and Head of the Unity of the Church Universal is, as such, the Chief Shepherd and Head of the Unity of the Brethren.' The statement continued: 'At the same time we disclaim the idea of our Saviour being considered to hold any ecclesiastical office in the Brethren's Church.'[19] It was officially declared that if, in 1741, those at the conference in London who invited the Saviour to lead the church in person thought he had expressed his willingness to do so, they were mistaken.[20] This decision inevitably placed the whole principle of the lot in jeopardy. Some ordained brethren immediately suggested that it should be completely abandoned; others, sensing that there was still some residual value in this procedure, advised against such precipitate action, and their compromise view prevailed. One area in which it was suggested that it might continue to be helpful was in the case of appointment to office, in order to eliminate jealousy and rivalry. It was also argued that abandoning the lot completely might introduce the undesirable 'popular element' into church government. Finally, a form of words was accepted which would enable provincial conferences to decide when and how the lot should be applied in future. One immediate result of partly relinquishing the lot was that congregational admission from then onwards was to be by confirmation following a suitable course of training. Confirmed members of other Protestant denominations were to be accepted as members of the Brethren's Church, provided that they were suitable in the opinion of the ordained brethren. From this time, the use of the lot ceased to be a significant part of provincial organization.

Secularization of the provincial Place Congregational settlements

These institutions originated in the early expansive period of German religious and cultural ascendancy, Ockbrook, Derby, being established in 1750, Fulneck, Leeds, in 1755 and Gracehill, Belfast, in 1765. Dukinfield, founded in 1755, was originally intended as a Place Congregation, but because of difficulty in acquiring sufficient land in Dukinfield, the fourth one was established at Fairfield, east of Manchester, in 1784.

They were originally strictly organized and exclusive, since they were designed for the spiritual advancement of residents and as recruiting grounds for Labourers to work in the diaspora societies and foreign missions. They were believed to be holy places in that the Saviour, as head of the Unity, had chosen them and kept a special watch over their inhabitants.[21] Thus, the dogma continued, Place Congregations were a phenomenon of the eighteenth century, 'the like of which there never was . . . on them rests a peculiar Grace . . . they are so calculated that the Holy Spirit can be at full liberty in its Work'.[22] Zinzendorf had been entrusted with their establishment and subsequent development by the Saviour, advised where necessary by the lot.[23] Inevitably, great importance was attached to these dogmas, and when the British Place Congregations were set up, all much smaller than most continental examples, their establishment took place in a wave of evangelistic enthusiasm, ensuring a broad uniformity of practice with the continental network. One implication of this uniformity was that the institutions depended on the willingness of residents to subordinate personal inclination and a degree of personal freedom when necessary to ensure a common good, which was represented to them as obeying the will of the Saviour. For this discipline to remain acceptable to residents, the original evangelistic enthusiasm had to be sustained; otherwise the ideals of self-sacrificial service intrinsic to the whole complex structure of belief and practice would begin to crumble. This gradual process of decline was the experience of the British Province from the early 1770s, and was well advanced by the early part of the nineteenth century.

The separatist doctrine of the Saviour's close personal relationship with members of Place Congregations was a unifying concept essential to Unity philosophy, but the economic and some of the open religious activities pursued in them were increasingly exposed to the pluralistic and libertarian pressures of contemporary practice in British society.

Since these influences, with no real parallel in the Continental Province, were fundamentally incompatible with most of what the Place Congregations stood for, they inevitably assailed the delicately balanced and complex spiritual, social and economic activity pursued within them. This imported system, which had proved effective in fulfilling Unity aims in its original continental environment, had been set up in Britain when potential residents were united in evangelical zeal, but after the first few decades of expansion, contemporary attitudes in Britain did not nourish them.

The Place Congregations exerted considerable influence in their own localities during the period of expansion, and some converts, most of them young and about two thirds of them female, applied successfully to live there and found satisfaction in their disciplined communal lifestyle. Since, in practice, the majority of residents were unmarried and lived in the Single Brethren's and Single Sisters' Houses, dissension was to be avoided as potentially destructive. When Fulneck opened in 1752 the first residents were enthusiastic, but by the 1770s external influences were taking their toll and the Single Brethren there were becoming notorious for their unco-operative and divisive behaviour. This cumulative disturbance came to a head in 1772 and is recorded in detail and with anguish in the minutes of Elders' Conferences. There were visits by alarmed Unity leaders from Herrnhut, frequent consultations of the lot, and temporary suspension of the celebration of the Eucharist for the entire congregation. Calm was restored and superficially little changed, but this episode foreshadowed a time when the appeal of Place Congregational life would diminish year by year.

It must be emphasized that the rate of change was comparatively slow. In 1795, Conference members were concerned by the persistent tendency of Place Congregations to draw off the elite of adjacent societies, a development which was deplored as it tended to weaken still further the declining diaspora network. Since the 1760s this tendency had increasingly given cause for concern. It was one consequence of the initial Unity philosophy, which valued the exclusiveness of a small, ultra-devout community separate from the world, with challenging standards of religious practice achieved only by rigorous self-discipline. This reflected the role of Place Congregations as prestigious training grounds for men and women who would serve the Brotherhood as evangelists. By the early part of the nineteenth century, however, the Single Brethren's Houses throughout the province were in terminal decline: when the 1824 Provincial Conference made its report, the numbers were: Fulneck 16, Fairfield 9, Mirfield 5, Gracehill 5 and Ockbrook 3.[24] Corresponding numbers for

the various provincial Sisters' Choir Houses were not recorded, but anecdotal evidence, although showing a gradual falling-off, suggests a much
less serious state of affairs.

The Church's original assumptions about the organization and role of
the Place Congregations and the way of life which they enforced were
coming under increasingly critical scrutiny, and these reservations
surfaced at the 1824 Conference. This reflected not only church members' growing unwillingness to accept the constraints of regulated living,
but also the diminishing opportunities for apprentice training on lines
which had characterized Choir House life during the eighteenth century,
when admission of children to a Choir House had usually been synonymous with their being able to learn a specialized craft and practise it as
residents.

The artificial restrictions imposed upon relationships between brethren and sisters in these establishments were now being regarded as inappropriate. A memorandum submitted by Fulneck Labourers and
members argued that the traditional practice of taking children from
their homes and putting them in Choir Houses should cease, and even
went so far as to suggest that the entire system of division into choirs
should be abandoned. There was a mixed response to this radical proposal and, although the matter was not put to the vote, the conference
minutes suggest that the gathering as a whole was not yet ready to accept
it. Nevertheless, the statistics of residents in the Single Brethren's Choir
Houses quoted above prove that, over the past thirty years, the appeal of
these one-time prestigious establishments had declined dramatically.

The minutes of the 1847 Provincial Conference recorded further evidence that Place Congregations were continuing to decline in esteem.
Some deputies were concerned that priorities and practice were changing, while a Labourer from the Mirfield congregation, clearly puzzled by
their seeming irrelevance to the real world, asked what had been their
original purpose. This gave rise to a prolonged exchange of views in
which all the traditional and by then largely academic arguments about
their role as disseminators of spiritual enrichment in their local areas
were reiterated.

The extent to which innovation had already changed the nature of
settlements was illustrated by the complaint of one member of conference that the current policy of building boarding schools meant that
the proportion of children to adults living in places such as Fulneck had
radically increased; Town Congregations such as Dublin and Bristol
were more in line with the needs of the church, not being burdened as the
settlements now were with an overmighty presence of children. Choir

Houses had long since ceased to be the dynamic source of vital commercial activity which had sustained the communities during their early years. Even the Single Sisters' Houses were losing their popularity; although Fulneck, by far the largest survivor, still had thirty-nine members, the Single Sisters' House at Gracehill had only two resident Single Sisters. No statistical information about men was provided.

By the mid-nineteenth century, too, the provincial Place Congregational settlements, though largely unchanged in outward appearance, had deviated substantially from the spirituality of the original continental model. They were no longer vibrant centres of evangelical zeal and a recruiting ground for pilgrims called to worldwide service. No longer were there complaints that the Place Congregations were drawing off the spiritual elite from the societies. The residents were groups of like-minded respectable families who, although still congregational members, earned their living outside the settlements, regarding Sunday worship and occasional meetings in church as the sum of their religious observance. They lived and worked in much the same way as the God-fearing inhabitants of neighbouring secular villages and small towns, remaining in or near the settlements largely because the locations were aesthetically pleasing and the sense of fellowship reassuring. The available evidence suggests that, while their religious aim was still the worship of God and the practice of Christian virtues, their cultural ideal was no longer religious service, but the more limited civic aim of usefulness to family and society, a philosophy more in keeping with evolving Victorian Protestantism.

A similar process of secularization occurred also in the North American Province, being particularly evident in the Place Congregation of Bethlehem, Pennsylvania, and has been the subject of detailed research by American scholars. Still unsurpassed is the doctoral thesis of Hellmut Erbe, in which he defines this process as 'the ebbing away of the pilgrim spirit'.[25] Gillian Gollin, whose work has been referred to in the historiography, and Beverly P. Smaby,[26] also show that initially, at Bethlehem as in all the other Unity Place Congregations, the choir system had assumed responsibility for most of the internal spiritual, social and economic aspects of everyday life there. Uniquely, it had taken the social aspect to the point where both sexes, whether married or not, lived communally in either the Brethren's or Sisters' Choir Houses and all residents had shared goods in common.[27] In doing so the leaders and residents sensed that they represented the pinnacle of development within the Unity and knew that they were fully supported by Zinzendorf.[28] In time, the inevitable decline in zeal, the complexities of raising money to pay off Zinzendorf's debts, and competing religious and libertarian pressures in American society, had the same effects as in Britain. The communal buildings were converted for family use; the whole ethos changed, and 'religion was never again the central focus it had been during those first exciting years. The people of Bethlehem became a community in which each nuclear family concentrated on its own economic and social needs.'[29] This paralleled the developments in secularized Fulneck, demonstrating that by the mid-nineteenth century, the majority of residents in Place Congregations in North America and Britain still adhered to the same Christian beliefs and ethics, but in every other respect the two communities bore little resemblance to their eighteenth-century antecedents.[30] In effect, religious practices were regarded as more precisely linked to churchgoing.[31]

Further subtle congregational changes in outlook occurred when Place Congregational settlements became bases for boarding schools. As essentially commercial establishments set up in competition with those provided by other denominations, they functioned largely independently of their hosts' congregational life, and were not drawn into local religious and secular preoccupations. Thus, coincidental with the increasing secularization of life in the Place Congregations, their residents became aware of an emergent educational role for their community of a type which had not been envisaged by its founders. It was much the same for the general public who came to regard named settlements such as Fulneck, Fairfield, Gracehill and Ockbrook as virtually synonymous with boarding schools.

The evolution of a new hybrid provincial character

In order to understand the nature of British provincial thinking in the nineteenth century, particularly the dilemmas which underlay its decision-making, it is important to remember that the early British converts, and particularly their leaders, were encouraged to travel. They visited Herrnhaag and Herrnhut and spent time in British settlements on business and when taking part in evangelistic outreach. By so doing they became aware of the international nature of the Brotherhood, were on familiar terms with its German leaders, and accepted the ethos of the Unity as interpreted by Zinzendorf. This included the concept of Christ's leadership and the spiritual aspirations of those who lived in the Place Congregations, particularly their special relationship with each other in Christ as interpreted during the Herrnhaag period. Their co-operation with leading colleagues ensured that they had a sound knowledge of the model which was brought into the country, the dissemination of which in the early years involved a working relationship and personal bonds between the aristocratic German leaders and their converts, between artisans, British gentry and educated revivalists. This exciting period, too dependent on wealthy patronage and Zinzendorf's style of leadership to last, was preserved by the second and succeeding generations of Labourers during a more plebeian era in the form of memories of a golden age during the eighteenth-century revival, which represented to them the ideal to which the church should aspire, and from which it had fallen away.

Like all mythologies, it was modified with the passage of time. The less desirable aspects of the Herrnhaag era were forgotten or reinterpreted, and there was greater emphasis on influences from Herrnhut and the old Bohemian Unity, the orthodoxy of which was more acceptable to nineteenth-century thinking. Its significance lay in its preservation of a core of historical events and interpretations which defined the church for its members as a different kind of institution from the other Protestant denominations, from which in practice it was becoming virtually indistinguishable. There were various levels of awareness of this difference among its mid-nineteenth-century members, giving rise to the range of sensibilities and loyalties which caused tension in decision-making.

The story of the origins and early achievements of the Unity, based as it was on recent memories and bolstered by current practice and links with the continent, had its creative and exemplary aspects.[32] Those members of Anglo-German families and Labourers who regularly visited Germany and had influential positions in the British Province, cherished hopes of reviving the original zeal and extending the institutions which had been so influential a century earlier. The chronology of synodal records shows how seriously they struggled to achieve this. Within a relatively independent denominational framework which was proud of its continental links with the Unity, they tried to strengthen congregational spirituality, promote outreach in expanding urban areas, maintain awareness of early Unity history, generate support for foreign missions, and raise a large proportion of the funds necessary to sustain the province. There were other elements in the membership who, while agreeing that the province should work to regain the zeal of the eighteenth-century religious revivalists, favoured an independent British nonconformist style and the rejection of residual German practices.

Although there was common ground in areas of decision-making which related to the practicalities of provincial life, such differing interpretations of the nature of the church led to recurrent doubts about its identity and lack of assurance as to its way forward. These weaknesses were aggravated by developments in contemporary society, which required not only an intellectual response to new scientific challenges to religious orthodoxy, but, on a more practical level, conformist measures such as the setting-up of Sunday schools.

In such conditions the period from 1790 to 1883 was a century of very slow provincial growth and virtually perpetual compromise. What emerged was not a totally independent British denomination, nor was it, like the Continental Province, functioning on lines virtually unchanged since Zinzendorf's day, but it was an Anglo-German hybrid with elements of both. It remained linked to its motherland by virtue of its membership of an international Unity which made demands upon it, particularly with regard to missions, and still directed some areas of its spiritual life through its representation on Unity Synods and by the annual 'Watchwords' which were common to all the provinces. These links fostered the less tangible sentiments associated with the 'golden age' mythology, so that throughout the nineteenth century synodal reports consistently lamented the deficiencies of the present time and the loss of a former vitality which they always hoped to find the resources, manpower and spirituality to regain.

Conference and synodal landmarks: a chronology of the period 1795–c.1883

1795: reassessment by the province at the end of the eighteenth century

The 1795 Fulneck Conference Report[33] gives an impression of how provincial leaders perceived the first half-century of Unity work in Britain. Their discussions affirmed with pride the rapid formation of town and country congregations during the period when German outreach after 1742 had led to the establishment of settlements and societies in accordance with Zinzendorf's perception of a Renewed Unity. Already aware that the initial enthusiasm for outreach and evangelistic fervour were diminishing, many of those present looked back to Cennick's time, the 1740s and 1750s, which they regarded as a benchmark of the Brethren's evangelistic success. Since then, they argued, efforts to expand the congregational structure on lines which had appeared promising in the 1760s had become progressively less effective. It was admitted that the province was feeling the effects of losing a generation fired by the urge for religious revival; many preaching places established at the height of the Evangelical Revival had been closed and few new ones had opened.

Reluctantly, the Brethren acknowledged that their organization was contracting its ambitions and being increasingly hindered by the difficulty of recruiting stewards for existing societies. They recognized that there were now obstacles to provincial expansion which had not been apparent in the early years, resulting from the restricted nature and size of the church's communant membership and the rapid growth of other Protestant denominations.

As well as providing a retrospective assessment of the first fifty years of Unity activity in Britain as perceived by those responsible for its future, the minutes of the Provincial Conference of 1795 reveal issues which were to shape subsequent provincial development. Its four main themes indicate where the province stood in relation to the original model, and foreshadow the emergence of the distinctive provincial style which had been implicit in the changes acknowledged during the 1770s and 1780s. Two of these, namely the problem of expansion and the question of respect for the lot, show that, while officially the organization still followed the Brethren's original aspirations, discussion was already revealing divergence of opinion and practice. The other two themes, education and missions, mark those aspects of Unity philosophy which were to be adopted wholeheartedly by the church as endorsements of its denominational identity and aspirations, and they remain the features with which outsiders are still familiar at the end of the twentieth century.

There were still signs of traditional aspirations, but with a subtle difference. Provincial reassessment at the turn of the century reveals ways in which the British Province was beginning to turn away from Zinzendorf's original perception of the role of the Unity and its institutional style. It was proposed to reverse the trend towards the dominance of Place Congregations by opening vigorous new societies in selected areas, and plans were drawn up for a society-forming evangelical initiative similar to that which had been so successful in the eighteenth century, but there was no suggestion that it was to be more than a means of increasing membership. Because of shortage of funds, the project was to be organized by Church Elders and financed where possible by a subscription levied on present society members. Although there is no evidence that this scheme began to operate, such an aspiration and its constraints typify the endemic conflict between a perceived need to expand and the problem of how to finance it and provide evangelists, a recurrent dilemma which the province never satisfactorily resolved. The immediate problem which it addressed, the centralization of congregations around the larger establishments, was simply part of the inevitable move towards denominationalism, which resulted from the church's failure to grow by establishing societies in new locations, and the concentration of its limited resources on those which were already viable.

On the other hand, the 1795 Conference was to have positive and far-reaching results for the future direction of the church in the British Province and perceptions of its character by both members and outsiders, since deputies explored ways to achieve spiritual outreach among the young through increased educational provision. Though not a new departure, being based on the structure already in place, this policy represented a major change of emphasis in provincial practice, and was in line with Unity thinking and development in the Continental Province at that time.

By 1795 the Brethren's educational facilities had already been opened to children of non-members as fee-payers in premises attached to, or near, existing congregational bases. Schools for girls were well established by then at Fulneck (1782), Dukinfield and Gomersal (1792) and Wyke (1794).[34] Apart from the provincial boys' boarding school at Fulneck, founded in 1753 by the transfer of the Lamb's Inn establishment, there was no further provision for them. Regrets were expressed that this was so, but 'there was a want of teachers duly qualified'. This suggests that a curriculum for girls was easier to devise, being based on traditional skills which would enable them to earn a living in the settlements and community and equip them for marriage, and that parents and young women themselves valued an opportunity to gain such security. The education of boys required more specialized teaching if they were to combine the spiritual and occupational skills which would enable them to live, work and serve within a framework consistent with the Brethren's expectations. In practice, however regrettable, those who aimed to follow a trade were drawn by necessity or inclination to find employment or apprenticeship elsewhere.

Provincial Sunday schools, perceived above all as religious institutions, were now being founded, the first having been opened at Fairfield in 1793, followed shortly by the second at Bedford, and during the nineteenth century most congregations set up their own. Like the provincial boarding schools founded by the Brethren, their Sunday schools reflected the increasing interest of British society in providing educational opportunities for the young, even though early experience suggested that they did not recruit many new congregational members. Various institutions for Sunday instruction which were primarily religious were already well established in both Protestant and Roman Catholic areas of Western Europe, some of these providing instruction in reading and writing. Those that emerged in Britain in the second half of the eighteenth century were chiefly the outcome of undenominational enterprise, later absorbed into the Methodist movement. They were located especially in rapidly expanding industrial communities making textiles,[35] and were the only religious institution which the public in the mass had any intention of using.[36] The first Methodist Sunday school, for example, was founded in High Wycombe in 1769, so the movement was well under way before the British provincial leaders initiated their own. Recent scholarship suggests that the impulse behind this nationwide development was more complex than might at first appear, and by the 1790s was partly related to contemporary developments in France, where the Establishment had been overthrown. The Quaker historian J. Walvin[37] argues that some early providers of Sunday schools hoped that the simple conservative and conformist religious instruction provided in them would diminish the possibility of social unrest in Britain during the French Revolutionary Wars.[38] Roy Porter[39] similarly argues that school complemented church for indoctrinating the children of the masses with ideals of obedience and conformity. By 1797 across the country there were 1,086 Sunday schools with 690,000 students, some of them adults. Although most contemporary leaders of opinion accepted that active religious involvement was a minority affair,[40] they were united in the view that religion and education were inseparable, justifying a denominational approach. Nonconformists preferred that children should receive simple Bible teaching, uncomplicated by the tenets of any particular religious persuasion,[41] and this had been the Brethren's position ever since their first catechism was published in 1723.

Another subject of debate in 1795, the province's enduring involvement with missions, was close to the hearts of conference members, who commented enthusiastically on 'the present stir among all denominations throughout Britain to establish missions to the heathen'.[42] They rejoiced that the existing missions of the Brethren and the work of their Society for the Furtherance of the Gospel, founded in London in 1741, were well known among leaders of opinion in other societies.

Other sources confirmed grounds for optimism about Unity missions, though many other religious organizations, such as evangelical elements in the Anglican, Congregationalist, Presbyterian, Baptist and Methodist Churches, were participating in this field of activity.[43] As early as 1778 Methodists had been encouraged to volunteer for missionary service in Africa, and in 1786 in Bengal. By the end of the eighteenth century several British denominational missionary societies had been formed – the Baptists in 1792, the Congregationalists' London Missionary Society in 1795, the Anglican Church Missionary Society in 1799 and the Methodist Missionary Society in 1813, reorganized in 1818.[44] The latter, despite a comparatively late start, soon began to make an enormous contribution to Christian missions. Some indication of the large sums of money which were being contributed for British missionary activity in general during the early part of the nineteenth century can be gained by considering the amount subscribed to the Congregationalist London Missionary Society. For the period 1815–20, £115,619 was given; the total collected between 1816 and 1850 amounted to £1,627,208, and there is no evidence that this society was exceptional in its capacity to attract funds.[45]

This was far from being the real cost of missions; the true cost was in human life. It has been argued that the devotion, courage and self-sacrifice with which British men and women missionaries of all denominations went out to serve their fellow men was a testimony to the quality of the lives of devout nineteenth-century Britons at their very best.[46] Tragically, large numbers died within a few years of starting work, usually as a result of contracting virulent tropical diseases. But this did not appear to deter others from embarking on the same hazardous course, among them a number of British provincial members who had responded to the call to this work.

1824: *the desire to preserve a heritage and the need for change*

The minutes of the Provincial Conference at Fairfield in 1824[47] mark a change of emphasis within the province, particularly in matters of religious style. A significant development which facilitated administrative change was the establishment of an executive committee of British Provincial Helpers. The Provincial Helper, effectively the President, and his colleagues were authorized from Herrnhut to administer the province under the authority of the Unity Elders' Conference, but with much wider powers than before. This provided a context within which the principal inherited institutional structures of the 1740s and 1750s could be easily and speedily dismantled if the province did not wish to retain them in their traditional form. As we have seen, members' opinions of what was necessary varied, providing a source of dissension which persisted for many years. Although there were still, in the 1820s, those who wished to preserve as much as possible of the original continental model, the balance was changing, as strong arguments were being put forward by members who hoped to modify it as a result of congregational pressure for change and consequent recognition by ordained brethren that some inherited practices were losing support. The latter group argued that a perceived decline in spirituality among existing congregations was related to 'the probability that our constitution in all its parts did not suit the present times and the local circumstances of these kingdoms and that a simplification appeared desirable'. It had been common knowledge for some time that well-established German traditions were being dropped or questioned, but now some of these omissions were being officially recorded: a few congregations were no longer using traditional liturgies, and congregational singing was being allowed to become lethargic; the need for prostration after receiving the bread at Holy Communion was being questioned.

There was more general deliberation about the province's endemic problem, shortage of money. It was still not the established practice for collections to be made at all services; yet, in general, congregation members were regarded as parsimonious. Since much of what they did contribute was paid directly to their Labourer as salary, amounts raised varied significantly from congregation to congregation, and ordained brethren present were virtually unanimous that they were not being paid enough. It was left to John Carey, from Dublin, to link congregational parsimony somewhat unsympathetically with spiritual weakness, with no recognition of the limited income of most members.

In spite of criticism of congregational inertia and reiteration of the problems of finding the resources for expansion, the conference statistics show a slow but consistent increase in the number of congregations, though still in rural or semi-rural locations: Baildon had been settled in 1816, and Kimbolton in 1823, as conventional congregations in the evolving British denominational style with a full-time resident Labourer.

Impressive progress was reported in educational expansion. The newly established boarding schools were regarded as the real areas of provincial advancement, and in 1824 discussions at the conference about this aspect of the work of the province were positively optimistic: one speaker referred with pride to 'our numerous and extensive establishments for the education and instructing of youth'.[48] It was pointed out that, because of the large number of applicants for places, there was a risk that the schools might become too large and unwieldy, although viewed objectively most of these schools were small, with fewer than fifty pupils.[49] There was also a shortage of skilled teachers because other denominations were committing more resources to the establishment of schools and colleges and competing for well-qualified staff.

Still on the theme of education, though with a much broader canvas, Conference recommended that congregational members with children should be reminded that it was their responsibility to pray, read the Bible, and in every possible way concern themselves with the spiritual upbringing of their offspring. To assist them in this task it was intended to publish a short church history, and work had already started on this. In addition, Holmes's more academic history of the Brotherhood was soon to be available – the first volume was published in 1825 – and conference members hoped that it might acquaint many with both provincial and Unity history.

The failure of the church to attract many of the younger generation into membership was confirmed eleven years later when the Provincial Conference convened at Fulneck in 1835 took note of only a slight growth in the number of communicant members, from 2,596 in 1824, to 2,698. The earlier conference perceived this problem as a failure on the part of the institutions themselves, but in retrospect it can be seen as reflecting changes in society. The inability of congregations to retain young members into adulthood was to accelerate throughout the nineteenth century and beyond. It would have been no consolation to deputies to realize the extent to which this shortfall after years of teaching with a religious bias was common in other denominations in the early nineteenth century. The Wesleyan Methodists, for example, estimated that only about 5 per cent of their Sunday school pupils subsequently joined the church.[50]

1847: reappraisal by the province after a century of development

The Provincial Conference which met at Fairfield in 1847[51] coincided with a landmark in the life of the British Province. It was a little over a hundred years since the settlement of the first congregation at Fetter Lane in 1742, providing an opportunity to reassess the achievements and shortcomings of the first century of Unity work in Britain, where the consequences of change and innovation were now becoming much more apparent.

The Conference Minutes provide further evidence that the German model was gradually being dismantled in practice and that the church's aspirations and spiritual vitality continued to be weakened in the process. It is a measure of changes already established in the province that one of the first problems the conference discussed was that of denominational identity, a problem which had also been exercising the Methodists for some years.[52] They were concerned about how the Brethren were perceived by those outside the church, and questioned how far even its own members understood its uniqueness. It was generally agreed that the British religious public were familiar with and generally impressed by the boarding schools and by Unity missionary activity (which was still primarily German), but most people were not familiar with the church's history. Many British congregational members had only the vaguest impression of events on the continent from 1722 onwards and the vibrant, yet seemingly unrepeatable, expansion of the Brethren's mission in Britain during its first twenty years. Traditionalists argued that members would resist further debasement of the original institutional structure if they had greater knowledge of its early history. The unease which these deliberations reflected goes to the heart of the fundamental dilemma faced by the province. Its practices and institutional organization were evolving in response to local conditions and social change, yet it retained a perception of a unique identity and mission which distinguished it from the other Nonconformist denominations and reinforced its continental connections.

This ambivalence surfaced in other areas of discussion where German practices and even the fundamental pattern of their establishments continued to be contentious issues. The use of the lot, always a sensitive indicator of changing thinking and practice, was a case in point. Other continental traditions were being amended or tacitly ignored, particularly where they had been designed to apply rigorous and restrictive standards of religious dedication and conformity. The 'speaking with', whereby in the days prior to the monthly communion Labourers interviewed communicant members to assess their spiritual worthiness to attend, was being dropped. Band and class meetings in both Place Congregations and Town and Country Congregations had been abandoned. Society activity was scarcely referred to, having virtually ceased to be a provincial priority.

An apparently minor conference report on the state of provincial burial grounds provided further evidence of how far the original German thinking about the nature of Brotherhood was losing its hold. Though satisfied in general by the way they were being administered, it complained that inscriptions on gravestones sometimes deviated from the official style by the addition of epitaphs. In a few cases the principle that the church's graveyards were exclusively for members was being violated, and non-members interred after paying a substantial fee. The rigid uniformity and strict regulation of this traditional symbol of unity and equality in death, characteristic of the founders' perception of membership of the Brotherhood in Christ, were not in keeping with the British preference for a less regimented system. This divergence from tradition was disturbing to traditionalists, who looked back to the simpler perceptions of the mid-eighteenth century when, it was argued, the Labourers and all adult congregational members regarded themselves as of identical status in one Brotherhood and accepted that material arrangements should reflect their spiritual equality before the Saviour. This sense of unity was perceived to be disintegrating, and consequently there was discussion about how far the province had gone in effectively separating the Labourers, the initiators, from their congregations.

These Conference Minutes were exceptional in providing individual congregational appraisals by their resident Labourers. A few, including Bath and Mirfield, were reported to be in good heart, with members living disciplined, simple, pious lives devoted to their congregations and removed from worldly pleasures; but they were exceptions. Ordained Brethren elsewhere were dissatisfied in varying degrees with the spiritual condition of their flocks, despite admitting the existence of a core of really dedicated members. A majority of their congregations were believed to be looking for social advantage and, although they worshipped regularly on Sundays, they were unwilling to attend weeknight congregational meetings. Some Labourers reported ageing congregations not being replaced by the young.

Although in 1847 a great deal of discussion centred on material changes in the original concept of the Brethren's identity and religious practice, declining congregational spirituality was identified as resulting from the insidious infiltration of undesirable attitudes common in urban industrial society. One other development, prevalent in Northern Ireland and familiar elsewhere, was the loss of members by emigration to industrial areas, such as Belfast, where there was no congregation. Dukinfield and Salem, in Lancashire, were cited as congregations where industrialization continued to hinder growth, although it was claimed that all denominations were suffering from the spread of the factory system. A perceptive comment by the Malmesbury Labourer was probably applicable to most other congregations in or near industrial areas. He observed of members: 'There is great diligence in business, but a want of fervour of spirit in serving the Lord.'

Despite the unanimity of the ordained Brethren on this matter, late twentieth-century scholarship shows that the relationship between urbanization, industrialization and a deterioration of religious observance was really far from simple and was subject to local and regional variation.[53] Although there is considerable evidence that industrialization may have been detrimental, according to Watts there is as much evidence of mill owners using their position to encourage the spiritual growth of their employees by, for example, making regular church attendance a condition of employment.[54] How far this arrangement was motivated by a desire to secure a docile workforce or to save souls is difficult to say, but it would be unrealistic to assume that most providers of employment were cynics. Other factors may have contributed to the loosening of the bonds of formalized religion, including the drift away from village life[55] where workers on the estates of the gentry were expected to attend Sunday worship, and the sheer exhaustion resulting from long hours spent by whole families at work in factories. In the case of the Brethren, it is likely that Labourers were still yearning for the close association between work and religion which they rightly believed to have been more easily attainable in mid-eighteenth-century domestic industry.

It was already being recognized that the early congregational network, based on the original areas of evangelism, was beginning to hinder the church's ambitions for expansion. Leominster, Cootehill and Ayr were already classified as small, a euphemism for being only marginally viable, and several ordained Brethren commented adversely on the problems of communication inherited from the excessively scattered nature of provincial premises. Yet, despite the generally gloomy tone of the Brethren's congregational reports and the slow rate of congregational expansion which they revealed, there were some grounds for satisfaction in 1847. The number of communicant members in twenty-nine congregations was 2,764, a small increase on the 1835 figure of 2,698, and a few congregations were reported to be initiating tentative evangelism by setting up house-group prayer meetings on the American model.

There was concern, however, about the lack of enthusiasm for missions in many congregations. This was a sensitive area in the Brethren's perception of its role as a church, and was seen by Labourers as further evidence of congregational decline. Such criticism was probably unfair in some respects, as changes in the character of Place Congregations and the collapse of the provincial diaspora societies meant that they were not providing trained workers for the overseas mission fields as originally conceived by Zinzendorf and his colleagues. As a result, material support was limited and personnel were not volunteering in sufficient numbers to sustain synodal ambitions. The importance of a personal element in raising awareness of and enthusiasm for missions was underlined by one notable exception in the reports, that from Fetter Lane, whose Labourer reported that, because they were able to meet some of the missionaries personally while they were in transit through London, his congregation shared a deep interest in foreign missions.

These reflections from within the church can be seen in perspective by comparison with the overall picture of missionary activity in Britain by the middle of the nineteenth century. There were other missionary agencies based in London which held public meetings and had a significant influence on congregations of all denominations, particularly in the capital, but also in the country as a whole. The scale of the whole overseas missionary activity directed from London at this time, which helped to characterize the Victorian era as the last great religious age in English history,[56] can best be appreciated by reference to some other contemporary sources: by the early 1840s, for example, the Methodist Missionary Society had 382 missionaries on foreign stations;[57] by 1850 the Congregationalist London Missionary Society had 170 missionaries at work.[58] The British province of the Unity, where congregational numbers and resources were so small, could not hope to match numbers such as these; its modest contribution to the support of Unity missions was integrated into the work of the Unity as a whole, where German Labourers were always in the majority. It was an important function of provincial conferences to encourage ministers and congregations to greater efforts to provide money and recruit missionaries, and criticism of this and other aspects of provincial life must be seen in perspective as part of this objective.

The most positive source of satisfaction to deputies in 1847 was the contribution being made to provincial resources and prestige by its boarding schools, which were being well patronized by parents seeking a sound religious context for their children's schooling. It was in this field alone that the province was going from strength to strength, having perceived a need among families of comparatively modest means which, at that point in the nineteenth century, was not being met by the state or the prestigious public schools.

The 1850s and early 1860s: renewed search for a key to growth

At the Provincial Conferences of the 1850s[59] two major themes were predominant. One of these was the familiar endemic problem of the province's shortage of money and consequent failure to grow, a weakness which was becoming increasingly pressing. A clear and detailed exposition of this state of affairs appears in the Fulneck Jubilee Committee's celebratory pamphlet.[60] The writers regard the period 1825–55 as a time of comparative inactivity, in which we discern the working of a leaven of opinion in which we may either purify the whole or hasten its destruction. . . . It is doubtless a fact, much to be deplored, that our congregations have not increased in the ratio of the population at large, though we rejoice still to number amongst us the bearers of names which have been handed down for three generations.

In retrospect it is significant that the congregations in that area were consoling themselves for lack of growth by taking comfort in familial continuity, which was to be an abiding characteristic of the British Province. To conference deputies of the time this failure to expand was the most disturbing reality of provincial life, and appeared insoluble. The second problem was administrative change, and in retrospect, the administrative decisions taken during the period had the greater influence on the future character of the province because they accelerated the emergence of a hybrid provincial style.

The first of these considerations, the problem of finance, formed a gloomy background to all discussions, in the form of continuing awareness of the limitations under which the province was operating as a result of its small membership. By 1853 the number of congregations had increased from 29 to 32, an increase of only 10 since 1782, and membership had increased marginally to 2,865. (According to the 1851 census, the Wesleyan Methodists[61] had 6,579 congregations, with 302,209 members.[62]) Ordained Brethren's salaries, still variable, remained low. Some did part-time teaching in order to survive; others felt obliged to take out private insurance against illness and old age, and all hoped that sooner or later salaries would be standardized. Financial stringency continued to hinder the setting-up of new congregations since they could be formed only if they were financially self-supporting. In the case of Horton (Bradford), for example, a formal proposal that the society should be settled as an official Town Congregation was rejected, since its members were unable to raise the necessary money.

The administrative changes which had such a radical long-term influence resulted from the effect on the British Province of a general reassessment of Unity relationships, the most important development in the Brethren's Church during the 1850s. It was paralleled in the province by several key reforms which brought it nearer to the formulation of an independent style by expediting the abandonment of some aspects of its German heritage. After much disagreement and by a small minority, it was decided in 1853 to rename the long-established Provincial Helpers' Conference – the provincial cabinet – as the Provincial Elders' Conference, PEC, a rejection of former terminology and a step towards formal acknowledgement of the distinctiveness of the provincial approach to administration.

It was at this stage that a small group of Labourers led by John Carey decided to take the unprecedented step of publishing *The Fraternal Messenger*,[63] an unofficial monthly journal, as an open forum for discussion of the causes and implications of the uncomfortable provincial situation which had been highlighted once again in the 1847 reappraisal. Publication began in July 1850, continuing for three years, with a regular format combining news items, literary and devotional articles and readers' letters, together with a series of monthly discussion papers described overall as 'Characteristics of the Brethren's Church'.

Paper I, the first of thirty-one, presented as a starting-point a theme to which all readers could accede:

> The Brethren are the quiet of the land . . . better known on the continent than in England . . . where there is much apathy and indifference in society and even among many members of the church itself, which we would fain hope a little more information would dispel and turn into the liveliest interest.[64]

This central theme was continued in subsequent papers, expressed very explicitly:

> From the time of the renewal of the church for about twenty years her growth was rapid and extensive . . . The word of the cross was to them not only the hope of salvation, but a weapon of true and undoubted power to turn the world upside down from darkness to light. . . . During the last fifty years she has been nearly stationary, if not decreasing.[65]

This, it was argued, was because the major institutional features of the Brotherhood which had been introduced into England in the middle of the eighteenth century had since either collapsed or changed out of all recognition, whereas in the Continental Province they were prospering.

The writers then considered several specific areas of provincial activity. Paper XVI dealt with the diaspora, defined as, 'those in connection with our church who live scattered through towns and villages and are united with us in heart, but are not under the same church rules and regulations', that is, they remained members of their original church. It was estimated that, in 1850, the Continental Province had approximately 100,000 such adherents, and it was stressed that, 'this sphere of labour is quite peculiar to the Brethren and of exceptional interest', but that,

Such a diaspora is impracticable in Britain; the English character and mind would not be conformed to it. On the continent those who entertain doubts about their religious beliefs but are content to remain nominal members of the Lutheran or Reformed Church are susceptible to diaspora work. In Britain such individuals can simply form a new sect, and they are not susceptible to diaspora work.[66]

The original diaspora as understood by Zinzendorf and his associates had collapsed.

Paper XVII referred to missions. In 1850 an estimated total membership of about 17,000 church members (communicant and non-communicant combined) supported about 293 missionaries (including wives) to the heathen. The comment was made that this was a very large proportion of missionaries to church membership, yet most were sent by the Continental Province, and very few British and American members were now willing to take up this work, which was 'not in their honour'. Mission work in general was no longer as arduous as it had been in the early days, when severe privations were usually involved; 'in fact, most stations are quite comfortable and often better than in some home congregations'.[67]

Paper XVIII concerned education, and commented that even those pupils who had been born into the church appeared to know little about it, and the history and significance of the Brethren's Church did not stir them. Yet, in the opinion of the editors, schools should be missions among children.[68]

Finally, the papers from XXII onwards were devoted to the theme, 'Prospects for the Brethren's Church'. They included an exhaustive analysis of the role of the congregational settlements, in which the original ideal, as the writers saw it, had been 'to subject the whole life, all outward circumstances, to the control and direction of the spirit of the Gospel, to be a light to the world'. They heartily subscribed to 'this beautiful idea', while recognizing that the reality was now quite different, for up to half the people living there were 'political members only, and only nominally church members'. They commented that this was 'one of the most impeding circumstances', since it meant that Labourers had to work 'with expediency in mind'. Secularization was corroding the original idea, and they recognized with regret that they were compelled to accept that, 'the original plan is no longer working as it was clearly intended, for the church is a spiritual kingdom'.[69]

These comments from within the church reveal the extent of the changes which had taken place by the early 1850s. Since the major institutional features had collapsed, most of what really distinguished the provincial congregational network from the Anglicans and other denominations no longer had an obvious role in terms of what it had originally set out to be.

Faced by this daunting prospect, the writers recognized that the only hope for the future lay in cultivating the spiritual life of the 'real' church members as distinct from the 'political' members. As they put it, 'We must aim to become truly a church, and only a church, let every tie binding worldly minded men to a nominal union with the church be severed. . . . Some must be excluded and made to depart from the settlements.'

The question was then put, 'What has been the moving power of the church from the beginning? What enabled our first Brethen to overcome all obstacles? It was faith, love and enthusiasm, the conviction of the heart.' The group of true Brethren and Sisters to be found in every congregation were described as, 'the real people of the church who love the church and want it to have the power it had originally'.[70]

It is impossible to assess to what extent these monthly journals circulated among the Labourers and congregational members. The editors claimed to have about one hundred subscribers,[71] and never implied that their publication expressed the mind of the province as a whole. Nevertheless, they did present a coherent explanation for the province's persistent uncertainty about its identity, and helped to ensure that subsequent action could at least be based on reality. In practice, all the underlying changes, which were now well established, continued because there was no alternative, and so the province progressed steadily towards an independent denominational character.

This was further formalized when, after decades of uncertainty and carefully cultivated ambiguity, the 1856 Fulneck Conference confirmed that the British Province was from then onwards in reality a separate denomination. It no longer even recognized a theoretical obligation to continue to act as a diaspora-society-forming agency seeking to enhance the spirituality of Anglican congregations, as had been its original eighteenth-century brief.[72] This important declaration merely confirmed that the British and Continental provinces had been following divergent courses of development for some time.

The 1856 conference also proposed that, subject to the approval of the Unity General Synod in Germany, due in 1857, the British Provincial Conference should become the final arbiter of provincial affairs, gaining dominance over the Provincial Elders, whom it would re-elect at the opening of each succeeding provincial conference. The Unity General

Synod of 1857 agreed to this and other measures which granted virtual autonomy to the British Province, while retaining a purely nominal supervisory role for the central organization of the Unity. This transfer of decision-making to an elected body from within the provincial membership completely altered the balance of authority in the province. As a result, the British and Continental provinces became financially independent of each other and in 1859 in fulfilment of these changes, the Continental Province provided the final subsidy of £15,000.

Because of the independence resulting from these administrative decisions, the 1859 Provincial gathering in Bristol[73] became the first properly constituted Synod of the British Province. This synod made further important alterations to the original German heritage which represented a significant adjustment to the realities of British religious pluralism. It had been a matter of the utmost importance that members of the Brotherhood were not allowed to marry non-members. This was no longer to be the case provided that the non-member was Protestant, confirmed, and acceptable to the Labourer and Congregation Committee; any member marrying a Roman Catholic would be deemed to have left the Brotherhood.

Synodal discussions about training for ordination were closely linked during the 1850s with perceptions that the province had lost some of the dynamic which had characterized its earlier years, and that enthusiastic leadership was necessary to counteract this. In the early years of eighteenth-century expansion, both the mentality and the spiritual vitality of established congregations had depended on the supportive role of devoted lay Labourers. As a response to criticism by deputies that the province had 'slumbered during the last half century' and must return to 'the spirit of activity' which had characterized it in the 1740s and 1750s, a suggestion was made which had important implications for the future management of shortages of trained lay and ordained leaders. In an attempt to restore the successful evangelism of the early years, provincial leaders recommended that ordained brethren should now begin to recruit suitably devout laymen, who would share in pastoral oversight by holding Bible-study meetings, visiting the sick and teaching in Sunday schools. There had been some promising activity of this type in Northern Ireland, where a Scripture Readers' Society, with cells of interested lay people, had already been formed in various congregations. These were reminiscent of the eighteenth-century religious societies, though in 1853 their stance was exclusively denominational. Unfortunately this experiment, too, proved to be short-lived, its high point being when it employed eight itinerants, but by 1859 it was in debt and its five remaining preachers recognized that public response was diminishing rapidly; the society was doomed.

In 1856, however, there was some evidence among deputies of a will for congregational expansion, and various measures were proposed as encouragement for laymen willing to help. Such people were now to be allowed to preach with the permission of the appropriate Labourer and his close congregational colleagues, defined as the Church Committee. It was also tentatively proposed, but the proposal was not immediately acted upon, to form a Home Missionary Society to support anyone prepared to become an itinerant evangelist or a house-group supervisor. District conferences of the lay and ordained were to be set up, responsible separately for the North of England, Eastern Counties, West of England, and Northern Ireland, specifically to raise money and recruit new church workers, including boarding-school teachers, Labourers and missionaries.

Some slow progress was being made during this period; for example, the congregation at Horton (Bradford) became virtually self-supporting, thus qualifying for official settlement, and there was activity in Weardale where the future congregation at Crook was to be recruited. Nevertheless, deputies expressed the need for a new outpouring of the Holy Spirit in every provincial congregation in view of the alarming ignorance and ungodliness in the country as a whole. Many commented with concern not only on the traditional needs of lukewarm Christians, with a nominal religious connection and secure employment, but also on the desperate situation of the poor, neglected and distressed in society. In keeping with contemporary Victorian priorities and sensibilities, the plight of these people, located primarily in industrial areas, gradually began to draw the Brethren from their traditional narrowly defined evangelistic stance towards a more social and philanthropic gospel.

Under the impetus of the increased independence of the province, deputies to provincial conferences in the 1850s expressed a preference for shorter intervals between them. Labourers were becoming increasingly aware of the geographical and social deprivation of working in peripheral areas such as Ayr, Haverfordwest and Tytherton, far from kindred spirits, a problem caused by the original pattern of inherited networks. This, of course, had been recognized long before, but was now thought to be affecting the organization and sense of community of the province as a whole, particularly as its financial situation and human resources precluded more than marginal growth.

These related problems of isolation and failure to grow, highlighted by the increased autonomy of the province, were issues which continued to trouble members into the 1860s and beyond. Labourers, particularly those working in remoter regions, argued that the Provincial Elders' Conference ought to help maintain a sense of unity by making more frequent visitations. All were agreed that this isolation was threatening the identity of the whole province, increasing the likelihood that it might gradually disintegrate, becoming a loosely connected medley of virtually independent congregations. In 1863 there were approximately 3,000 members, an increase during the preceding decade of about 200.[74] As a separate, self-consciously independent denomination the congregational network was only just holding its own.

By the 1860s, after very few years of financial independence from Germany, new problems were beginning to exercise provincial leaders, centred on the two areas for which the church had become known to outsiders in Britain since the 1790s, namely education and missions. At the 1863 provincial Synod, some brethren, both ordained and lay, expressed uneasiness that the long-term financial viability and prospects of the province, as well as its sense of identity, were in danger of becoming too dependent on the prosperity of its boarding schools. They argued that the Unity had never been primarily an educational agency; it had come into existence as a spiritual body, ministering first and foremost to the religious needs of adults. If such a reversal of eighteenth-century priorities and intentions were allowed to persist, the schools might survive and the congregational network might simply wither away. This possibility was taken very seriously and, as a result, Synod decided to make even more determined efforts in the direction of Home Missions. An official Home Missions Society[75] was now set up, to be financed by congregational contributions.

In the circumstances of the time, therefore, the British Province needed to call upon its own membership for interest and financial support. If such a reawakening and increase of involvement were to be achieved it would require a strengthening of congregational purpose throughout the province, and to encourage such a development it was proposed that a provincial journal should be published. It would concern itself to some extent with Unity affairs, but would pay special attention to the activities and interests of the British province, as did its predecessor *The Fraternal Messenger*. This had enjoyed a short but controversial existence, but collapsed through lack of support. Now, a decade later, the Bedford Synod decided that an official monthly journal should be published, entitled *The Messenger: A Magazine of the Church of the United Brethren*, starting with a first issue on 1 January 1864, provided that at least 500 members subscribed. This was a relatively late and small-scale arrival at a time which was witnessing the emergence of a large number of similar religious magazines of varying quality and influence, typified by *The Nonconformist* founded in 1841. This magazine, with its academic style, came to be regarded as a leader of Nonconformist opinion, achieving a circulation of about 15,000, whereas the more popular and chatty *Christian World* reached 150,000.[76] *The Messenger* was more akin to *The Nonconformist* in style, with perceptive and wide-ranging discussion of Unity and provincial concerns.

Consolidation in the late 1860s and 1870s

Still concerned with adverse developments in British society and the related failure of the province to expand, the 1868 Fulneck Synod focused on the need for a clearer sense of provincial identity and increased involvement of congregation members in provincial responsibilities.[77] In previous synods this failing had been blamed for the perceived difficulties of expansion and financial and congregational viability. It was still felt that maintaining the purity of Christian doctrine was the best guarantee of the province's survival, enabling it at least to retain the loyalty of existing members, even if it could not attract many new ones. In these circumstances town congregations, rather than those in rural or semi-rural areas, had the greatest potential opportunity for growth, and it was recommended that the elite of the ordained should be stationed there. Such experienced men might also be able to stem the drift of the respectable working class from some existing town congregations, a development which had already induced some misgiving.

This climate of opinion represented a further step in the direction of marginalizing the small and remote congregations by the strategic concentration of limited resources in urban areas where they might be expected to produce the greatest benefit. It underlined once again the church's endemic problem of how to target inadequate resources in an organization with so many small congregations on the periphery of its potential influence. The sense of isolation of their Labourers and the concessions to expediency now being considered by the provincial administrative body were painful evidence not only that it was becoming impracticable to sustain let alone expand the network, but that, more crucially, its further reaches could not be maintained in good heart.

Paradoxically, there had been some advances which showed that a desire to expand was strong, despite the difficulties. The Home Mission Society, though getting very little money from congregational sources, was setting up a new congregation at Westwood, near Oldham, in a densely populated area. There had been evangelistic initiatives in places such as Crook in County Durham, Bakewell, Glasgow and Scarborough, well outside the traditional areas of the Brethren's influence, though with the exception of Crook they came to nothing.

Communication and publicity among the provincial membership were still seen as providing a lifeline in the current situation where finance was at a premium. *The Messenger* had been launched successfully on time, and in 1868 seemed likely to survive. To augment it still further as a source of information, the Synod decided to publish an annual Provincial Almanack, starting in 1869. It was to be the first ever English-language reference book to the affairs of the entire Unity, giving comprehensive and detailed information about its personnel and activities, listing, for example, the address of every congregation, the name of its resident minister and, where relevant, the times of services. All schools, both at home and abroad, were to be listed. In the mission sections the names of all serving missionaries were given, with the address of the appropriate station. Access to this text gave subscribers information about their place in the overall scheme of things, justifying pride in belonging to such an active international body. These two publications marked another important stage in the provincial strategy for development. By 1868 *The Messenger* had already acquired the status of a substantial, well-written monthly journal with wide-ranging international interests, including regular news reports from home and overseas congregations, and was now to be complemented by a comprehensive work of reference.

The 1870s began in a mood of limited optimism as to the future of the province, and the 1871 Fulneck synodal statistics and reports suggested that some progress was being made. The number of communicant members had increased to 3,253 in thirty-eight congregations of varying size. Fulneck was the largest, with about 300 communicant members. On the other hand, fourteen congregations, roughly one third of the total, were very small, with fewer than 50 communicant members; three more had between 50 and 60. The provincial boarding-school network was still very successful, particularly the two schools at Fulneck which were attended by children of ministerial families and missionaries. Thirty-four Sunday schools were operational,[78] and general satisfaction was expressed at their present state and future prospects. Synod agreed that the Bible was to remain the foundation of all instruction in them[79] and, like the boarding schools, they were to have a definitely denominational style. There was also slow but persistent progress in Home Missions;

a single ordained Labourer was to be stationed at Heckmondwike, a retired missionary was to serve at Brockweir; and an appointment was to be made at West Pennard. The continuing policy of appointing a Labourer and his wife to every congregation, a generous arrangement in view of the small numerical size of some, meant that close pastoral oversight was still possible and appreciated.

The urgency of the need for initiatives to reinvigorate the church was underlined by synodal recognition of the irreversible nature of social change related to urbanization. It was becoming increasingly clear that the larger the town the smaller the percentage of people who attended church on Sundays,[80] and it was in the area of spiritual commitment to the certainties of faith that most apprehensions lay. Deputies to the 1871 Synod were increasingly aware of the pressures on Christian denominations in general and the Brethren in particular, resulting from scepticism in society under the influence of radical new scientific theories, such as the theory of evolution.[81] Fundamental religious doctrines continued to be under fire, and members of such a small and scattered province were felt to be particularly vulnerable to what was becoming an increasingly popular supposition that the natural sciences could solve all problems, even the problems of men; that man and society could be brought under universal laws like the law of gravitation.[82] Ordained brethren recognized the need to clarify Christian doctrine for themselves in the light of this challenge, and Synod called upon them to make greater efforts on behalf of their congregations, who in turn were urged to be more co-operative. It is in comments such as these that the underlying sense of stagnation in congregational life showed itself. Ministers were inclined to blame the loss of evangelical fervour among members on their own pastoral shortcomings and lack of the knowledge to combat scepticism, although this change was not unique to the Brotherhood. Both inside and outside the Anglican Church, for example, the theology of conversion and personal salvation was increasingly being challenged and supplemented by other styles of religious thought, such as a growing emphasis on sacraments. There had been only a modest response to initiatives to recruit lay assistance for Labourers, but it was regarded as desirable to continue the pressure on lay Brethren to consider this form of service, even though the supply of ministers suggested that lay assistance was not an urgent need. In these circumstances it is not surprising that there were comparatively few new congregational members, but the alertness of Labourers to the need to face these difficulties probably ensured that existing members retained their allegiance.

Provincial awareness of a continuing need for renewal and expansion was evident in a decision to ease one rule which had so far been retained in congregational practice. It was decided that non-members were to be allowed to participate in what had been private congregational functions, such as lovefeasts and choir meetings. Such a relaxation of the original exclusive style would give Labourers the chance to influence visitors and perhaps induce them to join the Brotherhood. This decision was another sign that the province had its own priorities and was dealing with its problems in ways which had little reference to the original principles on which the network had been established.

Three years previously the Unity General Synod had decided that all provinces should take a full share in foreign missions. It was made known that the German Province, having provided the bulk of the personnel and finance for so long, was becoming less willing to do so, and was expecting much greater assistance from the British and American provinces. For this reason the deputies at Synod, in marked contrast to most of their predecessors, had the opportunity for a full discussion of foreign missions. They were aware that the British Province was still not contributing adequately to this defining area of Unity life. It was an unpalatable fact that the Mission Board, located in Germany and composed largely of Germans, received many more applications for mission service from its own countrymen, even though English was the language most widely used, since the majority of stations were in British colonies. It had long been accepted that few British members were willing to volunteer for overseas service, perhaps because missionary training at that stage was available only in Germany, where prolonged attendance presented a severe cultural obstacle to aspirants from the British Province.

The discrepancy between desirability and practice continued to trouble the province throughout the 1870s, and in 1874, at the Fairfield Synod,[83] attention was once more drawn to this provincial indifference. Some deputies commented on a growing conviction among mission brethren that the interest of the British Province in Unity mission work, never great, was rapidly declining. The explanation for this situation, which troubled the missionary fraternity as a whole, was not far to seek. The establishment of new congregations at home was regarded as a far more pressing need, partly because, with increasing mobility and rapid urban expansion, more members were being hindered by the limited range and numbers of congregations available to them should they move from their home congregations. There was the added problem of providing the means to recruit new members in large urban areas. As an example of this deficiency, Synod was presented with a memorandum by four members living in the Leeds area,[84] who deplored the absence of a congregation there and emphasized the need to break out from the geographical restrictions of the original largely rural and semi-rural congregational network. They pointed out that an increasing number of members, like themselves, were being compelled to earn their living in cities like Leeds, arguing that new Town Congregations should be established with the utmost urgency and Home Missionaries should be directed to such areas.[85] The four members also recommended that a major house-building programme within the existing settlements should be undertaken, because the position of congregations in remote and isolated rural areas was becoming an increasing handicap. Such aspirations, while voicing sentiments with which no one could disagree and which had been raised before, took no account of the current financial situation of the province, which precluded such developments. The harsh fact was that still, in the absence of wealthy patrons, the ordinary membership could not hope to finance such ambitious aspirations.

1883: a turning-point

When Synod met at Fulneck in 1883, it faced a further reminder of its identity as part of the Unity, a stimulus to reconsider its origins and fundamental character, and a demand that it should take steps to shoulder its wider responsibilities on the mission field. James Connor, an English member of the Unity Elders' Conference, came from Germany as their representative and gave the opening address.[86] He conveyed fraternal greetings on behalf of his colleagues, expressed a wish for much closer spiritual union between all three Unity provinces and advocated a return to some practices of the mid-eighteenth century, such as frequent lengthy congregational visitation by provincial leaders. This had been a strong feature of Unity administration during the period of German cultural ascendancy, when Zinzendorf and other leaders had travelled regularly from congregation to congregation, allowing ample time to make their visits effective and memorable. By this means they had helped to ensure that provincial awareness remained vivid and morale high.

Br Connor then announced that he had been commissioned to visit all British congregations as an expression of the interest in them of the Unity Elders' Conference, a practical gesture which was warmly welcomed, although making Synodal deputies aware of deficiencies in the Provincial Elders' performance in this respect. Regret was expressed by some that this eighteenth-century pastoral tradition of frequent visitation by both provincial and Unity leaders no longer seemed possible, yet Labourers were always being urged to strengthen their ministry by making frequent pastoral visits to the homes of their congregational members.

Despite these positive and encouraging sentiments from Germany, Connor's visit also generated some anxiety, and exacerbated some areas of tension. One of these was the result of his blunt assertion that the British Province's provision of missionaries was inadequate; he made it plain that one reason why he had been dispatched from Unity Headquarters to attend Synod was to encourage more men to offer to serve in overseas missions. Another centred on those who wished to see a more characteristically British church, and the tension was aggravated by overt disagreement among deputies about relationships between the British and German provinces. Many speakers, including this time the president of Synod, spoke openly of the need to build up a distinctive British style. Paradoxically, although this view had many supporters, Synod passed a resolution pressing for acknowledgement of the 'great importance of preserving and promoting our connection with our mother Church in Germany'.

As far as evangelism and the spiritual life of the province were concerned, the nineteenth century to 1883 was a period in which there was little growth, mainly as a result of financial stringency and the scattered nature of the Brethren's initial areas of settlement, and partly also in response to the changing nature of society, a factor which influenced all Christian churches. What made 1883 a turning-point was the announcement that the cherished boarding-school network was beginning to collapse; the girls' school at Wyke and the boys' school at Gracehill were clearly to be the first casualties. This was accompanied by an increasing abandonment of the original German organizational priorities, particularly as a result of the development of town congregations on the British denominational model. In spite of these changes, many members still hoped to keep what they regarded as the characteristic features of a unique heritage intact, so that the church became in many respects another British Protestant denomination, while retaining some distinctive practices and valued links with the Continental Province from where it had originated. Its increasing use of the name 'Moravian' bore witness to the identity which it nurtured with some pride. Thus, by 1883, with a communicant membership of just over 3,000, dispersed among thirty-six congregations, the province was on the brink of a third historical period characterized by educational decline, uneasy denominational consolidation, and an increasing uncertainty of identity in an organization which was unable to escape from being in some important respects a British–German cultural hybrid.

Evolution of the Brethren's provincial institutions, 1782–1883

Twenty-two mainly town and country congregations had been officially settled in Britain by 1782. Subsequently there was a slow but persistent increase, so that by 1883 fourteen more had been added, making a total of thirty-six. Those founded after 1782 are listed below with their settlement dates, in chronological order, in accordance with published Almanacks.

Fairfield, Manchester	1784
Woodford Halse	1796
Priors Marston	1806
Baildon	1816
Kimbolton	1823
Pertenhall	1827
Brockweir	1833
Horton	1838
Baltonsborough	1857
Crook	1859
Wellfield	1864
Salem, Oldham	1869
Heckmondwike	1874
Westwood, Oldham	1874

There were fifteen boarding schools, five for boys and ten for girls.

Boys' Schools	*Girls' Schools*
Fairfield	Bedford
Fulneck	Dukinfield
Gracehill	Fairfield
Mirfield	Fulneck
Ockbrook	Gomersal
	Gracehill
	Ockbrook*
	Ockbrook
	Tytherton
	Wyke

*There were two separate establishments for girls at Ockbrook.

The Period of Uneasy Denominational Consolidation, *c.*1883–1945 (I: 1883–1918)

When the provincial history of the period between 1883 and the First World War is considered as a whole, three main elements of provincial activity can be identified: namely, maintaining the congregational network, providing boarding schools, and preserving a fraternal relationship with the Unity as a whole through participating in its missionary activity abroad. It has been shown that these same elements had dominated the nineteenth century, varying in prominence as circumstances changed. The constants underlying them all were the inhibiting effect of shortage of money, and the tensions generated by on the one hand a desire to preserve the identity bestowed by the original founders and on the other the urge to be comfortably British. In treating these issues as separate elements in the pattern of provincial decision-making there is a danger of making artificial distinctions; they were inseparable, their constraints producing a frustrating whole in which it sometimes appeared to the participants that very little changed from one provincial synod to another. This is misleading; with hindsight there was progress, but it was never clear-cut. Although the elements interacted uneasily at times and the British Province became increasingly absorbed in its provincial responsibilities and organization, it continued to value its inheritance as part of the Unity, a distinctiveness which set it apart from other British denominations in some respects, separating it from the mainstream of Nonconformity in Britain. Its role was never as simple as that of a small British denomination in straitened circumstances, but during the twentieth century this separatist tendency was gradually reversed as the church participated more fully in ecumenical discussions and in some areas found it expedient to amalgamate with other denominations. In order to appreciate the fundamental differences which these later decisions represent, it is necessary to understand the position from which it moved and the reasons which compelled the policies of Synod to change.

Maintaining the congregational network

Records of provincial synods have repeatedly shown that provincial leaders were always acutely aware that financial problems relating to the small number of communicant members were preventing provincial growth. Acute shortage of money was endemic and exacerbated by the increasing amount needed for ministers' salaries and pensions. There was also the financial liability represented by the weaker congregations, some of which still could not raise sufficient money to pay their ministers and were being subsidized from general congregational income. By 1883, even the prestigious Place Congregations were not attracting the extra funds necessary for growth, and there was insufficient money to improve old and worn-out buildings in some of the older settlements such as Fulneck. In some areas adjacent to the settlements better houses could be obtained at the same rental as those within the settlements, and there was an urgent need to build new detached properties for congregational members. It was becoming increasingly obvious that provincial resources were inadequate to finance all these immediate requirements; the church needed a substantial increase in income to sustain its weaker congregations, maintain its fabric, and supply the infrastructure necessary to provide support for any new outreach requiring additional premises.

Another area in which the question of finance was a determining factor was that of keeping the membership in touch with provincial affairs and promoting a sense of unity within the province, particularly for its widely scattered ministry. One desirable solution would be to hold annual synods for spiritual inspiration and social reassurance, and a formal proposal to this effect was made in 1886. Although it was defeated then on the grounds of cost, there was no doubting the pressure for a change of policy, and at Bedford in 1888 Synod decided to meet annually from 1890.[1]

This mood was accompanied by a temporary surge of congregational expansion which persisted throughout the 1890s, easing the worst financial stringencies which had troubled the province in previous decades. The optimism which this state of affairs engendered was reflected at the 1893 Baildon Synod, where there was prolonged discussion about evangelism among adults. The PEC reported: 'If we interpret the feeling of the province aright there is an increasing desire on the part of the Brethren and Sisters to see this side of our activity as a church still further developed.'[2] During the decade these developments included new work at Shankhill Road, Belfast: the congregation at University Road, Belfast, became self-supporting. A prestigious Sunday school was built at Mirfield. Risely became a Home Mission Station; a similar new station was opened on the Queen's Park Estate, Bedford, in the form of a combined chapel and Sunday school building to serve the needs of a new housing estate. A new chapel was completed on the site of the old one at Bristol, and at Westwood, Oldham, an extension of the Sunday school was built. There was a welcome response to the need for men to enter church service: calls to serve as missionaries in Labrador, Surinam and Queensland were taken up, and Fairfield College had a full complement of students.

Later in the decade, these modest improvements were facilitated by one of the few substantial gifts of money received by the church: the 1896 London Synod authorized the use of part of a bequest provided by J. T. Morton to subsidize a British Provincial Rural Mission.[3] Two specially appointed itinerant missioners began evangelistic work in Gloucestershire; another became active around Tytherton, near Swindon; another was stationed at Kimbolton, near Cambridge, and one was posted to Culworth, near Banbury. In every case these were rural areas where there had been previous missionary activity and congregational settlement, including Tytherton and Leominster. By 1897 some laymen had joined the mission staff, making twenty-one in all, and a resolution of Synod in that year commended them on their successes in this much-needed and highly appreciated work.

The crucial financial support for rural missions provided by the J. T. Morton bequest proved to be short-lived. The 1898 Mirfield Synod heard with dismay that Morton had died and, although his will explicitly stated his wish that subsidies should continue, his family were contesting it. Their legal action succeeded. In practice, there had already been a great reduction in the amount of money made available, which had led to a serious deficiency in the General Home Mission Account and necessitated a substantial reduction in the scale of its operations, despite an increase in its income from congregational members.[4]

On the positive side, there were some improvements in the financial position of the weaker congregations; it was reported that Malmesbury and Baltonsborough – the latter near Glastonbury – had become self-sufficient; Horton (Bradford) and Salem (Oldham) were hoping to follow this good example, and the Bristol congregation had wiped off its debts. Sustained congregational effort, encouraged by the progress facilitated by the Morton bequest, ensured that for a short time heartening new initiatives became possible. The provincial will was there if resources were available, but there could be no ultimate escape from the endemic situation in which a small membership generated adequate finance to meet everyday requirements, but not sufficient to provide for provincial overheads and capital investment to fulfil ambitions for evangelism and educational expansion, and to honour the expectations of the Unity as a whole.

Provincial Synods were not exclusively dominated by the mundane details of maintaining the congregational network and anxious deliberation about its potential for growth. As the turn of another century approached, provincial leaders found themselves again caught up in renewed controversy about the way the province had evolved since the early period when the German style was established in Britain and the extent to which it had remained true to its heritage.

In 1890 one anonymous radical group, possibly Fairfield College students, prepared for circulation a leaflet entitled, 'Defects of Modern Moravianism and some Proposals for Reform'.[5] It recognized that a culture of obscurity surrounded the province, asserting that most people in Britain had never heard of the church, still less of its education, and advocating a vigorous advertising campaign. The central defect, however, was failure.

> Our want of success as a church in this country is variously explained, such as retention of customs from which the spirit has gone and the meaning is not obvious. Some blame the foreign name; others the laziness of the ministers. But behind these feelings is the chilling idea that Moravianism in Britain may be played out; . . . the eighteenth-century church had a distinct aim, a *raison d'etre* which was on the surface and clearly visible. . . . This favourable state of affairs no longer exists.

The golden age was referred to again, and the desirability of re-igniting the Christocentric passion of Zinzendorf, stressing personal devotion to the Saviour.

The development of fixed settlements and static separate congregations to the detriment of diaspora creation was seen in some quarters as the source of the province's problems. Support for this criticism appeared at the highest level; for example, the Provincial Church Book published in October 1891[6] had already expressed misgivings because an impression still prevailed in Britain that the institution of the settlement with its accompanying social organization had always been, and remained, the essence of the Brethren's Church. This belief, it was argued, was a mistake: in reality, during the early period, the Germans had not intended to plant their constitutional model in Britain, neither had they contemplated a separate (denominational) establishment in Britain because they had not wished to sever souls from the church of their ancestry, but 'simply and singly to ground them upon Christ and his Blood'. Much of what had been done since the middle of the eighteenth century was thus contrary to the original intention and had failed to prosper. In contrast, it was maintained, the Continental Province had never deviated from its original intention and still retained extensive networks of diaspora societies in various parts of Germany and several other countries such as Denmark, Norway, Sweden and the Baltic States, serving about 70,000 members. In 1876, for example, 64 mostly ordained brethren were engaged full-time among them. Since this arrangement had met the religious needs of so many people since the 1740s and was warmly supported by the Established churches, change seemed unlikely, and the Continental Province had every justification for regarding itself as securely based. By implication, the writer argued, the British Province ought to have followed the same lines.

This analysis was reiterated by others in the ministry, for example, in a paper read by Br Libbey to the congregation at Gracehill on 29 April 1897 and reported in the edition of *The Messenger* published on 5 June.[7] In it he argued that the church, by following a narrowly denominational course, far from making the progress it should have made, was growing narrower and weaker. The best work of the church in the British Province had been the undenominational work carried on in the days of Zinzendorf, when nurturing souls in societies had been the primary objective, and the spread of congregations a side issue. The British Province was in need of reassurance that it was indeed unique and had not lost its sense of heritage or its original vision. It is not surprising that there was emotional tension and some difference of opinion underlying much provincial discussion at this time. These arose from a conflict between on the one hand the way the church perceived itself in relation to its membership of the Unity of the Brethren, with worldwide connections, an assured history and well-respected role as a missionary organization, and on the other hand the practicalities of running what in many respects appeared to be a separate British denomination.

The following summary shows the overall position of the province as far as its Congregations, Home Mission Congregations, Boarding and Day Schools were concerned. The tables illustrate the provincial structure near the peak of its congregational and communicant membership.

British Province 1900

Communicant membership

Ayr	40
Baildon	130
Ballinderry	42
Baltonsborough	49
Bath	45
Bedford	194
Bedford, Queen's Park	22
Belfast, Univ. Road	115
Belfast, Perth Street*	50
Bristol	114
Brockweir*	32
Cootehill*	22
Crook*	36
Devonport	27
Dublin	69
Dukinfield	132
Fairfield	192
Fulneck	287
Gomersal	118
Gracefield	81
Gracehill	141
Haverfordwest	23
Heckmondwike	50
Horton	111
Kilkeel*	43
Kilwarlin	61
Kimbolton	36
Kingswood*	37
Leominster	64
London	160
Malmesbury	60
Mirfield	131
Ockbrook	120
Pertenhall	34
Priors Marston*	26
Risely*	35
Salem	108
Swindon	20

Tytherton	69
Wellfield*	32
Westwood	106
Woodford Halse	55
Wyke	58

*Home Mission Station

Note: All data are from published Almanacks. Total communicant membership for 1900 on basis of this list, 3,377. The Almanack for 1900 uses information collected the previous year and quotes 3,364.

Boarding Schools (boys)

Fulneck	80
Ockbrook	50

Boarding Schools (girls)

Bedford	30
Fairfield	50
Fulneck	50
Gomersal	33
Ockbrook	30
Tytherton	25

Note: These numbers refer to available places, not necessarily filled.

Day Schools entirely supported or carried on by the church

Baltonsborough (British Mixed School)	70
Belfast, Perth Street	150
Dukinfield (British School)	279
Gracefield	35
Gracehill	74
Salem	393
Twerton	62

Note: These are numbers of children attending.

Number of Brethren employed in the service of the British Province, including retired members on pension, Heads of Schools, Wardens, etc. – 65 men. There were no diaspora agents. At least 6 continental ministers were employed.

The new century saw no significant overall change in the congregational network. Expansion and contraction coexisted; new home mission stations were established; the once flourishing rural missionary outreach was in terminal decline. Some weaker congregations still continued to receive sufficient subsidy from the stronger to enable most to remain viable. Swindon was officially classified as a Home Mission Station in 1901; during the same year both Salem and Baildon congregations joined the ranks of the financially self-supporting.

Members of the PEC were making helpful and much appreciated congregational visitations more frequently than had been their practice during the previous decade. This, together with the start of annual synods further reinforced feelings of solidarity, particularly among the ministry. *The Messenger*, sufficiently successful to be published fortnightly, had developed as a substantial, frequently erudite journal, reporting and commenting with authority on provincial and Unity matters, although its influence within the province was debatable.[8]

The chronic shortage of money threatened the long-term survival of the Home Mission stations at Wellfield in Yorkshire and Crook in County Durham; Pendine in South Wales was on the verge of collapse. The new stations at Queen's Park in Bedford and Wheler Street in Manchester were progressing, though it was common knowledge that they were well subsidized by adjacent and well-established congregations.[9] In order to reduce expense and attempt to maintain established congregations, the province adopted a strategy which was to prove effective in the future. In 1902 the congregations at Pertenhall and Risely were placed under one minister, and in 1904 the two Irish congregations of Kilwarlin and Ballinderry were similarly amalgamated. Congregational amalgamation was a practical solution which was used increasingly as the shortage of ministers became even more acute, and has remained one option among others ever since, as the history of ministerial provision in Part Three demonstrates.

The Dublin Synod of 1907 reported increased congregational financial support for Home Missions, assisted by loans from the Bates Trust, which was used to help found a new Home Mission church at Twerton, and to extend the existing church in Bath. During the same year it was announced that the foundation stone of a new church at Hornsey, North London, had been laid, and the site for a proposed new church in Belfast bought.

Another decision of the 1908 Synod reflected the continuing ambivalence of the British Province about its German heritage when it confirmed that, in the interests of 'uniformity of nomenclature', it wished to style itself officially as the Moravian Church, instead of the Church of the United Brethren, by which name it had been known throughout Europe since the 1740s.[10] By so doing it accepted the primacy of the alternative name which had been used since the Brethren came into Britain and was already customary in the American Provinces. In effect, this official renaming of the British Province brought it closer to the other English-speaking provinces and amounted to further separation in spirit from the Continental Province,[11] which resolutely retained its original name. Though clearly acceptable to a majority at Synod, the original principle of a Unity of Brethren transcending national boundaries, in which the British Province was one component, was undermined by this change. In practice it merely recognized the current reality, underlining the British Province's desire to decide its alignment within the Unity while consciously retaining its identity as a denomination within the British Nonconformist tradition, a development which was paralleled in Wesleyan Methodism.[12] There is no evidence, however, of a desire to abandon the Unity and launch out on an uncertain future as a separate denomination.

It was ironical that a move which distanced the British Province in name from its roots in Germany should take place when it did, since the decision became an embarrassment when the nation went to war in Europe six years later. When anti-German sentiment was running high, the name 'Moravian' led to some misunderstanding among members of the general public living near settled congregations, who realized that the church was associated with a part of the Austro-Hungarian Empire which was now a German ally. Congregational men who enlisted sometimes preferred to describe themselves as Anglican or Nonconformist rather than admit to being Moravian.[13] The name has been a source of confusion among the religious public ever since, but having once taken this step there was no going back.

Decline of the boarding-school network

The last two decades of the nineteenth century saw the continuing decline of the boarding schools, coinciding with the growth of legislation for state education following the Education Act of 1870, the consequences of which were beginning to be felt by the 1880s. Not only did the Act introduce compulsory schooling for children of every social class, but it established guidance for curricula and made government inspectors responsible for ensuring that standards were met. This put competitive pressure on denominational schools from those under local authority administration. One result of government legislation was a substantial increase in the number of public boarding schools, so that there were many other options for parents who had been attracted from outside the denomination by Moravian education, and the ominous signs recorded in 1883 were shown to be well founded.

The 1886 Fulneck Synod reluctantly recognized that some schools, which had been such an important part of the church's work in Britain, were no longer attracting pupils in sufficiently large numbers. Several schools were already in a serious financial position owing to this falling demand for places, together with increasing costs of maintaining premises in line with current expectations. The boarding schools were no longer subsidizing the church as they had done for much of the nineteenth century; in fact the reverse was true, and school maintenance was making inroads into income from congregational sources as the church tried to ensure that the accommodation and standard of teaching available in its schools matched those obtainable elsewhere.

This was a significant financial blow, bearing in mind how much the province had benefited from their success in the early years, but progressive decline could not be halted. In 1890 Dukinfield boarding school closed, to be followed in 1891 by Fairfield boys' boarding school; there was continued decline in Gracehill boys' school; the girls' boarding school there ceased to be a church undertaking and was launched on an uncertain future by Br Traeger of Dublin on his own responsibility. A similar fate befell the girls' boarding school at Wyke in 1892, and the process continued into the early 1900s. The 1902 Synod, held in London, reported further decline in the boarding-school network, predicting the imminent closure of Gomersal Girls' School, which it agreed to a year later. Provincial leaders were reconciled to the irrevocable nature of this development,[14] since the newly appointed government Board of Education now had the authority to determine minimum standards of school accommodation. The Education Act of 1902 raised further apprehensions about the ability of the province to compete with developments in government-funded and denominational education. The extensive government direction and inspection for which the two Acts legislated meant that private schools could no longer be the ultimate decision-makers in matters of facilities and curriculum, and this requirement, together with the capacity to attract well-qualified staff and pay them appropriately, could be achieved only by reducing the number of establishments run by the church.

Relations with the Continental Province: conflicting mentalities

Provincial problems were dwarfed by ominous political developments in Germany which were set in motion in 1871, with disturbing implications for the future relationship between Britain and Germany. In this process, members of the British Province, unavoidably cast in the role of a British–German cultural hybrid, became exposed to conflicting loyalties which affected subsequent provincial history for at least eighty years and included complete separation from the Continental Province during two devastating world wars.

The cause of this unprecedented change of relationship was the final achievement of German unification in 1871 together with the protracted and turbulent process by which it came about. Because of the nature of the Holy Roman Empire of the German Nation, 'a welter of hundreds of competing states open to a host of political intrigues and [local] wars',[15] the German-speaking peoples developed few of the sensitivities which had been gradually emerging in Western Europe since medieval times.[16] Then, in the late eighteenth century, Germans felt the impact of the French Revolution and Napoleonic Wars, during which the French made determined efforts to break up the Holy Roman Empire, a process achieved in 1806 and ratified in Vienna at the general peace settlement of 1815. There it was replaced officially by a German Confederation comprising fewer elements – thirty-nine states – in which Prussian and Austrian influence predominated, theoretically on a fairly equal basis. The period between 1815 and 1871 saw these two struggling for supremacy, and during the 1860s and into 1871 Prussia, under its Chancellor Bismarck, directed three victorious wars, against the Danes, Austrians and French, in that order. The 'new' state proclaimed at Versailles in 1871 – a united German Empire whose first emperor was the King of Prussia, or more simply, Germany – can best be understood in terms of its sudden and violent creation.[17] From the beginning, the Prussian army was regarded as 'the architect of unification',[18] acquiring great prestige in the process, and unified Germany became a partnership between the authoritarian, military Prussian state and leading circles of the new industrial and commercial middle classes.

In contrast to other nation-states which came into existence during the nineteenth century, Italy being a leading example, the Germans were the only people who did not create their state from below by invoking the forces of democracy against the traditional ruling groups, but accepted the form of a unified state gratefully from above.[19] This enhanced national self-consciousness, since being German was now a matter of pride; however, in the resultant ethos of conservatism and faith in dynastic leadership as exercised by the Prussian emperor, German citizens lived increasingly in a world of institutions which sought to discipline them. Foremost was the army; its presence was visible everywhere,[20] augmenting all the regulatory elements associated with the rapid advance of industrialization and ensuring that Germany soon had the potential to develop as the major military and economic power on the continent.[21]

Concurrently with this decisive change in German society was another, described by Charles McClelland as, 'the strange story of erosion and collapse of the cultural ideal of England in German minds'.[22] The ideal had originally been an eighteenth-century construct, when, quite apart from the fact that a Hanoverian dynasty was well established in Britain, British institutions were held in high regard in the Holy Roman Empire and the post-1815 German Confederation. At that time Britain was admired for its political stability, religious toleration, industrial skills and Anglo-German cultural affinity; the best English traditions were regarded as 'Saxon', of German origin, so that a German–English alliance seemed 'natural'. Leading members of the academic elite shared these sentiments, in particular those who taught history in the Prussian University of Berlin, men of widespread influence. From 1825 to 1871 the Professor of History there was Leopold von Ranke (1795–1886). He, like other colleagues, was a strong Anglophile who valued British stability, seen by him as largely a result of the political domination of a cautious, responsible and generally benevolent aristocracy. He believed that British power was contributing to the success of the European nations in containing France's ambitions after the French Revolution and the Napoleonic Wars. Thus, over many years, most German historians agreed in praising Britain because of its cautious response to the contemporary trend towards political reform and democratization.

Ranke retired in 1871, and his influential successor was another Prussian aristocrat, Heinrich von Treitschke (1834–96), who, although originally an Anglophile, presided over the erosion and collapse of this cultural ideal as he adopted an increasingly nationalistic outlook, in line with many of his countrymen. Conscious that the newly unified Germany, despite its internal struggles, was now a contender in the late nineteenth-century competition among European powers for imperial territories, markets and overseas colonies,[23] he came to regard Britain as no longer a racially and culturally similar ally, but an alien and threatening competitor, giving way to demands for political reform and democratization. McClelland suggests that Treitschke's change of view within his lifetime occurred typically in German thought about England over a much longer period, affecting attitudes into the early twentieth century,[24] which saw Germans convinced of their own strength, politically, militarily and industrially, and wanting desperately to be a world power.[25]

This aspiration was visualized in a European context in which initially German military and political dominance would be established, and then the German economy would be enhanced by the acquisition of large areas of land to the east and the west. In the west, particularly, was land rich in mineral resources and economic potential.[26] Thus, Germany was prepared to go to war to establish herself as a *Weltmacht*, a great power, alongside other world powers which had established their position before she had achieved national unity, with the dream of establishing control over a new order in Europe.[27] Before 1914, Britain would be perceived as the world power with which Germany would need to contend in order to emerge as an imperial nation with wide overseas as well as European interests, and so would remain her principal enemy. An additional destabilizing landmark in the slide towards war was Kaiser Wilhelm II's dismissal of Bismarck in 1890. This was followed by a short and unsuccessful period of personal rule by the emperor, marked by a lack of caution, the details of which are discussed by Giles MacDonagh in *The Last Kaiser: William the Impetuous*, published by Weidenfeld & Nicolson in 2000.

Immediately before war broke out, the central powers of Europe, Germany and Austro-Hungary, were ranged against a Franco-Russian combination, and conflict between them would almost certainly have ended rapidly in German victory. This was why, in 1914, the British government intervened on the side of France and Russia.[28]

Relations with the Continental Province: missions

These changes in sentiment between Britain and Germany insinuated themselves into inter-provincial relationships in the form of a sharpening of official German attitudes. One early example was James Connor's contribution to the 1883 provincial synod mentioned above. Although he reiterated that bonds between the British and German provinces should be strengthened, as spokesman for the predominantly German Unity Mission Board he criticized his British colleagues and their congregations for their persistent lack of support for foreign missions. It was not so much their regrettable parsimony – that was amply compensated for by grants from the London Association in Support of the Foreign Missions of the United Brethren – but their failure to recruit sufficient missionaries to take a fair share of the burden of manning the mission stations, a deficiency which the Unity Mission Board was now demanding that the British Province should redress.

When Synod next met at Bedford in 1888, no statistical evidence was produced of any increase in the number of candidates for overseas missionary service, but a resolution was dutifully passed, to be forwarded to the Unity General Synod which was to meet the following year. It recorded that the British Province 'desired by every means possible to maintain its connexion and intercourse with the German Province', and that, 'Assurances were to be given to the General Synod that the British Province recognized mission work as an obligation to which it held itself pledged . . . particularly in the West Indies.'[29] The resolution also demanded that due recognition should be given for existing British contributions to the work there. Mindful of James Connor's assertion five years previously, Synod agreed on a placatory resolution promising that the province would send more men to the West Indies to join those British missionaries already active in that area. The decisions of the 1888 Synod show that, despite its limited financial capabilities, the desire of the British Province to participate effectively in Unity affairs was still strong, even while decisions regarding provincial administration were revealing pressure towards the formulation of a distinctive provincial identity.

A decade later, at the 1898 Mirfield Synod, further discussion of the vexed question of British participation in missions took place in anticipation of the Unity Synod due in 1899. Once again the printed extracts give no indication of any real progress, although articles in *The Messenger* showed a willingness to admit publicly what had long been known by provincial leaders. One article noted:

Our missions have been largely German and we are regarded as such throughout England (among interested non-members). We have sent only a small contingent of missionaries and the Mission Board has naturally and rightly been German. Our church has been hallowed by its connection with the missions which are known to many who know nothing of the British Province.

It was acknowledged that Mission Board attempts to secure more than the usual small number of British applications had failed, and that numbers still showed no sign of satisfying Unity expectations.[30]

There was also evidence of British resentment of the more assertive style emanating from Germany. Some of those assembled at Mirfield complained that the Unity Mission Board was hag-ridden by what they described in pejorative terms as 'German bureaucracy', claiming that, despite the fact that a large proportion of Unity mission stations were in British territories where the language of the mission was usually English, Britons sent to 'German' stations based there had sometimes felt unwelcome. Other deputies commented that the Unity Mission Board and local mission station leaders handled Germans wisely, but did not always know what to make of Britons, 'who were more independent and less accustomed to military rule'. Finally, there was a carefully understated recognition that, since 1871, German attitudes were changing. 'When our missions began, a German was a cosmopolitan. Now he is a member of a great nation and is proud of being such.' It was admitted that the Germans could also claim that, whereas the British Province had no missionary college, the German Province had two, at Niesky and Königsfeld.[31]

Matters were brought to a head when the 1899 Unity Synod, particularly concerned with missions, produced a comparative table showing the contribution of each province to this work. It emerged that the Unity employed 170 married couples and 32 single brethren or sisters, making a total of 372 people. Of these, 299 were German, 44 American and 29 British, so that Germans provided 83 per cent, Americans 10 per cent and British 7 per cent of mission workers. About half the members of the German contingent had been recruited from the continental diaspora societies.[32] This contribution greatly enhanced the numbers recruited from German Unity congregations and incidentally proved the practical benefit of diaspora-style evangelism.

The 1901 Ockbrook Synod discussed the establishment of a Provincial Missionary College,[33] largely as a result of the disclosure at the General Synod that only 7 per cent of Unity missionaries were British. No action was taken at that stage because provincial leaders claimed that they could not release serving ministers for overseas service, and maintained that there was a shortage of suitable candidates and insufficient funds immediately available for this purpose. Nevertheless, the acknowledged need was taken seriously, and the Bristol Mission College (discussed in Part Three) was founded in 1904.

Meanwhile, in a further attempt to stimulate congregational interest in missions the 1902 Synod decided to publish a monthly mission magazine.[34] The first edition of *Moravian Missions* was published in January 1903, and within three years monthly sales of 6,000 copies were usual. Clearly, *Moravian Missions* was circulating far beyond provincial congregations, and its popularity reflected continuing interest in missions among the religious public of the time, appealing particularly to organizations and individuals who contributed to the funds of the supportive London Association.

Striking statistical evidence of support for contemporary involvement was provided in the November 1903 edition of *Moravian Missions*, in an editorial entitled 'Some Facts and Figures relating to Foreign Missions'.[35]

	Missionary societies	*Active missionaries*
England	42	5,136
USA	49	4,110
Germany	15	1,515
Scotland	–	653

The statistics quoted originated from the Ecumenical Conference on Foreign Missions held in New York in 1900, and showed readers that England was well ahead of other nations, even the USA, in the number of missionaries of all denominations working abroad.

The First World War: the crucial event in the first half of the twentieth century[36]

Many in British government circles expected war with Germany long before the event. As early as 8 November 1908, the British Foreign Office Secretary, Sir Edward Grey, wrote to a friend, Ella Pease,

> The German Emperor is ageing me: he is like a battleship with steam up and screws going, but with no rudder, and he will run into something one day and cause a catastrophe . . . I don't think there will be war at present, but it will be difficult to keep the peace of Europe for another five years.[37]

Grey's estimate proved to be accurate.

The 1914 Provincial Synod which met at Fairfield in August coincided with the outbreak of war. In a hastily changed address at the opening ceremony, Bishop Hasse commented with despair, 'We are in the presence of something overwhelming, a sort of dread nightmare, only it is a reality . . . Brother will find himself arrayed against Brother on different sides. Will our Unity stand the strain? Will it survive such an experience?'[38] Nevertheless, it was decided to complete the immediate business.

Its agenda was still dominated by domestic issues which had plagued the province for decades in spite of episodic and temporary improvements. Even though communicant membership was 3,941, almost at its peak, around half of existing congregations were being subsidized to some extent from central funds. The remaining provincial schools were suffering because of competition from the rapidly increasing number of other publicly[39] and privately endowed schools, and some members of Synod questioned the justification for struggling to maintain all existing premises. A minority even rejected the principle that it was a necessary function of any church to run boarding schools.

The most recent evidence before deputies at this critical juncture in European relationships suggested that the state of the British Province and its prospects remained matters of some concern, not only to its own members, but also to Unity leaders as a whole. A generally pessimistic view of the British Province had been taken by the 1914 Unity General Synod held at Herrnhut a few weeks earlier, and its misgivings were conveyed to the membership by Brethren who had been present on that occasion. On returning from there in June, Bishop S. L. Connor interpreted continental provincial opinion when he wrote about the present condition and future prospects of the British congregations in *The Messenger*. He confessed that he thought of the province with sadness and considered it was passing through trying times. It had always been 'a hard-fought battlefield',[40] and now it was falling behind the American and Continental provinces. Connor lamented the steady leakage of members which persisted in some congregations despite a gradual but very small overall increase in numbers, and commented that many ministers were in danger of losing heart. He concluded: 'As a Province we have our grave financial difficulties, the rapid melting away of our once flourishing boarding schools, our constant calls for retrenchment and our insufficient strength to expand.'[41] The comment was subjective, but it illustrates the pessimism which still pervaded the leadership after more than half a century during which the province had suffered from endemic problems to which it could see no practicable solution. These concerns were of marginal importance, however, in view of the appalling fact that the Unity was split and that a human catastrophe was engulfing Western and Central Europe.

Although the nation may not have expected war to break out quite so suddenly and in the way it did in the summer of 1914, it was psychologically and physically ready for it when it came; the challenge was expected and the response full of zest.[42] In its opening stages the war was popular in the country as a whole, and the Christian churches in Britain tried to reconcile their principles with the pressures of increasing calls to patriotism. The role of the Briton, as portrayed by many religious and secular leaders, was as a defender of Christian values; for example, in September 1914 the Baptist Union Council declared, 'We believe the call of God has come to Britain to spare neither blood nor treasure in the struggle to shatter a great anti-Christian attempt to destroy the fabric of Christian civilisation.'[43] Similar views were expressed by Sir W. Robertson Nicoll in *The Tablet*, addressed to all young Nonconformists. They were reproduced in *The Messenger* on 19 September 1914. The writer argued that, 'Christian law has been treated by our opponents as of less than no account, and their code of conduct is infinitely baser than that of savages.' The war was portrayed as 'a war against barbarism of the most evil and remorseless kind'. Against this background of righteous indignation which permitted no middle ground, it was still possible for thinking people to express a less emotive and biased point of view, and members of the Moravian Church were well equipped to perceive the tragedy of the situation. *The Messenger* contained various thoughtful articles about separation from the Continental Province and conflicting loyalties, which reflected the anguish of both ministers and lay members. It also reported fierce anti-British feeling in Germany. In late November 1914 it published an article written by a Swiss businessman who had travelled from Geneva through Germany and Holland, and had finally arrived in London. He had observed that,

> In Germany, national hatred is directed not so much against France, she is thought to be the victim of her alliances, as against England. England they say is at the bottom of the whole trouble . . . What is particularly striking in Germany is the eagerness, the unanimous *élan* of the whole population.[44]

As Blackbourn has noted, 'Public declarations trumpeted the "ideas of 1914", presenting the German war effort as a defence of culture and idealism against "British militarism, French frivolity and Slav barbarism" . . . both protestant and catholic clergy sanctified the spirit of sacrifice in their sermons.'[45]

Optimism characterized the German military leaders as well, particularly in view of the precedent set by their unexpectedly rapid victory over the French in the Franco-Prussian War during the autumn of 1870, in which the French armies had been easily out-manoeuvred.[46] However, in 1914, they could not have predicted the civilian starvation, unprecedented casualties, and political and social upheaval which would result from a protracted struggle lasting four years,[47] for it soon became clear that the industrialization of Europe had developed to the point where millions of men could be mobilized for a prolonged conflict.[48]

As the war progressed, the scale of the slaughter unfolded in newspaper casualty lists which revealed neighbourhood losses resulting from the policy of encouraging friends and colleagues to enlist together, and the mood of the nation hardened. Discussion and controversy about who was responsible for starting the war was a feature of *The Messenger*. Views expressed were widely divergent; for example, a leading article published on 27 November 1915 was emotional and hostile.

> The fact that the cruel, callous and cowardly outrages of Germany and the unscrupulous and dishonourable methods she has now employed during the war have filled the minds of all true Britons with contempt and loathing for her cannot be overlooked when the question of future cooperation in missionary work with the German branch of the church is considered.

In contrast, in the issue dated 11 December 1915 Revd G. W. MacLeavy argued: 'By choice and divine calling we are Moravians, members of a Unity, of an international Unity, of a Unity that can suffer diversity of expression, even if at this time an English Moravian may be sick at heart.' Feelings of bitterness and a desire for revenge had to be ruled out; there was a fundamental difference of mentality. 'Germans have always been taught to idealise their own country; the German mind organises and develops that which is presented to it. British Moravians must accept that German Moravians will see things differently.'[49] An equally enlightened point of view was expressed by a German missionary working in South Africa with German colleagues who had not yet been interned. He sympathized with their opinion about who was really responsible for starting the war, and the futility of apportioning blame for atrocities. To the German missionaries, the preservation of the international nature of the Brotherhood was paramount. There had to be a post-war renewal of unity.[50]

Meanwhile, as the war was raging in Europe, appearing less and less like a crusade and more a subject for deep cynicism,[51] the British Province was still struggling with the same old background problems. When the Provincial Synod was held at Westwood in 1916 the number of communicant members was the highest ever recorded, at 3,959, but in spite of this the long-standing accusation of congregational apathy surfaced, and an increasingly pessimistic view of the financial prospects facing the province prevailed in the reports; for example, the provincial treasurer warned of the drainage caused by central funds being used to subsidize the remaining boarding schools, arguing that they required a much larger proportion of the church's free income than any other department.[52]

The head of Fairfield College argued that, in view of the current European catastrophe, the recently acquired title, 'Moravian Church' should be abandoned. 'It is not a foreign church as we all know, so why give it a foreign name? Our present borrowed title was always unfortunate and is now more unfortunate than ever.'[53] Other church members restated the need for post-war reconciliation between Britain and Germany, and this point of view provided a Christian answer to painful realities. Very little information is available from sources such as the minutes of the Provincial Board to indicate how the British Province responded officially to the divisions which threatened the Unity. Evidence of popular responses to the dilemma of British Moravianism during the war does remain, however, in the form of articles and letters in *The Messenger*. As a body of opinion these reflect the heart-searching with which many members reacted to the knowledge that they were separated from their spiritual roots and that their Brethren had become the enemy, in a war in which horrific fatalities were reported daily.

Such an ameliorative approach was referred to in an article in *The Messenger* dated 14 August 1917 by A. Ward. He maintained that after the war Moravians should go to Germany in a campaign of love in order to extinguish the campaign of hate. At the other extreme, there was strong feeling in favour of abandoning all connection with the Continental Province and amalgamating permanently with another British denomination. In February 1918, G. W. MacLeavy protested strongly against this in *The Messenger*. He argued,

> Why should we join the Anglicans; they don't know where they are. Why join a Free Church; they too are seeking a new order. Why not cling to our great idea of Union . . . We belong to as true a church as exists, but we are not worthy of our ancestors.

Whatever may have been the opinion of the church leadership in reports of the Provincial Board, evidence from the congregations themselves paints a different picture. It partly explains what was interpreted all too often in the official records as congregational indifference, and offers a unique insight into the wartime experiences of the various districts. Reports to the Provincial Board from the congregations for inclusion in the official record of provincial activity published during the war years were more detailed than had been customary, and are a valuable source of information as to how individual churches were responding to wartime conditions. These detailed accounts appeared first in 1915. The response of Fulneck was more eloquent than most, and reveals the spirit of the time, as this extract demonstrates:

> The Congregation has taken a very honourable part in all the efforts that have been made in this neighbourhood to meet the national urgency. Long before the latest enlistment enactments had been passed there was in our midst a very generous response to the call for men . . . Four of them we shall never see again. . . .
>
> We read in the papers forecasts of trade and conditions of life after the war – we would sometimes like to forecast the conditions of our Congregations when we shall live again in more normal times and when those who are now separated from us will have come back to their homes; we cannot venture to do so. But from what we have seen of those who on rare occasions have come on furlough from the battle-fields, we have reason to think that many who have faced dangers and horrors unspeakable, will return to us with a deepened sense of God and the need of Him, and that they will be among us a salt and a light.

The practicalities of life in wartime Britain are reflected in congregational reports, and show that the war was making an increasing impact on church life, particularly where hardships were being endured. By 1915, at Gomersal, the congregation was beginning to suffer from the effects of various local forms of national service, as well as missing members serving in the army:

> Overtime at the mills and the consequent fatigue have reduced our attendances at Divine Worship and curtailed our week-night efforts. The departure of young men for Army Service is noticeable in many ways. Yet with our regret at our temporary loss we rejoice that the call to duty and self-sacrifice has met with so willing a response.

Although no formal statistics are available, some congregational reports for 1915 include numbers indicating how far congregations were depleted by the absence of their young men, occasionally with an added comment that, though missed, they have done what was expected of them. At Dukinfield over thirty were in the forces, most of whom had been 'directly and closely associated with the work of the Church, School and Institute'. At Fairfield, 'over sixty' and at Westwood 65 regular members of church and school had responded. At Hornsey there were 18 men on the Roll of Honour, one of whom had been killed in action; at Devonport 20, with one loss.

Reports from congregations particularly affected by the war give fascinating insights into the wartime life of their locality. In Bedford, the report from St Peter's noted: 'The 68th Welsh Division is still in the town and many families have had soldiers billeted with them continuously.' Queen's Park, Bedford sent a more detailed account:

> The military have been in residence during the whole year and have considerably changed the normal life of the town; the billeting of soldiers has made it difficult for the 'house-wife' to attend church gatherings, the long and irregular hours of work on the railway and in the workshops have had the same effect in the case of men. We have been disappointed with the small success of an effort to draw the soldiers to our Services.

The congregation at Devonport was particularly aware of the tragic toll which the war was taking on the nation's manpower:

> Living in a garrison town and a naval port, seeing so much every day to remind us of this terrible war, the transports leaving daily with their precious burden of loved ones, the hospital ships arriving with their burden of wounded and sick men, in very quick succession, all these events tend to cast a gloom over the District, and the high pressure of work in the Dockyard and munition Factories have to a large extent crippled the many activities of the Churches in the district.

One report shows how the burden of responsibility for nursing the many wounded who were fit to be cared for in the community was shared by local organizations and volunteers. Ockbrook reported that the Sunday school was still occupied by wounded soldiers and that some of the Sisters were 'part of the efficient nursing staff'.

In contrast, the rural congregations and those in the Irish District reported that the war made very little difference to their day-to-day activities. Dublin and Gracefield gave an account of nursing work, camps in the neighbourhood and the sending of 'comforts' for the troops. Kilwarlin made no mention of the war, reporting a quiet uneventful year. In Leominster, Malmesbury and Tytherton the war appeared to have made little impact apart from the fact that the congregation had sent parcels to those on active service. Baltonsborough, another rural district, mentioned no effects of the war, but emphasized its difficulties as a congregation with a large percentage of aged and sickly members. Bath was another congregation with an elderly membership, noting that, before the war they had only three young men, all of whom had now enlisted. Riseley reported: 'A good deal of effort has been made by the church on behalf of the various patriotic funds in connexion with the war, and several members have suffered the loss of relatives at the front.' The congregation at Woodford, Eydon and Priors Marston was able to record: 'In spite of wars and commotion our life has pursued an almost normal course.' All these examples underline the diversity of congregational experience, no doubt typifying such variations in the life of the nation as a whole. Ironically, London Fetter Lane, which was to be destroyed in the next conflict, had suffered no damage in two air raids which 'did mischief in the immediate neighbourhood'.

It is understandable that provincial finances would be a greater source of anxiety than usual in the wartime reports and synodal discussions: the largest congregations, as these reports clearly indicate, were in areas where the war was making its greatest impact on time and potential resources because of the number of men on active service, whereas the smaller ones, often with ageing congregations, were virtually unaffected.

These reports from the congregations confirm the inherited pattern of settlement which had always strained provincial resources. Apart from the trust funds, money to maintain the province was derived mainly from a few congregations with a large proportion of younger men and women of working age, whose contributions in normal circumstances outweighed their expenses; there were others, mainly rural congregations with a small, often elderly membership, who had never found it easy to sustain their own establishments, let alone contribute substantially to the demands of the province as a whole.

By 1916 there was evidence of a distinct change of mood. The Yorkshire District reports made very little mention of the war, and this was true overall. Ockbrook, with a touch of resentment, summed up the tedious hardships which were affecting everyday life in Britain. 'Like everybody else, we are made to feel that we are living in wartime. Taxation, food, light restriction, frequent appeals, etc., all tend to impress it on the mind.' In 1917 the war was taking its toll, not only of men, but of physical and emotional resources, and there was sadness and resignation among the congregations. Fulneck reported: 'In common with all other Churches we feel the loss of so many of our young men. . . . We try to keep in touch with them as much as possible.' St John's (Upton Manor) was counting the cost:

During the year three of the men connected with the Church have made the supreme sacrifice for their country . . . Since the war began, of the sixty who joined the Forces, five have fallen, seven have been seriously wounded, eleven have been invalided, and one is a prisoner.

Horton (Bradford), however, gave some indication that congregations were beginning to look to the future as well as raising money for gifts to the troops, recording that a two-day Sale at Christmas 'for the After-War Building Scheme' raised £130. The report from Gomersal struck a philosophical note often missing in these accounts of wartime congregational activity:

The war has claimed its toll of our young manhood in service and in lives. Amidst all the sorrows and tragedies of this terrible war time, one thing is manifest, life is taking a deeper, more solemn note. Ears that were deaf are now hearing the call of Eternity. May the call lead them to Him who is the Life, the Truth and the Way.

When reports for 1918 were received, the war was over, but there was little reference to Armistice celebrations; Ballinderry was the only congregation to record that bells had been rung. Some reports looked back over the past year, but without triumph over the victory, quite the opposite in the case of Horton.

In reviewing the Congregation life in the fifth year of war, we share with others the sense of failure and regret. . . . We are glad to have maintained regular connection with the fifty men on the service list. . . . These were in receipt of the *Messenger* . . . and a personal monthly letter.

Wyke counted the loss. 'Seven of our forty-seven have died on service between 1914 and 1918.' Westwood expressed the joy of the congregation at 'giving a welcome to a few of our men who have fortunately secured their discharge from the army'. These last three reports encapsulate the tragedy with which the Moravian congregations and the whole nation had to come to terms, and their relief as they looked to the future at the end of the war.

The hardships of wartime did much to bring the endemic problems which had beset the province into a new perspective for a while, as ordained and lay members reassessed their values and looked forward to a future where, it was hoped, there could be Christian renewal in the building of a better society. In a very real sense the end of the First World War marked a turning-point in the history of the British Province, leaving a legacy of unease which would have been unthinkable fifty years previously. Peace did not solve these problems, but it created a different, ambivalent mood among those who had survived the horrors of the European tragedy. The optimistic mood of the immediate post-war period did not survive once the old realities reasserted themselves, but for a while at least the weight of provincial burdens was not quite so obtrusive in its deliberations, which lost some of the introspection which had too often focused the attention of its representatives on its shortcomings, to its detriment.

Meanwhile, in Central and Eastern Europe, violent revolution, partly but not entirely a response to the dreadful slaughter of the war years, pointed the way to an even darker future, graphically described in a review by M. Egremont of a book by G. Dallas, entitled *1918*.[54]

> The chaos of the revolution after the abdication of the Kaiser contrasted with German memories of the battered but hopeful nation at war, and an army people had believed to be invincible. A Poland revived by the peacemakers emerged as a buffer against Bolshevism, but a territorial irritation for Germany; and the new Czechoslovakia carved out of the ruins of the Austro-Hungarian empire, included the resentful Germans of the Sudetenland. The dream of German expansion to the east, which predated 1914, arose again, this time to reclaim territory lost in the defeat of 1918. With it came the volunteer Free Corps, pledged to restore order and pride, in a foretaste of Nazism.

For the Continental Province, these turbulent times were to form the gloomy backdrop to the efforts of their extended European Brotherhood to remain together; for the British and American Provinces they would confirm their need for closer fellowship to safeguard the future of the Unity throughout the vicissitudes which were to test this German-based organization for the rest of the century and beyond.

6

The Period of Uneasy Denominational Consolidation, *c.*1883–1945 (II: 1919–1945)

Post-war steps towards reconciliation with the Continental Province

Although British and American provincial leaders had gained significant institutional independence of Herrnhut, with congregational support, at a deeper level most did not wish to abandon their German cultural inheritance. The war had reminded them that there was a deep emotional bond which political disputes and fierce animosities experienced during the carnage of war could not erase; real Moravianism was German and could be preserved in Britain only in association with the Continental Province. Despite the fact that most British members could not speak German and did not fully appreciate the spirit behind the religious and historical events which had formed their church, they recognized that they represented a distinctive community within the British Isles which, after almost two hundred years, was still different in style and fundamentally different in tradition from other Nonconformist denominations. A similar distinctiveness characterized the Continental Province. There, members of the Unity were regarded by outside observers as a religious aristocracy, a family into which people were born but rarely adopted,[1] and which still contained a large dual membership with the *Evangelische Kirche Deutschlands* of a type which no longer existed in the British Province.[2] Interacting with these arrangements were the old-fashioned social inequalities of Central European society which, in Zinzendorf's time and still in the early twentieth century, continued to affect continental provincial development.

When the war came to an end in 1918, most British and German members felt a strong urge towards reconciliation, a sentiment shared by the two American provinces. It was imperative to restore the pre-war Unity with its dynamic international image.

The first post-war provincial Synod met at Fulneck in August 1919.[3] One deputy commented on the beauty and peace of the settlement as a context for what he called the gathering of the clans. No doubt many shared his sentiments, but for others they were tempered by a continuing conflict of loyalties deriving from the recent schism of the British and Continental provinces, and such people needed reassurance that Unity leaders were of one mind 'with reference to the events that have made the civilized world shudder'. Discussions were marked by an earnest desire for reconciliation with the Continental Province, although there were a few dissenting voices. *The Messenger* had already printed a letter from Br H. Robinson in the June edition in which he declared that he had no sympathy with playing brotherhood with the Germans; his sole concern was the survival of the Moravian Church in Britain as a completely independent denomination.[4]

There were others in Britain who sympathized with this separatist point of view as a result of the enormous military losses incurred by British involvement in continental quarrels,[5] but it did not gain widespread support at Synod. An editorial comment in the August issue of *The Messenger*, 'Many Men, Many Minds', argued that there was no evidence among those who attended of any deep-seated desire to break away from the Unity and amalgamate with another denomination. There was still pride in belonging to what was perceived to be the oldest international Protestant Church, and the Continental Province with its roots in Germany was regarded as an essential part of it.

Leaders of the Continental Province were of the same mind and, as an act of reconciliation, the first conference of the General Directory of the Unity since the war met at Zeist from 16 to 18 August 1919. The aim was to restore some degree of mutual confidence after five years of independent working, and to consider the possibility of convening a General Synod.

In succeeding years, the reports of the Provincial Board to the post-war synods reflected contemporary emphasis on building bridges throughout the Unity. In 1920 their report to the Fairfield Synod mentioned the Zeist meeting of the General Directory, at which the British Province had been represented by Br Libbey, and noted also that the province had recently sent greetings to the Continental Provincial Synod and that of the two American provinces. By 1922 Unity relationships were well on the way to normality, helped by the fact that the Unity was celebrating the 200th anniversary of its foundation. The Provincial Board reported to the Fairfield Synod in July that this important event was being celebrated throughout the Unity and that 'a great gathering' had assembled in

Herrnhut in June. A letter of greeting had been sent from the British Board, although it could not send a representative to join in the celebrations.

By this time, also, the need to restore the image of the Unity as an international fraternal body was recognized by all its members. Ever since the middle of the eighteenth century the Unity's leaders had consistently followed an ecumenical course with an evangelistic style transcending national barriers, denominational minutiae, political differences and social inequalities. This unchanging rationale had frequently been reaffirmed during the war, for example, by Walter Bourquin, a German missionary working in South Africa. In a letter published in *The Messenger* on 13 November 1915, he argued, 'For the heathen there should be no difference between German and British missionaries; they should be teachers, servants of God, who for that very reason are different from all other white men.' Unfortunately, such a view was not acceptable in post-war British government circles. In a statement on future foreign mission work for the forthcoming Unity Conference at Herrnhut in August, the Provincial Board foresaw that important staffing changes would be necessary. Some German missionaries had been interned during the war and forbidden by the British government to return to territories under their control. Inevitably the burden of supplying suitable men would now fall more heavily than ever before on the British and American provinces, where, for the first time, the newly ordained would face the likelihood of a spell on the mission field as part of their professional career.

On the positive side, contact had been re-established with the Continental Province, which, for its own part, was struggling to come to terms with post-war constraints, and there seemed every likelihood that the traditional emotional links with the Continental Province would be restored, ensuring that the British Province remained firmly associated with it.

Post-war provincial development: an unfulfilled search for a new role

Alongside this movement towards reconciliation, the immediate affairs of the province demanded urgent attention. Its role in Britain continued to be uneasy. Post-war denominational consolidation implied preserving at least some of the unique characteristics of the original continental model; indeed, it could be argued that from this time onwards the province was led by those who wished to preserve what was left of it at all costs. The Moravians in Britain were becoming increasingly concerned with survival. Among the deputies assembled at Fulneck in 1919 there was evidence of an aspiration for spiritual renewal to compensate for the comparative stalemate of the war years. The ministry felt that the growing influence of laymen in the province allayed to a large extent the fears of those who had doubts about its future, although it was proposed and accepted that, because of shortage of money and students, the Bristol Mission College and Fairfield College should be combined. Synod could not agree which should close; persuasive arguments were put forward in favour of both, but no final decision was made. For the time being, therefore, both remained open, but their prospects were uncertain.

It was agreed that protracted efforts during previous decades to ensure the growth of the church had failed, and that in future a systematic attempt should be made to concentrate resources where it was strong, rather than cherish lost causes such as those congregations which were both small and in decline.[6] Many members of Synod supported the principle of ruthlessly closing dwindling congregations which, for many years, had been subsidized without making significant progress, and it was agreed that cash released by such restructuring could be used to pay better salaries to attract and keep first-rate men in the ordained ministry. However, opposition remained strong; no firm decision was made and, as at previous Synods, the uneasy status quo was once again allowed to continue. One important step forward was taken, which had considerable practical and symbolic significance in the light of what happened later: women were to be accepted as members of church committees and district conferences, and as deputies to synods.

In his opening presidential address to the 1920 Fairfield Synod, Bishop H. R. Mumford commented on the social and political unrest resulting from the war. He believed that life had simply become much harder and, like many contemporaries, was already looking back on the Edwardian era with nostalgic affection. In an effort to rally his audience by speaking of the nature of spiritual power and the church's need of it, he reminded Synod of the expansive period when Zinzendorf was in charge and the Brotherhood had looked out upon the world in their day and seen its great need everywhere. In contrast, too many contemporary British Moravians were parochial in thought and work, detracting from a heritage 'which we would do well to guard and cultivate, not only for ourselves but for the sake of the whole church'.[7]

On a more mundane level, Synod agreed that, if the traditions of the church were to be upheld and if it were to regain vitality, more ministerial students were needed. Most serving ministers were sons of the manse, and it was hoped that more candidates would come from lay families within the congregations to solve the problem of shortages, especially on the mission field. Since the war, only British, American or neutral nationals were permitted to work as missionaries in British-controlled territories. Consequently, British missionaries were having to do work previously undertaken by Germans, and were grossly overworked.

The Moravians, in common with other denominations, had lost a significant proportion of their young men, and there was worrying statistical evidence of declining communicant membership from the high point of 3,959 in 1916 to 3,590 in 1920. The age profile of congregations had changed, too, with the proportion of women and older men being greater than it had been in 1913. This reflected wartime casualties and loss of young men as potential founders of Moravian families, as well as changed attitudes in society as a result of the war, which had led to an increasing tendency to question the value of religious observance.

Despite this, there was an urge towards new beginnings in the province, exemplified by Bishop Mumford who, in his opening address to the 1921 Baildon Synod, said that for some years the need had been felt and frequently expressed, that subjects of wider than domestic interest should be part of the regular work of Synod. There was a desire that the province should find its true place in organized Christianity, and fill it.[8] He urged those present to appreciate that no community could live for long on its past, no matter how good that past might have been, and as a new role was now required in British society the province should undertake self-examination.

One strategy which had been considered episodically since the 1880s was intercommunion and possibly union with either the Anglicans or the Free Churches. Members of Synod had not been enthusiastic then and were not enthusiastic in 1921, believing that the distinctive heritage of the Brotherhood would not admit of its being subsumed within either body. Deputies had lived through the traumas of 1914–18, sharing an unprecedented sense of loss, and were now rediscovering deep emotional bonds with German colleagues, so that a deliberate act of provincial suicide, no matter how reasonably argued, would be unthinkable. Despite recognizing that the British Province was stagnating, with its numbers diminishing and its educational network in decline, deputies shared a strong urge to continue as a separate, though minute national denomination, distinctive in being part of an international Unity. This theme and the search for a new national role continued, being raised again at the Ockbrook Synod in 1922,[9] when J. E. Hutton read a general discussion paper entitled, 'The Possible Place and Influence of our Church as a Branch of the Christian Church in the British Isles', and reached the same conclusion, but could offer no tangible proposals for change. The province simply had to continue as it had been before 1913; there was no alternative.

By this stage some disturbing realities of the post-war situation had become apparent. There appeared to be no prospect of a return to the comparatively healthy state of affairs which had been such an asset in the nineteenth century when the boarding schools were subsidizing provincial activity. In 1922 there was renewed discussion in *The Messenger* about the diminishing number of boys' boarding schools.[10] Of the five which had been in operation at the turn of the century, only Fulneck had survived, and even that was half empty, when other local denominational schools founded at about the same time, such as the Quaker school at Ackworth, Yorkshire, were full. Editorial comment in *The Messenger* dated 22 November argued that for some time there had been a noticeable and worrying undercurrent of antagonism in the province towards Moravian academic institutions. This was possibly linked to the fact that, apart from the children of ministers and missionaries, whose education was subsidized, few congregational members could afford private education for their children. In contrast, from the much greater number of Methodists, the equally small proportion who could afford to pay fees nevertheless enabled several boarding schools to flourish. In the same article it was also reiterated that existing Moravian schools, like their defunct predecessors, produced few new congregational members. Finally, and probably inevitably, teachers in Moravian boarding schools were inadequately paid, so they tended to move on, and pupils had to contend with frequent staff turnover.

The pessimistic mood deepened as the hopes of the immediate post-war years proved as difficult to implement as previous efforts at renewal. Br Mumford, in a *Messenger* article dated May 1925 on 'Ministerial Supply', commented that in scope and influence the province was weak; it was financially sound; it could exist, but do no more. It had little to offer ministerial candidates except hard work without the hope of becoming a bishop or being in charge of a big city church. He then observed, 'We are regarded by those outside with sympathetic interest as a queer sect with continental connections.' Editorial comment in *The Messenger* dated August 1925 on the Bedford Synod of that year surveyed its proceedings, and the general state of the province, with gloom. Even Synod had been characterized by spiritual lethargy; there was widespread contentment with comfortable mediocrity and acceptance that nothing much could be done to change the obvious and seemingly irreversible decline. Much had been said, for example, about the problem of the supply of ministers, but no action had been proposed. It was well known that 11 of the 41 ministers working in Britain were over fifty-five, and that there was serious wastage in Fairfield College, involving those beginning, but failing to complete their studies, one *Messenger* writer asking if anyone cared. Other denominations were experiencing the same problem of a shortage of ministers; the number of candidates for the ministry had been declining for some time, and this was particularly the case regarding men of higher educational attainment. The whole population, it was argued, whether churchgoing or not, was being affected by the spirit of the age, and the trend of modern life was away from organized religion.[11]

If these criticisms were justified, provincial lethargy and widespread contentment with comfortable mediocrity were understandable insular responses to the cataclysm of the Great War and its immediate aftermath. This was certainly not the case in the Continental Province. Bishop C. H. Shawe attended the May 1925 Continental Provincial Synod at Herrnhut, and reported on the enthusiasm of the deputies, not only from Germany but from Holland, Switzerland, Poland, Czechoslovakia and Denmark. He noted that the diaspora was still very active, particularly in parts of Germany, Switzerland and Poland, where there were large numbers of diaspora societies. Members were not enrolled as full Unity members, but derived spiritual care and nourishment from it and, through the diaspora, Unity influence extended far beyond the confines of its statistical membership.[12]

Deliberations on these matters continued to be part of synodal discussion throughout the 1920s, but did not lead to any new initiatives. The province, now with a pessimistic recognition that as a separate British church it was in decline, coasted along, economizing here and there, plagued by recurrent uneasiness that in scope and influence it remained weak. In 1930 a leading article in *The Messenger* explicitly admitted what had long been implicit in synodal discussion that for years they had been talking about church extension with the tacit assumption that it was dead.[13]

From time to time, however, articles in *The Messenger* showed that some members, particularly the ministry, recognized what was really missing. G. W. MacLeavy, writing in March 1930 after a prolonged visit to the German Province in 1929, described how Moravians there were still suffering the effects of severe inflation. Despite such hardships they 'still . . . believe that God has a use for them and still they ask for closer relations with the British Province'. Of German piety he wrote:

> It is beautiful and serene. At its best I have seen nothing like it. One might compare it to the trust of a child, but it is not the fellow of innocence. Ignorance of the world has not bred it and sorrow cannot destroy it. This piety is not the spirit of a recluse and laughter and play are no stranger to it. Yet you could not transplant it to England. Ours is a different atmosphere. We are more matter of fact in our attitude to life.

Recognizing that this contrasting style went to the heart of the dilemma which faced British Moravianism so painfully throughout the 1930s, he recommended the interchange of visits, 'so that British and German Moravians can really get to know and love each other'.[14] In practice this was difficult for ordinary congregational members of that generation, and reflected the long-established reality which had been central to the evolution of the British Province from the beginning, namely that, with few exceptions, only provincial leaders and mission workers were in a position to fulfil such a role consistently enough to make meaningful personal contacts between members of the different provinces. One exception did occur eight years later. An entry in the Ockbrook Congregational Diary dated 4 September 1938 contained a report by Sr L. King of her experience as one of the 'Moravian Pilgrims', twenty-five in number, who spent ten days visiting the Continental Province at the end of August. The keynote of her report was the immense friendliness and enthusiasm with which they had been greeted everywhere. 'The link between our continental brethren and ourselves should have been strengthened by this personal contact.'[15] Visits such as this did something to counterbalance ministerial unease.

The church was driven back once again on its own preoccupations, and these were pessimistic. By the time of the 1935 Fairfield Provincial Synod, communicant membership numbers had fallen to somewhat below 3,500, a reduction of about 460 since 1916, numerically equivalent to two substantial congregations. Br W. Smith read a paper on church extension, concluding, as several of his predecessors had done, that Moravian congregations in the British Province were not merely small in numbers, they were defeatist in spirit as far as extension was concerned. He questioned the role of the Moravian Church in Britain, asking what it had to offer the world that was not already provided by other denominations. In answer he could only fall back on what had been introduced in Zinzendorf's time, and accept that everything new which the church had to say had been said in the 1740s.[16]

This theme continued for the rest of the decade. With reference to the 1938 Baildon Provincial Synod,[17] for example, a leading article in *The Messenger* in July commented, 'For many years writers about Synod have sung its praises . . . much more rarely has any writer said anything about any definite and concrete measure of reform and progress that has brought new life and hope into every congregation.' The same writer referred to the pitiable numbers who attended worship and 'terrible struggles to maintain financial stability', which in his opinion robbed ministers and people of any opportunity for Christian joy.

The possibility of union with the Anglicans or Free Churches was raised again, but the inevitable loss of identity which would result from this was still not acceptable. It was admitted that opposition was strongest among the laity rather than the ministry, so that, apart from a few special occasions, the laity of different denominations in any one locality scarcely ever met. This intractable characteristic of British society was a severe obstacle to the prospect of early Moravian assimilation into another denomination.

Some members of Synod thought the church was doomed if the field of view were limited to the British Province alone, but saw grounds for optimism if overseas missions were included.[18] Missionaries on furlough usually addressed Synod, and it was the view of some that, 'in this work lies our salvation'. Of all sessions it was those devoted to missions which had the greatest appeal, and it was missionaries who were still regarded as the real Moravians. Although this was almost certainly a valid judgement, it did not in practice help the British Province to recover a sense of identity, and by 1938 all these issues were once again overshadowed by international events.

The Second World War: the international dimension

In retrospect, the period from the outbreak of the First World War in 1914 to the end of the Second World War in 1945 appears as an age of catastrophe. It included an unprecedented world economic crisis accompanied by widespread unemployment. The catalogue of disaster was particularly severe in Germany, as Meyer[19] explains:

The Germans experienced a succession of crises between 1918 and 1933 that were extraordinarily difficult and diverse, particularly in contrast to the relatively stable tempo of the preceding generation. The Germans had not yet adjusted to the facts of defeat and political upheaval, when they were subjected to three additional forces: the peace treaties, with their stunning territorial and economic losses; the immediate, acute threat of communism to a conservative and bourgeois society and its hearth-dog of nationalism; and a catastrophic inflation. An interim period of stability, restored in 1925–29, was then shattered by the Great Depression and its concomitant political and nationalistic aggravation. These facts do not justify what happened in German thinking and actions, but a recognition of them is indispensable to a clear evaluation of recent German history.

In Spain, Italy and Germany, liberal democracy was replaced by totalitarian regimes which seemed better able to address the social and economic challenges of the age.[20] These economic factors were a major cause of the emergence in Germany of National Socialism. Until 1928 the National Socialists remained on the fringe politically, but when Germany was subjected to the Great Depression, parliamentary democracy there was placed on the defensive, and this gave the Nationalists, led by Hitler, the opportunity to bid for power. After Hitler became Chancellor as its party leader in 1933, the Germans were offered a renewal of the idea of a great leader, a political genius who would find and impose solutions to the domestic crisis which seemed beyond the reach of ordinary mortals and fallible institutions.[21] There was a significant improvement in the lot of most of the population, but National Socialism was associated also with violent antisemitism, doctrines of teutonic racial superiority, and aggressive policies towards neighbouring states,[22] driving Germany and eventually the entire European continent headlong in the direction of renewed armed conflict.

From 1933 onwards international tension gradually increased as German aggrandizement included reoccupation of 'lost' Rhineland territory and absorption of Austria and Czechoslovakia during the latter part of the decade, and by the early months of 1939 members of the British Province, too, were expressing alarm. In February, 'J. C.', writing in *The Messenger*, condemned what he described as the devilry of German antisemitism and the progressive curtailment of individual liberty in Germany in the interest of what was widely perceived there as a quest for national regeneration.[23] Similar criticisms were expressed at the June Westwood Synod, particularly by Bishop C. H. Shawe. In his opening address he observed that not since the Great War had ordinary people been so fearful and anxious. European society was having to face once again the seemingly endless clash of interests between totalitarianism and democracy.[24]

Crisis point was reached when the Germans invaded Poland on 1 September 1939 and the German government refused British and French demands for withdrawal. Declaration of war followed and European conflict was resumed on 3 September 1939. For the second time the Unity was split and members were recruited to fight in opposing armies. On the British side the mood was one of sombre and stern resolution, for war was seen as the only way of dealing with German armed might and overtly aggressive intentions. Similar sentiments were expressed in *The Messenger*. In the earlier years of the decade popular opinion had been in favour of some compromise with German aspirations, but it was now clear that none was possible and a renewed continental nightmare had to be faced. Various articles written by young Moravian conscripts argued that for them this was the case, and confirmed that their serving colleagues felt the same.[25]

In common with others in their forties and older, many congregational members had already lived through the trauma of the First World War, and grimly remembered its opening stages when the people of Europe had responded euphorically to a call to duty. In contrast, those taking up arms in 1939 were not as receptive to a renewal of 1914-style idealistic rhetoric.[26] They no longer entertained the conviction that 'God is on our side', having experienced the horrors of modern warfare and the vulnerability of civilians. Further, their vivid recollections of the troubled 1920s and 1930s suggested that another victory over the Germans would not necessarily lead to the kind of permanent political settlement associated with long-term domestic stability which had been envisaged in 1918.

'Quaestor' acted as spokesman for this older generation. In April 1940 he observed that any mention of the wonderful things which were going to happen to the world in general and Europe in particular when this war was over would be received sceptically by many who remembered how many fervent hopes had remained unfulfilled after its predecessor. It concerned him deeply that the British people were now fighting the Germans for the second time in a generation and that, as in 1914–18, something deep, primitive, and destructive had been stirred up.[27] When he wrote this, there had been as yet no major military engagements against the German armies, so that provincial members had ample time to regret, write and preach about renewed severance from the Continental Province and worry about the fate of fellow Unity members. The dilemma faced by some provincial members, both ordained and lay, was that they had close personal connections with members of a nation which must once again be regarded as a mortal enemy; they belonged to the same Unity, had worked on the same mission fields, and had attended the same synods. As in the First World War it was not easy to establish the stereotype of a legitimate target against which to channel a sense of just outrage; the war would be fought against people, not against a regime in isolation. Moreover, the affairs of the province, though in some measure independent, were still bound in with a working organization which embraced both the Continental and American Provinces, the latter still a neutral country.

Prolonged meditation on the anguish of provincial severance was abruptly marginalized when, during the months of May and June 1940, the deceptive inactivity of the early months of the war was shattered by a massive German attack. This led to an unexpectedly rapid and over-whelming victory of German forces over the combined French, British and other Allied armies, replicating the *Blitzkrieg* launched against the French alone in 1870, and suggesting that Hitler's war aims were fore-shadowed by the German leaders of 1914.[28] The June edition of *The Messenger* carried a supportive open letter from the American Moravian bishops expressing shock and distress at this catastrophic turn of events and noting that,

> Our oldest Provinces are within warring countries, and many of their members are in the ranks of opposing armies. Our European Diaspora and Czechoslovakian churches have already felt something of the blight and destruction of terrible warfare ... Once again, our beloved Brethren's Church is experiencing the shock, the confusion, and the demoralising influence of war.

The leading article of the same edition, headed, 'The Blast of the Terrible Ones', regarded as positively satanic the stunning successes of the strategies of the German High Command in France and the Low Countries. 'No longer do men waste time and speech in arguing about the existence of Satan, of the Devil, of satanic and diabolical forces. For they are at work everywhere, concentrated in an orgy of passion, hatred and fury.' On the other hand, some of the ministry, particularly those familiar with the pre-war continental province and especially its German members were doubtful about such over-simplified condemnation. It was these Brethren who had known most intimately and worked with the people behind the symbols. While denouncing the warped philosophy of Hitler's New Order for Europe, which in principle was the same as that of his pre-1914 predecessors, they could not accept that the Germans collectively were evil. Br F. H. Mellowes, for example, writing in November 1940, argued that it was impossible for him to accept that he was a member of a 'good' Christian civilization engaged in a struggle against evil, embodied as Germans. The well-known fact that approximately 90 per cent of the people in Britain were at best neutral to Christianity invalidated such a simplistic dichotomy.

> In the eyes of the ordinary German who has an element of security and a sense of dignity and who feels the whole weight of German might behind him, is there anything at all to attract him to a democratic country, to make him wish to change his National Socialism for our democracy? The answer is, 'No'.

Recent research supports this point of view. It is now recognized that even those who resisted Nazism because of doubts about Hitler's leadership were enthusiastic about German military success from 1939 to 1941. Patriotism, not dedication to human rights, was a primary aim of the resistance. As long as the choice seemed to be between victory and resistance they usually opted for victory, and in doing so implicitly supported the acquisition of rich land to the east and west for economic exploitation. Only after it became clear that the choice was between defeat and resistance did they join or rejoin the resistance movement.[29]

Sentiments such as those expressed by Br Mellowes were no doubt shared by others within the province and outside it, but what was not fully appreciated at that time among British non-combatants was that the German victories had resulted primarily from the outstanding professional skill of German soldiers at all levels. The German army had proved invincible because of their superior tactical and technical skills.[30] This, and not the deployment of superior numbers, had been decisive, and it was a worrying thought that, after the subjugation of most of Western Europe, the war could well become a concentrated struggle between Britain and Germany. In the summer of 1940 that seemed likely.[31]

The Germans launched extensive air attacks on major British cities, particularly London, throughout the autumn, winter and spring of 1940–1, although the widely feared invasion by forces massed in France, which would certainly have overrun the country, did not materialize, mainly because the German army began to regroup in eastern Germany and Poland in preparation for an invasion of the USSR, a drive to the east on classic pre-1914 lines. This was launched on 22 June 1941, and from then onwards the German–Soviet war became the major military contest whereby Europe's fate would be decided, 75 per cent of German casualties would be caused,[32] and at a micro-level the congregational structure of much of the Continental Province would be either totally and permanently destroyed or severely ravaged. Later that year, after the devastating Japanese attack on the US Pacific fleet at Pearl Harbor on 7 December 1941, the USA became fully involved as British allies. The trepidation with which British Moravians, like the rest of the nation, viewed this extension of the conflict was reflected in a leading article in January 1942

> The flames of war have now enveloped most of the earth's surface, and the conflagration has passed beyond the control of human wit and reason. It cannot be extinguished, it can only burn itself out. But before that happens there will be loss, bloodshed and suffering beyond all computation and imagining.[33]

During 1942 and 1943 the Allies, reduced in Europe to the control of one embattled island, could only exert a peripheral influence on German land forces. However, they gradually won the Battle of the Atlantic by destroying 70 per cent of all German U-boats, whose depredations had been seriously interrupting the flow of essential supplies. This victory was crucial because defeat would have wrecked the allied war effort. At the same time, the British and Americans began a campaign of aerial bombardment of major German industrial cities, which included the first 1,000-bomber raid on Cologne on 31 May 1942. In the following months the allied bombing offensive rose steadily in both geographical extent and intensity, and it was not long before this strategy was extended to include the wholesale obliteration of non-industrial German cities by fire-bombing in an attempt to terrorize the civilian population[34] and cripple the German military industrial infrastructure, though subsequent research has revealed that its impact on industrial output and civilian morale was less than was thought at the time.[35]

The serious long-term implications of such catastrophic urban destruction were not widely appreciated by contemporaries, and there were few public expressions of outright disapproval at first, but when this campaign intensified and was linked to demands for German unconditional surrender, there were some protests.

A *Messenger* article, published in April 1944, only two months before the Anglo-American invasion of France, quoted a recent declaration by the Religious Society of Friends in London, which questioned the need for the Allies' insistence that the war could only end when the German armed forces surrendered unconditionally. The Quakers proposed that an offer should be made to the Germans to co-operate in immediate, negotiated peacemaking, in order to avoid months of horrific urban bombing and further extensive devastation by warring armies. Suggestions such as this from minority religious groups, but apparently not the Moravians, and a few exceptional Anglicans, notably Bishop George Bell of Chichester,[36] were not acceptable to allied politicians, and the Germans suffered attacks of increasing ferocity as invading allied forces from both east and west gradually liberated occupied countries and penetrated into Germany. Despite the fact that their major cities had been devastated and the internal economic life of the civilian population seriously disrupted, the Germans fought loyally and with formidable efficiency, but during the first few months of 1945 it was evident that German land forces would soon be overwhelmed by sheer weight of numbers. In the end, Russian Red Army units linked up with the American forces coming from the west, on the banks of the Elbe.

German unconditional surrender in May 1945 was a turning-point; it brought an era of German history to an end. Most German cities were in ruins; the entire military and economic structure of the country had collapsed; but what created a global sense of revulsion was the appalling state of the concentration camps. Their liberation, according to one historian, 'revealed horrors which were beyond human imagination and comprehension',[37] and the repercussions of these events continued long after 1945.[38] After six years of war, an exhausted Europe faced the gigantic task of post-war reconstruction.

The Second World War: the domestic dimension

Routine congregational life continued much as it had throughout the inter-war period, and long-standing weaknesses persisted; yet even in that unpromising context some ideas were put forward which were destined to become the basis of future advance. In 1939 there were forty-two congregations and 3,239 communicant members, an average of 70 per congregation. Although a few, such as Fulneck, were much larger, most were only a little above or on the average, and a few were well below it and only marginally viable even when heavily subsidized. (In comparison, the Continental Province had a mere twenty-four congregations for 8,022 communicant members averaging 334 members each.)[39]

This familiar state of affairs was the central issue in a June 1939 special report on congregations in the British Province, where it was noted that,

Many of the congregations are small and find the task of carrying on the life of the church a continuous struggle, for the workers are few and the resources limited. . . . No other religious denomination would keep resident ministers for groups of people the size of some of our Congregations. . . . Is the church acting wisely in heavily subsidising these congregations? . . . The facts suggest that an overhauling of our church system appears to be indicated . . . but even more important, there must be a spiritual revival and revolution.

This admirable aspiration, set as it was in an increasingly sceptical and secular society, was unfortunately bedevilled by a continuing crisis of identity. In April 1939 an article in *The Messenger* by C. Forster entitled, 'Where do we Stand as Moravians?' raised a fundamental issue for debate as the British Province was compelled once more to face the implications of its connection with Germany. He quoted a dictionary definition of the church: 'The Moravian Church was founded in Herrnhut in Saxony in the year 1722. It claims to be a direct continuation of the Church of the Bohemian Brethren, but this is doubtful.' He agreed, and suggested that the Moravian Church was a sect that dissented from the Lutheran Church in the early eighteenth century. It did not have ancient origins and no one who compared the Unitas Fratrum with the post-1727 Renewed Unity in attitude and practice would dream they were the same church. He then called for a public decision on the issue of 'Just what is the Moravian Church and where does it stand?' as a basis for what it could hope to do in the future. Understandably there was no official response to this article, yet it showed that there were those in the province who were still troubled by the church's uncertain rationale. The debate continued in correspondence published regularly in the magazine during wartime as articulate opinion-makers pondered the familiar questions of the church's identity, why it was so small, and what was its future in Britain. A comparatively new trend in these deliberations, stimulated by the emotions of wartime, was the suggestion that it might be reconstructed in some way. In a *Messenger* article under the same title published in September 1939, Br Forster followed up his earlier article by suggesting that the British Province should consider union with the Congregationalists, because the two churches seemed to him to be similar in spirit.

It was not only the question of the church's identity which provided an impetus to debate about the future of the British Province. Just over a year later *The Messenger* published a letter on the theme, 'Why is our Home Church so small?',[40] the final sentence of which invited a response from readers offering their reasons. In 1942, Br S. L. Connor looked at the wider perspective, writing on the theme, 'Church Unrest and Criticism', when he noted, 'In many minds there is deep concern for the present condition and future prospects of our church.' He took some consolation from the fact that its problems were shared with other denominations. 'Now when we think of the weakness of our present-day Moravian Church and deplore the decline in membership and attendances, we must not forget that the same symptoms appear in all the other Church communities of the land. . . . The truth is that the whole spirit of the age is one of indifference, not to say hostility to the Church [as a whole].'[41]

His colleagues were concerned, also, about the state of the Sunday schools. The editorial in *The Messenger* of October 1942, referring to the most recent statistics which showed continuing decline, noted:

> In our judgement the most disappointing, alarming and desperate condition is our utter failure to increase our membership from the only hopeful source, the Sunday School. From forty Sunday Schools, only forty-five young people were added [during the previous year]. At this rate we are forced to face the fact of a gradual decline and disappearance of our Church. This was stated a few years ago in the PEC report. Simultaneously a total loss of thirty-five in adult membership indicates we do not draw on the general public to enlarge our borders.

Lucy MacLeavy reported in December 1942 that she had attended a conference convened in London to discuss post-war reconciliation with the Germans, and called on provincial members to recognize their special responsibilities in this healing process when the time came. She emphasized that, despite the war, it was vitally important that Moravians in Britain should not think of themselves as a national church, but as members of a renewable international Unity which still retained its roots in Germany. For her, ultimate reconciliation with the German Province was essential.

During the next two or three years other provincial members contributed to this broader debate about options for the future of British Moravianism, and their ideas were aptly summarized by Br W. Smith in *The Messenger* of April 1943. Discussing the prospects for the post-war Moravian Church, he argued that few Moravians could contemplate its future without serious misgivings. He suggested a radical way forward similar to that of Br Forster. He started with the premise that the purpose for which God had called the Moravian Church into being in Britain had been fulfilled and that many congregational members did not really believe that they belonged to an Anglo-German international church. The accepted mythology that they did should be abandoned. Instead, because the existing British province was virtually indistinguishable in day-to-day matters from other Nonconformist denominations, there was no longer any need for a separately organized Moravian Church. The province should participate with the other Nonconformists in a reunited Christian Church which could have a powerful unified role in post-war Europe.

Although nothing immediately practicable emerged from this debate – and in wartime conditions this was not surprising – it voiced a growing conviction among thinking members that, in abandoning its diaspora and organizing itself as a separate denomination, the British Province had seriously endangered its long-term prospects of survival. This misgiving had been raised publicly towards the end of the nineteenth century and still carried weight. One contributor to the discussion advocated a return to the eighteenth-century idea of an ordained minister as primarily a supervisor of house groups of members, so that the Christian influence of such informal groups would permeate adjacent populations, a suggestion which would have endeared him to the evangelists of the 1740s.

The idea of amalgamation of denominations was not new, but in the early months of 1943 it was being considered seriously as an option, even at government level. The Prime Minister had recently spoken on this subject, and in a leading article of May 1943 the editor of *The Messenger* argued strongly in favour of denominational amalgamation. This, he argued, was perhaps the best way forward, enabling congregational members to cast off the burden of routine sameness, littleness, stillness and ineffectiveness, and was to be perceived generally as a possible way forward by some Christians in post-war Britain.

In March 1944, shortly before the April Fulneck Synod, a leading article in *The Messenger*, entitled 'Begin at Home', expressed the hope that there God would make his will known to the church, 'that we may believe there is yet a real work of evangelism for us to do in our forty congregations . . . The English Province needs new inspiration to energise its general lethargy and effectiveness. The problem is ourselves.' These features of church unrest and criticism inevitably featured at Synod with little agreement on remedial action. A month later, under the heading 'Synod 1944', the editor of *The Messenger* admitted that it had been an enjoyable and refreshing experience and commented with obvious relief that no one had seriously proposed that the Moravian Church should be amalgamated with another. In spite of that, in his opinion, a feeling of disappointment remained; along with others he had hoped that new ideas might emerge about instituting more evangelistic preaching, strengthening congregational spirituality and attracting the young:

> This is just something that we all needed and it didn't come off. . . . Underlying all our fine phrases is the conviction that there must be something the Church has to deliver to the people and that we do not seem to know what that something is.[42]

Overshadowing this deficiency, another urgent domestic problem emerged as the year progressed, namely the shortage of replacement missionaries resulting from wartime restrictions on student training. Two in the West Indian Island of Antigua who were well past the age of retirement had been compelled to continue to carry sole responsibility for two very large and growing congregations. To replace them and others, an increase in the number of men sent out from Britain was needed urgently, an objective which could only be achieved by transferring them from full-time congregational ministry. In December 1944, therefore, it was suggested that a few serving British ministers might take up short mission contracts of, say, two years, and while they were away their home congregations would be served by their colleagues. No immediate action was taken because such a scheme would leave the British Province under-staffed.

In June 1945 the Provincial and College Boards argued that, to maintain staffing in Britain at the pre-war level, the province needed about ten new ordinands within the next four years, yet only three or four young men were known to be returning to college after demobilization, and no new candidates had offered for church service. Despite this critical impasse, the Provincial and College Boards were not then willing to act on a revolutionary resolution of the June 1944 Synod, that women should have a more significant role in church life and that ultimately their ordination might be possible.[43] Nevertheless, the passing of this resolution was an important augury of the ordination of the first woman in 1970.

Another suggestion which foreshadowed future policy, being capable of considerable extension, was the idea of two or more adjacent congregations sharing one minister in order to release one or two provincial staff for short-term appointments to overseas missions. It would be easy for two congregations to share one minister for a limited period, provided that they were warned in good time. There were also exchanges of ideas about increasing opportunities for the provincial laity to serve the church more actively. It had been noticeable for many years that most provincial synodal deputies represented the ministry; this was felt to curtail lay influence on provincial development, and the balance should be altered. The possibility of ordaining men who would retain a lay occupation, while acting as non-stipendiary ministers, had not yet been publicly aired, but within twenty years it became essential. The first of a series of appointments of this type was made in 1974 because the shortage of full-time ministers had become acute.

All these options were primarily matters for discussion in the prevailing atmosphere of wartime, but post-war developments made it necessary for them to become accepted policy rather than contingency plans, and formed the basis on which the future pattern of provincial administration would be structured and on which the viability of the British Province would increasingly depend. As yet they lay in the future; there were now more pressing concerns, and in June 1945, a month after the end of the war in Europe, the Provincial and College Boards wrote to all congregations, urging young men to come forward for ministerial or mission service now that the European war was over.

Effects of military action

Some indication of the events and decisions occasioned by wartime conditions can be found in the Minute Book of the Provincial Board,[44] who received information from the whole province and discussed the minutiae of the church's response to such varied issues as wartime damage to property and inter-church preparations for post-war reconstruction. These accounts of the results of enemy bombing of churches and their property show that the British Province was comparatively little affected.

The first reference to enemy action occurred in a minute of 26 November 1940: 'We agree to send a letter of sympathy to the Bristol Congregation, which was exposed to a severe and destructive air raid on the night of the 24th.' There is no indication of damage to the premises. It was a different situation in 1941, when a wire came on 19 April from Br Lloyd in Ballymena, regarding Cliftonville: 'School destroyed, Church windows and doors gone. Manse rather badly damaged. Can the Conference assist with necessary immediate repairs?' The Board agreed to send £35 for repairs and £10 for the minister's personal loss.

On 12 May 1941 the news was much more serious. 'Br N. Pennington informs us . . . that the Fetter Lane offices and adjoining property including the Chapel were destroyed during the night of May 10/11.' Br C. H.

Shawe was deputed to investigate, and reported on 15 May that the destruction appeared to be complete and there was little prospect of anything being saved from the wreckage. An official notice was sent to *The Messenger*. For the time being Br J. Connor attempted to carry out duties such as visiting, but resigned as minister of Fetter Lane in August, being unable to continue, and the work was taken over at the end of September by Br Shawe at the request of the Fetter Lane Committee. Behind the bare facts of the official record lies an untold story of the sheer hard work of trying to hold a community together during repeated attacks on London. Since the establishment of the London congregation there on 10 November 1742, these buildings had been intimately associated with the earliest period of Moravian activity in Britain, had witnessed its development, and by the 1940s housed important early records. The loss of much that was associated with this historic inheritance had naturally created widespread dismay, but did not detract from the continuing rich mythology of the site and its special place in British Moravian consciousness.

During the nights of 25 and 26 April 1942 there were raids on Bath, in which the minister's house was damaged, and was believed likely to be beyond repair, a fact reported at the committee meeting of 29 April and confirmed by Br Birtill. This appears to have been the last major damage sustained by church property as a result of enemy action, but it was thought prudent by the Finance Committee to advise on 11 October 1943, 'that those congregations that have not insured against war damage should do so'.

Something of the concern felt by the Provincial Board about the dangers of ministerial service in London during the war years is recorded in July 1944 when the call of Br E. Wilson to Hornsey was discussed. At this period the British air offensive had been carried into Germany, and there was little danger of concentrated German air raids on British cities, but by then the V1 and V2 guided missiles were being deployed against southern England, some reaching London targets. When the Board met on 24 July it had been proposed to defer the moves of ministers for a month because of the possible danger to Br Wilson's family from a move to Hornsey, a suggestion which worried the congregation. They submitted that, 'whilst the services might be suspended the pastoral care of the congregation is all important in this period of danger', and proposed that someone else should be sent for three months. The Board agreed to adhere to its proposal and consult with Br Wilson as to whether he might prefer to go without his family and begin in September as originally arranged; alternatively, Br Shawe would reside in London for the month of September. The discussion reflects a general recognition that the war was moving into the final stage when even a month or two could make a big difference to the level of danger.

The British Province as a whole was remarkably fortunate that its property did not sustain more damage. When, on 13 April 1945, the North American Province offered help in the reconstruction of British churches damaged during the war, the Board recorded, 'We are grateful for this offer, but reply that damage to local Churches was not so great as to warrant our accepting it, and for new provincial offices there are as yet no plans.'

Wartime co-operation with the American provinces

During the early years of the war in Europe the North American Province expressed its concern for its British Brethren with sympathy and offers of help. In August 1940 the Board noted a report from Br Stocker, 'on the readiness of Moravian families in America to accept British Moravian children who might be evacuated'. The Board did not feel that an official Moravian evacuation should be organized, because of the government's decision to limit overseas evacuation as much as possible, but agreed to make the offer public through *The Messenger*. This magazine was the medium, also, for the publication of the Canadian District's expressions of sympathy and encouragement received by the Provincial Board on 17 September 1940. It is moving to realize how much practical help was offered by individual congregations on a very personal level. On 11 February 1941 it was noted that £13 2s 10d had been collected by the congregation in Edmonton, Canada for 'relief of any Moravians in England who may have suffered through the war', and on 19 February details were recorded of payments to three individuals from this gift.

In 1940, when America was still not involved in the conflict, the Board was in touch with the American bishop, Br S. H. Gapp about Text Book material and he took a prominent part in subsequent arrangements. On 12 July it was recorded that,

> We have asked Br Gapp to secure the proofs of the German Text Book for 1942 (the one for 1941 having been completed), if he can do so, and send us proofs of the American version. If it is not possible for him to obtain the German copies, we should invite America to produce its own Text Book and offer to purchase what we require from there.

At this time the editor was already working on the 1942 edition. There was a change of editor, Br Blandford taking over in October, by which time, 'Half the copy for 1942, received from Germany, is now, Br Gapp reports, on its way to England.' In 1942 3,000 copies of the 1943 Text Book were being printed in England. In January 1943 Br Gapp reported that no material had been received from Germany for the 1944 edition, and the British Province arranged a contingency plan. The Board recorded, 'We request Br Blandford to prepare a text book for next year, making use of an old text book and putting in new readings from Scripture together with a fresh selection of hymn verses.' By 11 March 1943 the texts for 1944 had been forwarded from America by Br Furstenberger, but without readings. Br Furstenberger continued to send the texts and proofs for 1945 and 1946 editions, which were edited in England by Br Blandford.

A further area of co-operation between the British and American provinces was in overseas missions. The General Directory at Herrnhut, through which Unity missions had been organized, was now inaccessible, and decisions were required from time to time to keep them viable. The American provinces, with British agreement, took the initiative in maintaining a sense of unity among those provinces which could remain in contact, and Br Pohl,[45] of the South American Province, assumed the role of Executive Chairman of the General Directory in January 1941, retaining it until the end of 1944.

On 28 January 1942 Br Pfohl, in his capacity as Secretary of the American Provinces, forwarded a copy of two resolutions passed at the Synod of the Southern Province, one affirming its faith in the continuity of the Unity, the other extending greetings to the conferences and boards of the various provinces. Similar expressions of fellowship and greetings were noted in both January and December 1943.

The first occasion on which a decision on behalf of the American-based General Directory was made by the other provinces of the Unity, was recorded in the Minute Book of the British Provincial Board on 4 October 1943. It resulted from an application by the Province of South Africa West for permission to authorize ordinations: 'On behalf of the Provincial board of South Africa (W.) Province, Br Schmidt applies to the General Directory for permission to authorise ordinations in the Province during the war. We agree to give our vote in favour of granting this permission.' On 12 January 1944, it was recorded that:

Br Pohl [*sic*] reports the decision of the General Directory respecting the application to ordain Brn in the SAWP, viz. that the two candidates named may be ordained and further, that future candidates may be ordained until the South Africa West Provincial Board is able to communicate with the Herrnhut Mission Board.

Other types of decision were needed from time to time. The Provincial Board's Minutes show how information was circulated and consultation maintained to enable discussion to continue and some progress to be made. On 13 September 1944 South Africa West was again the subject of consultation in difficult circumstances. Br Schmidt had requested the opinion of the General Directory on questions arising from the claim of the church in South Africa West to independence. The Board agreed to send a letter to 'Brn Pfohl and Gapp' with their views, but these were not recorded in the minutes. On 13 November 1944 it was noted that, 'Br Gapp forwards a copy of a letter sent by the North American PB to Br R. Schmidt of South Africa West on the interest of the North American Province in the property held by the Missionanstalt.' It also recorded a resolution by the North American Province, as part of the General Directory, that the British Mission Board be requested to assume temporary administration of South Africa West till after the war, when the General Directory could again function in its entirety. By this time, also, the province felt that responsibility for chairing the Directory should be shared as it had been before the war: on 29 December 1944 the following note was minuted by the Provincial Board:

> Br. Pohl (12 Dec) writes expressing his readiness to relinquish his office as Executive Chairman of the General Directory . . . and suggesting that the rotation of the position should be resumed. Next in order would be the German Province, but as they are at present precluded, the turn of the British Province would come next. We should be willing to accept the responsibility, if that should be the wish of both American Provinces, but we should be equally happy if they suggested either that Br. Pohl should continue in office or that the Northern Province should provide the Chairman.

On 22 February 1945 it was recorded that, as both the American provinces had renewed their request, Br Shawe accepted the office of Executive Chairman of the General Directory from 1 March 1945. Military conflict in Europe ended with a total German collapse on 8 May 1945 and by June it had been agreed between the British and American provinces that an early meeting of the General Directory was desirable, but probably not practicable before 1946. In the meantime the British

Province intended to re-establish contact with the continent and submitted a preliminary draft of an agenda for discussion.

Post-war reconciliation with the Continental Province

Even in wartime the province was alert to any movement in Britain in support of European post-war reconstruction, having a more direct interest than most other denominations in the rapid re-establishment of Christian relationships with the continent, although it must be emphasized that all denominations were prepared to co-operate in this work, and did so.

Br Shawe reported to the Fulneck Synod in 1944 on the Moravian Church in Czechoslovakia (British Auxiliary), referring to the steady receipt of sums of money which would be ready for help to the church on the day of victory. He referred to the help which the British Province had been able to give to Czech refugee children and some adults. Hospitality had been given by Fulneck, Ockbrook, Bristol, London and Fairfield. He continued:

> Br. Vancura is head of the Reconstruction department but we know little of the present conditions of our church in Czechoslovakia. From the little that has become known, chiefly through Switzerland, it would appear that the German occupation has not directly attacked the Churches; we even heard that Moravians had organised a new congregation at Bielohrad. Post-war needs will have to be considered in connection with the efforts shortly to be organised on behalf of all the Protestant Churches on the Continent.

Synod passed a resolution that, at the earliest possible opportunity after the war, the Provincial Board should establish contact with the German provincial network and bring its needs to the attention of members of the British Province so that they could help. One practical result was that the Provincial Board, with the support of the Finance Committee, agreed on 11 October 1944 to a positive preparatory step by issuing an appeal for a fund of £750, to which provincial funds would contribute £250, in aid of the British Council of Churches' appeal for a newly formed society, 'Christian Reconstruction in Europe'. This organization had branches in America and many neutral countries as well as in Britain, and collaborated with the Department of Reconstruction and Inter-Church Aid set up by the emerging World Council of Churches, in Geneva.[46]

Positive news from Germany reached the British Province early in 1945. In March an editorial entitled 'Our Church on the Continent' appeared in *The Messenger*, quoting *Feuilles Vertes*, the journal of the Moravian Church in Switzerland. This reported the observations of Swiss visitors who had recently returned from Germany, verifying the vast extent of devastation and disruption generally and Moravian losses in particular. Whereas in 1919 every German congregational base was intact and as accessible as in 1914, in 1945 most, including Herrnhut, were either badly damaged or utterly destroyed. Many, such as Berlin, Ebersdorf, Gnadau, Gnadenberg, Herrnhut, Kleinwelke, Neudietendorf and Niesky were cut off in the Russian zone of occupied Germany.

This grievous loss was not all: other old-established congregations such as Breslau, Gnadenfeld, Gnadenfrei, Guben Hausdorf and Neusalz had simply ceased to exist because, when the region came under hostile Polish administration, all ethnic Germans living there had been expelled.[47] They had been caught up unwillingly in the severance from German political control of territories which had been predominantly German-speaking for centuries, and in this manner nearly a quarter of the country's pre-1938 territory, where some 9 to 9.5 million people had previously lived, ceased to be part of it.[48]

As news of the fearful disaster which had overtaken the Unity heartland spread throughout the British Province, many people, despite their revulsion for well-publicized German atrocities, experienced deep and perhaps unexpected compassion for fellow Unity members – a good augury for future reconciliation. In April, Bishop Shawe, already Executive Chairman of the General Directory, was appointed as the church's representative on the newly constituted Committee for Christian Reconciliation in Europe, which was to be based in Geneva. Over a long period his personal contribution, and therefore that of the British Province, to the rebuilding of the Unity was enormous. His German counterpart was Br Baudert, who agreed with the desirability of convening a Unity Conference as soon as possible, but at Bad Boll in Baden-Wurttemberg, by then the new provincial headquarters on account of wartime damage at Herrnhut.

Soon after the unconditional surrender on 8 May 1945, more detailed information became available, and British provincial leaders, including Br Shawe, travelled to the continent to re-establish contact with Unity headquarters in Germany, and begin the process of reconciliation. Once hostilities ceased there was no delay in this process. On 21 September Br Shawe reported to the Provincial Board that the Swiss had promised their help in communicating with Br Baudert and their support in any effort to

re-establish the Moravian schools in Germany. The possibility of a Unity
Conference in Switzerland in 1946 which Br Baudert might attend was
being considered.

One heartening indication that relationships were moving forward
was recorded by the Board on 1 November 1945:

> A letter of greeting (the first since the outbreak of war) was received
> from Br. Baudert. He writes that the Board is now settled in Bad Boll,
> and looks forward to attending a Unity Conference in the not too
> distant future. He reports that efforts are being made to restore some
> of the Church activities by re-establishing the educational work. This
> accords with our suggestion made to the Christian Reconstruction
> Committee in Geneva.

The patient work continued during the next few months; the Unity
Conference was to be arranged for July 1946, with a prospect of Br Gapp
and Br Pfohl attending the Synod of the British Province on their way to
this conference. By 19 March 1946 it was recorded that the amount so
far collected for Christian Reconstruction in Europe was £1,200 18s
10d, of which £213 2s 9d was for Czechoslovakia. A sum of £250 was to
be allocated for the general purposes of the World Council Committee
administering the fund. The enthusiasm of the British Province for this
work shines through the simple record. There was no inkling in those
early days of the problems ahead when Herrnhut and other continental
congregations would become virtually inaccessible behind the Iron
Curtain set up by the occupying Russian authorities.

When the Provincial Synod met in Ockbrook in July 1947, two
significant greetings were received from Germany which epitomized the
current situation of the Continental Province.[49] Br Baudert's message of
fraternal greeting from Bad Boll mentioned that *The Messenger* had been
received there with news of the forthcoming Annual Synod of the British
Province. He gave thanks to the Lord that the German Brethren were
reunited with others from abroad, and expressed the gratitude of the
leaders of the Continental Province for the hard work done during the
war by the other provinces to sustain Unity Missions. His letter contained a warm tribute to the selfless devotion of Bishop Shawe and the
help he was currently giving to their province. The second letter, dated 4
July, from Br Schmidt on behalf of the Eastern District Synod of the
United Brethren currently meeting in Herrnhut, expressed regret that the
German Brotherhood was now split because of the division of Germany
into three zones, but thankfulness that the Unity had held together. He
sent hearty greetings and expressions of brotherly love.

The Report of the Provincial Board to the Baildon Synod in 1948 recorded in its section on the Unity the two synodal meetings of the German provinces the previous year, with their expressions of brotherly love to the other provinces of the Unity. The Board's comment on the situation in Germany was prophetic: 'The work in Germany goes forward with true heroic zeal, but not all the difficulties are physical. There are reports of incidents and conditions in the Eastern Zone which cause grave disquiet.'

The patient work of rebuilding links with the continental provinces went quietly on, and in 1952 the report of the Provincial Board to the Dukinfield Synod showed considerable progress. Regarding the Unity it was recorded that,

> Br. Shawe has been at Bad Boll for consultations with the Boards of our Church in Western Germany, and with the Directorate of the Mission Institute of which he is a member and in which the British Province has an interest in respect of Mission Funds. On the same occasion it was possible to visit Berlin for a meeting with the Boards of the Moravian Church in Eastern Germany, whose need of contact with, and prayer of, the whole Unity is specially great.

It was to be virtually forty years before unrestricted relations between the western and eastern districts of the Unity could be re-established, but even under the restrictive East German regime some visiting was allowed by groups of ordinary church members, particularly through the work of the women of the church. The Provincial Board were able to maintain friendly contact in an official capacity, as routine greetings were regularly exchanged at synods and the work of resolving problems which affected the whole Unity continued.

Part Three

Renewed Creativity

Part Two has surveyed the development of the British Province from 1742 to 1945, while exploring some themes which have recurred throughout the period. It has been argued that the form of Christianity which the Brethren established in Britain, though firmly based on Lutheran Protestant doctrine, was associated with innovative social institutions. At first they were welcomed in Britain in the current atmosphere of enthusiasm for a religion of the heart, but in the longer term their aim of working with members of existing churches through diaspora societies, and regarding their settlements primarily as structured communities of the devout and training-grounds for evangelistic outreach, had a limited appeal for British people. In common with other Protestant Churches, once the fervour of the eighteenth-century Evangelical Revival had worn itself out, provincial congregations lost much of their original spiritual dynamic, a situation which their leaders endlessly regretted and sought unsuccessfully to change over the next half century and beyond. Those who took up positions of responsibility gradually transformed the original institutional organization into one which, while remaining true to its origins in some respects, also reflected the influence of nineteenth-century developments in British Nonconformity. Consequently, by the middle of the nineteenth century, an Anglo-German style had emerged in the British Province which was in some respects a continuation of the original eighteenth-century establishment, but which differed from it in many aspects of its aims and organization.

The study then followed the experiences of the British congregations through two world wars, showing how efforts were made by provincial leaders to maintain relationships within the Unity and to play a significant role in the re-establishment of German connections when peace came, despite the problems of the Cold War. In essence, then, while presenting a chronology of prolonged transition, Part Two has explored specific areas of the church's experience in which continuity and change are most evident.

Part Three is more directly thematic, with an element of retrospection which provides a detailed exposition of some subjects which have been introduced in Part Two. It still emphasizes continuity in the church's history, while concentrating on the significance of earlier policies and decisions for the period after the Second World War. Other mainly post-war developments are considered, both for their impact on the province itself and its relationship with the Unity, and as areas of ministerial and lay involvement in the interdenominational Christian community.

Initially the church's provision for the training of ministers is discussed, showing how, since the establishment of a training institution in the mid-nineteenth century, the British Province has responded to changing needs and contemporary practice, including in recent times the deployment of non-stipendiary ministers and the ordination of women. A second theme centres on congregational life; after a brief survey of aspects of church life which are common to all denominations, it examines two major elements which are specifically Moravian, namely, the contribution to provincial life of Moravians who came to Britain from the West Indies between the late 1940s and the 1960s, and the influence of the Moravian Women's Association on congregational spirituality and support for missions. Other developments are then discussed which have been primarily the work of church leaders and interested members, and have kept the Moravian Church in touch with the thinking and practice of other denominations and enabled the congregational network to survive. These include ecumenical discussions, which are now becoming increasingly prominent, and some local amalgamations between provincial congregations and the United Reformed Church, paralleling developments in the Continental Province, where some Unity congregations are sharing premises and working with the Landeskirche, the state church of the region.

7

The Ministry (I)
Professional Training for Provincial
Ministers and Missionaries

The Brethren's tradition

The early use of artisans as ministers and missionaries was a provisional arrangement on the part of the Unity to meet the perceived needs of a rapidly expanding organization. It caused surprise among other denominational leaders in the mid to late eighteenth century, particularly as the well-known missionary enterprises of the Jesuits had always been conducted by men who had undergone the most rigorous and specialized intellectual and spiritual training. The Brethren's ordained artisans were devoted to their calling, and some achieved outstanding results, but many could not meet the demands of the situation, despite a deep faith and commitment, and so the proportion of artisans in service was gradually and unobtrusively reduced.[1]

As soon as possible, therefore, institutions were set up to increase the proportion of educated men. From 1739 onwards, young aspiring ministers were required to attend rigorous academic courses at the newly opened Unity Paedagogium (Grammar School) at Marienborn, which from 1808 was located at Niesky. Successful students then transferred to the Unity Theological College, founded at Barby in 1754 and relocated in 1818 to Gnadenfeld, where it remained until 1945. Graduation from Theological College was usually followed by a period of teaching, either in the Unity Paedagogium or in some other school, prior to ordination on being called to full-time ministry or mission service.

This approach to ministerial training accorded with the orthodox Lutheran view of the ministerial role, at the heart of which was the recovery of sound doctrine, which could only be taught by those educated to demanding standards. To preach and to maintain an effective disciplined Christian ministry required training, books and character.[2] By the end of the eighteenth century, therefore, an increasing proportion of Unity ministerial and mission staff had studied at Marienborn and Barby, and the tradition of an educated ministry became established.

A related development took place in the British Province. From 1742 onwards 'labourers on souls' were a mixture of academically untrained craftsmen and a small minority of college-educated Germans and Englishmen. Initially the German group occupied a greater proportion of senior positions, but as time went on there was increasing participation by educated Englishmen who had graduated from the Unity Theological College at Barby. These men inevitably had a greater sensitivity to and deeper sympathies with German culture and outlook than was possible for those who had not undergone this training. As a result they acquired the all-important Anglo-German mentality which they passed on to succeeding generations of the ordained. Nevertheless there is evidence that, well into the nineteenth century, a large proportion of British Labourers had not yet undergone the rigours of an academic education. In 1833 the Anglican clergyman Thomas Grinfield published a memoir of Friedrich Rampftler,[3] a well-known provincial Unity minister, in which he wrote:

> Mr. Rampftler combined with his ministerial activity a habit of more extensive and varied reading than might have been expected in a pastor of the Moravian Church. And I mention that habit more particularly, not merely as a feature that marks the individual, but also as a habit which doubtless had its share in producing that superiority in the pulpit by which he was distinguished.

Professional training in the British Province

Brief reference has already been made to the fact that, early in the nineteenth century, some English Labourers (referred to hereafter as 'ministers') and congregational members were pressing for an English Theological College. This was part of the process by which the province was reducing its German institutional connections and evolving as a distinctive, separate and self-governing denomination. An English theological college with locally recruited staff and students, it was argued, would ensure a more 'English' ministry, a view which accorded with the developing national consciousness of the early Victorian age. A first tentative step was taken during the 1820s when a few older pupils at Fulneck School were offered advanced training on the lines of Niesky Paedagogium prior to study at Gnadenfeld. According to the minutes of the 1824 Provincial Conference there were seven such boys, though what became of them is not clear. It seems that this arrangement did not lead to the formation of more than an embryonic theological course, and it was dropped.

There had been a precedent for establishing further training at Fulneck. The memoir of Peter LaTrobe, son of Christian Ignatius LaTrobe,[4] includes a reference to a temporary expedient during the Napoleonic War.

> He was still of a very tender age when he was sent to the Provincial Schools at Fulneck. . . . Here he distinguished himself . . . and creditably finished his course of studies in the school. The college of the Brethren on the Continent being at this time closed against English subjects in consequence of the war, a temporary Seminary was instituted at Fulneck for the benefit of those who either were designed for the ministry of our Church in England, or were desirous of securing the advantage of a more advanced education. Having completed a course of studies in this Institution . . . he was, in the year 1813 appointed one of the tutors in the boys' academy at Fairfield.

No other record of this seminary has been found, so it has not been possible to establish how long it lasted, though it seems reasonable to assume that access for British students to the continental seminaries was re-established after the war ended in 1815.

It was not until 1856 that another effort was made, involving Br England, minister of the Bedford congregation, who agreed to accommodate and prepare two or three zealous young men for ministerial or mission service. Since he was expected to continue his normal congregational duties, his well-intentioned experiment collapsed after a year. By this time the desire for a permanent theological college in Britain was growing. The need for an educated ministry was raised again at both the 1853 and 1856 Provincial Conferences, and in 1858 an article was published in the *Fraternal Record*, successor for two years of the *Fraternal Messenger*, entitled, 'An Educated Ministry at Home and Abroad: The Requirements of Our Day'.[5] The anonymous writer recognized that many sections of the community were receiving a better education, and contended that those in charge of congregations should have their minds similarly extended. There was evidence, also, that 'semi-literate missionaries were far from rare', demonstrating that they were really incapable of teaching and leading. Goodwill was no longer enough.

The recent achievement of provincial autonomy spurred those attending the 1859 Provincial Synod to try again. They decided to set up a Training Institution at Fulneck and appoint a full-time salaried tutor to organize a two-year residential training course for two students at a time, beginning in 1860. It is a measure of its national character that from 1860 onwards theological college training in the British Province remained in the northern heartland where members of the Brotherhood were most densely concentrated.

This important synodal decision brought to an end the traditional preparation for ministerial or teaching service in Britain. This had produced a core of educated Germans augmented by British men also trained in Germany, working alongside a majority of long-service colleagues who had not been called upon to study to this level. British students tended to be drawn from ministerial families in which the father or grandfather had been partly educated in either Niesky or Gnadenfeld. As sons of the manse these young men had already attended Fulneck School, usually as boarders, and so had been enveloped in Unity tradition for many years. Some of them now remained in the settlement for a further two years to be trained for full-time church service. This training was to involve an initial period of teaching followed by a lifetime's employment as home-service ministers or overseas missionaries, or a combination of the two. In principle, therefore, entrants between the ages of sixteen and eighteen were looked upon as trainee teachers. After completing all or most of their two-year course they would be called upon to teach for a number of years in one of the boarding schools of the provincial network. By the time they were in their mid-twenties they would be expected to re-enter the Institution to take up ministerial training, followed by ordination on a call to a particular congregation or to the mission field. In effect, teaching in a Brethren's school was visualized as a valuable prelude to ministerial service at home or overseas.

The arrangements were far more flexible in practice than the initial outline plan provided for, and the number of students proved to be more variable than had been foreseen.[6] When the Training Institution opened on 10 October 1860 three students were enrolled for teacher training. Two of these were English born, and the third originated in the West Indies, probably the son of a missionary. In 1861 there were seven English students, three of whom were hoping ultimately to enter the home-service ministry and three who intended to become missionaries; a seventh man, a German, was also enrolled prior to service in West Africa. He, like his predecessor from the West Indies, stayed for only one year. This type of mixed entry became a feature of student admissions, complicated even further by recurrent brief appearances of Germans who had already qualified for mission service at Niesky and had been sent for a few months to improve their English before serving in Labrador or the West Indies. As a result, admissions varied greatly from year to year: although the usual range was three to five, in 1867 there was only one, whereas in 1873 there were ten, mostly from Germany and the West Indies. In practice, far from being an exclusively English institution, for the first sixty years of its existence about a third of its students came from Unity institutions overseas for a variable period of instruction before entering service as teachers or missionaries. Most English students favoured a permanent career in the schools or the home ministry, only a minority aspiring to long-term service on the mission field, despite the regular presence in the student body of men committed to this work, who contributed an international ethos to the institution.

As time went on it became increasingly obvious that the Training Institution was not producing as many student teachers as had been anticipated, a weakness accentuated by the high withdrawal rate from school service of those who had been called into it. The province was not alone in this: failure of men to take up or, when trained, persist in teaching for more than a few months, was a national problem provoked by the growth of the industrial and commercial economy. By the mid-nineteenth century this had created a seemingly insatiable demand for employees who were sufficiently literate and numerate to fill clerical and minor supervisory posts. Railway companies were particularly competitive, offering employment with better pay and prospects for promotion than school-teaching,[7] and the growth of a national rail network made it practicable to find alternative work, especially in the vicinity of northern industrial cities.[8] Not surprisingly the church was exercised to find adequate replacements to make up for these persistent losses. By 1868 the Fulneck Training Institution had been in operation for eight and a half years, during which it had trained six ministers and nine boarding-school teachers from its English applicants, though some had subsequently declined to serve either in the church or in its schools.

Denominational training at Fairfield College, 1875–1958

Provincial leaders were not entirely convinced that Fulneck was the best location and considered moving the Institution to a city or large town closer to a major secular university college such as Bristol or Manchester. As there was no general agreement it was decided to retain it in Fulneck for the time being, and tuition continued there until 1874, when a decision was made to move it to the Fairfield settlement, a few miles east of Manchester. There it would be renamed the College and would make use of the academic facilities at Owens College, Manchester

The move was made in the summer of 1875. The aim was for students to be taught some aspects of natural science[9] as well as arts subjects at a higher level, so that they would make more effective boarding-school teachers and perceptive ministers, being familiar with science and technology as well as traditional subjects. Several northern cities were establishing science colleges at about this time because of widespread concern among industrialists for the future of British industry and commerce in the face of increasing foreign competition, and also as a visible expression of the civic pride of a new industrial and commercial elite: Newcastle College of Physical Science opened in 1871, and both the Yorkshire College of Science, in Leeds, and Firth College, in Sheffield, opened in 1874.[10] Owens College, having been founded in the 1850s, was already well established and prestigious, with a broadly based curriculum which included the sciences, and was more appealing and accessible by the time the Fulneck Training Institution was transferred to Fairfield. The congregation at Fairfield, like its predecessor at Fulneck, could function as a secure home base and also furnish a convenient and instructive example of how a provincial church functioned; all students were encouraged to teach in the Sunday school.

For a few years after 1876, little use was made of the Owens College courses, because entry was conditional on having passed the examinations set by the Matriculation Board of London University, and many Fairfield students had not reached this standard. At that stage, most studied elementary science, mathematics, Latin, Greek and German in their college base, augmented by attendance at Owens College lectures as non-examinees working up to Matriculation standard. Failure to achieve this did not necessarily preclude them from future church service, as the qualifying examinations for the ministry were conducted by the college principal and a representative of the Provincial Board. Nevertheless they still regarded it as desirable that a few very able youths should go to Germany for further education in the Paedagogium and Seminary, that an interchange of teachers between the British and German schools within the Unity should be encouraged, and that, after enlargement, Fairfield College should open to non-Moravian students, though development along these lines was slow and hesitant.

There was progress: a few students were gaining London Matriculation, so that in 1883 a more formal relationship with Owens College (since 1880 elevated to Victoria University) was established, and the period of study was increased from two to three years so that as many as possible could register as full-time undergraduates, with the option of either a science or an arts degree course. After graduation they were encouraged to do some teaching in provincial boarding schools and re-register later for a further two-year course of ministerial or missionary training given by Moravian tutors. Soon rather more than half of the clergy and teachers employed by the British Province had received college training, at either Fulneck or Fairfield. While they were students, some met and eventually married young women from the congregation, there-by assisting in the creation of wholly Moravian ministerial families. A few students preparing for church service expressed a preference for German tuition and transferred to Gnadenfeld. With this in mind the 1883 Synod discussed the desirability or otherwise of educating some British students in Germany. It was generally agreed that, in the past, the province had benefited from such an arrangement, some deputies arguing that British ministers educated in Germany raised the tone of the provincial staff,[11] even if Fairfield College lost some good students by this arrangement; others recommended that a few German students should come to England for training. The President of Synod, Bishop W. Taylor, probably expressed the majority view when he argued that the English college education was essential 'to build up our English type of Moravianism', a significant comment which reveals how far mainstream provincial thinking was moving.

By 1888 most ordinands were taking degrees at Victoria University and then studying theology and Moravian history and practice at Fairfield College. The total number involved at any one time, though small, was sufficient to maintain current staffing levels, although a number of deputies to Synod still argued that a proportion of these graduates should proceed instead to Gnadenfeld for theological training, after which they should return to Britain and teach for a period prior to ordination and congregational appointment. This arrangement, it was believed, would prevent severance of a vital and precious link with the church's continental heritage and maintain a significant German cultural element in the ministry. Others argued that such a decision would threaten the achievement of the British Province in providing its own college, particularly since views on some aspects of church life were different in the two provinces. As a compromise it was agreed that if some students wished to go to Gnadenfeld for their theological training they might be considered, provided that they learned the necessary German, but there is no evidence that more than a small number did so. This continuing debate highlights recurrent ambiguities in the province's sense of identity and reveals the extent to which influential members of the British Province still valued the German heritage. While such strength of feeling for the German connection remained, it was unlikely that the province would ever become completely anglicized.

In the first decade of the twentieth century there was a decline in the number of applicants for admission to Fairfield College. This was particularly unwelcome in view of a temporary shortage of ministers, insufficient men being available to replace older, experienced colleagues on the verge of retirement. To fill the gap, efforts were made to recruit trained clergy from the German and American provinces, but without success.[12] During this decade, also, Victoria University (from 1903 renamed The University of Manchester) founded its own Faculty of Theology, to which ministerial candidates were eligible to apply. This meant that, as well as reading for an arts or science degree, they could take a second degree course in Divinity. Additionally, although the Provincial College Diary is imprecise about the periods involved, Moravian students were sometimes encouraged to study for several months either at the United Free College in Glasgow or at Edinburgh New College, a policy which provided a stimulating social and intellectual contrast to the routine of Manchester University and Fairfield.

The year 1910 was a landmark in the history of the college, with special celebrations marking the fiftieth anniversary of its foundation at Fulneck on 10 October 1860. Lists were published of students who had registered in either Fulneck or Fairfield during this period and had subsequently entered either the home or foreign service of the province.[13] Between 1860 and 1910, 134 men had been registered as students, of whom 60 had subsequently taken up posts in either the schools or the home ministry. A further 27 had gone overseas on missionary service, accounting for 87 of the entire entry. Unfortunately, no fewer than 47 of the 134 had either failed to complete the training course (10), or, having qualified, had resigned from subsequent church service in the ministry (5), the mission field (8) and the schools (24), the last figure illustrating the availability of tempting alternative employment elsewhere. This was a serious loss when set against the considerable cost incurred by the province in providing them with free accommodation and training. Further, of the 27 registered students who had joined missionary congregations overseas, only 12 were English, the other 15 being Germans whose attendance at the college was primarily to learn English. The evident reluctance of British newly ordained ministers to serve in foreign missions, a mere 12 over a period of fifty years, was well known in the province and always noted with regret, although it was counterbalanced to some extent by the increasing proportion of well-qualified Fairfield graduates joining the home ministry, a marked improvement on the academic standard achieved by many of their predecessors in the 1860s and 1870s.

The definitive style of the college had now been established. From around 1910 onwards students who were admitted for training became registered students at Manchester University for three years and read either arts or sciences for a first degree. They then studied theology, Moravian church history, and other Bible-based subjects at Fairfield in preparation for ministerial or mission service, using college facilities and tutors for the most part. After two years they were usually regarded as ready for full-time service and ordination. This style continued throughout the next few decades, apart from a brief interruption in 1916, when the college was closed for the duration of hostilities because all the students had volunteered for military service, a patriotic action which was highly regarded by the church and college authorities.

After 1919, when it reopened, few students applied for places, and in 1924 it was being predicted that, for each of the next few years, only one student per year would graduate.[14] This was considered inadequate, even in the light of the report to the Dublin Provincial Synod of that year that provincial communicant membership was declining, from 3,607 for 1903 to 3,491 for 1923. Moreover, defections of new and expensively trained ministers into other more socially prestigious and better-paid denominations, where they found ready acceptance, was taking away some of the best men[15] and increasing the likelihood of there being insufficient ordained men to maintain the principle of one per congregation.

Br G. Muff (a prominent Moravian layman and Member of Parliament, later Lord Calverley) made a radical and thought-provoking contribution to discussion of this shortfall by asking, 'Need the care of one congregation be a full-time job?'[16] He argued that any two adjacent congregations could easily share one minister if current shortages of trained men made this necessary; indeed shared ministry might become widespread. It was also revealed by the Principal of Fairfield College, in an article in *The Messenger* entitled, 'Something that Concerns Us All', that, although more students entered college from ordinary congregational families than from a ministerial background, more than half of them either failed to complete the course or subsequently defected to another denomination, in contrast to a quarter of those from ministerial families. As a result, the serving ministers were still predominantly sons of the manse.

'A.H.M.' wrote in April 1925 that 11 out of a total of 41 serving ministers were over fifty-five years old; so that the province was facing the prospect of an ageing ministry as well as a dearth of enthusiastic new young ordinands. He pointed out that maintaining a virtually empty college was very expensive in terms of outlay per candidate – there were only three in residence. In August, another contributor, Br H. Hassall, discussed 'The Supply of the Ministry', maintaining that other denominations were experiencing similar problems because potential students for ministerial training, like the population at large, were affected by the spirit of the age and moving away from involvement in organized religion.

Despite these fears and the severe economic depression of the late 1920s and early 1930s,[17] student numbers unexpectedly increased, so that Fairfield College enjoyed a period of stability when ten or more became the norm. In 1932, there was a full complement of twelve students in residence, and again in 1939, when the number included a German and a Dane who were spending a year in Britain to learn the language. This comfortable situation was to change irrevocably when once again the demands of national service took their toll.

During the Second World War admissions virtually ceased, picking up quickly in December 1945, when six men were registered. The small number of students trained during the late 1940s was insufficient to ensure the long-term supply of ministers, and in an article entitled 'Supply of Ministers' in *The Messenger* of September 1947, Br Hassell, the college principal, drew attention to 'a dearth of applicants of high intellectual and moral calibre'. This publicity was the prelude to an intensive recruiting campaign by Br G. W. MacLeavy, directed particularly at the Northern Ireland congregations, but no new candidates had come forward by the end of the year. Seven students were then in residence.

The numbers were maintained for several years, but the situation was not as viable as the numbers alone suggested. The report of the College Advisory Board to Synod in 1950 recorded that the future supply of ministers was still a source of anxiety, even though ten students had been registered for the session 1949–50, two of them students from the North American Province. Their contribution in making the other students and the neighbouring congregations aware of fellowship within the Unity had been greatly appreciated, but inevitably they had returned home. Two of the others had received a premature call, one to Jamaica and another temporarily to Gracehill, and they would not be able to return to college in the next session to complete their training.

The Board reported concern, also, over the financial situation of the college. Before 1946 it had never been self-supporting, and during the inter-war period had been subsidized from provincial and mission funds to the order of about £900 a year. After 1946, special and exceptional post-war government grants to ex-servicemen had temporarily put its finances in credit, but these grants were almost at an end, and once again, in 1950, the college was in deficit. Congregational subscriptions and donations, an important traditional source of revenue, had decreased by 50 per cent since the war, three-quarters of the congregations making no contribution. This meant that the average amount that each congregational member gave directly to the training of the ministry was about twopence-halfpenny a year. When the College Advisory Board next reported to Synod in 1952, the situation was unchanged, with only eleven congregations supporting the college directly and a total contribution of about £30 a year, which represented 1.5 per cent of the cost of maintaining it. The bulk of its income still came from general provincial funds, including mission funds.

By this time the Board was perturbed once again by the lack of candidates, and in these circumstances alternative strategies to meet future ministerial shortages were now being publicly considered. It would soon be impossible to maintain the traditional provision of one full-time minister to every congregation. Realists recommended congregation-sharing, supplemented by the appointment of lay preachers, or 'ministerial assistants', to ease the burden on existing staff, even if this provoked some congregational resistance. Again this prophecy of doom was followed by some slight improvement in student numbers, and by 1954 five students were enrolled, a revival which proved unsustainable because a year later numbers had begun to fall again, to three, then two, and by 1957 it was recognized that the decline was probably terminal, a prediction fulfilled in 1958, when the college was empty and in debt, with no applicants for places. Passionate heart-searching took place, especially among serving and retired ministers, who understandably felt emotionally involved with the fate of this family-size institution; the 1958 Fairfield Synod authorized what was euphemistically styled 'temporary closure', widely interpreted as permanent. In April of the following year, with the situation unchanged, the Provincial Board grimly noted that for the first time in many generations, arguably in the entire history of the college, permanent closure seemed inevitable, a daunting prospect when more than half of serving ministers were over fifty. The finality of closure was confirmed symbolically a few years later when the Church Service Advisory Board reported to Synod the disposal of the college library.[18]

Ministerial training since 1958 in an ecumenical environment

The closure of Fairfield College marked the end of an era in the British Province. For virtually a century sons of ministers and missionaries had been educated in Fulneck School, from which those intending to take up ministerial service had progressed to the Training Institution or, after 1874, to Fairfield College, to be joined there by young laymen drawn from Moravian congregations. A minority of these ordinands had attended Moravian schools and colleges in Germany for part of their education and ministerial training. All these conservative institutions had been influential in sustaining Anglo-German Moravianism among existing ministerial and lay families, thereby generating dynasties with a family tradition of church service, either at home or abroad. Since the number of students had always been small, often ten or fewer, living together with the principal and his wife, the atmosphere and daily practice had always been that of a closely-knit Moravian family with shared interests and objectives. At the same time, continuing awareness of belonging to the whole international Unity had been strengthened by German students coming for a year to learn English, students from the American Province undertaking part of their training at Fairfield, and missionaries paying visits when home on furlough, no doubt with recruitment in mind.

This intimate Moravian collegiate 'family' may have been somewhat introverted simply because it was so small, but it had successfully produced a body of men who remained deeply devoted to traditional Moravianism. Most accepted the principle that the British Province needed to be institutionally independent of the German homeland, yet the eighteenth-century style stemming from Herrnhut was still an enduring influence on their thinking and feeling about the church. Because the number of serving ministers in Britain had never much exceeded forty at any one time, personal relationships based on shared family, school, college and congregational experience generated a closely-knit network, strong in nature and international in range. It is not surprising, therefore, that for these people especially, the closure of Fairfield College was viewed with regret and apprehension, fears being expressed that it would lead to the emergence of a new generation of ministers trained in non-Moravian institutions, with results which could not be predicted.

The worst anxieties of those who surveyed closure with horror were not realized. After what proved to be a temporary interruption in demand for Moravian ministerial training, two applications were received in 1962, followed by a few more later in the decade, although the total numbers involved did not justify reopening the college. Instead, arrangements were made for them to attend colleges of other denominations near their homes, such as St John's (Anglican) College in Nottingham and the Northern (Congregational) College in Manchester. Northern College, whose prevailing ethos still reflected the decidedly middle-class nature of much traditional Congregationalism, had prepared students to degree or certificate level since mid-Victorian times. It provided spacious though austere accommodation as a context for rigorous academic training, reinforced by a requirement that all students must preach in a Congregational church every Sunday during term-time.

As a result, Moravians living in the north who applied for ministerial training in the early 1960s attended Northern College, joining a student body of about 60. Even this, like all the other Nonconformist colleges, was arguably too small to cope with the complexity of theological training. In 1962 the college accepted the first two Moravian students after the barren years (1958–61) when no men came forward for the ministry. Inevitably, during their four years of study, they and their successors experienced the ambiguous and potentially uncomfortable juxtaposition of two different historical traditions, even though they profited greatly from the academic discipline and communal social life. A sense of alienation from their familiar Moravian tradition was fostered unintentionally by the college requirement of regular Sunday preaching in a Congregationalist setting; so that, at the end of their training, the traditions and usages of Congregationalism had become as familiar to them as those of Moravianism. Added to this was the absence of any tutor qualified to advise them on the finer points and complexities of the history and practice of the Moravian Church, a serious but predictable deficiency. In consequence, Moravian students training for the ministry in this or any other non-Moravian denominational institution needed a very strong commitment to Moravianism if they were to maintain their original intention. The extent to which some subsequent defections from the ministry can be ascribed to the pressures experienced in these institutions must always be speculative, but training within a different denominational framework inevitably left students with some conflicting loyalties.

This possibility was recognized by the Provincial Board, who arranged for a compensatory period after college training, when young graduates, before ordination, were appointed as student assistants to a senior

Moravian minister for one or two years. In this role it was hoped they would acquire deeper knowledge of the history and traditions of the church[19] and also participate in day-to-day congregational activity. This arrangement meant that during the 1960s a new type of Moravian minister began to emerge, who was less steeped in Unity traditions than his Fairfield-trained predecessors.

There were a few exceptions to this new pattern of non-Moravian ministerial training. One or two men studied for a year at the Bethlehem Seminary in the USA; one worked for a year on the Labrador Mission, gaining work experience before returning to Northern College to complete his training. These men became familiar with American Moravian-ism, complementing the process by which British society in general was becoming increasingly drawn towards America, and coinciding with the period when the isolation of Eastern Europe prevented normal relation-ships between the British and American provinces on the one hand, and the Unity centre at Herrnhut on the other. Further evidence of this more flexible pattern of training was already evident in 1966, when the Church Service Advisory Board commented to Synod on the gradual emergence of a group of older and more experienced congregational members who had come from other employment to be trained for church service. Though few in number, they were being engaged actively in the congre-gations as Lay Pastors, while at the same time receiving theological train-ing, though not at that stage necessarily being considered for ordination.

The ecumenical, as opposed to the traditional Anglo-German, outlook which Moravian ministerial students were now experiencing became even more characteristic of tuition in Northern College during the 1970s after it transferred from its original base at Whalley Range, Moss-Side, Manchester, to Rusholme in the same city. There, in Luther King House, and in premises owned by the Baptist Church, the student body was a mixture drawn from seven different British denominations – Congrega-tionalists, URC (after 1972), Unitarians, Baptists, Methodists, Angli-cans, and one or two Moravians.

This arrangement became the norm, with groups of students of differ-ent denominations being taken together through a non-denominational and overtly ecumenical three- or four-year course. Though perhaps becoming progressively less academically rigorous, it became much wider in scope and more suited to the perceived managerial and pastoral needs of contemporary congregations. Students tended to be older men and women, now augmented by graduates preparing for a second career; so that the average age of the student body was about thirty-five.

Moravian students were, of course, a tiny minority, isolated in denominational specifics from the main thrust of the teaching, which remained mostly in the hands of URC men, who still could not offer distinctively Moravian scholarship. As a result, by the end of the twentieth century, many ministers entering the Moravian Church were well equipped to make the difficult decisions necessary to take the British Province forward towards the beginning of the twenty-first century when further amalgamations with other denominations might become inevitable.

The report of the Church Service Advisory Board to the 1992 Ockbrook Synod restated current policy regarding ministerial training and in particular the church's relationship with Northern College: 'It has been the policy to maintain the long-standing tradition of training in the Manchester area, whilst at the same time making use of facilities in other parts of the country where it is appropriate.' The report included an appreciation of the role of lay preachers in congregational life, and ended with a comment on changes in ministry which summarized the current situation:

> The future of the ministry is inextricably bound up with the future of the Church. Synod will hardly need reminding of the significant changes that have taken place in the shape of ministry over the past forty years: the emergence of the mature student as the norm rather than the exception, the fuller share taken by sisters in the work of ministry, the growth of the non-maintained sector.

Two years later, the report of the Board to the 1994 Salem, Oldham Synod commented frankly on some of the problems inherent in the training of ministers in a non-denominational college, and outlined the practical steps being taken to minimize their effect.

> We are conscious of the isolation felt by our students in establishments belonging to other denominations, and have attempted to offer the necessary support through an Advisor, through the fellowship of a local Moravian congregation and by bringing them together with the probationary ministers, at annual conferences where personal and theological concerns can be shared and dealt with. . . . It is the policy of the Board only to recommend acceptance of applicants of the highest calibre, whether for the maintained or non-maintained sectors, and to tailor training arrangements to the individual requirements of each. Some thought has been given to the criteria employed in the recruitment of non-maintained ministers and to the wider opportunities open to this form of ministry.

This report also gave evidence of recent opportunities for closer co-operation with and representation of the church within the decision-making structure of both Northern College and the Manchester Christian Institute at which some non-maintained ministers had been trained. This would enable Moravian recommendations to be included in discussion of matters which affected their students.

The Bristol Mission College 1904–1926

The few prospective missionaries who came forward from the province before 1904 were trained either in the Fulneck Training Institution or at Fairfield College. On 7 April of that year, what proved to be a short-lived Mission College was established at 10 Beaufort Road, Clifton, Bristol, in a large private house, the lease of which was made possible by a gift of £5,000 from Br J. Purser, a member of the Dublin congregation. He believed that the British Province needed a separate establishment for this purpose, open to applicants from Moravian and other denominations. The college provided both teaching and residential facilities for the principal, Revd A. J. Heath, an experienced missionary, his wife, responsible for domestic arrangements, and the students, three being registered in 1904, thereby establishing a pattern which was retained throughout the entire history of the college. Bristol was chosen because no suitable accommodation appeared to be available in any of the provincial settlements, and the excellent medical school of Bristol University was easily accessible to students who aspired to be professionally qualified medical missionaries.

The college course, which originally took three years to complete, was extended to four in the early 1920s. Within this framework there was considerable flexibility. Some students studied for one of the three years at the Glasgow Bible Training Institution, which was not a missionary college, but a centre for the 'firing of evangelists'.[20] After completing the Bristol course, some students completed their training at Livingstone College,[21] an Anglican missionary college at Leyton in London. This institution dating from 1901, a foundation of the Society for the Propagation of the Gospel, trained both men and women for missionary service in Africa. Among other subjects they studied elementary medicine, in order to equip them to work as pioneers in remote tropical areas, teaching them how to look after themselves and give the population basic medical advice, a course of training deemed necessary for most Moravian non-medical missionaries. In addition, and provided at Bristol, were courses in First Aid, Book-keeping, Building, Carpentry, Hygiene,

Elocution, and Teaching Methods, to prepare students for the practical problems likely to arise amongst what were regarded as half-civilized societies. This essential preparation for the more mundane requirements of mission life was a subordinate part of the Bristol syllabus, taking up about a third of it, the rest being along conventional academic lines, including Biblical Studies, Christian Doctrine, English, History, Geography, Greek (studied at Bristol Baptist College), and the History of Moravian Missions,[22] to further the overall aim of sending educated men overseas, not merely technicians. It was expected that these men would act on the college dictum, backed by the accumulated wisdom of all denominations, that patient pastoral labour was the basis of ultimate success on the mission field.[23]

A year after the college's successful inauguration, when six students registered, it was expected that at least this number might become the norm, which would necessitate larger premises. It was decided, therefore, to make further use of the Purser gift by buying a larger detached house in Cotham Road, where the staff and students took up residence in May 1907, after which the college remained in this location until 7 October 1926, when it was amalgamated with Fairfield College, and the Cotham Road premises sold two years later.

During its 22-year existence, Br Heath supervised and arranged for the further training of 39 registered students, 22 of whom were Moravians, 13 non-Moravians, and 4 were foreign students of unspecified denomination. Although many entrants completed their courses to an acceptable standard, 15, having failed to satisfy the tutor, withdrew from mission training. There is no evidence, however, that any who qualified at Bristol and began mission service abroad decided later to resign on other than health grounds.[24] The minutes of the College Board show that in 1925, within a year of amalgamation, 5 Moravians and 8 non-Moravians who had trained in Bristol were still in active service; 7 more resident students were currently undergoing training, indicating that, shortly before the end of its independent existence, the student body was still as large as it had been during the first few years, even if in the interval the numbers had varied considerably.

Evidence from the minutes of the Joint College Advisory Board, 1911–50, shows that, unlike the majority of students at Fairfield, the educational background and innate ability of Mission College students, most of whom came from the laity, varied widely. A few, who had been well educated prior to entry, had studied to degree level at the Medical School of Bristol University. After graduation they had taken the mission course, living throughout their training at Cotham Road for a variable period of up to eight years. At the other end of the educational scale there were examples of men with modest educational qualifications who, having completed elementary school training, followed by study in evening classes after work and experience with youth organizations, had successfully completed Methodist Local Preachers' examinations, but had been unable to compete successfully for a place in the Methodist colleges because of the high standard required of all candidates for the Methodist ministry. It is not surprising that some of the latter, no matter how conscientious, soon realized that they could not cope with the course, and abandoned the idea of working overseas as missionaries. It was in this respect that the contrast with Fairfield was so marked: there, by 1904, many students had passed London Matriculation on or shortly after entry, and by the 1920s it had become the norm; so that they were registered for degree courses in either arts or sciences at Manchester University.

Throughout the whole period, 1904–26, the attitude of the provincial authorities to the two colleges and their attitude to each other were at best ambiguous, because the College Board was never in agreement about the need for two separate establishments. On accommodation grounds the house in Cotham Road could only provide 8 study-bedrooms, whereas Fairfield could provide 14, with some unused space in the attics which could be converted if necessary. Since the maximum number of students in Fairfield at any one time had been 12, it could easily provide for the mission students, as it had done from 1860. On the other hand, although it was undeniable that the opening of the Mission College had incurred more expense, very few English Moravians educated at Fairfield had taken up mission work in the pre-Mission College era, a mere 12 between 1860 and 1910. With the opening of the Mission College, where admission of non-Moravians was possible and acceptable, there had been a notable increase in English student applications, leading to the deployment over a 22-year period of 23 qualified missionaries, a marked improvement on the rate between 1860 and 1910, and at the time of amalgamation applications were not falling off.

Even the location of the two colleges had been a source of recurrent disagreement from as early as 1912. Although acceding in principle to the wishes of the Purser family that a Mission College be a separate institution, the 1912 Synod ordered the College Board to report on the desirability or otherwise of retaining Fairfield College in its present form, and to explore options for amalgamation. It had been suggested that the undergraduates might instead be educated at Bristol University and housed in that city in a Moravian hostel.[25] After graduation they could return to Fairfield for ministerial training. A year later some College Board members contemplated amalgamating the two colleges at Fairfield to restore the pre-1904 state of affairs; others doubted whether this would work because of the different aims, atmosphere, style of living and intellectual standing of the student bodies in the two institutions.[26]

Despite all the uncertainty about the most effective and financially prudent method of running two separate establishments, the training of teachers, ministers and missionaries using Fairfield and Bristol continued until 1926. Then, at last, Synod decided that the entire student body would be best served by learning and living together at Fairfield College, an arrangement which was retained without any major alterations until 1958, since when no special provision has been made for missionary training.

At the beginning of the twenty-first century, therefore, Moravian ministerial training in the British Province is being adapted to the contemporary situation, as the province faces the reality of dwindling numbers and the eventual likelihood of more amalgamations with other denominations. One very significant feature of the present system of ministerial training is that it is producing men and women for the ministry who have a deep regard for the church's history and tradition, combined with a realistic approach to its future needs and prospects.

The Ministry (II)
Non-Stipendiary Ministers, and the
Ministry of Women

Emergence of a non-stipendiary ministry

The need for a creative approach to ministry

When, in 1951, Lord Calverley and others argued that the principle of a full-time minister for every congregation was in danger of becoming untenable, reiterating a point of view which had been raised from time to time since the 1912 Synod, they recommended filling the gaps by recruiting and training lay preachers and others to share the administrative burden carried by serving ministers. The subject was debated with an increasing sense of urgency during the 1950s, because it seemed clear that a crisis was approaching, but no action took place, even when there were no longer any students at Fairfield College and none in prospect. Towards the end of the decade a leading article in *The Messenger* of September 1958 lamented, 'Never has the British Province been in a grimmer situation. Our liquid assets have gone. The College is to be closed temporarily for lack of suitable candidates. There is neither men nor money for extension . . . hard facts have to be faced.'[1]

One minister who faced them was Norman Driver, in a May 1961 article entitled, 'Looking Forward to Synod'. He emphasized the need for occasional congregation-sharing as a temporary palliative to avoid congregational closure, and proposed that the province should establish a permanent part-time, non-stipendiary ministry. This would consist of ordained men who would take charge of a congregation while continuing in full-time secular employment, an idea which was by no means new, having first emerged in the Anglican Church in the mid-nineteenth century. The 1961 Synod did not take up his proposal, but explored an alternative arrangement whereby full-time ministers could be allocated to districts in a team ministry, visiting congregations in rotation on the basis of a plan similar to that of the Methodists, assisted by lay stewards 'in charge' of each congregation for routine day-to-day matters. It was thought that this might prevent congregation-sharing and closure where there were too few ministers in the teams to base one man permanently in each manse. This scheme was abandoned after prolonged discussion of its implications; but clearly, the growing crisis in ministerial supply had to be faced and a radical change of policy adopted. Further exchanges of ideas took place during the mid-1960s, and in July 1968 the Provincial Board announced publicly in *The Messenger* that, because of continuing concern about the future supply of ministers, some new form of auxiliary ministry was now being considered.

Discussion of this idea was not confined to the Moravian Church, though because of the small numbers involved it may have appeared disproportionately so to its leaders. The Church of England was finding that the continuance of what for centuries had been regarded as a sacred office and a full-time salaried occupation serving the whole country was being threatened by a continuing decline in the number of candidates for ordination.[2] In 1970 the church broke with tradition by taking the principle of a non-stipendiary ministry into its official institutional structure.[3] From that date bishops were authorized to ordain and licence deacons and priests who would continue to live in their own houses and follow secular occupations in addition to their ministerial duties. It was acknowledged that such a ministry was needed in order to maintain the parochial system where its existence was threatened by shortages of full-time clergy. It was motivated not by any theological principle, but by the need to fill gaps in staffing.

Statistics for the Church of England non-stipendiary ministry and the nature of its participants provide a useful comparative perspective from which to review subsequent Moravian experience, which was broadly similar. The first ordinations of Anglican non-stipendiary ministers took place in 1972, when 12 were ordained, and from then to 1986 around 1,437 men and 150 women joined this ministry. Most candidates were from the teaching and other professions, managers, administrators and other non-manual groups, thus corresponding to the social categories of the male membership of the Church of England. Annually, they represented 10 per cent of all ordinations in 1975, 20 per cent in 1976, and thereafter regularly about 25 per cent.[4] Between 1971 and 1981 about 10 per cent transferred to the stipendiary ministry after variable periods of service in a non-stipendiary role. The ages of ordination during the same period show that the vocation appealed mostly to those of mature years, being respectively: under 40 years, 19.4 per cent; 40–59 years, 62.1 per cent; and 60 years and over, 18.5 per cent. From the beginning, the Church of England insisted that non-stipendiary ministers must reach the academic standard of the General Ministerial Examination necessary for candidates for the full-time ministry, which may have inhibited many less well educated candidates from applying.

The establishment of a non-stipendiary ministry in the British Province

The example and subsequent experience of the Anglicans and others provided a stimulus to the Moravians to adopt this solution to their own problem. In 1972, the Church Service Advisory Board report to Synod presented a detailed recommendation of the idea of supplementary ministries:

> Many denominations have introduced this kind of Ministry in recent years, and we feel that this matter should be considered by our Church too. By 'supplementary ministry' we mean ordaining for part-time service in the Church, brethren and sisters who would not expect to come into regular Church service. . . .This unpaid, part-time ministry might appeal to those already in full-time occupations or professions who would do Church work alongside their daily occupation. . . . Secondly, brethren or sisters retiring comparatively early would undertake a similar service to the Church, and who by their former training and experience would be well equipped for part-time ordained service.

Synod accepted this proposition as one of the measures under the heading, 'Steps towards Renewal',[5] namely, 'Strengthening the number of leaders by instituting a suitable course of training and making opportunities of service known, for members willing to accept a call to ordination and appointment as unpaid part-time ministers.' They would then assist full-time ministers within a district or take charge of a nearby congregation, and if necessary undertake a course of training outside the college system. The wording of the resolution indicates that the proposal was perceived as a cohesive measure, extending the involvement of congregational members in spiritual leadership, while alleviating the problem of ministerial shortage.

The policy was quickly implemented: Michael Rea, a professional engineer, became the first non-stipendiary minister, being ordained as a deacon at Ockbrook on 1 December 1974 and subsequently called to

Priors Marston. On 15 January 1975, Dorothy Moreton was ordained at Fulneck, setting the seal on the church's recognition of her many years' service as a medical missionary in Tanzania, as well as giving her the opportunity to serve the congregation at Leominster. From then onwards a succession of other Moravian lay men and women were ordained as non-stipendiary ministers and called to congregational service: Marjorie Grubb in January 1979, to serve Woodford Halse and Eydon; Kenneth Evans, February 1985, Heckmondwike; Robelto Bruce, 1984, London District; Clarissa Johnson, June 1989, Hornsey; and Beth Torkington, July 1989, Wheeler Street.

As in the parallel case of the Church of England, it was felt necessary to ensure that the establishment of non-stipendiary ministers did not threaten the academic standard associated with ministerial training. In 1974 the Church Service Advisory Board's Report to Synod noted that non-stipendiary ordination should not be made too easy and should be conditional upon the completion or continuance of a definite course of study. In 1976 the Board reported: 'The Supplementary Ministry is now an established and valued part of our work,' yet it also pointed to the difficulty of providing suitable training, as each case was different, and ready-made courses were not easily available. It is a measure of the chronic understaffing of the congregational network that, by the early 1990s, these seven ordained men and women constituted a quarter of the total serving staff, a proportion similar to that in the Church of England recorded above.

Again like the Anglicans, it took time for congregations to accept that those in this ministry were just as much priests as those in the full-time ordained ministry, and the view that non-stipendiary ministry was a second-class institution had adherents in the early years.[6] Traditionalists still hankered after one full-timer per congregation, leading to a response in a November 1991 *Messenger* article by a member of the Provincial Board, who recalled that, although it was sixteen years since Michael Rea, the first non-stipendiary minister, was appointed, 'there still seems to be some uncertainty within the Province about the nature and purpose of this sector of the ministry'.[7] He then vigorously defended the principle of extending the ministerial base in this way, by emphasizing the exceptional degree of commitment involved for a congregational member in full- or part-time employment to submit voluntarily to a course of rigorous training, outside working hours, in preparation for prolonged periods of ministerial work during week-nights and weekends. He reminded critics of the existence of considerable numbers of non-stipendiary ministers in other denominations. He did not quote examples, because the position in the Anglican Church was well known. Further statistics were given in a report by a Moravian delegate at the General Assembly of the United Reformed Church in July 1995. He wrote in *The Messenger*[8] that one-fifth of the ordained ministry in the URC, 200 from a total of 1,000, were non-stipendiaries. Further, this body of ordained men and women were caring for 1,800 congregations, an arrangement necessitating frequent doubling-up of adjacent congregations under one minister. Because of current trends in society which were leading to a shortage of applicants for full-time ministry, the tradition of one congregational base for one full-time minister, though theoretically still desirable, was of necessity gradually being abandoned.

Published accounts of the Anglican experience in the 1970s and early 1980s suggest that the relationship of non-stipendiary ministers with colleagues was sometimes uneasy; in the church they sometimes felt themselves to be 'second-class priests'.[9] The position of the Moravians was better in that each one was usually in full charge of a congregation. By the late 1990s, it was evident that serving non-stipendiary ministers in general, including the Moravians, were being given the opportunity to create a new sense of group identity within the more conventional ministerial structure, confident in the assurance that their numbers would increase rather than diminish. They and their families were usually well known locally, since by the terms of their engagement they were not called to live elsewhere after ordination, unless they particularly requested it. Their ministry, therefore, had a degree of stability and permanence not usual among their full-time ordained colleagues, and because they were volunteers their status was enhanced. The familiar and tactless concept that an ordained minister was paid to serve no longer applied; inescapably, the non-stipendiary minister was recognized as undertaking a labour of love. He or she was seen as being 'in the world', and thereby more experienced in facing the problems and tensions between Christian commitment and secular working life than a full-time serving minister, no matter how perceptive. The hope was that the non-stipendiary minister was also recognized as such among those with whom he worked during business hours, providing potential opportunities for extended service among them. In practice, the experience of non-stipendiary ministers in the workplace and even in the church was more ambivalent than might have been expected, particularly until the principle became established.

By the end of the century the Moravian Church was becoming increasingly appreciative of the unique contribution which these men and women could bring to its ministry. It was realized that the body of expertise gradually being gathered by the seven non-stipendiaries in the province could well be amalgamated to design a training course specifically for this type of ministry, as well as encouraging young people to consider such an option much earlier. If that could be achieved, the non-stipendiary ministry would no longer be regarded as suitable primarily for those already well established in their secular careers. Such a prospect demonstrates the commitment of the church to this flexible and realistic system of ensuring the continuity of ministry, and is a tribute to the success and dedication of those who have responded to the call.

The ministry of women

It was traditional practice in the Roman Catholic and Protestant Churches, that the ordained ministry was composed entirely of men, the pre-Reformation bodies insisting also on their celibacy. In contrast, Unity-ordained men, like those of the German Lutheran Church from which it arose, had been free to marry and positively encouraged to do so. Much of the work of ministerial staff at home and abroad was regarded as a partnership between a married couple whose distinctive and subtly different skills contributed essential elements to the religious societies, mission stations and settled congregations which they were called to serve. Nevertheless, though it was policy that a male missionary should be married to ensure that heathen women could find a congenial confidante, only the men were ordained as Labourers.[10]

The role of women in the eighteenth-century Unity

From the early days of the Renewed Unity, wives were sometimes required to work independently on the periphery of Unity activity. There is a fascinating example of this in the memoir of the ordained Labourer Philip Heinrich Molther.[11] He was nominated by Zinzendorf to work in America, and in preparation for this he went first to Herrnhut and finally to Marienborn,

> where everything relative to my future plan was settled and I was married to Johann [*sic*] von Seydewir [*sic*] on 5 September [i.e. 1739].
> . . . As circumstances required my setting out without her, it was resolved she should follow me with the next company that was to go to America.

Molther went to London, expecting to cross the Atlantic in January. An accidental fall prevented this and in March 1740 he was informed that because of the delay he was to remain in London. Further illness intervened and he was still in England when his wife came to London in August on her way to America. Molther continues:

> It was left to me to let her proceed or keep her with me; but being convinced in my heart that it was the will of our Lord that she should go thither, and finding her willing to go, I accompanied her on board where we prostrated in prayer before our Saviour and covenanted with each other to be and remain his, after which we took an affectionate leave.

Molther himself was recalled to Marienborn in September and then sent to France. It was three years before he and his wife were reunited to work together.

> In April 1743 I returned to Marienborn where I found my wife who had arrived from America a few days before me. I received her as if she was given me quite anew by our Saviour. After some time we travelled together to the Synod which was held at Hirschberg. There we were appointed to visit the awakened souls in Switzerland.

In the early days of the Brethren's work in Britain, the work of the wives of German leaders was recorded routinely by the diarists. Fetter Lane saw the participation of a number of prominent women in the routine work of the congregation and its outlying societies, where they shared the task of spreading the German philosophy and worked alongside English Labourers. The diary for 9 August 1743 records a 'Widdows' Love Feast' at which Sister Spangenberg 'spoke exceeding sweet to them and Mrs Beadle was Inducted into the Office of Warden of the Widdows'. Though not in charge of the induction service, Sr Spangenberg, as wife of one of the leading Germans ministering in England, had a prominent teaching role in the organization.

The task of supporting the ministry, shared with German women by the wives of prominent English Labourers such as Sr Holland, was not easy: it demanded tact as well as concern for the spiritual welfare of women members, who were sometimes critical. An unusually frank record in an account of a routine meeting for spiritual and general oversight of the women of the Fetter Lane congregation describes a minor altercation involving the wife of Schlicht. It illustrates the outspokenness with which women in the congregation were prepared to question their leaders' actions, and the difficulty of imposing the Brethren's standards on some English members, even those who had been privileged to visit the continental settlements.

> Friday Augt 19th 1743.
> Sr Holland and Claggett spoke with the married Women and was very much pleased with them. Sr. Schlicht spoke to the Single Women. Mary Bowers told her that she had been very much displeased at her at Herrnhaag, because she would not lend her a guinea to buy some cloath. Mrs Ewsters spoke very hard to Sr Schlicht.

There is evidence that wives of Germans who were serving in Britain, in effect as Unity missionaries, took a prominent part in the sacrament, beyond that which would have been permitted in the Anglican Church. On Sunday, 1 January 1750 it is recorded that,

> Br. Boehler . . . consecrated the blessed Vehicles, both of the Body and the Blood of our Saviour by chanting the very Words of Institution. Then he and Sister Boehler dispensed to the Sisters, and Br Gambold and Br Latrobe to the Bn.[12]

Such participation by the wives of ministerial Labourers was probably regular practice: an account of a sacrament held at Fulneck on 26 January 1755 records that the elements were administered to the Sisters by Br and Sr Hauptmann.[13]

The role of women as Choir House Labourers

The leadership of British women as Labourers was always regarded as extremely important. As soon as possible they took charge of daily routine alongside the Germans, fulfilling a vital administrative and pastoral role in the Single Sisters' and Widows' Choir Houses and among the women generally. The Fetter Lane diary records the service of some of these women. In August 1743 Hannah Westerman left the Yorkshire congregation to serve at Lamb's Inn. On 23 September 1743, 'Molly Bower gave a Love Feast to a Children's Band.' In January 1749 Anne Odle died of smallpox on a visit to London from Bedford. She had joined the Brethren in 1744, aged thirty, and 'had been a Labourer among the Single Sisters there since the beginning of their Oeconomy'.

It is invidious to isolate the role of women as administrators and organizers of the work of these eighteenth-century oeconomies from

their pastoral duties. Part of the Choir Labourers' responsibility was to
ensure that the women under their care had employment which suited
them and enabled them to maintain themselves financially, and the
women were expected to accept their judgement.[14] Some responsible
women were nominated to negotiate suitable markets for the products of
the sisters' oeconomies, travelling where necessary to deliver the fine
needlework and other handicrafts for which the settlements soon gained
a high reputation; but leading women were responsible, also, for the
welfare of the sisters in their charge. They supervised the spiritual lives of
choir members, and travelled between the Place Congregations where
they were based and their associated societies, to encourage or admonish
the women and ensure that the high spiritual tone and sense of commitment were maintained throughout the whole locality.

In the early years German Labourers were usually firmly in charge of
the newly established Choir Houses, and their leadership continued for
some years. Sr Mary Cathrine Vogelsang was in positions of responsibility in the Single Sisters' Choir at Grace Hall (Fulneck) between 1752
and 1765, and her memoir remains in the archive at Gracehill, in
Northern Ireland, where she died.[15] It provides a profile of one lay
woman from an artisan family, who was groomed by the Zinzendorf
family for a position of authority and responsibility in the British
Province.

She was born at Lidon in the island of Rügen in 1719, and by the age
of twelve was living uneasily with her widowed mother, who 'put me to
good pious people to learn to weave'. Having stayed with them for four
years she returned to her mother's house and set up in business working
from home as a weaver. Here she had her first contact with two brethren
from Herrnhut who 'called at our house on their journey', but it was not
until two other brethren were sent to work in the neighbourhood that she
was converted and recommended to visit one of the congregations. In
1742 she journeyed to Herrnhaag, accompanied by 'Br Shickt' [sic], and
in September settled into the Single Sisters' House. 'Here a quite a new
period of grace began with me. The Holy Ghost discovered to me my
hidden corruption,' and on 5 January 1743 she was received into the congregation. Later that year it was proposed that she should marry and go
to Pennsylvania, but her life took a different direction.

> Our dear Savr. showed me daily my poverty and necessity and granted
> me a true confidence to cleave closely to his blood, merit and passion;
> and from this time it was first right weighty with me to be a Single
> Sister and to enjoy my Choir-Grace.

In the same year I came into the wash-kitchen of the Orphan-House, and had the pleasure to become acquainted with the late Countess de Zinzendorf, who proved a real and abiding blessing to my heart. In general this period was particularly blessed to me, and I felt so extremely thankful and blessed in the Mother's lap, that I wished for nothing else but to die in the nest, where I would daily keep Sabbath, and had to converse with no-one except with my faithful Friend.

On 27 October 1744 she partook of the Lord's Supper and was confirmed as a Single Sister. She remained there until Herrnhaag was vacated, moving in October 1748 to Holland, where she lived in the Pilgrim-House and was 'taken among the intercessors', and again in January with Zinzendorf's Pilgrim Congregation to London. For the next eighteen months she worked in the linen-room in the Count's house in Bloomsbury Square, was sent to Fulneck for a short time as Sr Anna Mary Archer's assistant while the Count's household was in Germany, but in 1752 she moved to Fulneck as the Interim-Labourer of the Single Sisters' Choir and later took charge. In May 1756 she was called to Herrnhut to attend the Synod, at the close of which she was 'blest Deaconess' and returned to Fulneck on 18 December. She worked in Fulneck until May 1765, when she was called to Ireland as Choir Helper to the Single Sisters at Gracehill, where a Choir House was being built, and remained there until her death on 16 December 1787.

This profile gives a significant insight into the kind of women who worked in positions of responsibility in the years of enthusiastic expansion. Like many of her male counterparts she was an artisan by training. Obviously a woman of initiative and devout inclination, she left her home area and travelled a considerable distance to experience life in one of the Brethren's congregations, a form of service which suited her well. Her response to the discipline of Herrnhaag is an excellent illustration of the system and its effect on those who embraced it. There was some flexibility, enabling women to reflect before accepting a call to marriage, and her decision to become a Single Sister resembled that of taking the veil in a nunnery. She went by prayerful stages to a final confirmation of her vow by acceptance to the Lord's Supper, and settled to a sheltered life, wishing for nothing more than to remain 'in the nest', practising devotion to the Saviour and serving the community by her work.

Her call to the work of a Labourer shows how important it was to Zinzendorf that those who were placed in authority over the women in Choir Houses and congregations should have approved experience. Being known personally to Zinzendorf's wife through her work in the linen-room, she was chosen to remain close to the family and continue the same work when the Pilgrim Congregation, Zinzendorf's personal entourage, moved to London; so that by the time an assistant Labourer was required in Yorkshire, first temporarily and then on a permanent basis, she was well schooled in appropriate disciplines and thinking. A woman with the right spiritual training and mentality became leader of the Single Sisters in the newly established British settlement. This is made abundantly clear by the supplement to her personal memoir written by the Labourer at Gracehill in 1787, after her death:

> The opportunity she had had in former years of being so much about the late Disciple not only proved an extraordinary Blessing to her own Heart but a School in which she profited greatly, in imbibing those Principles our Saviour had given him relating to the Congregation and her Choirs and the leading the same that they came like a second nature to her.

Such comparatively rare insights from memoirs which remain in the archives confirm that appropriate spiritual qualities were of greater importance than formal training, at least for Labourers in the women's institutions. The influence of Sister Mary Vogelsang at Fulneck is explored further in Chapter 12.

Women in charge of others in the settlements had more responsibility than merely to maintain good order and ensure the smooth running of communal life. The House Orders of the Fulneck Single Sisters' Choir House (1783)[16] show that officially appointed room-overseers and their assistants were responsible to the Choir House Labourer for the mutual consideration essential to communal living. Both were expected to maintain 'the spirit of love and peace, so that all the company for whom they are responsible may shine in this respect as examples to the other sisters and induce the rest of the sisters to follow them'. This was a pastoral role equivalent to that of their male counterparts.

Evidence from the eighteenth-century records, therefore, shows that women had a positive role in Unity institutions. Those who were appointed as Labourers in the Choir Houses were key figures in the organization, since these establishments trained and provided wives for men called to service at home or overseas; in fact neither men nor women were allowed to marry outside the Brotherhood and remain members of it. Between 1752 and 1786 115 sisters married out of the Single Sisters' Choir House at Fulneck,[17] and all of these would be approved marriages. The statistics give no details of why people went elsewhere; many sisters who moved from Fulneck to other congregations remained in Britain, but three went to Holland, six to Germany and five to America. It is reasonable to assume that, though some remained single, a high proportion of these women married into the service of their Saviour in Britain or abroad as working partners to dedicated brethren. In this way, women who became Labourers in the Place Congregations, being disciplined in Unity thinking, ensured that the training of others who were to work alongside the men was appropriate to their supportive spiritual role, and in the first decades of the mission to the British Province, like Sr Mary Vogelsang, they were mostly Germans.

Conservatism in a denominational organization

In the early years the role of leading women in Unity affairs was more active and responsible than was common in Established churches. Women shared in leading the ritual observances of the various congregations and societies to which they belonged, with opportunities consistent with Zinzendorf's philosophy. He came from a family tradition in which wealthy women of strong character were active in decision-making at the highest level, and he was prepared to accord considerable status and authority to the wives of his leading colleagues. Partly, also, Unity perception of what was appropriate to women's religious activities reflected the enthusiasm of the Evangelical Revival. When the early evangelists set up networks of house groups, converted women were central to their structure and spiritual success, becoming conspicuous as pioneers in the establishment and expansion of Methodism.[18]

Public attitudes to women in church service have usually reflected the conventions of the current generation. The report entitled *Religious Worship in England and Wales*, by Horace Mann, submitted to the Registrar-General as part of the 1851 Census of Great Britain[19] described the Moravian Church administration with an air of surprise and a hint of disapproval:

> The chief direction of the affairs of the church is committed to a board of elders, appointed by the general synods, which assemble at irregular intervals varying from seven to twelve years. Of these boards, one is universal and the others local, the former being resident at Herrnhut, and maintaining a general supervision over every part of the society – the latter being specially connected with particular congregations. Bishops, beyond their power of ordination, have no authority except

what they derive from these boards . . . There are *female* elders, who attend at the boards; but they do not vote.

The italicizing indicates just how remarkable Mann found this inclusion of women at a high administrative level. It is obvious that they had as respected a place within the Unity organization as contemporary assumptions and practice would allow, and at least their views were likely to have been heard officially and taken into account, since there is no suggestion that they were mere observers.

As provincial congregations of the late eighteenth and early nineteenth centuries gave way to pressures towards denominationalism, so the role of women within the church gradually conformed to stereotypes common to Anglican and Nonconformist denominations, the minister's wife practising the vital supportive pastoral, organizational and social skills expected of her. Only on the mission fields could a woman expect to be a spiritual leader in her own right, and by the late nineteenth century women were becoming increasingly numerous in overseas missions run by all the British Protestant denominations. The Anglican Church Missionary Society, the interdenominational China Inland Mission, and the Congregational London Missionary Society, for example, were all employing women, often on a fairly large scale. Between 1891 and 1900 the Church Missionary Society alone recorded that 54 per cent of its new intake of mission staff were women.[20] Outside these areas of service, women had little opportunity to take a leading part in ministering to the needs of congregations. Several women who enquired about entry to the Bristol Mission College[21] were passed on to the Anglican Livingstone College which trained both men and women for medical missionary work in Africa, it being contended that their natural skills were most suitably employed in nursing, for which an academic theological training was inappropriate. Some well-known women with professional skills who went out as missionaries alongside male colleagues lost their salaries when they married, but were still expected to fulfil their former role.

The ordination of women

Despite their continuing involvement in the mission field, and genuine recognition by the church of the skills of women and their contribution to church service, ordination in the British Province, as in other major Christian denominations in Britain, remained restricted to men until the twentieth century. There were signs at the beginning of the century that a change was imminent, when the pioneers of a radical new approach to ministerial appointment emerged, arguing that women, too, should be ordained. Leading spokesmen were members of the old Dissenting denominations, who had a well-established reputation for challenging traditional ideas and practices. The Unitarians were the first to ordain women, by 'inducting' the German aristocrat, Gertrud von Petzold, to the ministry of Narborough Road Free Christian Church, Leicester, in 1904. The Congregational and Baptist Churches followed the lead of the Unitarians in 1917 and 1918 respectively and, although the number of women involved in each denomination was very small, the principle that women had a role in the ordained ministry was accepted.[22]

An early intimation of a change of policy by the Moravian Church came during the Second World War, in a resolution at the 1944 Synod which recognized the place and value of the ministry of women and welcomed the appointment of a woman assistant to the minister at Dukinfield.[23] It requested District Conferences to consider in principle the acceptance of suitable women candidates for the ministry and report to the Provincial Board with a view to the matter being placed on the Agenda of the next Synod. The Report of the Board to Synod in June 1945 on Women in Church Service revealed very clearly how controversial was the whole question of the role of women in the church and how divided the membership on the issue.

> The Reports sent to us on this subject preclude the framing of any proposal that might be expected to command general assent. It is clear that there is a great divergence of opinion on the question of an ordained ministry of women; less difference on the value of the service they may render in special work; and virtual agreement on the need of special training if they are so employed. It might perhaps be said that while most members would recognise the full spiritual qualification of women for ministerial service, there is a general feeling that the practical difficulties would prevent any more than the occasional exceptional use of such service.
>
> We should, however, state that whatever openings may be denied to women at home, there is a growing demand for women in the Mission Field, as doctors, teachers, social workers, and deaconesses. It may be that the ministry of women will at present be most profitably exercised in some such way.

This cautious approach could not last; the Continental Province took the lead, and both the 1953 and 1957 Unity Synods at Herrnhut declared that, in principle, the ordination of women was not only permissible, but desirable as a great service to the church.[24] By 1968 there was already one ordained woman serving in the Herrnhut District.

Two years later, impelled to some extent by this precedent, but also by a critical shortage of men and irreversible changes in secular society regarding the role of women, the British Province moved in the same direction. A motion before the Ockbrook Synod in July 1970 proposed that Synod recommend the acceptance of women for the full-time, paid, ordained ministry of the British Province. It called upon the Church Service Advisory Board (CSAB) to implement the resolution by accepting suitable women as candidates and, without recorded evidence of dissension, the proposal was adopted. As a result, Sr Emily Shaw, Warden of Fulneck Choir Houses, wrote to offer herself for ordination, and the Provincial Board referred her application to the CSAB.[25] On 28 October 1970, therefore, Bishop J. Foy ordained her at Fulneck, where she had already served as a lay preacher in the Yorkshire District, so that ordination was for her an extension of the service she had already given to the church in various ways. Her ordination was recorded in the Programme and Agenda of Synod 1972 (Fulneck), as 'an occasion of great interest' at which many visitors were present. It concluded, 'Sr Shaw must have felt that she had the Church with her.'[26] She later shared her excitement at the privilege of being the first woman minister (called to take charge of Woodford Halse, Egdon and Priors Marston congregations) with readers of *The Messenger*, in an article for the October 1973 edition entitled, 'The Challenge of being a Woman Minister'.[27]

The ordination of Sr Dorothy Moreton, already referred to in the non-stipendiary section, followed on 15 January 1975, and from then onwards the composition of the ministerial team gradually changed, so that by 1998, out of a total of 24 ministers in active service, 7 were women, almost 25 per cent. This was a very high percentage in comparison with the other British denominations. The Unitarians, for example, who had been in the forefront of the movement to ordain women, had 83 ministers in 1986, of whom 10 were women; the United Reformed Church (formed by the union of Congregational and Presbyterian Churches) had 1,838 ministers in 1983, of whom 149, i.e. 8.1 per cent, were women. Even the Baptists, who had been prominent among the pioneers, had only 3 per cent of women, a mere 61 out of a 1985 total of 2,029 ordained ministers. Methodism, too, has not attracted many women candidates in proportion to the whole, so that in 1985, although 188 women had been ordained, they represented only 5.4 per cent of the total ministry.[28] By the late 1990s the figure was over 10 per cent. The

Moravian readiness to welcome ordination for women in proportion-ately large numbers was probably initially a response to the difficulty of recruiting sufficient suitable male candidates from such a small denomi-nation and the virtual impossibility of attracting them to it from other churches. These women are now appreciated for the distinctive qualities which they bring to their ministry.

The women ordained into Moravian Church service in the British Province, like those of other denominations, have tended to be of mature years, bringing a wealth of experience to their ministry, particularly in the pastoral sphere, even if in the natural order of things they would have fewer years of service than those ordained in their twenties. By ordaining both men and women, a proportion of whom had non-stipendiary appointments, the province has avoided collapse, since most congrega-tions have been able to retain a minister they could regard as their own, still the favoured option. The diminishing number of full-time ministers has not become unreasonably stretched, and has been enriched by the addition of a varied and experienced group of second-career or joint-career colleagues. In this way the province has kept in line with current practice in other Protestant denominations, including the German Lutheran and the Anglican, in which the ordination of women dates from 1994, and was attained only after fierce and prolonged disagreement.[29] Women ministers now have a significant number of female colleagues throughout the Unity and in ecumenical consultations with ministers of other denominations.

Although opportunities for ministerial service are now more diverse and flexible, the number of young men applying for ministerial training is still declining nationally, and it is still a minority of Christians who have chosen to accept women into their ministries; 75 per cent of them still regard ordination as the prerogative of men. Both the Roman Catholic and the Orthodox Churches maintain their traditional policies, and these seem unlikely to change in the foreseeable future.[30]

Developments in Congregational Life since the 1950s

Meeting the needs and responsibilities of congregations in a changing society

During the 1960s the churches in Britain began to recognize the emergence among the population as a whole of profound and probably irreversible changes in social attitudes, with serious religious implications. Moral and ethical values based on traditional Christian teaching, including its definition of Christian marriage and the family, were being questioned and rejected by increasing numbers of the younger generation of adults, who were defining their culture, sexual relationships and spirituality outside the formal establishments and teaching of the Christian Church. One aspect of this was the increasing freedom of choice demanded by women, particularly with respect to a career outside the home, and its acceptance by men as a practical solution to the financial demands of a mortgage and the raising of a family in an affluent society where prosperity was becoming linked to consumerism and both were regarded as desirable on social and economic grounds. A corollary was the widespread acceptance of easier divorce and the validity of sincere relationships outside Christian marriage, with consequent increase in the number of one-parent families as a result of marital breakdown and the temporary nature of many extra-marital relationships. Those outside the churches rejected their forms of worship and what they perceived as the basis of their faith. Without necessarily denying a spiritual dimension to life they were looking for something which they could regard as more relevant to everyday experience in the modern world.

Another change in British society dating from the period of post-war reconstruction had an impact the significance of which was scarcely recognized at the time. From the 1950s onwards, significant immigration was being encouraged: as well as those from the Caribbean Islands and Africa there were immigrants from Eastern Europe, Pakistan and Far

Eastern countries, all of whom expected to make a better life in a more highly developed and affluent industrial country which advertised its need for their skills. While the influx of Christians from other countries enriched the churches, this movement of people from various ethnic groups and different faiths led ultimately to the racial, cultural and religious prejudices which are in danger of becoming entrenched in parts of the country sixty years later. As succeeding generations have sought asylum and acceptance in Britain, or simply to join families already in the country, they and their children and grandchildren have given rise to a multicultural society which now challenges the Christian churches to reassess their relationship with people of other faiths.

Changes in style of worship

Changes of such magnitude, having initially created a crisis of confidence in the churches, gradually led clergy and laity of all denominations to address the problem of making the Church appear more relevant to the needs of modern society. One line of thinking focused on attracting people to churchgoing by introducing a less formal, 'popular' style of worship, giving rise to revisions of old hymn books and a number of books of eminently singable religious songs and meditations, with simple, emotive words. The latter have been widely appreciated, particularly in Nonconformist churches, and not only by the young. Orders of service and liturgies have become much more flexible as a result of the modernization of traditional wording and the introduction of new forms. New translations of the Bible have appeared in which the vocabulary and concepts are designed to be more accessible to a new generation of readers. Despite its cherished tradition of singing hymns which differ from those of other denominations, the Moravian Church, too, is currently reconsidering what is appropriate for congregational use today.

Attracting and retaining young people

Because it is becoming increasingly crucial to attract the next generation of members, church youth work has been emphasized increasingly in recent years. It is now acknowledged as vital to give the younger members of individual churches a sense of sharing in one community rather than just belonging to the church they attend, and the various denominations have their own policies to ensure that their young people meet together regularly. To further this aim, the British Province of the

Moravian Church has appointed a Provincial Youth and Children's Officer to correlate its work with young people throughout the province, particularly by organizing annual Summer Schools, a Provincial Youth Forum and conferences. One important aspect of this recent work is the initiative to re-establish and retain contact with former members of provincial youth groups and to make relationships with the young people of other provinces of the church. Another aspect is the co-ordination of the work of the Provincial Youth Forum and the Young People's Missionary Association (YPMA), so that all the young people of the province are aware of the needs of Unity missions and are working to raise funds to provide practical gifts to meet particular needs. Regular YPMA reports in *The Messenger* not only list its financial achievements, but emphasize its philosophy that members should take personal responsibility for translating their faith into action. In this way the young people of the province are following the well-established pattern of the Moravian Women's Association.

Changes in congregational participation in church life

Throughout the last half of the twentieth century church members have been urged to take an even more active part, not only in the traditional fellowships and devotional groups of their particular 'church family', but also in supporting a newer style of participation in the organization of church life, based on membership of teams and focus groups rather than formal committees, a reflection of changes which have been taking place in business and corporate life. This has meant that lay groups now have a more positive function in the work of individual churches and in the Christian life of their locality. Formal and informal interdenominational activities have been encouraged and have become particularly strong in urban areas, the concept of 'churches together' having considerable appeal when regular church attendance is dwindling and Christians are increasingly aware of the need to speak with one voice. The Moravian Church has been closely involved with the Churches Together in England Forum, sending delegates to its conferences and publicizing their reports on the difficulties and issues to be faced by the various denominations in working and worshipping together.

Most churches have appointed a Social Responsibility Secretary to represent their own congregations in discussions over the churches' response to local social problems. The Moravian churches have participated actively in these aspects of congregational life, strengthening local bonds with other denominations. In the Moravian Church the Social

Responsibility Committee also produces a calendar of special days and weeks in the church year during which specific issues are to be discussed at congregational level.

Provincial congregational fellowships, special-interest groups and activities for special celebrations follow a similar pattern to those which make up congregational life in any denomination, since all seek to promote a sense of community and common purpose in serving God. It is beyond the scope of a broad study such as this to consider them in detail, even though they are the mainstay of day-to-day life in congregations. In this chapter, two areas of change which have made an unprecedented difference at congregational level are explored in some depth, since they have resulted directly from the British Province's position as a member of the worldwide Unity. The first is the immigration and settlement of Moravians from the Caribbean, particularly during the 1960s, which had considerable initial impact locally, and soon involved the establishment of some joint congregations with other denominations; the other is the adoption of the North-American-style Moravian Women's Association by the women of the British Province. Since its inception, this organization has worked tirelessly to promote provincial understanding of the church's international character and support for Unity missions.

Caribbean Moravian immigration and settlement

Post-war opportunities for Commonwealth immigrants

Immediately after the Second World War inflation and unemployment were endemic in the Caribbean Islands, with few opportunities for personal advancement until the British Parliament passed the Nationality Act of 1948, guaranteeing British citizenship to Commonwealth immigrants, including those from the West Indies and from the Indian subcontinent. Later the same year a small contingent of 492 Jamaicans landed in Britain, to be followed by others at rates which soon averaged about 20,000 a year; so that by 1957 the Caribbean community in Britain numbered about 100,000.[1] The early arrivals tended to be men looking for work who, in the case of married men, were joined later by their wives and families. All were responding to opportunities created by an expanding economy requiring a substantially increased labour force, a state of affairs typical of the European Economic Community as a whole from the late Fifties and throughout the Sixties.[2] Already in the late 1950s some families who had come over with the first contingents were well settled, many of them with jobs, and therefore they were in a position to provide temporary accommodation for relatives who wished to settle in a country which appeared to offer the prospect of a more prosperous life, particularly to those with a sound education and professional skills. Some of those who remained in Britain found it unexpectedly hard to establish themselves: although work was comparatively easy to find, subsequent promotion was harder to achieve, and for the first time in their lives they encountered racial prejudice.

The British Province was slow to recognize the significance to the church of this influx of people from the area in which they had established missions two hundred years previously, and from which many immigrants with Moravian connections were coming. It was not until May 1956 that the Provincial Board noted having received an invitation from the London Council of Social Service to a 'fact-finding' conference in June, 'in connection with the problems arising from the entry into the country of so many West Indian immigrants'.[3] They agreed to ask the Hornsey minister, R. G. Farrar, to attend. Presumably as a result of this meeting, in March 1957 a brief comment in *The Messenger*[4] noted that Caribbean Moravians were beginning to migrate to Britain, implying that there were not many, and that some were already attaching themselves to British Moravian congregations.

Br Farrar welcomed a few newly arrived Moravian immigrants to his church, who said that many others living in more distant parts of London would not easily be able to make personal contact, and that there were contingents in both Birmingham and Manchester. It became clear that a much larger number of Caribbean Moravians might well be coming to London, in which case the province should respond by ensuring that as many as possible attended either Hornsey or Upton Manor, the only congregations offering a regular weekly service, the other congregation, Fetter Lane, meeting less frequently. There was an obvious opportunity for the province to respond to this initiative on the part of the newcomers, and to work among people who had been strangers in a strange land, and were now settled and actively seeking a place in the Christian community. In the spring and summer of 1958 letters by J. K. Berry and P. Gubi appeared in *The Messenger*,[5] expressing concern for the spiritual welfare of these Moravians from overseas, and emphasizing the urgent need for the church to contact them.

The work of Kirby Spencer and his colleagues

In October of the same year Br J. Kirby Spencer and Br P. Gubi were called to Hornsey and Upton Manor respectively, bringing them both into a sphere of ministry where they became keenly aware of this opportunity which provincial leaders were failing to exploit. At this stage Br Gubi was working part-time in Church House as manager of the Moravian Mission Agency Ltd., and until November 1959, when he was ordained, he was Lay Assistant to Kirby Spencer for the work at Upton Manor.

This move, though not primarily in response to the arrival of Caribbean people, placed them both in a position where they felt morally obliged to augment their normal congregational duties by a voluntary itinerant ministry to house groups which were being set up in a manner reminiscent of the eighteenth-century style of the church. During the next few years both men began to follow up the names and addresses provided by Br Farrar, and responded to new initiatives; for example, a few Caribbeans were attending Upton Manor from adjacent areas of East London such as Hackney, Leytonstone and West Ham, necessitating considerable effort on their part, in order to worship with fellow Moravians, so that it was vital to try to retain their loyalty.

By the early 1960s the amount of extra work involved was enormous, because it had become apparent that the number of Moravian immigrants was increasing rapidly, particularly into London, since there, as elsewhere, they often changed their address several times before finding a permanent home. Volunteers who assisted with the distribution of literature during those years recall the hard work involved in trying to target communities where Caribbean Moravians and other immigrants were living, in the hope of attracting them to the fellowship of the nearest church. The fact that many were widely dispersed hindered regular contact, and increased the clerical work involved in tracing individuals and retaining their interest in church membership. In March 1961 a *Messenger* editorial drew attention to the expanding work of Kirby Spencer who, though handicapped by lack of a car, was already setting up networks of house groups in Stoke Newington and Paddington.[6]

Early in 1961 the scope of this eighteenth-century-style outreach extended to Birmingham as a result of a contact made by Br Gubi in his capacity as Mission Agency Manager. With the agreement of Revd K. Beck, Minister at Sparkhill Methodist Church, he arranged a meeting to which he invited as many local Caribbean Moravians as could be traced. Seven attended this inaugural meeting, a response justifying a regular monthly Sunday afternoon service, enabling Br Gubi to take morning service at Upton Manor, travel to Sparkhill, lead Moravian worship there, then return to London, benefiting from an arrangement where someone else deputized at the Upton Manor evening service, or if necessary for the whole day.

The Provincial Board regarded all this outreach as a secondary and voluntary activity on the part of Br Kirby Spencer and Br Gubi until a Synodal resolution was passed in 1961, 'That the Provincial Board be directed to set apart at the earliest opportunity a brother to carry out the Ministry among West Indian Moravians in England.'[7] In September the Provincial Board agreed to call Br Kirby Spencer officially to the West Indian work[8] and for the time being to take it on a part-time basis in addition to his full-time ministry at Hornsey. They considered the possibility of providing him with another house to facilitate this. Even so, the Finance Committee failed to give this work any real priority in terms of resources and manpower, and were still suggesting in November that the two ministers should undertake the West Indian work alongside their congregational responsibilities, as it was difficult to find the money for a full-time appointment. In December, however, the Provincial Board decided that this plan was unworkable, and that the West Indian work was so urgent and vital that every step should be taken to implement Synod's directive that a full-time appointment should be made.

From August 1962, therefore, Kirby Spencer was relieved of responsibility for the Hornsey congregation and provided with a new house in Finchley and – of crucial importance – a car. This gave him some flexibility, but did little in practice to enable him to concentrate on the Caribbean ministry, because the Provincial Board expected him to cope with all the work in London and the Midlands, now including Birmingham and Leicester, as well as being assigned to Church House as the new manager of the Moravian Mission Agency, a task taking up three full days a week.[9] Simultaneously, Br Gubi was called to Lower Wyke in Yorkshire, and Br W. Mortimore took charge of both Hornsey and Upton Manor, preventing him from assisting Br Kirby Spencer in other than exceptional circumstances. Synod passed a further resolution in 1963[10] that the appointment of a 'Minister to Moravians from Overseas' was to be a full-time one from the beginning of the following year.

Shortly before these events the rate of Caribbean immigration had increased still further because of fears that Parliament was about to reduce it drastically, an accurate forecast, as the passing of the Commonwealth Immigrants Act of 1962 restricted entry to those with employment vouchers, awarded on the strength of their vocational or professional training, and in 1965 the number of vouchers was limited to 8,500.[11] One result of this for the British Province was that many of those who came to England from a Moravian background during the 1960s already had good professional qualifications in their own country, and were emigrating in the expectation that they would find equivalent work, which many did, to the subsequent advantage of London congregations.

Br Kirby Spencer's report to the 1963 Synod gave deputies an informative picture of the current situation. It was emphasized that West Indian Moravians had 'strong denominational allegiance'; the devout would go to great lengths to join a Moravian Church rather than another Free Church congregation. The immediate policy of those working with the immigrants involved forming groups of keen Moravians in monthly worship and fellowship, active through an elected committee. The opinion was strongly expressed that it should not be part of the ultimate policy to establish separate Moravian 'black' congregations, but that existing congregations, in London, for example, should become diaspora centres.

The report included figures from June 1963, showing totals in direct contact with Kirby Spencer. Ninety-three others had been in contact on one occasion but their present whereabouts was unknown.

London	451
Birmingham	126
Leicester	74
Bristol	31
Huddersfield	14
Total	696 firm contacts

[At that time there were *c.*2,936 congregational members in the British Province.]

It was further reported that some West Indians were members at Hornsey and Upton Manor and attended regularly. Deputies to Synod were informed in detail about the work of the London societies; the report gave times of meetings and numbers attending. These groups used Methodist facilities for their monthly meetings: at Stoke Newington, since November 1960 a group of between 20 and 45 members had been meeting in the High Street Methodist Church; a West London group of the same size had been meeting since February 1961 in Denbigh Road Methodist Church near Ladbroke Grove, or periodically for socials in

Fearnhead Road Methodist Church, Paddington; another group of between 8 and 20 members held the only Moravian service south of the Thames at Streatham in Riggindale Road Methodist Church; this dated from December 1962. In Birmingham the monthly meeting, with an attendance of between 20 and 50, was in Sparkhill Methodist Church. Negotiations were being conducted to rent the large Methodist manse belonging to the Sparkhill Circuit at a nominal rent as a Moravian Church House, for the use of the minister when visiting Birmingham, and as a meeting place. The arrangement in Leicester was rather different. Local Moravians were invited to the 10.45 a.m. Methodist service in Wesley Hall, which was often conducted by Kirby Spencer. Afterwards an informal Moravian Fellowship was held.

The 1963 report affirmed the value of what was being done, saying that the very nature of this outreach among West Indian Moravians had borne witness to the fact that the Moravian Church was still active. It concluded with the following comment:

> This work has proved to be a most exhilarating and satisfying ministry, yet at the same time bewildering in its complexities, scope and opportunity. A 'shepherd of souls' is part of the work of the minister, but when his flock is so large and widely scattered there are many who look up and are not fed.

On 1 January 1964 Kirby Spencer took full-time charge of the work, a new part-time lay appointment being made to the Managership of the Moravian Mission Agency. Br Kirby Spencer worked exceptionally hard to form house groups for those he managed to contact, posting a monthly circular letter to all in London with a fixed abode reasonably near a Moravian congregation or society, and to all known immigrants in provincial towns where facilities were being set up. Summarizing progress made so far in the June 1964 edition of *The Messenger*[12] he reported that he had made contact with 1,069 Moravian members, some of whom had been in Britain for ten years, although most had arrived within the last five. At least one pastoral visit had been made to 712 members. Classified by geographical area, there were 674 known members in London, of whom he had visited 488; in Birmingham he had visited every one of the 140 Moravians, while of the 114 known Moravians in Leicester he had visited 72. During the past few weeks new outreach in Wolverhampton and West Bromwich had enabled 6 of 28 members to be visited. At that time he was also aware of a further 100 or so Moravians scattered throughout the province, including some in

Manchester, but he had only been able to visit 6. He was well aware of what remained to be done, but could claim credit for recruiting voluntary helpers to lead house groups or societies, to encourage members and to plan services and outings; these groups continued to meet in Stoke Newington, Paddington and Brixton. In Birmingham he had 10 helpers, and in Leicester 6. The majority took their work seriously, reporting cases of illness and other problems. In his view many were capable of conducting services, and some had already done so. The Report of the Provincial Board to Synod, July 1964, admitted that 'there has been a considerable extension of the work since it was placed upon a full-time basis'.

In October of 1964 Br J. Chester drew public attention to his achievement, arguing that, at the present rate of progress, Br Kirby Spencer would be in touch with a number of Caribbean Moravians equalling about half the existing white communicant members in the province by the time the 1966 Synod met. Tragically, the immense burden carried by Kirby Spencer was beginning to undermine his health, and the fairness of expecting him to carry this workload alone was questionable; indeed the appointment of an assistant was an urgent necessity.[13] By the end of the year he was too ill to work, and resigned on 4 February 1965 for health and family reasons.[14] In March he was relieved of his work as minister to the Caribbean Moravians, being called instead to the Swindon and Tytherton congregations. The work in London was reorganized: Br Mortimore, then at Hornsey, took on Upton Manor too, with the help of Br H. R. Williamson who at that stage was in charge of Fetter Lane, Upton Manor, and what became Harlesden United Reformed and Moravian Church. Both were asked to do as much as possible over and above their routine duties, but Br Kirby Spencer was not replaced, a decision which laid the Board open to subsequent accusations of short-sightedness and failure to take full advantage of a unique opportunity to enrich the life and character of the province.

The period of consolidation

In July 1965 Br P. Gubi was called from Wyke to serve in Birmingham and Leicester, living in the former manse of Sparkhill Methodist Church, which was now used as originally envisaged, with some rooms serving as an administrative centre and for weekly services. Soon a larger, more formal meeting-place was called for, and it was arranged that premises would be shared with nearby Ladypool Road Congregational Chapel, which had a residual white congregation. This became the core of a future Moravian congregation of the British Province, the Sparkhill manse being renamed Moravian House as planned.

The 1966 Synod was given the latest information on the progress of the societies, the majority of whose London members came originally from Jamaica or the eastern West Indies. In particular it was reported that the West London Society, now meeting in St George's Presbyterian Church, Brondesbury, had provided regular pulpit supply to a church with a declining indigenous population and no minister. During the last eighteen months an increasing number of Moravians had been worshipping there, in addition to the meetings of the West London Society. At St George's the two denominations co-operated fully and willingly, providing the nucleus of a future joint congregation. Similar optimism was shown in Birmingham, where the arrival of Br Gubi was enthusiastically received. Increasing use was being made of the presence of a resident minister including weekly services in Sparkhill Methodist Church. The Birmingham society was not strong financially, and the expense of providing a full-time minister was borne by the province. There were hopes for a future opening at Aston, and for union in a joint ministry with Mansfield Road Methodist Church, near which many West Indians were living.

In 1966, however, Br Gubi was transferred to Bedford, from where he was still expected to continue the work in Birmingham and Leicester. A year later he was moved again, to Kimbolton and Queens Park in Huntingdonshire; at the same time Br A. Wright was called to Birmingham and Leicester, so that once again there was a full-time Moravian minister living and working in Moravian House.

The three London Societies meeting in 1968 reflected a steady consolidation of the Caribbean network within the Moravian Church, and a continuation of the association with other Nonconformist churches, particularly the Methodists. The meetings at High Street Methodist Church were associated with Hornsey; the South London Society associated with Upton Manor met at Mostyn Road Methodist Church, Brixton; Brandesbury was well established as a Presbyterian congregation in association with the former West London society.

The church based in Moravian House became officially recognized as Sparkhill United Church (URC/Moravian) in 1975, providing a precedent for future similar amalgamations. During the same year, also, after much discussion, the members at Leicester decided that they, too, aspired to congregational status, which was confirmed in 1976, the congregation initially being linked with that at Ockbrook. It did not have its own church building, but services took place at Wesley Hall Methodist

Church. This congregational structure remained in place for the rest of the twentieth century, its members generating a characteristic vitality, particularly in the London area where all the Moravian congregations soon became and remained predominantly supported by men and women from the Caribbean, attracting new members from among former non-Moravians living in the surrounding districts who were drawn to their characteristic style of worship.

The province was offered an unexpected opportunity for growth and renewal, but in retrospect did not take full advantage of it, though it is only fair to say that this fault was not limited to Moravians.[15] Br Kirby Spencer was of the same opinion, maintaining in June 1964: 'Such a ministry as I am set apart to do is more than worthwhile. The tragedy is that we did not find the means to begin it years ago.'[16] The experience of inadequate resources leading to missed opportunities was true also in other areas such as Leeds, where there were substantial numbers of Moravian immigrants from the Caribbean islands, notably St Kitts. A society was founded in association with Fulneck Moravian Church, but members living in the Chapeltown area of the city, for example, were unable to travel conveniently to services and meetings on the outskirts of Pudsey. As they settled into their own locality they joined the Methodists or one of the Pentecostal churches and their contribution to Christian witness and social concern in the locality forty years later is testimony to the energy and commitment brought to these congregations by people from the Caribbean.

In retrospect

During the early years both the immigrant communities and those among whom they were settling were uncertain in their responses to the changes in society which resulted from a substantial increase in the number of British citizens from other parts of the world. Some groups of Caribbean Moravians, particularly the young, felt insecure in British society, as Sr V. Barker explained in an article in *The Messenger* in October 1966.[17] Her theme was that, although many adults appreciated the provision made for them by the British Province, only a small proportion of the 12- to 20-year-olds did so. She anticipated that, as a result, the overall Caribbean membership would decline when the first generation had died out. She also noted that most Caribbeans had little real contact outside the church with non-Moravian English people; such as there was tended to be a superficial and often uneasy relationship at work or in lodgings. There was, in her view, very little social interchange. Her comments show that the difficulties for both communities were very real at first, and inevitably the lengthy process of interaction proceeded at its own pace.

The successful integration of Caribbean Moravians into the provincial congregational network had implications for the future development of the British Province. An unpublished paper by U. R. Bruce, 'To the Memory of Revd Kirby Spencer: The Missionary to the Overseas Moravians',[18] paying tribute to his work with immigrant members of the church, appends a copy of a 1964 sermon by Br Foy, preached at Hornsey, entitled, 'A Revival of Home Missions'. Foy reiterated the well-known argument that the policy of church extension in the traditional sense of providing a resident minister and a fixed congregational base in a new area had come virtually to a standstill; the province had neither the men nor the financial resources to sustain it. In view of this, the province could extend its influence only by reverting to the well-tried and typically eighteenth-century Moravian method of using a few congregational bases as focal points for itinerant evangelical and pastoral outreach, leading to the creation of new networks of religious societies open to the spiritually sensitive of any denomination. In Br Foy's view, the work of Br Kirby Spencer in London, then at the pinnacle of his influence, and that of Br Gubi in Birmingham, proved that this approach still worked.

In 1970 among the resolutions of Synod was one which added a note on Moravian Societies to the Book of Order of the British Province, 1966 edition, as Section 21a, listing the recognized societies. In reality most of these were immigrant groups. The Provincial Board reported to the Bath Synod of 1976 on the promotion of one of these societies to congregational status:

> One striking feature of recent Synods has been the way in which almost every Agenda has welcomed a new Society and sometimes a new Congregation composed largely of Moravians from Overseas. We are happy to note that this Agenda welcomes in addition to a new Society, [i.e. Harold Road, formed from the members of a recently closed church] a new Congregation, a Society which has proved itself and has a representative here among us, the Congregation elect of Leicester.

The Report of the Provincial Board to Synod 1978[19] provided further evidence of the successful integration of members from the West Indian communities into the British provincial network. In particular, the Board reported that the church had been represented on a working group of the British Council of Churches on white-led and black-led churches, initially by Sr Clarissa Johnson of Hornsey and more recently by Sr Valerie Barker of Fetter Lane.

In a section of the same report headed, 'The Church in a Multi-Racial Society', the Board reiterated the church's commitment to its responsibilities, recognizing both the difficulties faced by the church and the valuable contribution of the Caribbeans to British Moravianism:

A consultation on Moravian work in multi-racial communities was held at Spark Hill United Reformed/Moravian Church, Birmingham, in March 1977. The purpose of this consultation was to reach a better understanding of the spiritual and social needs of Moravians from overseas and how these could be met.

During recent months, one of the disturbing features of our national life has been growing racial tension, showing itself particularly in the rise of such movements as the National Front.

[The report re-emphasized the commitment of the church to the essential oneness of all humanity, noting that many members had signed the Affirmation against Racism prepared by the British Council of Churches.]

During the past twenty years or so, since Brethren and Sisters from the West Indies began to settle in this country, British Moravians have tried to welcome them into the Churches. We have to confess that sometimes acceptance has been slow, but we believe that over the years understanding has grown and that the brethren and sisters from the West Indies, and their children born in Britain now feel themselves to be fully a part of the Church in the British tradition.

We acknowledge gratefully the strengthening of life in the Church that they have brought.

One of the best indications of this strengthening influence is to be found in the report of the British Province to Unity Synod in 1988, where it was recorded that one ordained minister and two students were from a Caribbean background, 'reflecting the enrichment brought to the province by brethren and sisters from the Caribbean'.

Despite Sr Barker's pessimistic forecast in 1966, the existing Caribbean Moravian congregations are still flourishing at the beginning of the twenty-first century and are a well-established part of what has been defined as the 'free churches'[20] of urban Britain. Over the last forty years these churches have formed an important hub of effective community life, giving immigrants a sense of 'belonging' in contemporary Britain.[21] Immigrants, especially women, were able to find more outlets for social and spiritual activities in Moravian congregations than in secular voluntary organizations, and many members still travel considerable distances to worship in the familiar style and with other Moravians. Churches such as Hornsey are now welcoming a second and third generation of young adults, some of whom are non-Moravians living in Britain, who have been attracted to the church community.

A different problem now faces these congregations in which members from the Caribbean islands form the majority of the membership. After upwards of thirty years working in Britain many older members are facing retirement, and the pull of their original homeland where they still have family is strong, as also is the attraction of staying in the country of their adoption, where they have children and grandchildren, friends and colleagues. Over the years, those who were not happy in Britain have returned, and some of their children, also, have opted as adults to settle in the islands which they have traditionally regarded as 'home'; but the ones who remain, and the next generations of their families, are accustomed to a very different way of life from that in the Caribbean islands. For many, Britain is the only homeland they have known. The decisions which they make in the next few years may well determine the future of the congregations they support. Although their numbers are very small compared with the total number of Caribbean immigrants (477,000 in 1996),[22] their impact on the tiny British province of the Moravian Church has been considerable, numerically, financially and spiritually. They are valued because of their contribution to the work of the province as a whole and their capacity to introduce a vibrant new dimension into congregational life.

The work of the Moravian Women's Association[23]

Since the middle of the eighteenth century, the majority of communicant members in the British Province have been women, most of whom, until the latter part of the twentieth century, have been restricted to a supportive rather than a leadership role in congregational affairs. Yet women, both in the Moravian Church and in other Protestant denominations, have traditionally carried out a great deal of congregational work in the churches; the early Methodists, for example, where the ratio of women to men was 2:1,[24] organized themselves in a similar way. This convention has provided an effective use of members' traditional skills and enthusiasm, but given them only a minimal influence on the decision-making process.

Establishment of the Moravian Women's Auxiliary in America and Britain

Women in the American Province (North) had participated in congregational activity along similar lines until, in the 1920s, a provincial organization led by and composed of women Moravians was established, initially in Winston-Salem, North Carolina. It was entitled 'The Moravian Women's Auxiliary' and consisted of a network of congregational societies, with a regular programme of meetings common to all. When Br C. H. Shawe and his wife Eileen visited the province from England between August and November 1948, they were so impressed by the achievement and popularity of this organization that they decided to recommend the idea to British congregational members. At the 1949 Bedford Synod they both commented on their American experience, describing how the Auxiliary furthered the spirit of fellowship and enlarged the horizons of its members, thus laying the foundation for a British counterpart in which Sr Shawe was to undertake a leading role.

Sr Shawe introduced the idea enthusiastically to other leading Moravian women at Synod and in the province. The interest which she awakened is recorded in the accounts of those who were approached by her, such as Sr M. L. Britton:[25]

> Soon after her return from America she enlisted the support of Sr Mary Birtill and myself. The call came to me as I left the church one Sunday. 'Could I have a few words?' . . . She outlined her plan and asked for my help. My reaction was lukewarm to say the least, but I did promise 'moral support'. Little did I realize at the time that I should be caught up in the adventure of a lifetime! As the three of us met together in the following weeks to talk the matter over, the vision of Sr. Shawe came alive and we became convinced we should go forward.

Sr M. Spencer has described the events at Synod which led to the setting up of the provisional committee:

> I vividly remember Sr Shawe speaking enthusiastically about her idea during a lunch break and asking my opinion as a young minister's wife. I told her it was a good idea if she could get an organizing committee. At this she immediately stood up and announced that she wanted to meet all the ladies present before the next session. We all trooped back into the Church and again Sr Shawe told of the Women's movement she had found in the States. We all agreed it would be

wonderful to start a similar organization – studying the Bible and meeting on the same day each month would give us a bond of unity in study, prayer and fellowship. Later, after talking to the Crook ladies, I was able to write and tell Sr Shawe that being an isolated congregation we all felt this would draw us closer to the other sisters in the district.

This initial enthusiasm typified the spirit in which the women who had met at Synod approached the task of publicizing the idea among the congregations.

The formal inauguration of the MWA in the British Province[26]

Because Sr Shawe met with such a wholehearted response among other women in the London area and deputies at Synod, a conference of women invited to be members of a provisional committee was arranged at the Shawes' home in Hornsey in September 1949 to discuss the proposal, *That an effort be made to form a Provincial Women's Organization to bind together the women of our congregations in closer fellowship and service.* They agreed unanimously to replicate the American model with the overall aim of nurturing the spirituality of women of all ages in the British Province, and set up a formal committee, under the presidency of Sr Shawe, with Sr M. Gilchrist as secretary. The committee included a vice-president and treasurer, secretaries who were to be responsible for the mission and devotional aspects of the organization, and representatives of the Districts. Members were charged with the task of discussing the formation of circles in their own localities.

Despite some initial misgivings among those who ran the established women's meetings and groups who already raised money for missions, there was an appreciative response to this initiative throughout the province, and the first official meetings of the British Moravian Women's Auxiliary took place in January 1950 with about 500 taking up membership. Other interested women were to be accepted as members, regardless of religious affiliation, and this open welcoming of women from other denominations became a feature of the organization.

By February 1950 31 circles had already been formed. Plans were set in motion in May to produce a news-sheet for sisters who were too frail or lived too far away to attend meetings, and in the autumn of that year the first District Rally was held at Cliftonville, Belfast. Synod that year welcomed the inauguration of the MWA, expressing good wishes for its future development.[27] In October 1950 the central committee circulated a reminder of its aims, which were designed to make women more aware

of the significant spiritual and material contribution they could make to
church life and encourage them to take on responsibilities within the
church, an area in which at that time they were perceived as diffident and
unaware of their potentiality:

> The Moravian Women's Auxiliary is a Provincial Women's Organiza-
> tion uniting all Moravian Women in closer fellowship with one an-
> other and in the wider service of God, particularly in the following
> ways:
>
> 1. By seeking to associate in our fellowship both those who are mem-
>   bers of the Church and those outside it;
> 2. By co-operating with Ministers and Committees in congregations
>   by fostering the spiritual life of women;
> 3. By promoting social activities and leadership through the accept-
>   ance of responsibility in any phase of the Church's life and work;
> 4. By helping the Church financially;
> 5. By promoting study of the Bible and of Moravian Missions.

The constitution

At congregational level women are grouped into 'Circles' – social groups
of varying size – with more than one in a congregation if numbers
warrant such extension. The organization is democratic, with a written
constitution that has been updated periodically as a result of discussion
and approval by the circles. The 1997 version coincided with the change
of name from 'Auxiliary' to 'Association'.[28] The Provincial Central
Committee, with its District Representatives, also has an Executive
Committee comprising the President, Vice-President, Secretary and
Treasurer, Devotional Secretary, Quarterly Secretary and Home and
Overseas Secretary, elected for three years, with a restriction that they
may only serve three years in the same office.[29]

Circles meet monthly. At first it was considered desirable that they
should all meet at the same time, but this arrangement has been adapted
over the years to meet the needs of individual congregations. Each circle
has its own committee, its leader being assisted by two secretaries, one to
promote the devotional side of circle activity, the other charged with
bringing to the attention of members contemporary religious and secular
issues both at home and overseas, with some emphasis on the church's
missionary activity, but not excluding other needy causes outside the
church. To facilitate this, two sets of detailed notes, one devotional,

the other missionary, are published and distributed to all circles for the ten months of the year during which they meet, providing the secretaries with suitable material to assist members to share the same concerns at the same time. The theme for the devotional notes and the project for the year are chosen annually, and the ten sets of papers circulated each year include a newsletter written by the president or vice-president.

The status of the MWA within the church structure is ambivalent. This became obvious quite early in its history when in March 1959 the inter-church Consultative Committee of Women's Church Organisations asked the Provincial Board to appoint a Moravian representative. The Board approached the MWA, who felt that, since they were not an official provincial body, they had no authority to appoint a representa-tive, whereupon the Board agreed to ask Sr S. W. Twine, the current president, to serve.[30] Further evidence of this ambivalence is that for many years the MWA did not report officially to Synod, but sent a greet-ing and received a cordial acknowledgement. Greetings are received from the Provincial Board at the Annual Rally, and a member of the Board is present to convey them.[31] The committee have always worked closely with the Provincial Board, asking their advice about suitable fund-raising objectives. In September 1958, for example, the Board made four sug-gestions, two of which were for furnishings and equipment, one for the repair of the Nain Missionary Boat, and one for a subsidy for A. J. Lewis's History of the Church.[32]

The success of the organization during its first twenty years is reflected in its membership statistics. There were thirty circles in December 1967, with 459 full members and 115 associate members, a total membership of 574. In December 1968 the numbers had increased to 493 full members and 131 associate members, a total of 624, though there was a plea for more young members. The policy of encouraging sisters to take part in Christian events and witness in their wider locality was reflected in the fact that, by then, many circles included women from other denominations.

The evolution of regular events

The importance of rallies as a focal point for members in the same district was soon recognized, and the first one for the Irish district was held at Cliftonville in 1950. This led to the practice of holding an Annual National Rally, the first one taking place at Hornsey in 1955 to celebrate the organization's fifth anniversary.[33] When a second was held at Ock-brook the following year the Annual Rally became an institution, being held in the various districts in turn following the annual meeting of the Central Committee. Between 300 and 500 members, from the whole province, meet for these events at one of the Moravian settlements. Each rally begins with a service at 3.00 p.m. followed by tea, and provides a spiritual and social occasion which gives participants a renewed sense of fellowship. The Irish District rallies are still separate events, but MWA members from England are welcome to attend. In 1997, for example, there were guests from Birmingham and Westwood.

On the second Saturday in October another annual gathering, styled 'the Away Day', takes place. The Away Day provides opportunities for many of the women of the church to meet together and establish a specifically Moravian relationship outside their home congregations while undertaking some joint activity. As originally conceived, each had a theme, introduced by a keynote speaker, followed by a series of discussion workshops based on it. In the afternoon the members shared in the service of Holy Communion, followed by a high tea, before departing for home. This scheme, which began as primarily an opportunity for study and group discussion, had developed by 1981 into a more varied occasion, with workshops on such interests as music and flower-arranging in addition to the more traditional religious and social themes. Subsequently, an additional and more informal Fun Day, centred on a particular Circle, has become a feature of provincial life, and people make their own way there for an outing in the locality.[34]

A further opportunity for spiritual growth, taken up by a minority, is the annual Retreat.[35] A group of three women visited Ampleforth Abbey in 1983 for a 'mini-retreat' as an experiment, and the first retreat was held there in 1984. Over the next sixteen years these annual retreats became increasingly popular and it was decided to run two each year, one at the weekend and one mid-week. The second centre chosen was the Bristol Diocese Retreat House at Almondsbury, Gloucestershire, and weekend retreats soon became an established aspect of MWA activities and provided spiritual inspiration. Sr M. Shaw, who participated in the 1986 Ampleforth Retreat, described in *The Messenger*[36] how she was moved by the contrast between their simple celebration of Holy Communion in the Retreat House and the Abbey services across the way, with their plainsong, candles and crucifixes. Over the years a pattern of retreats has developed whereby responsibility for administration, spiritual content and much of the programme itself are undertaken by members. The result is that each one involves study and discussion, worship and relaxation, the whole providing a rich experience of fellowship.

The achievements of the MWA

This nationally and locally integrated association has continued to pursue its original aims, strengthening Moravian women's sense of group identity and providing them with responsible offices and leadership roles within the framework of church organization. While being careful not to regard itself primarily as a money-making organization, an important aspect of its awareness of the province's obligation to the wider Unity has been the raising of funds for immediate areas of need at home and abroad.

Circles began to 'adopt' missionaries as early as 1950, and also created closer congregational links with the Continental Province. In 1951 twelve MWA members visited Zeist, Bad Boll and two other German congregations, a particularly important aspect of renewing personal relationships in a province which had so recently been at war with its German brethren and sisters. In this way members were enabled from the beginning to gain first-hand knowledge of the wider Unity and its responsibilities. The personal approach was successful in that the following year ten German sisters spent a fortnight in the British Province, visiting Hornsey, Fulneck, Fairfield, Ockbrook and Bristol.

In 1951, also, when a hurricane devastated Jamaica, money was raised and dispatched. Early fund-raising activities included the scheme whereby the MWA raised £576 to furnish the new mission flat in Moravian Church House, London, which was inspected by the Central Committee in June 1957.[37] In March 1958, a successful scheme to supply clothing for Jamaica was recorded, and the President's report for 1969 confirmed its continuing stability.

The President's report for 1971, the twenty-first anniversary year, shows that there were twenty-seven circles in the British Province and two circles in Labrador, with 490 full and 98 associate members, a total of 588. More than 500 members had met at Ockbrook for the anniversary celebrations, and the special Anniversary Project had raised £131 for work in each of six different provinces of the Unity. Other traditional fund-raising and philanthropic projects were reported: £25 had been donated from central funds to the Sikonga Appeal. The knitting of blankets was evidently an on-going activity, providing a resource for areas of need. Another sign of the quiet effectiveness of the commitment of women in the church was reflected in the comment on the amount of local social work being undertaken by members as reflected in circle reports. In her July 1972 letter the President reported that the allocation for the British Province from the MWA's 21st Anniversary Project went to the refurbishment of the kitchen at Church House.

Another important aspect of the work of the MWA has always been its international role within the Unity. Much of this, routinely, was derived from the regular mission reports studied in circle meetings alongside the devotional aspects. Particularly significant is the link with Herrnhut established during the Cold War period. In 1972 money was available from Central Funds for a special project, and it was decided to send £20 to Herrnhut, where the Herrschaftshaus was to be rebuilt as a home for handicapped children. Other more substantial donations were made subsequently.

1973 was a time of reassessment associated with preparations for the forthcoming 25th Anniversary in 1975. To help with future policy a questionnaire was circulated to all circles covering the MWA's aims, organization, activities, approach to various problems, and its member-ship, with a view to deciding whether alterations might be desirable. It was hoped that the questionnaire would reveal what the organization meant to its members and how they felt it could make more impact on church life. The results made it obvious that members felt content with the established arrangements, which had reaffirmed the value of the new life which the MWA had brought into the church. One regret was expressed – that they still seemed unable to attract new and younger members. This was a problem area where the questionnaire could shed little light. Viewed retrospectively, this was not surprising, and did not reflect adversely on the quality of what the Moravian Church was offering, but marked a trend found increasingly in all church and secular organizations and attributable more to the changing role of women than to the failure of existing members. By that time secular society was pro-viding wider opportunities for higher education and training for all, and its accepted norms had moved towards a different role for women, in which younger women in particular increasingly needed and wished to combine family life with a career, consequently having little time avail-able for those activities which were traditional among generations of women who expected to centre their lives on domestic concerns.

The occasion of the 25th Anniversary in 1975 was regarded as an impor-tant landmark, and the philosophy of social awareness, always at the centre of the MWA's thinking, was reiterated in the letter of the presi-dent, Sr Janet Rea, in October:

When we have to spend so much time in fund-raising efforts for our own congregation and doing jobs on our own property it is so impor-tant to be outward looking and to keep in touch with other Moravians, and I feel that the MWA is an important way of doing this, but even more important is keeping in touch with those people round us, church folk and non-church folk alike, and I hope we take every opportunity to do this.

By this time, many members were corresponding regularly with 'adopted sisters overseas' and giving considerable time to social contacts outside their own church, especially with the elderly. In order to help the organization to keep in touch with overseas sisters and housebound people in the various localities, the *MWA Quarterly* was published, a magazine which summarized the latest news and provided an abbreviated version of the devotional and mission topics studied in the circles. Publicity for members' work in these traditionally female caring roles was facilitated in this way, and made an impact which would have been impossible without a formal framework. As part of this widening of relationships with women in other provinces, the connection with America was strengthened. In 1975 members celebrated the fiftieth anniversary of the foundation of the MWA in America, and four years later Sr Olive Linyard represented the British Province at the Joint Moravian Women's Conference at Bethlehem, Pennsylvania.

The projects for the year 1976–7 illustrate the significant contribution made by MWA members to the international missionary undertakings of the Unity. Each year a theme was chosen, for study and practical support, the current one being 'Building'. This fitted the project to build a church in Katumba, Sumbawanga, a refugee camp for about 57,000 political refugees from Burundi. They already had a site and the church would cost £5,300, of which the Danish Mission Board would pay half. The MWA promised £500, and by October 1977 had raised £1,000 for the new church at Katumba.

Recognition of the MWA's contribution to church life

Reporting for the *Moravian Messenger* on a recent National Executive meeting in September 1982, Sr D. Barker noted the continuing interest of provincial women in the MWA. There were circles in thirty-two congregations,[38] some of the associate members being younger women in employment, who formed 'semi-circles', meeting in the evening with their own separate leaders and secretaries. It was at this point, after over thirty years of activity, that the organization gained a greater degree of official recognition: the Fulneck Synod of 1982 not only authorized the Central Committee to elect representatives to serve on interdenominational committees dealing with the work of women in the church, but also passed a resolution inviting it to submit a regular report (designated a 'Memorial') to Synod.

The first memorial was submitted in 1984, summarizing the history of the MWA and outlining its regular activities. The strength and vitality of the organization was evident from this account of its recent achievements, the specifics of which now reached a wider audience. It had 444 members and 150 associate members, who received a quarterly circular with news and devotional material. Since the previous Synod its members had raised £1,250 for Nain, Labrador, £1,500 for women's work in Tanzania, £600 towards training a teacher at Leh school, £570 for the Indian Medical Fund, and £100 to send a barrel of goods to Br and Sr Craig. The Association had strengthened its links with sisters overseas when eleven sisters had attended the International Women's Conference in Winston-Salem in June 1983, and in 1984 a successful retreat at Ampleforth Abbey had been attended by twenty-four sisters.

Widening contacts with the Unity

The memorial presented to the Bath Synod of 1990 reported the celebration rally held at Fairfield to mark the fortieth anniversary of the MWA and presented a retrospective account of its activities and money-raising projects. One significant element in this memorial was the account of overseas visitors to the British sisterhood, given particular significance by the recent breakdown of communism in Eastern Europe. It recorded the steady, on-going work to build a relationship with sisters in areas where for many years normal contacts had been difficult to achieve.

> Over the past five years we have entertained seven sisters from Eastern Europe (East Germany and Czechoslovakia). They have stayed with us for two weeks, attended Retreats and Rallies and seen as much of our Province as time and their stamina allowed. This has proved a wonderful experience for both them and us, and has given those who met them a greater insight into and understanding of, the recent dramatic events in their countries.

Their remarkable achievement in maintaining contact with East German Moravians and regularly supporting the children's home in Herrnhut, while their country was still under communist control, resulted from their persistent determination to work with the communist regime on terms which were acceptable to it. This ensured the granting of visas to women to visit the British Province for official conventions, the deciding factor being that it could justifiably be argued that the visits were not social.

September 1993 was the occasion of the first European Women's Conference at Ebersdorf, Thuringia. The British Province was represented by eight women who were part of a group of about forty from the various European provinces. A second conference was held at Nova Paka, Czech Republic, in 1995, a third at Herrnhut, 11–15 September 1997. Fifty-three women of the Moravian Church met there, including ten delegates from the British Province and a contingent from the USA. When the fourth European Moravian Women's Conference met in Zeist, 7–11 October 1999, a leading role was taken by Sr K. Ward of the American Province (North), the first woman bishop of the Moravian Unity. Sr G. Gribble, writing in *The Messenger*,[39] was impressed by the multilingual fellowship and the sense of belonging to a long tradition, which was enhanced by the *Conference Hymn Booklet*.

> The inclusion of a number of hymns from the Moravian tradition enabled us to sing praises in strange tongues to familiar tunes. The sharing of the Watchwords in various languages served to remind us of the unity we enjoy daily when reading the same words of Scripture, although separated geographically and by language. Our common heritage was evident in many situations, not least by our being in Zeist, a gem of a Moravian scttlement, built in the 18th Century on the meadows in front of the Castle.

The work and fellowship of the MWA has done a great deal to ensure that women have become increasingly aware of the continuing vitality of the Unity in a world where international relationships are increasingly important to the Christian churches, and have experienced at first hand the satisfaction of making a practical contribution to its overall aims. The projects of the MWA in the British Province, raising about £7,000 annually by the year 2000, have helped many mission stations and individuals. They have provided resources ranging from pigs for Rajpur to drugs for Tanzania, from helping with the tuition fees for a Nicaraguan student in London to supporting teacher training in north India. Nearer home they have paid for the redecoration of the Chapel at Church House. Increasingly they have looked beyond purely Moravian interests to more general projects involving the welfare of women and families, including research into breast cancer and the support of street children in Columbia.[40] In total, they have raised £98,000 for the causes they have supported.[41]

Throughout its history the Moravian Church has maintained its fellowship through the 'Watchwords' and weekly accounts: leading members of the provincial ministry and laity, working throughout the Unity, have brought its message of community to local congregations to make them aware of the lives and needs of its missions and to encourage them to deepen their spiritual experience. In the early years of Unity expansion, some privileged women from Britain travelled to the continent to visit the settlements there, or to the Americas and other mission fields to render service, but never has there been such an opportunity for all women in the British Province to contribute so directly to its work. Over the past fifty years the MWA has aimed to foster personal contacts between women of all nationalities within the Unity, to encourage commitment, and to give practical support to Unity projects. For those who cannot travel, the association provides an opportunity to take an active part in the work of the wider Unity; its study notes and projects provide an equivalent of the eighteenth-century correspondence between the provinces, which in its day was a unifying element whereby ordinary members of the first Place Congregations and Societies became knowledgeable and committed participants in Unity activity in the wider world.

Ecumenism and the British Province

Although the eighteenth-century Protestant Revival had stimulated an interest in mission and consequent awareness of the need for fellowship among Christians of different denominational traditions, it was not until the twentieth century that a movement arose with a strong sense of the need for Christian unity.

The twentieth-century worldwide ecumenical movement

A comprehensive short summary of the ecumenical movement and its position at the end of the twentieth century is that by Geoffrey Wainwright in *The Oxford Companion to Christian Thought*.[1] He shows that the need for churches to work towards common ground was articulated at the World Missionary Conference in Edinburgh in 1910, when leading members of the predominantly Anglo-Saxon Christian churches determined to develop practical co-operation between churches, which would remain independent in other respects. These objectives were explored further between 1921 and 1961 by the International Missionary Council, and over the years many Christians came to believe that disunity was damaging the Church as a whole and that it was vitally important for all denominations to explore vigorously all avenues which would lead to areas of agreement in which they could work together.

The Orthodox Patriarch of Constantinople, also, was sensible of the advantage to be gained in the aftermath of the First World War if Christians spoke with one voice on issues of freedom, peace and justice, and in 1920 proposed a fellowship of churches, similar to the League of Nations, an idea which appealed also to the Swedish Lutherans, who were already working towards a Universal Christian Conference on Life and Work, to be held in Stockholm, in 1925. These proposals acknowledged that the areas in which churches could work together harmoniously were likely to involve 'practical Christianity' devoted to seeking freedom, peace and justice for all nations.

Meanwhile another strand in the search for common ground was represented by the Faith and Order Commission which had its inception at the Lausanne Conference in 1927, and held conferences at Edinburgh in 1937, Lund in 1952 and Montreal in 1963. Two of its early concerns presaged those which have characterized later discussions on ecumenism, namely, a search for ways to organic church union, and for a common mind on matters of Christian theology, tradition and renewal.

The aims and initiatives of the 'Faith and Order' commission overlapped those of the 'Life and Work' movement (1925) in the person of Archbishop William Temple, and a World Council of Churches was proposed tentatively in 1937. A provisional committee, set up at Utrecht in 1938, laid the first foundation for the World Council of Churches, and after the Second World War the founding assembly was held at Amsterdam in 1948. It included Anglicans, Baptists, Calvinists, Congregationalists, Lutherans, Methodists, Mennonites, Moravians and the Salvation Army, 147 churches officially constituting the Council. Its growth can be measured by the fact that, at the time of the Canberra assembly in 1991, 317 churches, drawn from every continent, were members.

Some idea of the breadth and complexity of the WCC can be gained by looking briefly at a few of its most significant conferences. Of major importance was the realization in 1954, as a result of the Cold War, that the churches were divided not only by questions of doctrine, but by social, political and cultural factors. At New Delhi in 1961, the Orthodox Churches in the socialist countries joined the Council, and the twentieth-century missionary movement became fully integrated in its concerns. The fourth world conference on Faith and Order in Montreal in 1963 showed the full effects of Orthodox participation, as did the presence of Roman Catholic observers. From 1964 the Roman Catholic Church recognized that other churches, despite their defects of doctrine, sacraments and order, were significant in the 'mystery of salvation'. The resultant dialogues, which have continued ever since, have aimed to establish common ground in areas of broad agreement and to tackle disputed aspects of dogma. Social and doctrinal issues have both been the focus of conferences. In 1968 the assembly at Uppsala faced world conflicts such as the growing gap between rich and poor nations, racism and the moral ambiguities inherent in new scientific discoveries. At Louvain in 1971 the meeting of the Faith and Order Commission discussed on-going studies on baptism, Eucharist, ordination, worship and the nature of scriptural authority. Throughout the 1970s and 1980s these two strands of social concern and doctrinal practice have been central to the work of the WCC, and experience has shown that, while the churches can often speak with one voice on questions of justice and morality, questions such as those concerning the Eucharist and the ordained ministry still remain barriers to full communion.

The Moravian Church is a charter member of the WCC, and through the years its representatives from the British Province have contributed to conference discussion and ensured that congregations have been kept in touch with ecumenical thinking through reports to Synod and contributions to *The Messenger*. Their work exemplifies the role played by individual members of provincial churches, the ministry and the Provincial Board in ensuring that British Moravians have a voice in the broader concerns of the worldwide Christian churches.

The twentieth century has seen steady progress towards consensus among Christians concerning areas in which churches can work together. Martin Reardon[2] has suggested that during this period three factors have acted to modify denominational thinking about unity as the various churches interacted. While each tradition rediscovered its own roots and traditions, separate churches became more willing to learn from each other and discover what their traditions had in common, and responded to the need to seek reconciliation in a global society and pluralist world. He points out that the early Protestant idea of Christian unity originated from the need for missions to work together, and was not envisaged as uniformity, whereas the 'Faith and Order' approach was based on the Pauline perception of organic unity – the Church as one body, an idea which many Christians now regard as unrealistic. Christian thinking has been developing towards recognition of the need for a visible common identity, based on communion, which would nevertheless respect their distinctiveness and independence, the 'unified diversity' expressed by the Lutheran World Federation in 1977. Reardon suggests that the widest agreement yet was reached in the Fifth World Conference on Faith and Order in 1993, 'Towards Koinonia in Faith, Life and Witness'. He comments that, while there is little visible progress towards the recognizable common identity which the concept of *Koinonia* (communion, fellowship) represents, there is wide agreement on areas of common faith grounded in scripture and the Nicene Creed, in common life, expressed in baptism and the Eucharist and nurtured by a common ordained ministry, common witness, common decision-making and a shared commitment to the search for justice, peace and the integrity of creation. He points to progress resulting from the work of the World Council of Churches, including a new stage reached in 1995 when

Pope John Paul II invited other churches to discuss how his primatial ministry of unity might become acceptable to those who reject his claims to supremacy.

The achievements of the ecumenical movement at the end of the twentieth century mark several areas of progress.[3] There has been a growth in charity and joint prayer and action between Christians divided by confession and institutions, with some shared liturgies and intercommunion. In 1995 the papal encyclical *Ut unum sint* committed the Roman Catholic Church to ecumenism and affirmed the obligation of all Christian churches to evangelization. As new issues arise and new areas of religious, political and social development become prominent, the ecumenical movement continues to respond to the immediate needs and changes within the Christian churches in search of its ultimate goal.

The leaders of the twentieth-century Moravian Church, too, have always been involved in these discussions, since the church has a tradition of working across national and denominational boundaries in the interest of furthering the gospel, both as a revivalist community and in foreign missions; the ecumenical outlook is essential to Moravian thinking and practice.

The eighteenth-century Unity: an ecumenical philosophy

Zinzendorf's own experience was ecumenical and his main intention for the Unity was to raise a community of dedicated Christian evangelists to reawaken existing denominations and from these people to supply missionaries to the heathen. As a result, the philosophy of the church has always been one of openness towards other Christians. For Unity members, the essentials of faith were the religion of the heart and the dedicated life, and they were committed to the awakening of those they regarded as nominal Christians to deeper spirituality.

A. J. Lewis[4] has pointed out that the ecumenical basis of Zinzendorf's philosophy was that Christians should become one by their shared spiritual experience of Christ, the 'unity of His wounds'. Such unity, for Zinzendorf, was not a matter of intellect, creed, ritual, order or even service, but a unity of the heart. As far as denominations were concerned, he had no interest in organic union, since he recognized the value of variety in thought and practice, which provided different channels for different temperaments, regarding denominations as a manifestation of divine wisdom rather than a human invention, and teaching that membership of a denomination was not the same as being one of the flock of the Lamb.

This ecumenism, fundamentally evangelical, involving the need of the sinner to accept salvation, a new relationship with the Saviour and subsequent obligation to spread this gospel to revive the existing churches and convert the heathen, was in some respects similar to the core beliefs of all Christians, in that it placed belief in and commitment to Christ at the centre of faith. On the other hand it differed considerably from twentieth-century ecumenism which, though always acknowledging the centrality of Christ and the need for evangelism, has looked towards areas in which the churches can work together in a multi-faith and agnostic or atheistic world. This has led to concentration on progress in areas where the churches can speak with one voice on ethical and social issues, and a willingness to worship together in ways which a conservative such as Zinzendorf would not have accepted as central to Christian experience.

Early provincial ecumenical activities

In British provincial Place Congregations, as in those on the continent, members led a disciplined life, and a strict demarcation applied between men and women who met the criteria of membership and those who were attracted to the Brethren or had not yet achieved sufficient grace to be fully accepted. In the early societies, however, this exclusive attitude did not apply, since their members were men and women from established denominations who wished to enrich their spiritual experience. Their original nature was that of a house-group, which expanded to form a community which worshipped together, so that they were not envisaged as training grounds for an elite. Their leaders, who were already trained evangelists and preachers, needed to work freely with those they sought to influence.

It is clear from early nineteenth-century records that some local Labourers were working amicably with other evangelical churches, not only with the Anglicans, and were welcomed as part of the local support system and as preachers. The Diary of the Congregation of the Brethren at Plymouth and Plymouth Dock for the years 1808 and 1809[5] illustrates the friendly working relationship between the Brethren's congregations and other churches. The entry for 18 December 1808 recorded:

Brother Traneker having been appointed a member of the Committee of the Assylum [sic] for Female Penitents, established at Stonehouse, he attended for that purpose and was introduced by the Revd Mr Hitchins. All the evangelical Clergy and dissenting Ministers in the 3

Towns, are members of the same by means of which they keep up a friendly intercourse with each other.

On 15 January 1809 the diarist noted that Brother Traneker preached on behalf of the Asylum at the request of the Committee, 'to the largest auditory he ever saw in our chapel'. There were regular accounts of his preaching at the Asylum itself throughout the whole of that year.

The Brethren's policy of exchange preaching with other ministers is confirmed by the records for 16 July 1809 and 30 October 1810, where Br Traneker wrote in the first person:

16 July. In the evening I delivered a testimony of our Saviour's love to the sinners in the Methodist Chapel at Bideford, which was also the case the following Monday evening. On Wednesday I preached by request in the dissenting Chapel at Northam, and on Friday in the Methodist Chapel at Bideford, and on Sunday in the Independent meeting at Appledore.

30 Oct. The Revd Mr Hitchins attended the evening preaching. This Gentleman is the Minister of St. John's Church in this town, and labours in great blessing, and he is also a sincere friend of the Brethren.

It is reasonable to suppose that such co-operation with other local churches continued informally; certainly the Provincial Conferences became apprehensive about the effect of some Unity tenets on their members and friends from other denominations, as the minutes of the Fairfield Conference of 1847 show.[6] The appropriateness of continuing to regard the Augsburg Confession as a 'creed adopted by the Brethren's Church' in the British Province was debated by the conference, and apprehensions arose because of a perceived need to adopt it as a whole, if at all. A resolution was passed that, 'if such a reference must be made, to insert a clause stating that the Congregations in this province are not required to adopt it', the grounds being that some articles were likely to offend many members and 'many of our Christian friends'. On the other hand, it was also deemed inappropriate to 'commit the Brethren's Church to the articles of the Church of England,[7] or to any of the other protestant confessions of faith'. The tension between maintaining doctrinal individuality and the desirability of finding common ground with other denominations was already explicit in provincial thinking, and a committee was set up to consider the matter further.

Participation in twentieth-century ecumenical discussions

Apart from ideological considerations such as those described above, the British Province's failure to grow has resulted increasingly in problems of viability as a separate denomination. This is a problem which it shares with other Christian churches, as well as the whole Unity, and reflects the growing tendency of European and American society towards secularization, and the diminishing ability of members to fill and maintain large churches. The problem has exercised British provincial leaders for most of the twentieth century, and representatives of the Moravian Church have been in regular talks to examine the possibility of closer connections with other churches, being more urgently motivated than many other Nonconformists to find a way of survival which would solve the problems of expensive premises, shortage of ministers and dwindling congregations in a minute denomination. On the other hand, as the British Province has developed a denominational character and outlook, there has been continuing expectation by Moravians that their church will be recognized and valued by other churches as conventionally Protestant in its doctrine, but with a special identity derived from membership of the Unity. This has led the province to retain its awareness of difference, while seeking always to work with other denominations towards the common ground which they share as Christian churches committed to preaching the one gospel. On practical and ideological grounds, therefore, the Moravians have insisted on their freedom to co-operate with any churches, regardless of their relationships with each other.

On the eve of the outbreak of the First World War the churches in Britain were already pledging themselves to an international involvement in problems of Christian belief and practice, and the Moravian Church was preparing to be in the forefront of such discussions. The report of the PEC to Synod in August 1914 included the following statement: 'Along with all the Churches of our country we have associated ourselves with the preliminary work being done in view of a "World's Conference on Faith and Order", which it is proposed to hold in the coming years.'[8]

During the war years some discussion continued. In 1916, the Provincial Board reported to Synod that the church had been officially represented on the United Committee of Anglicans and Nonconformists in connection with the proposed World Conference on Faith and Order, a work which could not be carried forward until the international situation clarified, and for which no report was issued. There was no such barrier to talks between the Free Churches on the subject of closer links between denominations, and these continued in spite of the war. In 1916 it was reported that the Moravians had been represented on a Joint Commission of the Free Churches dealing with the question of Christian Unity,[9] but no formal reports were to be presented, apart from a general statement entitled 'Towards Christian Unity', until some definite findings were available. There were reservations on all sides, well summarized in the proposal placed before Synod,

> That this Annual Assembly of the Moravian Church in the United Kingdom expresses its general approval of the proposal to bring the Evangelical Churches of England into greater unity, provided that this does not interfere with the autonomy and the main features of each constituent Church or Churches. It hereby appoints two of its members to serve on a United Committee to consider the implications and possibilities of a Free Church Federation and to prepare a Scheme for submission to the Denominations concerned.

Two resolutions welcomed the proposal,[10] the second with the proviso that it

> did not preclude or be antagonistic to closer cooperation with the Church of England or the international fellowship of Christian Churches and their cooperation – in conformity with the traditions of our Church, to endeavour to secure the practical accomplishment of this wider ideal of unity.

Relations with the Free Church Federal Council (FCFC)

The Brethren appointed to attend the 'Special Committee of Non-conformist Churches' produced a report to the 1919 synod, as a result of which Synod voted to join the 'Federation of the Evangelical Free Churches of England', still retaining their right to practise intercommunion with other denominations, and the Provincial Board's report at Fairfield in 1920 mentioned the church's representation on this body. Thereafter, brief reports of attendance at meetings occurred regularly at the Synods which followed, with indications of goodwill and some progress on a variety of common interests. The important thing was that the Moravians were represented and had a voice in any on-going discussion.

The end of the Second World War gave a stimulus to the activities of what was by then the Free Church Federal Council. The reports to Synod show the variety of issues on which the Free Churches were by that time concerned to work together, and indicate that they did not regard themselves as an inward-looking body concerned with doctrinal wrangling, but were seeking to speak with one voice on social issues and questions of religious freedom. They recognized that, although some member denominations were comparatively small, they could be influential as a group, particularly in domestic issues, but also in consultation with like-minded organizations abroad. The representatives' report to the 1945 Fairfield Synod showed that the Federation had discussed the domestic issue of Religious Education in the national school system. It had also set up a committee which had been considering how to persuade members to link up their own denominational plans with those of the Council. As a body, the Council had given support to statements of similar bodies in America, 'with a view to securing recognition throughout all states of the religious freedom regarded by us as an essential in a modern community'.

At Ockbrook in 1947, the reports of the representatives described how the Council was engaged in making the task of post-war reconstruction among member churches more effective by setting up administrative arrangements to co-ordinate the work of the FCFC. In particular, general approval had been given for a scheme to divide the country into twenty areas the size of one, two or three counties according to their size.

Throughout the late 1940s and into the 1950s the reports show the FCFC working steadily to publicize the churches' concern for moral and spiritual issues. In 1948, for example, they endorsed the position of the Churches' Commission on Gambling, arguing against the introduction of a State Lottery. In 1949 the emphasis was on youth, particularly the need to secure extended scope for chaplaincy to the Cadets and state-sponsored youth organizations. The Council had co-operated with the Church of England to push forward improvements for the moral care of young soldiers serving their training period in Germany. In 1950 the Council reported that it had publicized its stand against atomic weapons and gambling, and in support of Sunday Observance, and had claimed the need for an appropriate Free Church share in the appointment of chaplains in public institutions and Pre-Service Units.

At this point, also, the FCFC was conscious of the difficulties involved in negotiating with the Church of England. The 1950 report to the Bath Synod phrased this tactfully: 'The most difficult point dealt with by a special Commission – and at the same time the most delicate point – was the preparation of a statement relating to the possibility of inter-communion with the Church of England.' Another commission had been set up on which Br Shawe, the Moravian representative, had been nominated to represent the smaller Free Church bodies, which was to consider the problem of relations between church and state, since the Church of England was contemplating changes in the position of the Establishment, and the Free Churches wanted to investigate the issue from their own point of view. The report of the Provincial Board to Synod in 1952 clarified this issue further: the Church of England wished to maintain its prestige and authority as the Established church, but gain greater freedom from Parliament. In 1946 the Archbishop of Canterbury had suggested that the Free Churches should take episcopacy into their system to facilitate intercommunion, and as a result of a conference in Oxford in 1950, had produced a pamphlet 'Church Relations in England'. At this stage there was no available report of Free Church discussion or response, and in any case, the involvement of the Moravians as members of the FCFC was separate from their on-going direct discussions with the Anglican Church as an independent denomination, which are outlined below. It was beginning to appear that little progress could be made in the attempt to solve problems of doctrine and practice, but that there were considerable prospects of working together on social issues.

When Synod met at Hornsey in 1956, the FCFC report reflected contemporary changes in the attitude of society to formal religion. All member churches were under financial strain, and the Council was advocating consideration of a policy whereby one denomination would build a church and all Free Church people would support it. Such a proposal was unlikely to be implemented, but was a sign of the times. A call for spiritual unity was made, particularly a plea for an adventurous response to fulfilling the churches' common mission in evangelism. There were five practical recommendations to facilitate joint enterprise: complete recognition of each other's churchmanship; free transfer of all in full membership from one church to another; common access of all members to the Lord's Table; mutual recognition of the fully accredited ministers of each denomination as Ministers of the Word and Sacraments, and finally supplementary membership.

In 1956 the report of the FCFC representatives summarized the essential function of the FCFC in united evangelism, namely in the areas of relationships between church and state, education, matters of religious liberty and rights of conscience, and against the social evils of gambling and intemperance. At the same time it welcomed the increased opportunity given by membership of the British Council of Churches for fellowship and co-operation with the Churches of England, Scotland, Wales and Ireland, and expressed the conviction that a united approach to the government on matters of interest to all the churches would carry weight.

The report emphasized that there was no conflict of interest, or rivalry, and that both organizations were needed.

Between 1959 and 1961 the FCFC reports recorded an attempt to establish a Free Church Union. It was argued that there was need for union in those villages where some denominations were struggling without a minister, and in new towns and on housing estates, where united witness was necessary for greater impact. A commission had been appointed in September 1958 to consider the possibility, and an executive was to get in touch with the four largest denominations, with the proposal that six Methodists, three Baptists, three Congregationalists and two Presbyterians were to be commissioned to serve. In practice there had been problems over the terms of reference, and the commission was in abeyance until September 1959. In September 1961 the Special Commission came to the conclusion that the difficulties were insurmountable and that any attempt to establish a Free Church Union would be unlikely to succeed, but that Christians should continue to extend ways of working together. This failure was reported to the 1963 Baildon Synod by the FCFC representatives, and the principle of looking for ways to extend co-operation between the Free Churches was endorsed.

A retrospective account of the first twenty-five years of the FCFC presented to the 1964 Synod gave members an up-to-date summary of the achievements of this interdenominational body on which they were represented, confirming the value of working along with other churches in areas where there were united aims, and where controversial arguments over doctrine and religious practice could be avoided. An example from the 1964 report to Synod illustrates what the church felt could be achieved by a united approach. Conversations had taken place with the Director-General of the BBC and Head of Religious Broadcasting to ensure that the interests of the Free Churches were safeguarded in the planning of religious programmes by the BBC and ITV. Representatives were looking for common ground with Anglicans and Roman Catholics on the question of denominational schools and religious education, in order to present a united front to the Ministry of Education and Government, while safeguarding principles which were part of Free Church life. The Council had also expressed concern for the underprivileged, supporting World Refugee Year and the Freedom From Hunger Campaign, and had urged the government to give more aid and reduce the amount of money spent on armaments. It was clear from these reports that membership of an ecumenical body was providing the Moravian Church with a voice in the wider issues concerning Christians in society, a strategy which it has continued to value.

Reports of various committees involved in the province's relationships with other churches within the United Kingdom have continued to feature in synodal reports throughout the last fifty years. It would be inappropriate to give an account of these individually in a book which aims to examine broad patterns of provincial history, but a few extracts will exemplify the work which has gone on steadily in the background of provincial life, and made the opinions of the Moravian Church known to other denominations.

In 1976, at the Bath Synod, the report of the Inter-Church Relations Committee outlined proposals of the Churches Unity Commission. 'The Commission, representative of eight denominations, is in being for three years. It has drawn up a set of ten propositions for the constituent Churches to examine, with a view to acceptance as the way forward to visible unity.' The propositions and appended notes were not available with the report, but their acceptance had been recommended to Synod by the committee. At Ockbrook, in 1978, the Inter-Church Relations Committee reported that the Synod of 1976 had accepted the ten propositions outlined in the book *Visible Unity* and authorized the Provincial Board to sign the Act of Covenant. It was reported that progress had been slow and that the Moravian Church was the only one to have accepted them. The Roman Catholics had refused and the propositions were still being discussed by the other churches. It was commented that the church should regard signing as a first step, and meanwhile congregations were urged to participate in local ecumenical activities.

The Provincial Board reported to the Fulneck 1982 Synod that it had represented the church at all the meetings of the Churches' Council for Covenanting, adding, 'In addition there have been many requests from other Churches within the framework of the Covenant for members of the Provincial Board to speak about the Moravian Church from places where there is no Moravian Church nearby.'

In 1988 at Lower Wyke and Wellhouse it was reported:

Perhaps the closest links this year have been with our Methodist friends and colleagues, who in May celebrated the 250th Anniversary of John Wesley's conversion. . . . We are very happy to have a Methodist, Dr Lewis Burton, as our preacher at the opening service of Synod this year. He is, in happy symbolism of our times, also Executive Secretary of the West Yorkshire Ecumenical Council of which we are members.

Relations with the Church of England

The report of the Church of England–Moravian Church Working Party at the Ockbrook Synod in 1992 is of considerable interest, since it typifies reports to various synods about the progress of talks about a closer relationship with the Anglican Church.

> The exploratory nature of these talks in which we have been learning from each other and explaining our position on matters of faith and order, has now to some extent moved on into the task of setting down in approved texts those things which we share in common. . . . We have been greatly helped in our discussions by the pattern of Church Unity set out in the Meissen Declaration of 1991 between the Church of England and the Evangelical Church in Germany – especially in the theological basis of the Declaration.

Warnings were given that it was important not to assume that use of the same terms implied the same practice, and the comment was made that conversations between the two churches went back over a hundred years to the 1870s.

When Zinzendorf sought political and religious recognition for the Unity in Britain and in the American colonies, it was to the bishops of the Church of England that he turned for support. It was to Anglican congregations and ministers that the Brethren appealed at first when they wished to establish a society network similar to that operating in conjunction with the Lutherans in Germany. As the province gradually developed into an independent organization with its distinctive British style, this link was not maintained as originally envisaged, and it was not until 1878 that a serious attempt was made to begin discussions about closer ties between the two churches. Surprisingly, there has been comparatively little progress until recently.

No attempt will be made here to give an account of the convoluted history of Anglican–Moravian conversations, since two publications are already in print which deal fully with the issues and summarize the current state of the relationship at the end of the twentieth century. Colin Podmore's 1991 article in *One in Christ*,[11] and the 1996 *Fetter Lane Common Statement*[12] published jointly by the Church of England and the Moravians, illustrate the difficulties and stumbling blocks. They clarify areas in which agreement has been possible to enable the two churches to work amicably towards common aims. Both provide exemplars of the problems which beset the Christian churches when they wish to acknowledge their fellowship in Christ and speak with one voice to the secular world, but retain a keen awareness of the distinct beliefs and practices which identify them individually.

According to Podmore, one major fundamental problem is that of the Moravian episcopacy, which has been an issue since discussions first began, Anglican reservations centring on the questions of its original validity and subsequent continuity. In 1889 the Moravian archivist at Herrnhut published a report, in answer to a query by the committee of nine bishops set up to consider the question, which pointed to two gaps in the Moravian succession, in 1500 and 1553. Although this committee was happy to accept as valid the transfer of the episcopacy of the old Unitas Fratrum to the Renewed Church in 1735, and not concerned about the apparent gap in succession, the members were not unanimous on the validity of the original consecrator's orders. Subsequently, in 1901, the committee which then discussed the matter decided that the episcopal succession dated back only to 1553, and that Moravian orders could not be recognized by the Anglicans.

Podmore identifies two ways in which the dialogues are of general interest; they illustrate how Anglican attitudes to unity have changed over the years, and they reveal the questions to be resolved and pitfalls to be avoided in discussions about unity. He shows how dialogues between 1908 and 1920 discussed the establishment of an interchangeable ministry, but made little effective progress, and how between 1920 and 1936 the two churches' views on the goal of unity diverged. The situation was further complicated by the fact that the Moravians' association with the Free Church Federal Council after 1948 resulted in their being categorized by the Anglicans as a 'Free Church'. He concludes that the Moravians currently stand in a 'bridge position' between the Church of England and the Free Churches, being a Free Church with a threefold ministry and bishops consecrated in a personal succession.

The Fetter Lane Common Statement of 1996 clarifies the relationship between the two churches at the end of the twentieth century, and summarizes their shared interests, differences and joint commitments. It identifies their first common interest as dating from Comenius' visit to England in the 1640s and attempt to promote unity and reconciliation between the two churches. (It should be noted that this was part of Comenius' wider commitment to pansophism, the notion of a unified Church throughout the world, which would be central to the establishment of colleges for the promotion of universal knowledge in a Christian framework. He received a sympathetic hearing in England.[13]) Further, he bequeathed his church-in-exile to the care of the Church of England, who subsequently encouraged collections on behalf of the Bohemian Brethren-in-exile.

The *Common Statement* describes the calling of the two churches to full visible unity, and records ten points on which they can agree in faith. In brief summary, the two churches accept the authority of the Scriptures and the Niceno-Constantinopolitan and Apostles' Creeds; they share a common tradition of 'spirituality, liturgy and sacramental life'; they share a definition of baptism and a tradition of following infant baptism by confirmation; they believe that the celebration of the Eucharist is the feast of the new covenant, in which Christ unites the believer with himself, shares his risen life and sacrificial self-offering, and is the means by which, through the power of the Holy Spirit, the Church experiences the love of God and the forgiveness of sins; they proclaim the gospel of redemption by grace through faith and that justification leads to good works and love; they believe that the Church and its members are called to work for the furtherance of justice and peace, since God has made peace through Jesus 'by the blood of his cross'. The Church is constituted and sustained by God, and is not the creation of individual believers; it is a sign and foretaste of God's kingdom, but as a human organization constantly needs reform and renewal. All members of the Church are called to participate in its apostolic mission, but the ordained ministry, an office of divine institution, exists to serve the ministry of the whole people of God. Both churches have the threefold ministry of bishop, presbyter and deacon, with the same role and significance. Finally, the ministry of oversight (*episcope*) is defined as a gift of God to the Church, and exercised in personal, collegial and common ways in both churches, though oversight functions have varied in both traditions.

Their *Statement* is based on the determination of both churches to acknowledge their agreements and commitment to full unity, to resolve outstanding differences and to 'intensify' relations. It recognizes that the two churches belong to the One, Holy, Catholic and Apostolic Church of Jesus Christ and commits both of them to specific steps to draw them closer together.[14]

The Agreement sets out the issues still to be faced by the two churches, and addresses the question of how two churches of such different sizes might live in unity and retain their distinctive identities. It is revealing to outline these issues a little more fully, since they epitomize the wider problem of inter-church discussion and moves towards unity in the twenty-first century, a time when the Christian churches are increasingly aware of their need to co-operate if they are to speak with conviction in a multicultural and increasingly secular world. The two churches recognize their need to nurture both their traditions, among which they specify matters of religious practice and style and their ways of remembering their historical traditions, and commemorative festivals. They also recognize their need to respect the wider organizations of which each is a part, the Moravian Unity and the Anglican Communion, together with other ecumenical partnerships. Other major issues on which further discussion is needed include questions of ministry and episcopacy, the latter problem being still unresolved, and they admit to differences of opinion about the means of exercising authority and sustaining the distinctive ethos of each tradition.[15]

The way forward

The progress of discussions on church unity in general was exceedingly slow during the second half of the twentieth century, since each denomination has its preferred forms of worship, and differences of emphasis, and occasionally of belief. Representatives of the Moravian Church faithfully maintained the Moravian presence and voice in these discussions, and it is important to recognize the steadily continuing work of the churches in the direction of mutual understanding and joint worship. The reports of the Faith and Order, Inter-Church Relations Committee exemplify this on-going process. This extract, from *The Messenger* of May 1998, records a particularly significant occasion that was shortly to take place:

> One of the Committees associated with the work of the Inter-Church Relations Committee is the Church of England–Moravian Contact Group. At the February meeting, the Committee was brought up to date with the number of joint services having taken place so far, and the main signing of the Fetter Lane Declaration in Manchester Cathedral on the 7th November 1998 at 11.30 am. The work continues with the Contact Group, although the Church of England Council for Christian Unity is concerned at the span of discussions it has undertaken as it approaches the possibility of talks with the Methodist Church. The Moravian Church has been asked to send an active observer to these discussions and Br David Newman has agreed to represent us.

In principle, the Christian Church as a whole has increasingly recognized that members must respect individuality and diversity and concentrate on the areas in which they can and should speak with one voice. The names of various initiatives directed towards this end may alter, but the regular information reaching Moravian congregations from their representatives has ensured, and continues to ensure, that the shared concerns confronting contemporary Christians continue to be discussed in individual congregations and that members become increasingly aware of the part they can play as members of a wider Church of Christ.

At the beginning of the twenty-first century the British Province of the Moravian Church is aware of its need to continue to be represented in ecumenical discussion, to which it is wholly committed in principle. Christian Unity as a goal is valued by all Christian churches, but many problems still remain to be resolved, and Moravian representatives are working towards this end and ensuring that the views and interests of the church are heard.

These discussions take place against a background of urgent efforts on the part of all the Christian churches to find common ground. The January 2001 edition of the Roman Catholic magazine *Priests and People*[16] is devoted to the theme, 'Christian Unity: What are the Prospects?' and contains articles by representatives of the main churches in Britain. The assistant editor points to unresolved problems and the need to keep making fresh starts, warning of the danger that Christians will be beguiled at the level of personal friendliness and neighbourliness into persuading themselves that there are no significant barriers to unity. Paul Avis, giving the Anglican perspective, is convinced that the deep spiritual unity between the Christian churches cannot be destroyed and must be the basis for progress. He notes the major agreements which the Anglican Church has made with other churches between 1991 and 1999, including the Fetter Lane Agreement, and outlines their common pattern (as described above), including the determination to seek to overcome obstacles on the way to the goal of visible unity. Jenny Carpenter, writing on behalf of the Free Churches, after surveying the causes and history of dissent, points frankly to areas where some churches are still uneasy and recognizes others where they already co-operate, particularly over concerns for the environment and racial justice. She points to the United Reformed Church as a leading force in the commitment to unity, and to the significance of the 'Churches Together in England' movement, particularly their current theme, 'Journeying Together in a Common Life'.

The two concepts of unity in diversity and working together on issues of common concern form a sound basis for the future, since they acknowledge the central importance for Christian churches of speaking out over issues which represent Christian faith in action. The concept of a united Christian Church seems far distant, if it is achievable at all, since all value their traditions and stand by the principles which led to their distinctiveness, but the Moravians in Britain, despite their small numbers, seek as high a profile as possible in these discussions, regarding themselves as a unique denomination with a contribution to make.

The second issue facing the Moravian Church, and related to the need to co-operate with other denominations, is a practical one consequent upon the diminishing number of church members in the British Province. The church still has thirty-five congregations of which four are now joint congregations with the United Reformed Church. Several others either share a minister or hold their services in the premises of other churches. These amalgamations and compromises, the former paralleled on the continent by similar amalgamations with the Lutheran Church, probably represent the only way forward for the Moravians, but threaten their distinctiveness. In this practical sense, it has been possible for the church to acknowledge that its unity with others in Christ is sufficient for all to worship as one united Church. The Moravian element is still nominally distinct, but amalgamation necessarily involves subsuming some of its traditional identity in the greater whole in the interest of survival, a pattern which exemplifies the problem and challenge of Church unity.

Part Four

Moravianism

Introduction

Like all other secular and religious institutional organizations, the Unity of the Brethren has always had its distinctive style. This evolved in response to changes of outlook in European religious society as a whole, to which it has reacted in the light of its own beliefs and traditions. At first it was both energetic and flexible, as its eighteenth-century leaders experimented with a wide range of practices which, although not new in Christian history, appeared idiosyncratic and were sometimes controversial. When pressure of public opinion forced Unity style into more orthodox channels it became less extreme, and from then onwards evolved by combining residual elements from its original Central European homeland with practices resulting from its adaptation to changes within Protestantism. This style can be defined as Moravianism.

Parts Two and Three have followed events in the province, as described in provincial accounts, from the establishment of the first mission to the end of the twentieth century, illustrating not only the experiences described there, but also the tensions and changes which arose from interaction between a growing desire to conform to British denominationalism and the appeal of the Moravians' Anglo-German tradition. Part Four examines the original characteristics of Moravianism and outlines ways in which it changed over two centuries, in order to shed further light on important aspects of the nature and history of the church in the British Province. It examines the original devotional style practised in the Renewed Unity in its contemporary setting, and looks more closely at the traditions within which and from which it originated, providing further evidence of how the German element initially dominated the provincial network and then gradually gave way to a characteristically British practice in which the residual German elements were cherished as symbols of an individual identity.

Discussion of the distinctive Moravian experience centres primarily on the written word, since communication on paper and in print was at the heart of the Brethren's organization. In order for the Pilgrim Congregation led by Zinzendorf to communicate its beliefs and credentials to ordinary members and those who wished to serve as Labourers, it was essential to establish the history, doctrines and way of life which they perceived to characterize the Renewed Unity. The written word, expressed in hymns, liturgies and litanies, and in the network of news from other European congregations and the mission fields, was at the centre of the Brethren's message to interested outsiders and believers alike. Congregational diaries and sermons circulated from Herrnhut maintained a uniform spiritual experience throughout the organization, since they were read aloud in meetings. The devotional works published by and for the Brethren were the main source of their understanding of the spiritual aspect of their faith and community. Their religious fervour was grounded in these expressions of communal experience which also provided resources for personal meditation on devotional texts and traditional imagery. In this respect their spiritual experience, like that of all religious organizations, was partly an expression of devotional priorities derived from their beliefs, and partly the result of the devout individual's visionary and imaginative interpretation of received wisdom. Emphasis has been placed on the eighteenth-century Unity's idiosyncratic use of language, since this was an important aspect of bonding during the formative years of Zinzendorf's lifetime, when fervour and expansion were at their height. Without the ecstasy which it induced and the sense of brotherhood and sisterhood which it fostered, the dynamic which established congregations, societies and missions during the 1740s and 1750s could not have occurred. The early devotional material, reinforced by regular usage, served to make the members aware of the continuity of the Christian traditions from which it was derived, to familiarize them with new material unique to their Brotherhood, and to bind together those who shared its symbolic rituals and imagery. Its influence persists in the specifically Moravian aspects of present hymnody and practice.

Equally important to their vision of community was the education of their own children and those who came into their congregations, and an examination of their early provision for schooling reveals the style and beliefs which they inculcated in the young to safeguard their spiritual nature and provide future workers and leaders of the Brotherhood. These children, in addition to a basic education which fitted them to earn a living, became familiar with the international ethos of the community to which they belonged. Along with adult members of the societies and congregations, they were kept in regular touch with the activities of the whole Unity. Although Moravian education in the British Province changed in the nineteenth century with the development of boarding schools as a commercial enterprise, the church continued to provide generations of children with a Moravian education until these schools became independent organizations.

The publications which the Brethren used, and the letters from other parts of the Unity which were so central to their communal devotional life, give unique insights into habitual ways of thinking which confirmed their shared identity and strengthened the bonds of membership. They were the written sources by which leaders of the German mission established the organization's credentials and the definitive style of its satellites. Their role and forms of expression have changed with the changing nature of provincial and international Moravianism, and these residual elements are being superseded gradually by new forms judged more appropriate to modern worship, but they remain a distinctive feature of the church today.

Moravian Hymnody and Litanies

One characteristic feature of Moravianism by which its evolution is revealed is the Unity's published hymnody, which can best be understood when considered in the framework of Western European Christian hymnody as a whole. The practice of setting religious poetry to music for singing dates from apostolic times, and the motives underlying it have always been the same. They were reiterated by Luther (1483–1546), an acknowledged expert in this field, who also welcomed the supporting role of musical instruments, in line with contemporary use of organs in Roman Catholic churches. For Luther, hymnody, although a valuable vehicle for the worship and praise of God since it aided the exercise of devotion, was primarily a medium for spreading the gospel. His hymns, therefore, conveyed a message which was presented vividly and dramatically in the style of folk-song, with a fairly rapid beat and without ornate language and other poetic refinements. They were designed as a confession of faith rather than a way of creating a mood or conveying passionate emotion,[1] and were uncommon in their time because they were written in the vernacular. The importance of this new development can hardly be exaggerated, for most existing models of sacred poetry used in the day-to-day services of parish churches and monasteries, and in innumerable devotional texts, were written in Latin, as they had been for a thousand years. Latin, as Duffy argues, was the language of spirituality:

> The highest form of prayer was uttered by the priest at the sacring, the moment of consecration at the mass. It was part of the power of the words of consecration that they were hidden, too sacred to be communicated to the lewed (common people), and this very element of mystery gave legitimacy to the sacred character of Latin itself as higher and holier than the vernacular. Moreover, since the word of scripture and the liturgy came from God, they were held to convey power even to those who did not comprehend them.[2]

In this respect, therefore, Latin was one aspect of priestly domination which militated against lay understanding, and it was the latter which Luther wished to encourage.

His influence was decisive in shaping Protestant hymnody during the Reformation,[3] and he encouraged German poets to compose works for this purpose, initially for a revised Mass and later to accord with the different format of religious observance which gradually emerged. The long line of Lutheran publications began with the *Achtliederbuch* of 1523 which contained extracts from the Psalter, paraphrases from other passages of scripture, transcriptions of Latin office hymns and antiphons, pre-Reformation congregational hymns which had been set down originally in the German language, and original hymns. Luther himself made a substantial contribution to the flow of new hymnody, and this formed a basis for subsequent hymnals through the centuries right up to the present time.[4] Nor was this development restricted to Central Europe. The earliest borrowing of non-native Protestant music for English settings occurred about 1539 with the publication of Miles Coverdale's *Psalms and Spiritual Hymns*. This book was based on the hymnody of Johann Walther, who collaborated with Luther in Wittenberg in laying the foundation of German Protestant hymnody.[5]

Luther, in contrast to Calvin in Geneva, was not averse to borrowing secular melodies and adapting them for use as hymns, and many examples of such reuse have been traced. He saw this as a means of preserving old melodies and giving people material that would displace unwholesome songs. He therefore appropriated beautiful melodies for sacred use, asking, 'Why should the devil have all the best tunes?'[6] As a result, Lutheran hymn-tunes were popular and reassuringly familiar. A good example is a melody for 'O sacred head sore wounded', now famous for its role in Bach's St Matthew Passion, but originating as a secular love-song, 'My mind is in turmoil, and a young woman has made it so'.

From the *Achtliederbuch* onwards, Lutheran hymnals provided music for the hymns, and the melody line was usually printed in the range of the male voice with the tenor in the lead. At first each hymn was given its own tune, though occasionally tunes were matched with several hymns. Later, and particularly during the seventeenth and eighteenth centuries as Lutheran hymnals swelled to immense proportions, many more texts were sung to the most popular melodies. The extra expense of printing the tune for each hymn was avoided by publishing hymnals containing words only, tune books with a numbered collection of tunes being printed separately. The appropriate number in the tune book was then indicated in the text, a practice adopted in the eighteenth-century

Unity and other hymnals. As in Lutheran hymnody, the composer of the tune and the writer of the vernacular text were frequently the same person.[7]

Reformation-style hymnals for congregational singing were published by both the Czech and German wings of the Bohemian Unity, the best known and most influential German text being Michael Weisse's 1531 hymnal.[8] It was based on the 1519 Czech edition in use at the time, included several of his own compositions, and had an unusual format in that there was subdivision by titles, beginning with the seasons of the church year. It used only a small number of familiar tunes from pre-Reformation and secular sources. In subsequent editions, new religious poetry was written to fit a restricted repertoire of melodies which were radically different from melodies used in contemporary Lutheran hymnals, and in this respect, too, Bohemian Reformation hymnody differed from the Lutheran which, in the early years, favoured new tunes for new texts.[9] The old Brotherhood, also, sang in the vernacular, i.e. Czech or German, probably in unison and without any instrumental accompaniment. It made extensive use of antiphonal arrangements in which parts of a hymn were allocated to separate groups in the congregation who responded to each other or to a soloist.[10] Thus, despite some differences in style and content, the old pre-Reformation Unity gave hymn-singing a similar role to that assigned to it later by Protestant Reformers.

The evolving hymnody of the Continental Province

The eighteenth-century Brotherhood drew on both Czech and Lutheran sources, elevating and extending them to accord with the beauty and sophistication of current German practice. The Pietist movement had already given fresh impetus to the composition of new hymns,[11] and concurrently music was one of the fine arts in which Germany could claim real distinction, especially after 1700, Dresden being one of several prestigious centres.[12] Unity hymnody developed on a massive scale under Zinzendorf's leadership, laying down the musical tradition of harmonized singing that was to dominate it throughout the eighteenth century and into the nineteenth. The singing of complete hymns was normally confined to the weekly Sunday public services. Most services were private, and referred to as 'meetings', being restricted to congregation or society members; often on these occasions single verses of a variety of hymns were used as responses in prayers, as praises, and even interposed in sermons, to illustrate a particular subject. This devotional style, beloved of Zinzendorf, attained its most sophisticated form in the Singing Service,[13] in which a scriptural theme was elaborated at length by skilful selection of appropriate extracts from many sources. Like the Bohemian Unity, the eighteenth-century Unity clung tenaciously to the principle of writing new texts to well-known melodies.

The early settlers at Herrnhut used the Lutheran hymnals in circulation at that time, and the earliest text issued by Zinzendorf came into use in 1725. It was based mainly on Johann Anastasius Freylinghausen's 1704 hymnal,[14] and was a characteristic Pietist product, Freylinghausen being an influential colleague of Francke at Halle and a leading contemporary hymn writer.[15] It contained only 23 hymns taken from Old Bohemian Unity sources. The so-called Marche hymnal appeared in 1731, followed in 1735 by the first hymnal of the eighteenth-century Unity. This contained a total of 972 pieces; 747 were from various sources, including many from the Lutheran Pietist tradition, and 225 were original compositions by Zinzendorf, exemplifying his Christocentric style and constituting a major landmark for this new religious organization – its own official hymnal. It was a vehicle for a prolific outpouring of individual and congregational fervour and reflection, as well as providing a basic tool for extensive evangelical outreach in Europe and overseas. Further editions were published in 1737 and 1741 with substantial appendices, eight and twelve respectively.

Concurrently, the practice of instrumental accompaniment to harmonized hymn-singing underwent rapid development, for, in contrast to the Bohemian Unity, the new Unity did not limit itself to unaccompanied congregational singing, but made extensive use of wind instruments, trumpets, trombones,[16] horns and organs, in keeping with the elaborate musical traditions and contemporary practice of German-speaking society. From as early as the mid-sixteenth century there had been a continuing tradition of organ-building in Germany, exemplified between 1545 and 1630 by several generations of the north-German Scherer family, whose organs were installed in Lutheran churches in cities such as Lübeck, Stettin and Hamburg.[17] They were succeeded by, among others, Arp Schnitger, the greatest organ-builder of the late seventeenth and early eighteenth centuries, who found inspiration in the work of the distinguished Scherer family, rebuilding some of their organs as well as constructing 150 new ones, many with three and four manuals. There were other organ-builders in Germany, Italy and France, so that, by the 1730s, most sizeable Lutheran and Roman Catholic churches had one, and their congregations were familiar with organ-playing for its own sake as well as to accompany choral and congregational singing.[18] It was taken for granted, therefore, that organs would be used in Unity devotions.

The Brethren also participated in the long-established and extensive German tradition of wind instrumental accompaniment to choral and congregational singing: from the first decades of the seventeenth century groups of trumpeters had been used to accompany congregations and choirs.[19] An example from the Roman Catholic tradition shows that, in Vienna, there were groups of instrumentalists and choral singers capable of performing polychoral works like those for seven choirs and trumpets published in Valentini's *Messa, Magnificat et Jubilate Deo* (1621). Subsequently, the use of trumpets in sacred music spread quickly from the imperial court in that city, so that over an ever-widening area of both Catholic and Protestant Central Europe the instrument became regarded as appropriate for any solemn festive occasion.

These continental developments did not extend to seventeenth-century England and Scotland, where, as Davidson comments,

> the advent of Puritanism was silencing choral singing and organ music in the church. Popular sentiment against the organ (in particular) was felt in English churches for the next two centuries,[20] although during the latter part of the seventeenth century organs were built in the larger cathedrals.[21]

As a result, when the Unity arranged for the installation of an organ in Fulneck and Fetter Lane in 1747 and 1748 respectively, it was found necessary to call upon the German-speaking organ-builder, John Snetzler,[22] who subsequently established a workshop in London and spent a lifetime building and installing some 88 organs in Britain.[23]

Meanwhile, on the continent, choral singing in four parts was introduced, the antiphonic tradition extended, and solo singing widely practised, and musical scores for religious devotions were composed, so that, from its early years, there was a sophisticated musical background for Unity religious poetry far beyond the experience of the old Unity. At religious services an exciting alternation occurred between the presiding liturgist (cantor), the chorus (choir), the Brethren, the Sisters, the congregation as a whole, the instrumentalists and the preacher, providing for the participants a heightened sense of community in devotion similar in scope and variety wherever the Brethren settled. Corroborative evidence for the British Province is provided by John Sharman in his manuscript 'OLIM' (1863), deposited in the archive of Fulneck School. He recalled his experiences there during the period 1813–18, when he was a pupil and worshipped in the settlement.

> Fulneck has had directly and indirectly a vast civilizing influence, and of the agents employed in this good work, music has been by no means the least effective . . . horns, bassoons, trumpets, and the organ. The Germans are, with the exception of the Slavonic tribes, the most musical race in Europe, and the first settlers in Fulneck brought with them the beautiful melodies sung in the German churches from the time of Luther, and thus gave to the thousands who flocked to their ministrations, the first opportunity of comparing sound church music with the he-hawing then universally practised in English churches. The Brethren were probably the first who introduced the quartet of trombones into Yorkshire.[24]

Because of the rapid development of the Unity into an international body, limited at first mainly to Protestant Europe but extending overseas during the 1730s and 1740s, it soon became necessary to publish hymnals in languages other than German, an increasingly important aspect of Unity expansion. In practice, the existing German-language texts and tunes were taken as definitive, and translations were carried out in such a way as to ensure no change to the tune. This perpetuated the long-standing preference for producing new texts to old melodies, which inevitably caused linguistic problems about which some non-German speakers felt strongly, but were overruled. In the 1749 English-language hymnal, published by James Hutton in London, there is a printed copy of his correspondence with Zinzendorf on this point, in which the Count firmly defended the principle: 'when sometimes twenty languages unite in the Praises of the Lord, that Nation would be at a loss, which out of care to preserve the Neatness of Poetry, had altered the Tune, and with it the Harmony with the Chorus'. Hutton's complaint about the poor quality of translation in some of the copious recent material sent from Germany was regarded as irrelevant.

The range of languages involved in these translated hymnals is well illustrated by the following table derived from John Julian's *Dictionary of Hymnody*,[25] showing the total number of editions published and the period of time involved between the first and the last. Only European texts are included for the sake of simplicity, because over the years numerous hymnals were published in local native languages for use on the mission fields, and attempting to quantify them is outside the scope of this book.

Language	Number	Period of time
Bohemian	5	1756–1829
Danish	5	1738–1829
Dutch	several	1738–1856
English	12	1742–1969
Estonian	3	1741–1791
French	2	1747–1880
Lettonian	5	1742–1874
Swedish	1	1819
Wendish	1	1741

Although a large amount of religious poetry was written and published in the early years, there do not appear to be printed records of hymn tunes until 1784. Before then, the published hymnals contained some general suggestions for tunes suitable for particular verse forms; they were obviously well known, many being derived from Freylinghausen, and relatively few in number.[26] This disparity between tunes and verses is clearly illustrated in the case of the next Unity hymnal to be published in 1754, *The Small Hymnal*, which contained 3,000 hymns, mainly of one verse, with an index of only 242 melodies,[27] and in this respect can be regarded as another characteristic Zinzendorfian product. It ran to three editions up to 1772, by which time the desire grew to replace the Count's enthusiasm and devotional style with a more orthodox approach in keeping with the Lutheran tradition and as a means of reassuring the German religious public after the excesses of Herrnhaag. This became the special task of Christian Gregor. His 1778 hymnal was another religious landmark, followed in 1784 by a tune book containing 261 melodies, still showing the influence of Freylinghausen's melodies of 1704 and later.[28] Together these two texts became the foundation of the Continental Province's hymnody and remained in general use until 1927. The present German-language hymnal was issued then, and even as late as 1930, British visitors commented on the use of the same tune for large numbers of hymns.[29]

This, then, was the context in which the hymnals of the British Province gradually evolved. In principle there has always been a strong overflow of continental hymnody into the British repertoire, and very little back to the continent in return, despite the fact that later English-language editions gradually incorporated a variety of hymns from the Church of England, Methodist and Dissenting churches, most of which used a different tune for each hymn. The Wesley brothers were deeply impressed by this continental hymnody and the fervour with which it was sung. This led John to borrow and adapt music from contemporary Unity hymnals for use in his own early publications.[30]

Hymnody of the British Province

In the early 1740s, congregational and society members were handicapped because they could not read the German texts of current Unity hymnody and had few alternatives from other denominations.[31] There was a 'hymn vacuum'[32] which was filled partly by the work of talented English members such as John Cennick who wrote their own hymns, and partly by combined efforts such as that quoted previously from the Fetter Lane Diary of 6 October 1743, when Br James Hutton wrote some verses and the German Labourer Br Schlicht set them to music. There was also a system of somewhat crude translation from German originals, organized by the Unity. Several hymnals edited and printed in London by James Hutton between 1742 and 1749, mainly from this material, went a long way towards meeting the deficiency. In retrospect it is evident that their quality suffered because of the hasty production and unplanned nature of their material, but they were accepted enthusiastically in the emotional climate of the Brethren's congregations and societies during the 1740s.

This was a critical period in Unity development during which the Herrnhaag style, with its obsessive emphasis on Christ's atoning death and need to show gratitude in active service, was having repercussions wherever their missions were being established and becoming known in evangelical circles. Hutton's first collection of 1742, a slim volume of 187 hymns, 90 of which were from Germany, reflected this style. Successive editions of 1743, 1746, 1748 and 1749 contained progressively larger numbers of examples, mostly from Herrnhaag itself, in lengthy appendices. They clearly appealed to him, and there is every sign that they proved attractive to other congregational members and to the German hierarchy in London, some of whom were 'graduates' of Herrnhaag. After 1749 Hutton's private publications ceased because of the furore unleashed by sensational revelations about the Herrnhaagian literary, spiritual and social style, with its 'blood and wounds' theology and overt eroticism. It was decided to wait a few years and then publish an official English-language hymnal which would perform the delicate task of moderating the more offensive 'blood and wounds' elements from the Herrnhaag style, while retaining as much as possible of its original motivating power, which had inspired an outpouring of evangelistic and missionary fervour and expansion.

A similar process was also taking place in the Continental Province, for the same reason, when the first English provincial hymnal, a vast collection, was published in London in 1754. As an expression of modified Unity spirituality it was intended to present a reassuring balance of the familiar and the new. It now contained a major, though still largely German, component from traditional biblical, pre-Reformation and orthodox Protestant sources. This had a calming effect on religious public opinion in the capital, so that succeeding hymnals were published there without arousing further controversy.

The 1754 hymnal laid the foundation for subsequent provincial hymnody. It was followed in 1769 by a shortened, more portable edition of 257 hymns, all taken from its predecessor after its compilers had eliminated further traces of the Herrnhaag style thought likely to give offence. The text thus represented a further stage in a return to Protestant orthodoxy in line with contemporary Unity thinking. It was followed in 1789 by a new hymnal for use in Britain and British colonial territories with a new format modelled on Christian Gregor's 1778 German hymnal, which divided the contents into 40 sections on related themes, an arrangement which became standard in the British Province and persisted into the twentieth century.

Gregor's text also introduced new hymns and others which had been reworked since their original appearance. In the preface to the British hymnal, the editor, John Swertner, acknowledged his debt to Christian Gregor, noting that the German hymnal 'had met with much approbation both in our congregations and with other sincere Christians abroad'.[33] Because it had incorporated many new translations from the German, Swertner also reiterated the difficulty of translation when the text was expected to be compatible with definitive German tunes. The book contained 887 hymns of which 453 were translations, and this arrangement, by which a substantial proportion were imported from the continent, remained in force throughout the next century. Because of this, and the controlling influence of Gregor's format, this 1789 text was recognizably the parent of subsequent English-language hymnals in both Britain and America. It also perpetuated the use of German tunes, one factor ensuring that British provincial hymnals continued to evolve quite differently from those of other Protestant denominations in Britain.

This evolutionary process continued into the next century, with the publication of a new provincial hymnal in 1801. Further editions were published in 1826, 1849 and 1886. The latter, like its predecessors, was for the use of 'the Protestant Church of the United Brethren or Unitas Fratrum', and about a third of the contents were translations from

German, continuing a trend in which the proportion of translations, though still large, was gradually being reduced. In the preface it was stated that a number of recently written hymns had been added, which brought the text more in line with the hymnals of other denominations, and this, it was argued, gave it a more English flavour. In two other respects the new provincial hymnal adhered to conservative influences from the continent: it retained both the tradition of having the same tune for a relatively large number of hymns and the format of 1789. As a result, the difference between English and German hymnals was slight for much of the nineteenth century, because the Continental Province was still using Christian Gregor's 1778 text. The 1886 text was reissued in 1902 with minor adjustments, and then in 1912 a revised hymnal with a completely different order of contents was published, which described itself in a new way: the contents were no longer 'for the use of the Protestant Church of the United Brethren' as they had been since the mid-eighteenth century; they were now *The Liturgy and Hymns authorised for use in the Moravian Church in Great Britain and Ireland*. From then onwards the church retained the title permanently in its hymnals, and under this superscription the text was modified and reissued in 1960. This edition was still in use at the end of the twentieth century, though another edition was being prepared.

Hymnals as a measure of British provincial development

An examination of the content of successive hymnals, selective though it must inevitably be, provides an insight into changes in doctrinal emphasis and style of worship authenticated by the British Province from the mid-eighteenth century onwards.

Because it contains a predominance of English translations from German, the 1754 hymnal is a separatist, essentially German publication unique among hymnals available in London at that time. It is entitled *A Collection of Hymns of the Children of God in all Ages, from the Beginning till Now: In Two Parts designed chiefly for the use of Congregations in Union with the Brethren's Church*. In the preface the editors state that, 'The Brethren's grand topic in their Hymns, as everyone may see, is the Person and Propitiation of Jesus Christ,' and that 'they continually betray a burning Propensity to Propagating the Gospel of Peace'. The key word here is 'propitiation', Christ's appeasement of God for the sake of sinful humanity. In short, the 'grand topic' is Christ's atonement.

Part I contains 695 hymns, mostly from biblical, pre-Reformation,

German and other Central European sources, described collectively as 'Hymns of the Church of God in preceding Times'. They are classified as follows:

> Anthems out of the Bible; taking the form of direct quotations not
>   expressed in hymnal form
> Scripture hymns
> Hymns of the Primitive Church, including Pre-Reformation
> Hymns of the Ancient Brethren's Church (51)
> German hymns of the sixteenth century
> Old hymns of the English church (94)
> German hymns of the seventeenth century
> English hymns of the seventeenth century
> German and English hymns of the late seventeenth and early eight-
>   eenth centuries.

The sections which derive from church practice rather than scriptural sources will be illustrated to show some ways in which their content reflects changes of emphasis.

In Part I, a separate section, numbered 246–97, is classified as 'Hymns of the Ancient Brethren's Church', which with one exception, no. 297, are translations from German, each hymn being preceded by the opening line of the original German text. These hymns contrast markedly in content and mood with the hymns in Part II, written on the continent in the 1730s and 1740s. The earlier hymns are calmer, being less dominated by the atonement and the consequent duty of the convert to adore the person of Christ and make sacrifices in his service. A typical example is no. 270:

> The goodness of our God is great!
> For Blessing he did us create,
> He knows his chosen People all,
> And helps them free from Adam's fall.
>
> He does his people sanctify,
> Moves them to blest things constantly:
> Draws them to Christ his Son and so
> Instructs them all his Will to do.
>
> Whoe'r hears Christ's word heartily,
> And keeps it as it ought to be,
> Believes it and confesseth free,
> He gets a healthy Soul thereby.

He that with God so takes a part,
And hath the trust within his heart;
He's no more an accursed Man,
But an holy and blessed one.

The Sacraments of Christ, which are
Giv'n by his faithful Minister,
Make us truly partake of his
Pure Innocence and Holiness.

Who in this Blessing doth persist,
And walks as a Soldier of Christ,
To him is promised the crown
Of th' holy ones before God's throne.

This hymn is similar to the later Brethren's hymns in its gospel message of salvation and the convert's duty to do the revealed will of God in order to receive his due reward in heaven, but there are significant differences of content. The notion of God's foreknowledge and choice receives more prominence than is customary in the Brethren's eighteenth-century hymns, and the mediation of the ordained minister in the distribution of the sacraments is not emphasized by those who later meditate on their direct knowledge of Christ and access to his person. Descriptions of the redemptive act sometimes seem formulaic in these earlier hymns, which typically praise God without claiming an intense personal relationship between the worshipper and the Saviour.

Hymn 291

Because the Day is at an end,
And night doth now its shade extend;
To thee, O Lord, our Hearts we raise,
And thee for freshest Mercies praise.

Our Calling's Labour to fulfil,
Strength thou hast lent us all the while:
And to exert the gifts of grace
There hath occurr'd both time and place.

Yet we are of Defects aware:
Forgive them, Lord, the Children spare:
Thro' Christ as from all guilt acquit,
And take us to thy care this night.

The majority of the hymns entitled 'Hymns, mostly German in the Sixteenth Century' (nos. 298–336) are by Luther, as a footnote to p. 168 confirms. Since their emphasis is mainly on doctrine, they use simple, unemotive language, and each hymn contains a message. Hymn 304 is typical:

[1] When Adam fell, the frame entire
Of Nature was infected:
The source, whence came the poison dire,
Was not to be corrected,
But by God's grace which saves our race
From their entire destruction.
The fatal lust, indulg'd at first,
Brought Death as its production.

[3] By one Man's guilt we are enslav'd
To sin, death, hell and devil:
But by another's Grace was sav'd
Mankind from all this Evil:
And as we all by Adam's Fall
Were sentenc'd to damnation,
So the Man-God has by his Blood
Regain'd our lost Salvation.

[5] Christ is the Way, the Light, the Door,
The hope and life eternal;
Our strongest Shield, t'obtain the field,
The Helmet of Salvation.

German hymns are further represented in Part I (nos. 432–81) by a section entitled, 'German Hymns of the Seventeenth Century', covering the period of the Pietist movement. These are much more emotive than the Ancient Brethren's hymns and show some of the characteristics which were to be exaggerated in the mid-eighteenth-century Brethren's hymnody. They emphasize the crucifixion, Christ's boundless love and the call to fervent devoted service, thus marking the emergence of evangelical revivalism in Central Europe. They differ from the hymns of the Herrnhaag era primarily in their language and imagery, which are more restrained than that of the Renewed Brethren during the 1730s and the 1740s. Verses 1, 2, 3 and 8 of Hymn 444 express concepts which are more characteristic of Part II:

Jesu, thy boundless Love to me
No thought can reach, no tongue declare:
O knit my thankful heart to Thee,
And reign without a rival there.
Thine wholly, thine alone I am:
Be thou alone my constant Flame.

My Saviour, thou thy love to me
In Want, in pain, in shame hast show'd:
For me on the accursed Tree
Thou pouredst forth thy guiltless blood:
Thy Wounds upon my heart impress,
Nor ought shall the lov'd Stamp efface.

O that my heart which open stands,
May catch each Drop, that torturing pain
Arm'd by my Sins, wrung from thy hands,
Thy Feet, thy Head, thy ev'ry vein:
That still my breast may heave with sighs,
Still tears of love o'erflow my eyes.

Still let thy love point out my Way,
(How wondrous things thy love hath wrought!)
Still lead me, lest I go astray,
Direct my Work, inspire my Thought:
And when I fall, soon may I hear
Thy Voice, and know that Love is near.

The attention of the worshipper is focused on Christ crucified, and the hymn expresses gratitude for his sacrifice and remorse for the personal guilt for which his innocence atones. There is some emotive emphasis on open-heartedness and a pictorial expression of the desire to experience physically the wounds and blood of Christ and to lead a life directed by his loving word and inspiration.

Other elements in Part I of the hymnal express an ascetic principle which accorded with the Pietist emphasis on creating a group of devout worshippers within the existing churches. This trend is typified by these extracts from hymns 451 and 452:

Hymn 451

[1] Farewell henceforth for ever,
Thou false World's empty mode!
Christ and his Grace's favour
Thy system doth explode.
In Heaven's my conversation,
Where souls in him possess
A rich remuneration
For their poor services.

[4] O let my soul be buried
Within thy open side!
So 'bove all hurt be carried,
In thy rich ocean wide.
. . .

[6] Shelter our souls most graciously
Within thy open'd Side;
Move them from every harm away,
And in thy Safeguard hide: . . .

Hymn 452

[1] Haste, Lord, within my worthless heart
To form thyself a Shrine!
For me a poor and simple worm
Thou shed'st thy Blood divine,
Therewith to save my guilty soul
From endless pain and woe.
. . .

The section, 'English Hymns of the Seventeenth Century' (nos. 482–536) again represents a difference in tone. Most of them are written in a simple, gentle style without excessive emotion. A typical example is no. 531, a hymn of twelve verses composed by Joseph Addison, (1672–1719) which opens:

[1] When all thy mercies, O my God,
My rising soul surveys;
Transported with the View, I'm lost
In wonder, love and praise.
. . .

The same mood is represented in no. 613, a hymn of two verses.

[1] I know the weakness of my soul;
But Jesus is my Stay;
My kind Redeemer has engag'd
To lead me in his Way.

[2] And he'll for ever be the same
Tho' I to change am prone;
My welfare still he will promote,
Who chose me for his own.

Part II, entitled, 'Hymns of the Brethren in the Eighteenth Century', contains 460 largely unclassified hymns and single verses, mostly if not entirely from German or other Central European sources. In a combined alphabetical index at the end of Part II, the tune number allocated to each item is cited, with reference to a separate 'Table of Tunes'. Ninety hymns use tune 9, ninety-eight hymns use tune 8, and there are other examples of such multiple use, showing that in 1754 it remained customary for many hymns to be sung to the same tune, and that this aspect of the dominant Unity style was retained regionally.

Since its overall style is still exciting and at times feverish, Part II probably reflects the reality of current Unity spirituality better than Part I. There is the same lavish praise for and preoccupation with the detail of the Saviour's self-sacrificing death on the cross, linked with effusive expressions of confident willingness to serve him as a means to eternal life. Collectively, these 460 hymns and the accompanying single verses, all from Unity sources, represent without fundamental change a yearning to say the well-loved emotive things in many slightly different ways, and they were popular because they were repetitive and reinforced the familiar tenets of the faith.

Many of the hymns in Part II take the form of a personal conversation with the Saviour, conveying thankfulness for his atoning death, confidence in his leadership and willingness to serve him. The first and third verses of no. 3 typify the combination of adoration and gratitude which remained strong features of communal devotions:

[1] Jesu, our glorious Head and Chief,
Sweet Object of our Heart's belief,
O let us in thy Nail-prints see,
Our Pardon and Election free;

And in the op'ning of thy pierced Side,
Freely go in and out and feed and hide.

[3] And now, dear Lord, I thee entreat,
(Thy Child that twines around thy Feet,
That can't without thee live an hour,
Thee, my Soul's Husband, Rock and Tower;
Whom above all Things even myself I love)
O let me in this Language still improve.

In hymn 72 the emotional mood of devotion is sustained.

[1] O Lamb, O wounded bleeding Lamb!
My heart's a-thirst for thee,
And pants and gasps for thy sweet Grace;
Each moment water me.

[2] Look with thy tender piercing Eyes,
And search my ev'ry Thought,
And all the turnings of my Heart;
Look on the Worm thou'st bought.

[10] I am thine own, for thou hast bought
Me with thy dearest Blood;
Since I'm so precious in thy Sight,
Do with me as seems good.

This willingness to serve as the Saviour demands is a frequent theme, expressed typically in verses 23 and 27 of Hymn 3, where verse 23 emphasizes how the calm of reflection leads the nourished soul to active service:

[23] The Soul at first a Calm enjoys;
Then feasts; and next to Action flies,
Where Faith's unconquerable Might
Undaunted meets its glorious Fight;
She works . . .

[27] At Jesu's Word each Witness flies
To open all the blinded Eyes;
And when we call, the Lord is near . . .

Thankfulness, another recurring theme, is often associated with intimate contemplation of the Cross and echoes of the Sacrament, as in the following verses:

Hymn 40

[6] Nothing's sweeter than this Matter,
That the Lamb has dy'd for me;
None can truly tell its Value,
Here, nor in Eternity.

[7] O my Saviour, Let me ever
Feed on what thou'st done for me;
O let nothing but thy off'ring
Be of any weight to me.

[8] Thus reclining, always twining
Like a Worm about thy Feet,
I shall feel it every Minute,
That thy Blood alone is sweet.

Hymn 42 illustrates how this certainty of redemption and willingness to serve are often associated with indifference to the beguiling influence of worldly pleasures as the soul rejoices in its new life in the country of the redeemed who have been called by their Saviour.

Hymn 42

[1] O tell me no more
Of this World's vain Store,
The Time for such Trifles
With me now is o'er.

[2] A Country I've found,
Where true Joys abound;
To dwell I'm determined
On that happy Ground.

[7] Great Spoils I shall win
From Death, Hell and Sin:
Midst outward Afflictions
Shall feel Christ within.

Both the individual and the community are utterly confident of divine leadership. The personal direction of the Saviour, a tenet of their belief as Unity members, is reflected here.

Hymn 216
[1] Thou who of old the Leader was,
And Guide of Israel's chosen Race,
Who by thy own almighty Hand,
Didst bring them safe from Egypt's Land
. . .

[3] That mighty Pow'r thou then didst show,
Assur'd we are attends us now;
Yea, much more tender watchful care
We thy thrice happy children share;
Thy guidance sure, tho' secret we pursue,
Thy Spirit's voice and Beck we ever view.

[6] Thy Guidance may we never leave;
To thee our Elder ever cleave;
Thy Blood-mark on our foreheads be,
That the deriding World may see
We thy blest people are, thy chosen train,
Bought with the price of thy so bitter Pain.

The sense of a journey undertaken and a just reward at the end for the one who follows the Saviour are illustrated in the first verse of Hymn 236:

Morning Star I follow thee,
Lead me here or lead me there:
Thou my Staff in trav'ling be,
I'll no other weapon bear;
Me may Angels guard from ill,
When I am to do thy Will:
So shall I with steady pace,
Reach the dearest City, Grace.

The sentiments expressed in these lines encapsulate the spirit of a missionary church whose emissaries were working in some of the most dangerous and difficult areas of the world for Europeans, and whose residential communities were regarded as a training-ground for world-wide service. It is significant that they appear in the section of the hymnal devoted to contemporary compositions.

Part II also contains 'The Church Litany', which featured regularly during Sunday devotions, and a somewhat enlarged version for use on special occasions, together with 'The Litany of the Life, Sufferings and Death of the Lord', which, as the name suggests, was a fully developed litany on a somewhat smaller scale than the Church Litany. There is also a select group of specially titled hymns, such as, 'The Church's Prayer to her Head and Lord', which have a litany-like response layout.

The 1754 hymnal, drawing on German and other Central European sources to an extent unique in contemporary British hymnody, was the foundation on which all subsequent provincial hymnals were built. It remains a very important publication for the understanding of eighteenth-century Unity spirituality as presented to English-speaking members, because it provided them with source material for public and private devotions. During the next two centuries succeeding hymnals retained a distinctively Anglo-German style. Changes were slow and irresolute, because the mid-eighteenth-century atonement style of the original Unity in its German homeland exercised a strong and persistent appeal, in spite of a desire in the British Province for modernization in line with contemporary taste, and a willingness to bring in new hymns. Much later, in 1886, after several intermediate editions, this German influence was still clearly evident, and it was not until the publication of revised hymnals in 1912 and 1960 that it lessened significantly. Even then, in comparison with other contemporary publications such as the *English Hymnal* (1904) and *Songs of Praise* (1925), provincial hymnody is still Anglo-German and separatist. Although there was a progressive reduction in the proportion of English translations of German hymns from about one-third in 1754 to about one-fifth in 1960, what is retained is still substantial, and influential because of its traditional and familiar role in the Brethren's worship.

The significance for the development of the British Province of this slow transition from a German to an Anglo-German style can be better understood in its context. Between 1754 and 1960, there were changes in the way in which British society interpreted the nature and content of religious poetry and its expression in hymnody. These strongly influenced mainstream denominational hymnody and had some effect on the Brethren's provincial hymnody.

By the end of the eighteenth century, ideas about suitable subjects for hymns and appropriate modes of expression were evolving under the influence of the English Romantic poets.[34] The first generation of these, Blake, Wordsworth, Coleridge and Southey, far from rejecting Christianity, were devout believers of one kind or another and found sources of inspiration in the Bible,[35] but to a much greater extent they celebrated a love of beauty in nature and recognized the value of freedom. As a result, the subject matter of hymnody became less centred on the salvation of a foul sinner washed clean by the blood of the Lamb, and more on the adoration of some aspect of the Trinity.[36] The most distinguished single example of hymn-writing to which this new and popular approach gave rise was R. Grant's, 'O Worship the King', based on Psalm 54.

> O worship the King
> All glorious above;
> O gratefully sing
> His power and his love;
> Our shield and defender,
> The ancient of days,
> Pavilioned in splendour
> And girded with praise.

As Watson says, 'This hymn is beautiful in its Wordsworthian perception of an active, living universe; . . . it illustrates *par excellence* how the hymnody of salvation has become the hymnody of adoration.'[37]

The Brethren's provincial hymnals were very slow to respond to these changes, and the many hymns which still dealt with the atonement did so in language little different from that of the mid-eighteenth century, as the following typical examples from the 1809 hymnal show:

Hymn 66. German

> [1] Immanuel's meritorious tears
> Assuage our ev'ry pain,
> His bitter suff'rings, cries and pray'rs
> Our fav'rite theme remain.

Hymn 409. German

> Glorious Redeemer, thou hast me
> To come to thee invited;
> Thy love, to love thee ardently
> Hath my cold heart excited.

Thy cross, thy shame, thy pangs, thy smart,
Thy wounds and bitter passion,
Now melt and captivate my heart,
And prompt my adoration.

Hymn 501. German [Single verse]

Lord Jesus, thy atonement
Be ever new to us;
Grant we may ev'ry moment
In spirit view thy cross:
O keep our garments pure,
In the temptation hour,
From sin's infatuation
Preserve us by thy pow'r.

The Brethren's customary emphasis on the atonement was a feature, also, of many hymns of English origin which were retained in the 1809 hymnal.

Hymn 416

[1] Teach me yet more of thy blest ways,
Thou slaughter'd Lamb of God!
And fix and root me in the grace
So dearly bought with blood.

Hymn 504

[1] O Lord, the contrite sinner's Friend,
Most wretched should I be,
Did I not know thy precious blood
Was shed for worthless me.
. . .

[2] . . .
More clearly to me manifest
The myst'ry of thy cross;
And for this precious Pearl may I
Count all things else but dross.

The criteria for selection were sufficiently long-established to ensure that hymns which maintained the Brethren's traditional focus still dominated the atmosphere and message of their hymnody, in spite of its use of a variety of source material. Since this edition reflects provincial thinking at a time when the Place Congregations were still flourishing, the 1809 hymnal is dominated by hymns of the atonement from both German and English sources. This emphasis demonstrates an exclusive attitude which does not follow the trend identified by Watson in the hymnody of other denominations, where the prevailing subject matter is no longer salvation through the blood of the Lamb, but adoration of the Creator and the celebration of a love of nature, beauty and freedom, the themes of Romantic poetry.

By the early nineteenth century, the eighteenth-century association of hymn-singing with dissent, nonconformity and evangelicalism was weakening. The emotive hymns of that earlier period were now generally regarded as rude and homely; something more refined was looked for, and this change in taste was evolving with exceptional vigour among Anglicans, who had hitherto been singers of metrical psalms and only marginally of hymns. At the beginning of the Victorian period, therefore, the writing of new 'Romantic' hymns became important in all the British Protestant Churches, changing the style of an evangelical and dissenting minority into an art form which had something in common with the more universal hopes and aspirations of the Romantic poets.[38] In this way hymnody became respectable and dignified, being drawn into a more central role in mainstream Christian experience.

Two of the leading writers of this genre were James Montgomery (1771–1854) and Reginald Heber (1783–1826). Heber, a distinguished clergyman of the Church of England who later became Bishop of Calcutta, began to publish his hymns in 1811. He had a strong sense of the dignity and majesty of God, with the result that his hymns are fervent, but do not emphasize the atonement.[39]

The son of a British provincial minister, Montgomery was educated at Fulneck School. He had originally been regarded as a prospective candidate for the provincial ministry, but instead went into publishing in Sheffield, where he lived for the rest of his life. Whether or not he was nominally a member of a particular provincial congregation as an adult is uncertain;[40] he was not active in the church, his funeral service was not conducted in one of the Brethren's churches, nor was he interred in a Unity graveyard such as Fulneck or Ockbrook, but in Sheffield. He was undoubtedly in close touch with leading church members among whom he was regarded as one of their own. His advice was sought in connection with the 1849 Hymnal, which in 1835 he had agreed to revise, though begging for more time. At the 1847 synod, Br Reichel gave an account of his correspondence with 'Br J. Montgomery' relative to the revision.[41]

There is no suggestion that Montgomery met the leading provincial ministers in this connection, nor did he edit the text, though he suggested the removal of some hymns from the earlier hymnal, added others and made some revisions.

James Montgomery became widely recognized as a significant poet of the Romantic period[42] and his hymns were included in various British hymnals, including those later published by the Brethren. There were 51 in the 1886 edition, and even by 1960, 30 still remained. Their inclusion indicates some change of emphasis in British provincial hymnody, and willingness to accept new conventions, since many of them reflected adoration rather than atonement:

> [1960 edn] Hymn 447
>
> [1] Songs of praise the angels sang,
> Heaven with hallelujahs rang,
> When creation was begun,
> When God spoke and it was done.
> . . .
>
> Hymn 448
> [1] Stand up and bless the Lord,
> Ye people of his choice;
> Stand up and bless the Lord your God
> With heart and soul and voice.
> . . .

He was also regarded as one of the greatest poet/hymn-writers on the subject of prayer,[43] understanding it as central to the Christian life:

> Prayer is the Soul's sincere desire,
> Uttered or unexpressed;
> The motion of a hidden fire
> That trembles in the breast.

As the nineteenth century progressed, hymn-writing in the Romantic style proceeded apace, with enthusiastic participation by members of the mainstream denominations until, in 1861, there was a pivotal moment in nineteenth-century hymnody with the publication of *Hymns Ancient and Modern*. It was 'astonishingly popular . . . the representative book of Victorian hymnody',[44] becoming the dominant text in the Church of England. After its appearance, the number of hymn-books published

in Britain multiplied rapidly and their contents gained variety and rich-
ness.

Despite these contemporary changes in attitude to hymnody and the
vibrant context in which new ones were being produced, the Brethren's
provincial hymnals still retained a substantial proportion of hymns in the
earlier tradition, a majority of which were English translations from
German. Of course, it is impossible to know how many were in regular
use, though it may be significant that the Continental Province retained
and used the 1778 Christian Gregor edition through the nineteenth and
into the twentieth century. The fact that these traditional hymns were
included at all suggests that they still met provincial needs. A typical
example from the 1886 edition is Hymn 501, a translation which begins:

> Lord Jesus, thy atonement
> Be ever new to us;
> Grant we may every moment
> In spirit view thy cross,

and the opening of no. 416, an English original, could well have been
written at the time of Zinzendorf:

> Teach me yet more of thy blest ways,
> Thou slaughtered Lamb of God!
> And fix and root me in the grace
> So dearly bought with blood.

These examples are characteristic of a text which was still very largely a
celebration of atonement, despite the inclusion of new hymns in a more
modern style by writers such as Montgomery.

The Anglo-German nature of provincial hymnody can be analysed more
accurately in the 1886 hymnal which, for the first time, printed the name
of the author of each hymn. With this information it becomes possible to
estimate to what extent this hymnal with its German atmosphere was still
rooted in the eighteenth century and the time of the Evangelical Revival.
It contained 1,323 hymns, 456 of which were German – from the Revival
period in the majority of cases. Many others had been written by mid to
late eighteenth-century members of the church. There were 151 by the
Zinzendorf family, chiefly the Count (1700–60), 59 by Christian Gregor
(1723–1801), and 49 by John Cennick (1718–55). Other eighteenth-
century contributions came from outside the direct tradition of the

Brethren and were less circumscribed in content. These included 76 by Charles Wesley (1708–81), 36 by John Newton (1725–1807) and 39 by Isaac Watts (1674–1748). Together with contributions by more recent nineteenth-century writers, the latter group represented some recognition of the movements which were taking place in other denominations, and reflected the change which was slowly drawing the province towards a degree of conformity with the English tradition which would have been unthinkable a generation before. Even so, the overall picture is still of a conservative evangelical style, with limited appreciation of more recent changes of sentiment in the religious public as a whole.

In other denominations in Britain where German hymnody was appreciated during the nineteenth century, successive editions of the Brethren's provincial hymnody appear to have had virtually no influence. It is true that John Wesley translated 33 hymns from the 1735 edition of the Herrnhut hymnal and introduced them to a variable extent in the series of hymnals published by the Methodists; but apart from that, the collection of hymns which was most used as a resource for mainstream hymnals during the nineteenth century was a seminal anthology of over nine hundred hymns originally assembled by Christian Carl Josses Bunsen, a Prussian diplomat and man of letters, who was Prussian Ambassador in Britain from 1841 to 1854. His 1833 anthology, published in Hamburg, inspired a number of brilliant young English women to become translators. Their work was far more influential than the readily available Brethren's hymnals in making the religious public more aware of the treasures of German hymnody.

Frances Elizabeth Cox (1812–97) was one of the earliest of these translators; she published *Sacred Songs from the German* in 1841. In 1855, Catherine Winkworth (1829–78), regarded as the most outstanding of the group,[45] published her collection of translations, *Lyra Germanica*, in which the hymns of Paul Gerhardt had a prominent place because she regarded him as the greatest of all German hymn-writers. These translated anthologies were widely appreciated, and one prominent feature of the new *Hymns Ancient and Modern* published in 1860 was the use of German hymnody mainly derived from the publications of these women.

This was the position by the turn of the century when among the religious public in general and Anglicans in particular, further changes in taste were occurring. One was a desire to move away from Victorian hymnody, another was exemplified in the writings of the aesthetic movement in literature, a prominent contributor to which was John Ruskin. His influence emerged most clearly in the hymns of Robert Bridges, whose *Yattenden Hymnal*[46] was published between 1895 and 1899. This, a beautifully printed book, was a small collection of one hundred hymns, many by Bridges himself, set to music from the sixteenth and seventeenth centuries. Its simple and dignified language expressed the beauty of religion which, for Bridges, was its chief attribute. He therefore excluded hymns detailing the crucifixion, preferring those dealing with heaven, natural beauty and the joy of life within a divine setting. His best known, a translation from Joachim Neander, appears in the British Province's 1960 hymnal as no. 323, and reflects Bridges' advocacy of beauty in words and music, preferably as in seventeenth-century plain-song. It reads,

[1] All my hope on God is founded;
He doth still my trust renew,
Me through change and chance he guideth,
Only good and only true
God unknown – He alone
Calls my heart to be his own.

The *Yattenden Hymnal* was followed in 1904 by a disastrous reissue of *Hymns Ancient and Modern*, by then used in so many Anglican churches that it could justifiably be regarded as their official hymnal. Unfortunately, in an attempt to conform to contemporary thinking, radical changes had been made to many well-known and loved hymns, a policy which provoked controversy among users. It was quickly followed by the publication of *The English Hymnal*, an early attempt to escape from the restrictions of official denominational hymnals and include all the best hymns of the English language, irrespective of source. The new book was significant for its use of tunes from the repertoire of English folk music, arranged by composers of the calibre of Vaughan Williams, to replace some of the traditional Victorian contributions which were increasingly being seen as dated. This book brought in new hymns expressing national and imperial pride, as well as admonitions for humility in the acceptance of the responsibilities entailed in this dominant role. Other new hymns expressed social concerns aroused by what was seen as widespread acceptance of materialism and inequality in society. The process was taken further in *Songs of Praise*, published in 1925, which advanced *The English Hymnal*'s non-denominational style still further, appealing to the common pool of Christian goodwill in all churches and stressing service and international understanding. Schools, most of which had no direct denominational connection, were also targeted. In all these respects, and particularly in schools, *Songs of Praise* was a great success, justifying the publication of an enlarged version in 1931, in which those sections dealing specifically with children's interests and a love of nature were expanded. In the preface to this edition the editor showed that he was well aware of the difficulties of producing a new hymnal to compensate for the increasing evidence of alienation from denominational hymnodies. Nevertheless, this was in his view the way forward, and the new non-denominational style continued in the BBC Hymnal of 1951, described as educative and undogmatic.

The scene was now set for preliminary work on a new Moravian hymnal, the first since 1912. Its compilers clearly recognized the profound changes of taste which had occurred since then. As a result, when the new hymnal was published in 1960, it conformed much more closely than any of its predecessors to the generally accepted style of contemporary hymnody as exemplified by *The English Hymnal* and *Songs of Praise*, while retaining some key aspects of its own separatist Anglo-German style.

Its editors drastically reduced overall contributions from traditional eighteenth-century Unity and British provincial sources, a change best illustrated by comparison with a few examples taken from the 1886 hymnal:

	1886	*1960*
John Cennick	49	11
Christian Gregor	59	5
Christian Ignatius LaTrobe	15	2
John Newton	36	8
Count Zinzendorf and family	151	32

James Montgomery's hymns were severely pruned from 51 to 30, and the hymns of Charles Wesley were reduced from the very substantial number of 76 in 1886 to a more modest 30. The most significant change was in the contribution of the Zinzendorf family, which had always been over-represented, despite the fact that their vocabulary had been modified considerably over the years under the influence of the Romantic and Aesthetic movements.

The new hymns which replaced these omissions came partly from sources already referred to. Catherine Winkworth was represented by nine hymns in 1886, but nineteen in 1960, Robert Bridges by four. There was only one by Rudyard Kipling, exponent of national honour and social concern, but it exemplified strong currents of opinion prevalent in Britain at the beginning of the twentieth century and still acceptable, particularly in the spiritual education of young people, until the collapse of British imperialism was complete.

Hymn 318

[1] Land of our birth, we pledge to thee
Our love and toil in the years to be;
When we are grown and take our place
As men and women with our race.

[5] Teach us the strength that cannot seek
By deed or thought to hurt the weak;
That under thee we may possess
Man's strength to comfort man's distress.

Percy P. Dearmer, editor of *The English Hymnal* and *Songs of Praise*, was represented by five hymns characterized by the non-denominational style of his texts. Hymn 11 speaks of the truth and wisdom enshrined in the Bible and its unique role as a model for the leaders of society:

[1] Book of books, our people's strength,
Statesman's, teacher's, hero's treasure,
Bringing freedom, spreading truth,
Shedding light that none can measure!
Wisdom comes to those who know thee,
All the best we have we owe thee.

Hymn 79 shows a completely different aspect of Jesus Christ from that which was so characteristic of the eighteenth- and early nineteenth-century provincial hymnals, with their emphasis on the devotion of the redeemed sinner to his atonement and wounds:

[1] Jesus, good above all other,
Gentle child of gentle mother,
In a stable born our brother,
Give us grace to persevere.

[3] Jesus, for thy people dying,
Risen Master, death defying,
Lord in heaven thy grace supplying,
Keep us to thy presence near.

Jan Struther, a contributor to *Songs of Praise*, was represented by two hymns, both of which demonstrated her non-denominational stance. Hymn 272 was written with a youthful audience in mind:

[1] When a knight won his spurs in the stories of old
He was gentle and brave, he was gallant and bold;
With a shield on his arm and a lance in his hand,
For God and for valour he rode through the land.

[3] Let faith be my shield and let joy be my steed
'Gainst the dragons of anger, the ogres of greed;
And let me set free, with the sword of my youth,
From the castle of darkness the power of the truth.

The romantic, crusading image appeals to desirable qualities of character and an unspecified faith in an equally unspecified truth, again a long way from the precise teaching which young people in the eighteenth-century provincial Oeconomies were given through their hymnody.

Many other, mostly pre-twentieth-century, writers were represented by one or two hymns; yet what still made this text different from all its companion volumes of twentieth-century hymnody adopted by other denominations was the survival, particularly in the Holy Communion and Covenant section, of hymns from the eighteenth-century German Unity tradition. These retained the forceful message of the original versions and some of their imagery, even though the language had been toned down. Most Protestant denominations preserve some images of the body and blood of Christ symbolized in bread and wine in their communion service and its associated hymnody, but a more specific survival of the Brethren's traditional directness remains here. A typical example is no. 513, composed by Zinzendorf in 1734:

[1] O glorified Head,
Since mortals may tread
The holiest of all,
And deeply abased 'fore the mercy seat fall;

[2] Admit us, we pray,
On this solemn day,
To thee to draw nigh,
And thy holy body and blood to enjoy.

Another, by John Cennick, shows similar characteristics:

Hymn 514
[1] Together with these symbols, Lord,
Thy blessed self impart;
And let thy holy flesh and blood
Feed the believing heart.

Johann Wilhelm Zander's contribution, no. 521, is a single verse:

Like the King of Salem,
Thou with wine and bread
Com'st to meet thy people,
Them to cheer and feed:
O preserve the enjoyment
Of thy blood and death
To thy congregation,
While we live by faith.

Finally, the covenant hymn, no. 554, written by the British provincial member John Swertner and published in 1789, retains the best of the authentic mid-eighteenth-century style virtually intact:

Now bless and praise the slaughtered Lamb,
Extol the great Redeemer's name,
Thou favoured congregation,
Which at the table of our Lord
Didst eat and drink with one accord;
Thou know'st thy destination
Is to abide in Christ by faith,
And to show forth our Saviour's death:
Walk then as children of the light;
Live to his praise by day and night:
    O Lamb once slain,
    We vow again
    Thine to remain;
Confirm our promises: Amen.

The tone of these celebrations of communion and covenant is not replicated in the 1983 Methodist publication *Hymns and Psalms*, which is a good representative of current Nonconformist practice. Alongside more recent hymnody, this hymnal typically uses a more symbolic eighteenth-century expression of the sacrament, such as that found in no. 596, a hymn by Charles Wesley:

[1] Author of life divine,
Who hast a table spread,
Furnished with mystic wine
And everlasting bread, . . .

It retains as no. 597 James Montgomery's 'Be known to us in breaking bread', which the Moravian hymnal does not use:

[1] Be known to us in breaking bread,
But do not then depart;
Saviour abide with us, and spread
Thy table in our heart.

[2] There sup with us in love divine,
Thy body and thy blood,
That living bread, that heavenly wine,
Be our immortal food.

The two hymnals do share the lovely communion hymn by Reginald Heber (1783–1826) set to a melody from *La Forme des Prières et Chants Ecclésiastiques* published in Strasbourg in 1545:

Bread of the world in mercy broken;
Wine of the soul, in mercy shed:
By whom the words of life were spoken,
And in whose death our sins are dead:

Look on the heart by sorrow broken,
Look on the tears by sinners shed;
And be thy feast to us the token
That by thy grace our souls are fed.

This evidence of selection from a common heritage serves to underline how, in the evolution of denominational hymnody, the underlying philosophies behind the publications of different churches still operate to reinforce those areas of practice and tradition in which their members are most aware of their individuality. As their hymnody reveals, this is an area in which the Moravian Brethren still remain committed to preserving the unique elements in their own history.

Litanies of the British Province

In *A Dictionary of Church Music*, James Robert Davidson describes a litany as a responsive order of prayer consisting of a series of biddings and petitions led by an officiant, with each article followed by a brief fixed response by the people, i.e. antiphonally. Being found in pagan rites, it is one of the most ancient forms of worship, and its simple device of repetition has for centuries been a means of securing the attention and united involvement of participants. Every word is crucial because it contributes some vital insight to the whole ritual.

The necessity of a historical perspective on the development of litanies has long been recognized by religious historians. Their collective view was exemplified by Alphonse Dupront when he wrote, 'I cannot conceive of a better way to cast light on the basic associations and impulses of religious life than by studying these various sorts of writing intended for collective meditation.'[47] The source of Unity litanies, therefore, like their hymnody, can be located in the early sixteenth century. The pre-Reformation Church made use of litanies, and Luther appreciated their value,[48] introducing two in 1529 which were very similar and defined as 'The Latin Litany Corrected' and 'The German Litany'. These and their appended collects were closely modelled on the pre-Reformation 'Litany of all Saints', excluding the invocations of the saints and intercession for the Pope and the departed,[49] and form the direct though distant antecedent of the familiar First Order of Worship, or First Litany, of present-day usage.

A Litany for Protestants: Luther's 1529 prototype

This, usually referred to as Luther's 'Great Litany', formed the basis for all subsequent Lutheran litanies. As in his hymns, Luther's turn of phrase was vivid and dramatic, expressed with clarity and simplicity without ornate language and other poetic refinements. Petitions were comprehensive in range and identified all the needs of the human condition. The style was antiphonal, every petition being followed by a united response by the congregation, with the opening and closing *Kyrie eleison* shared between the officiant and choir. This was rendered in its ancient form:

Kyrie eleison,
Christe eleison,
Kyrie eleison,
O Christ hear us.

Then followed the crucial words of Christian doctrine, that a tripartite yet inseparable Godhead should be petitioned for mercy and direct intervention in earthly activities:

O God, the Father in heaven, Have mercy upon us.
O God, the Son, Redeemer of the world, Have mercy upon us.
O God, the Holy Ghost, Have mercy upon us.

Next, after petitioning for divine graciousness, began the lengthy list of what may be described as doctrinal entreaties:

From every sin, Free us good Lord.
From every error, Free us good Lord.
From every evil, Free us good Lord.
From the snares of the devil, Free us good Lord.
From sudden and unexpected death, Free us good Lord.
From plague and famine, Free us good Lord.
. . .
By the mystery of thy holy incarnation, Free us good Lord.
By thy holy nativity, Free us good Lord.
By thy baptism, fasting and temptation, Free us good Lord.
By thine agony and bloody sweat, Free us good Lord.
By thy cross and passion, Free us good Lord.
By thy death and burial, Free us good Lord.
. . .

Subsequent 'more earthbound' entreaties for divine assistance included,

That thou would'st deign to preserve all bishops, pastors and ministers of the church in sound word and holy life,
That thou would'st deign to send faithful labourers into thy harvest,
That thou would'st deign to give peace and concord to all kings and princes,
That thou would'st deign to cherish and guard the infants and the sick,
That thou would'st deign to give and preserve the fruits of the earth,
. . .

The antiphonal response in this section was, 'We entreat thee to hear us.'
    Luther's 1529 prototype was then rounded off with the three petitions of the *Agnus Dei,* followed by a repeat of the *Kyrie Eleison.*

This, then, was the source not only of the subsequent Lutheran Litany but of others, so that its influence was Europe-wide. This litany was used by the Bohemian Unity from the 1560s and printed in their 1566 hymnal,[50] and, with contributions from the litanies of the Eastern Orthodox Church, it also provided a framework for the litany in the Anglican Book of Common Prayer (1549).[51] Later, Zinzendorf recast and extended it, publishing it for Unity use in 1744. The first English-language edition, a direct translation, appeared in London in 1746 and was republished with amendments in 1752 in the form of a slim book entitled *Some of the Litanies of the Brethren's Churches*, and was divided into two parts. Part I consisted of the Church Litany derived from Luther, followed by a series of six special litanies composed for the Unity during the mid-eighteenth-century expansive period, but gradually falling into disuse by the end of the century. These were:

Litania dei patris
Litania Domini Immanuelsis
Te Agnum
Litany of the Life and Death of the Man Jesus Christ
Litania domini Spiritus
Hymnus de Sponsa

All six were set for two choirs responding to each other, with antiphonal responses by the congregation as a whole or the men and women separately. The style was essentially poetic and literary; participation was meant to be an aesthetic experience, the language encouraging an outpouring of emotion.

This style also influenced the contents of Part II, which comprised hymns and poems chiefly translated from the German. The printed introduction summarized the rationale of the Unity in a hymn of ten lengthy verses, typified by verse 4.

The Doctrine of the Unitas
By Providence was meant
In Christendom's degenerate Days
That cold lump to ferment;
From Scripture Pearls to wipe the Dust;
Give Blood-bought Grace its Compass just,
In Praxis, Truth from show to part,
God's Pow'r from Ethic Art.

In verse 8 there was a further revealing disclosure about the Unity's attitude to itself:

> A chosen Flock must like the Sun
> Here cherish and there scorch.

This is an ironic touch in view of contemporary controversy and criticism which had been associated with the spirituality of Herrnhaag.

The Church Litany of 1754

Zinzendorf's version, 'The Church Litany', reappeared in 1754 at the end of Part II of the revised British Hymnal,[52] and from that time onwards, with further amendments, was the basis of all subsequent provincial publications. A comparison of this litany as published in London in 1754 and Zinzendorf's 1744 recasting of Luther's original text shows that the two texts were virtually identical apart from the additions made by Zinzendorf.

Zinzendorf's version followed much the same format as his illustrious sixteenth-century predecessor's, though with a substantial increase in length and elaboration. It began with the *Kyrie Eleison*, followed by the Lord's Prayer, then the crucial words of Christian doctrine with 'blood and wounds' language deriving from his time and not Luther's, in which, addressing God, '. . . and lead us not into temptation, but deliver us from evil,' there was a pause while the choir sang a characteristic mid-eighteenth-century Unity verse:

> Think on thy Son's so bitter Death,
> His five dear Wounds and thorny Wreath;
> For they have full Atonement made,
> For all the World a Ransom paid.

Zinzendorf then extended the original 1529 list of short doctrinal petitions to include,

> *From all Sin,* Keep us our dear Lord and God.
> *From all Error,* Keep us our dear Lord and God.
> *From all Coldness to thy Merit and Death,* Keep us our dear Lord
>   and God.
> *From the Devil's Power and Craft,* Keep us our dear Lord and God.
> *From Tumult and Sedition,* Keep us our dear Lord and God.

From the wicked World, Keep us our dear Lord and God.
. . .

From untimely Projects, Keep us our dear Lord and God.
From all Loss of our Glory in thee, Keep us our dear Lord and God.
. . .

Luther's simple and quite brief 'earth-bound entreaties' were likewise greatly extended and enriched, in Zinzendorf's terms, by choral verses sung only by the choir. The type of request fitted with those of 1529, although with insights and emphases characteristic of eighteenth-century Unity thinking and practical concerns, for example,

> *Bless thy holy Catholic Church invisibly, unite her visibly and bring*
> *   her together from the Ends of the World.*
> *Make the Word of thy Cross universal among all those who are*
> *   called by thy Name.*
> *Forgive our Enemies, Persecutors and Slanderers and turn their*
> *   Hearts.*
> *Keep the Single Brethren and Sisters chaste both in Body and Mind.*
> *Keep thy Eyes open on all thy Witnesses and Messengers by Land*
> *   and Sea.*
> . . .
> *Keep our Doors open among the Heathen and open those that are*
> *   still shut.*
> . . .
> *Have mercy on the Negroes, Savages and Slaves.*
> [Response throughout] Hear us dear Lord and God.

This, by no means the last petition, was immediately followed by a verse for the choir, one of several, representing eighteenth-century Unity taste:

> My God, thou see'st them flying,
> And thee denying,
> Through Satan's envious lying
> Defying thee.
> Remember Jesu's dying,
> Thy Son is he.
> . . .

After yet more petitions, this protracted and time-consuming text was rounded off with the *Agnus Dei* and *Kyrie Eleison*. Even then the end had not been reached; four more hymn verses were set as the concluding crucial words.

Nineteenth- and twentieth-century versions of Zinzendorf's 1754 text

The conservative quality of this text can be illustrated from the version published in the important new hymnal of 1886, in which both format and length were virtually unchanged. The early petitions, for example, covered the same ground in slightly different language; the congregational responses, also, were marginally modified.

> *From coldness to thy merits and death,*
> *From the loss of our glory in thee,*
> *From error and misunderstanding,*
> *From self-complacency,*
> *From envy, hatred and malice,*
> *. . .*
> *From the deceitfulness of sin,*
> *From all sin,*
> [Response throughout] Preserve us, gracious Lord and God.

Slight modifications also appeared in the 'earth-bound' entreaties, reflecting advances in mission work and alterations in doctrinal emphasis. Whereas the 1754 litany had petitioned:

> *Keep thy Eyes open on all thy Witnesses and Messengers both by*
>   *Land and Sea, let Spirit and Fire rest upon their Testimony;*
> *Keep our Doors open among the Heathen and open those that are*
>   *still shut;*
> *Have mercy on Negroes, Savages and Slaves;*

In 1886 this section read,

> *Watch over thy messengers both by land and sea;*
> *Prosper the endeavours of all thy servants to spread the gospel*
>   *among heathen nations;*
> *Accompany the word of their testimony concerning the atonement*
>   *with demonstration of the spirit and of power;*
> *Bless our congregations gathered from among the heathen;*
> *Keep them as the apple of thine eye.*

Choral interludes by the choir similarly show changes in language which alter the emphasis of the subject matter. In 1754 the first read,

Think on thy Son's so bitter Death,
His five dear Wounds and thorny Wreath;
For they have full Atonement made,
For all the World a ransom paid.

and the corresponding item in 1886 was,

Most holy, blessed Trinity,
We praise thee to eternity.
Thou Lamb once slain, our God and Lord,
To needy prayers thine ear afford,
And on us all have mercy.

The twentieth-century revision, defined in 1960 as the First Order of Worship, or First Litany, was essentially a contraction of the 1886 version, using the same vocabulary wherever possible, and otherwise a shorter simplified form. A present-day congregation member reading the 1886 text would recognize whole sections, word for word, while being aware of what had been missed out in other sections, such as this one from the 1886 text:

Thou Head and Saviour of thy body, the Church,
Bless, sanctify and preserve every member through the truth:
Teach us all to be subject to one another in love:
Grant that each, in every age and station, may enjoy the powerful
*   and sanctifying merits of thy holy humanity; and make us chaste*
*   before thee in soul and body . . .*

which became in the 1960 version:

Thou head and Saviour of thy body, the church,
Sanctify and keep thy members through the truth;
By thy holy humanity make us chaste in soul and body;
Teach us to serve one another in love.

As in the litanies of other Protestant denominations, there is thus a thread of continuity from the original Lutheran litany of 1529 to the present time. Sadly, the literary individuality and power of the original

English language translation could not be sustained because of inevitable changes in taste and usage in all forms of religious poetry. As far as the British Province is concerned, however, the litany in all its versions has retained a decidedly eighteenth-century quality dating back to 1754, and the language of the current First Order still illustrates the definitive style of the church. Although other litanies have been added during the twentieth century, they have always had a subordinate role, forming a homogeneous group with a broadly similar style which is only marginally different from the first. All retain a pleasing simplicity and clarity of expression suited to modern needs.

At the present time, a revision of the hymnal and litanies is being prepared, which will reduce the number of hymns and reflect contemporary changes in style and content which are now preferred by most Christian congregations. Hymns and meditative songs in the newer convention are already represented in the various modern publications used to supplement the official hymnal in many provincial churches.

The Role of Language and Symbolism in the Life and Worship of the Brethren's Communities in the British Province

One major difference between the fellowship and style of worship familiar to British Moravians today and that practised by their eighteenth-century predecessors is their use of language. The study of provincial hymnody, litanies and liturgies has shown the persistence of some traditional German material, but it is remarkable how far the language used in daily records and religious practice, as well as in these devotional texts, has changed since the eighteenth century.

This is rarely because they were translations from German and the first provincial leaders were working in a foreign language; it derives almost entirely from the imported mentality and symbolic conventions of the Brethren during their participation in the Evangelical Revival. An examination of this language and symbolism, therefore, illustrates the distinctive nature of what they brought to Britain, suggesting why it was so appealing initially, how it strengthened fellowship within the Unity, and why it was gradually abandoned in favour of a linguistic form which better fitted the indigenous tradition.

The language and symbolic practices of celebrations and festivals

The descriptions of congregational activities in the Fetter Lane and Fulneck diaries between 1744 and the early 1760s illustrate the unifying and uplifting role of verbal and pictorial imagery specific to the Unity in forging the relationship between the first German leaders and their British choir and congregation members. This imagery, quite different from that used in secular society and other religious groups, was attractive to British converts in the years when Unity expansion was at its most distinctive, disciplined and controlled, because it provided a new, more fervent expression of Christian devotion. It is nowhere better illustrated than in descriptions of special celebrations.

These were occasions for decorating the Brethren's meeting-places with greenery, flowers and pictorial representations of the community's relationship with the Saviour. They were expressions of shared fellowship which united German and British brethren and sisters in the celebration of significant Unity events and Christian festivals. By these representations of communal identity they created a perception of their relationship with their leaders, each other and their Saviour, which was for them the essence of their Brotherhood and sustained its vitality.[1]

One of the most revealing detailed accounts of special community activities in the Fetter Lane congregational diary describes the 'little childlike Hieroglyphicks' with which they celebrated Zinzendorf's birthday in 1749.[2]

> May. Wedn. 17. At 7 in the Evening was a Lovefeast for the whole Congregation on account of our dear <u>Ordinary's Birthday</u>, which was last Monday . . . He himself favoured us with his Presence, and after the Meeting was over, he was led by the Bn [Brethren] into the Room up one Pair of Stairs in the Chappel-House, which he unexpectedly found adorned with green Leaf-work on white Hangings, with natural Flowers, and a German Verse on the Sides of the Room, explaining and applying the Watchword. Here was another little Lovefeast, in the midst of which the Door was thrown open, and in the opposite Door which leads to the Gallery, discover'd an illuminated Picture,[3] wherein the Ordinary was twice drawn, first in a reclining Posture, as musing, and then as conversing with our Saviour and solacing himself in a Garden where the Fountains spouted Blood – pointed by him to the Emblems of the four Quarters of the Earth, which stood underneath, representing his several Places and Congregations . . .

> The S Bn [Single Brethren] next day had in their House a like Festivity. Their Room was made to resemble a hewn Rock, in two Corners of which were Fountains springing, and a flaming Heart pictured by one of them, with the Inscription 'I feel my Heart is glowing.' When all the Company was present and sung that Verse, 'That timorous Dovy can upon Occasion bid Mountains and Rocks give way', the Figure of a Rock in one Side of the Room open'd on a sudden, and discover'd the Picture of the Ordinary leaning on our Saviour's Breast, putting his Hand into the Sidehole, with the Words, 'Let me in Peace, Ask not what I do.'

Wed. 24. The Single Sisters in their Choir House expressed this Evening their Thankfulness for the Birth of our beloved Ordinary, by several little Devices, particularly some emblematical Pictures, suddenly shifting and successively presenting themselves to the Eye; the last of which represented the Ordinary in conversation with our Saviour, and the Choir of Sisters marching up from a Hill a little way off.

This account reveals the congregation's perception of their leader and their church, demonstrating the success of Zinzendorf's projection of his own personality. He was depicted by his followers not only as a reflective man concerned with higher thoughts, in a setting reminiscent of Gethsemane, but as one in regular personal conversation with the Saviour. It is known from other sources that he cultivated this image. The memoir of Br P. H. Molther, who spent some time in London, describes Zinzendorf's affirmation of his call to the ministry in these terms:

> . . . the late Ordinary arrived from St. Thomas in the West Indies. As soon as he had saluted me he said: 'My brother, I have spoken to our Saviour concerning you whilst I was at sea. He has ordered me to mention to you in his name that you are to go to Pennsylvania to preach the gospel in the whole country.' I replied: 'Here I am; may he do with me what is most pleasing to him.'

All the images in this congregational picture, and the extract from Molther's memoirs, expressed the brethren's recognition of their leader, Zinzendorf, as in an exceptional relationship with the Saviour: when Zinzendorf was pointing to the emblems representing the Brethren's establishments throughout the world he was doing so as director of the entire Unity missionary enterprise, under Christ.

The Single Brethren's picture represented the count as akin to St Peter by its parallel to the rock on which the Church was to be built[4] and portrayal of Zinzendorf in the posture of the beloved disciple, leaning on the Saviour's breast. It included other biblical associations such as the faith that can move mountains and Moses' smiting of the rock, traditionally associated with Christ's wounded side from which gushed blood and water. The picture was elaborated by one of the currently popular images of the 'side-hole', the side-wound of the crucified Christ, here intimately accessible to their leader, who was to be left at peace in his mystical relationship with the Saviour.

The Single Sisters' devices were not described in detail, but the depiction of their Choir marching towards Zinzendorf and the Saviour

suggests regimentation and obedient conformity, and was the only portrayal of the community in the whole description of the celebrations.

Similar pictorial tributes were mounted at Fetter Lane in honour of the
birthday of Zinzendorf's son, Christian Renatus (Christel), on 11 September 1749,[5] shortly after his move to London from Herrnhaag when
that community was dispersed:

> In the evening the English Congregation expressed her Joy at the dear
> Christel's Birth by a Love-feast in the Chapel, wherein some Musick
> made on that Occasion was sung, and an illuminated Picture was
> placed at the lower End, prettily representing Christel as leaning on
> our Saviour's Breast and then surveying the several Congregation
> Places, conformable to those Words in the Ordinary's Hymn on that
> Occasion,
> > Served as if of Steel thou wert,
> > But charmed as a Love-sick Heart.

Such pictures appear to have been confined to celebrations of the birthdays of Zinzendorf and his son. Accounts of birthdays of leading brethren and other Labourers indicate that they were celebrated modestly
and affectionately by the sharing of a meal and fellowship. These special
representations suggest that members of the Brotherhood truly accepted
that its authority from Christ as Chief Elder was mediated through a
close personal relationship between the Zinzendorf family and the
Saviour, a unique and essentially mystical communion, elevating these
leaders to a position of privilege.

This feature of eighteenth-century Unity mentality is borne out by
Zinzendorf's occasional statements and by those of his senior colleagues.
At the 1754 London Synod, for example, Zinzendorf expressed the belief
that Jesus of Nazareth visited the Oeconomy – used in this sense to refer
to the whole Unity network – and was bodily among the members. He
declared further that the Saviour had always had among men a secretary
to whom he communicated his thoughts for transmission to others.[6] He
did not overtly make that claim for himself, but the community believed
that the Saviour had revealed his divine plans for the Place Congregations to Zinzendorf and had entrusted him with their execution. The
Congregation at Herrnhut was reminded of this by Bishop Johannes von
Watteville on 17 May 1760, shortly after Zinzendorf's death. Speaking
of Place Congregations as a divine conception, he said,

Our Saviour made use of this, His Disciple, as the Founder of this new Phenomenon of the Kingdom of Jesus Christ . . . Our Saviour hath entrusted the Heart of the Disciple with the fundamental Principles of these Villages of Christ and the Rule after which they are to be carried on.[7]

There are occasional references in the congregational diaries to symbolic practices in the Brethren's ritual, including clothing worn for particular services. On 19 February 1749 the Fetter Lane diarist recorded that,

> At 6 in the Evening the Lord's Supper began. The Congregation being met, Br Boehler and Biefer came in, cloathed in that solemn Dress, which is at present usual on this Occasion in the other Congregations, viz. a long white Talar or Surplice, tied round the waist with red Ribbon (our Saviour had on a golden Girdle, but our whiteness is girt only by his Blood.)

It is not clear whether this symbolism of the cleansing blood of the Saviour was a new departure for Fetter Lane or whether the diarist was recording the custom because the account would be kept in the Herrnhut archive, to which copies of all diaries were sent annually. The same diarist described a new practice in the women's dress in an account in July 1749 of Zinzendorf's visit to Yorkshire, which had been related to the London congregation by Br Boehler:

> After that a general Lord's Supper, of 200 communicants at which the dear Ordinary officiated, the first time that he has done it in an English Congregation . . . It was mentioned that, at that Communion, all the Sisters had on the Exoutie or Cap usual in the Congregation, which is so simple, and a Memorial of the Napkin wherewith our Saviour's Head was bound; this was the first time that among us such a whole Assembly had been so dress'd, but which soon encouraged a second, for at this present solemn Meeting, the Sisters in London did the same.

This is a significant example of the adoption of a German custom by English congregations during the years when the Brethren's mission was expanding and being received enthusiastically, their converts wishing to join wholeheartedly in Unity practice. It must be remembered that men and women from these congregations were participating in excursions to the continental centres along with their German colleagues and becoming familiar with their style.

The description in the 1760 Single Brethren's Diary[8] of the baptism at Fulneck on 7 April of a new member, John Angel, is interesting both as an illustration of the ritual and for its retention on this formal occasion of some 'side-wound' language, which was by that time much less evident in the diaries.

> First the Brn LaTrobe, Abraham and Worthington appeared in Albis when Br LaTrobe spoke with great unction concerning the sacred Institution of Baptism and its Power and Effect upon a human Heart. Then Br John Naylor, Choir Servant, and Chr Goodman who was baptised in the Congregation at Bristol brought in the Water and Abraham and Worthington brought in the Candidate who had also a Talar on without Girdle and was seated between Abraham and Worthington, then Br LaTrobe addressed himself to the Candidate and said: 'Is it your Intention to devote your Soul and Body to him who has redeemed you by his Death and Blood, to renounce all the Works of Darkness and be baptised into his Death and henceforth to live the Life of Christ, &c.?' Answer: 'Yes.' Then the Candidate kneeling down, Br LaTrobe drew near and in the Name of Jesus reclaimed him by the Imposition of Hands as the Property and Reward of God's Torment and Blood Shedding, and afterwards overstreamed him with the penetrating bloody Bath of Regeneration out of Jesus' Side, three times, in the Name of the Holy Trinity and called him John Renatus. Then the Candidate prostrated with Abraham and Worthington during a powerful Breeze of bloody Grace and when he arose on his knees, his baptismal Cap was put on him by Br Abraham and afterwards the Blessing of the whole Congregation but especially that of his Choir was imparted to him by the Imposition of Hands, and while that Verse was sung: 'The Saviour's Blood and Righteousness His finery in the Wedding Dress' Br Abraham bound the red Girdle about him after which he was led out of the Hall and went to rest.

The white talars worn by the officiating brethren and the binding of the red band as a symbol of the convert's regeneration were tangible representations of the Brethren's communion with the Saviour and the believer's regeneration by him. This description shows that the right to wear the red band of the redeemed was conveyed at baptism. For them, the placing of the baptismal cap and the laying on of hands by the whole choir symbolized the candidate's full acceptance into the community of the redeemed and his entering into a deeper relationship with his fellows. The lines of the quoted hymn illustrate what the Brethren believed to be the essence of their relationship with Christ. Such marriage symbolism pictured their perception of the intimate bond between the baptized member and the Saviour. The language and ritual of the occasion were part of the formal framework which bound the members of the Place Congregation to each other and to the whole Unity.

An example of the retention of emotive language when recording the central events of the Christian year is the description of Easter celebrations in the 1760 house diaries of the Single Brethren in the Fulneck community, where the tone changes from the practical language of most routine entries describing daily activities. Here again the ritual practices were expressions of communal faith and experience. The Brethren's diarist recorded the whole festival:

> April 3rd. In our Morning Blessing we felt an earnest of what our agonising Friend would be to us this Day, and throughout the whole Day was felt a powerful Gethsemane Breeze. In the Evening we entered with Body and Soul into the Sacramental Transactions and dolorous Liturgies of our Lord on this Day. First the Holy Pedelavium comforted us richly and render'd us pleasing both to our Friend and Selves. Afterwards we sat us down to the Agape with our Spirits watching every Bloody Drop flowing from our incomparable Friend in Agony, and at last enjoyed that which words cannot utter without a Holy Shuddering of the Fraim. The body and Blood of Christ.
>
> 4th. Our Choir spent in Stillness attending with our Souls on every Act of an tormented Lover, till 3 o'clock in the Afternoon when we assembled with the Congregation about his Cross and kept Lit: [Liturgy] to our Birth Place, made by the Soldiers aweful thrust. After which our Hearts were greedy in Joseph's Work to join.
>
> 5th. Our Morning Blessing was round the Corpse of our dead One, and his Graves Vapours was powerfully felt. We also saluted our Brother Abraham whose birthday is today. In the Evening we had our Ev'ning Blessing in our Choir Sleeping Temple where our dear Abraham spoke on the Watchword 'His faithfulness was declared in the Graves, In the Sabbath Rest'. but Cou'd not utter his Thoughts for the tenderness of his Heart, therefore kneeled down and with Tender Sighs and Tears uttered what could not be done in Words, in behalf of the hallowing of our Sleeping Temple, ev'ry Bed and Inhabitant thereof, with that divinely aweful Presence of him who was stretched cold in the Sleep of Death, and whom we have hitherto so graciously enjoyed in our Sleeping Liturgy.

6th. We visited the graves of our departed, when 2 belonging to our Choir were called to Mind: Isaac Holland, a Gr. Boy and Benj. Hepworth a Youth being gone to the Church above since last Easter.

This description takes the reader to the heart of the religious experience which held the community together amid the vicissitudes and problems of everyday life. When they joined in worship they were experiencing a mystical union with the Saviour who was their friend, sharing some aspects with the whole Place Congregation and others in the intimacy of their choir. At Easter the whole community abandoned the practicalities of daily living in order to concentrate as individuals and in fellowship on the central mystery of their faith. This was the spirit of the Brethren's Church, and while it lasted its members retained the dynamic of Zinzendorf's original vision.

Imagery from hymnals of the 1740s

The earliest English-language hymnals, printed for the Brethren's British congregations by James Hutton before the publication of the official 1754 hymnal, accurately reflect the rapid expansion of the emotive imagery of Herrnhaag and the beginning of its modification after the disbanding of that community. Some characteristics of this period in Unity history have been described previously, but in a general manner appropriate to their context. It is not until the imagery itself is examined that it is possible to appreciate just how different it was from that used by other Christian churches and evangelists during the Evangelical Revival.

In one sense there was nothing new, since most of its esoteric elements are represented in medieval mystical writings and occasionally in other eighteenth-century hymns such as A. M. Toplady's 'Rock of Ages' (1775), which has persisted in English hymnals.[9] These have little in common, however, with the Brethren's unbridled and emotional outpouring of verse in the supplements to the hymnals of the late 1740s. What happened at Herrnhaag was a two-way process, which simultaneously created and fed on a unique perception of the individual Christian's intimate relationship with Christ in this particular community. This language, embarrassing though it was to the Unity subsequently, was of primary importance at its height, since it was shared by members and defined their exclusive group identity and spiritual aspirations. For a few heady years it spilled out into the whole organization, including the British Province, as the expression of an energy which ensured the establishment of a worldwide network which has remained the church's distinguishing characteristic.

In this sense it was the high point of the community's expansion, because without the cohesive fellowship of Herrnhaag the Unity would have been less effective in establishing its missions and societies. The language itself, in which the love of God and fellow Brethren was expressed, became inseparable from the call to revive Christian communities and evangelize the heathen, and was the dynamic for the self-sacrificing sense of worship, service and purity of vision which inspired the Brethren to achieve so much in so short a time. To regard it as little more than introverted indulgence would be to undervalue the sincerity of its exponents and to underestimate its role in sustaining the concentrated activity to which its emotionalism gave rise. Its excessive use of fanciful images and its individuality were the threads which bound its devotees in an intense experience which led them to sacrificial service in gratitude to their Saviour. These qualities suited the Unity's perception of itself as an elite which made it comparatively difficult for those outside to gain full membership, and which maintained a strong sense of divine calling. Its counterproductive aspect was that it appeared alien to outsiders, so that the relationships it engendered were easily misunderstood. This led to the abandonment of the Herrnhaag community and the modification of Unity style into a compromise more conformable to the Herrnhut original and acceptable to outside observers. Once this happened, some of the spirit and intense fellowship of the early Unity was irrevocably lost.

The characteristic imagery arose from a personal response to the sacraments[10] and the crucifixion, and was given added significance by the Brethren's belief in Jesus Christ as their Chief Elder. Its theme was the adoration of Christ on the cross, emphasizing his flowing blood and the wounds sustained for the redemption of sinful man. The side-wound was a potent central image because it gave access to the heart of the suffering Saviour, the water which flowed from it along with the blood, and the air with which it was deemed to be surrounded. This gave rise to conceits which described the worshipping souls in terms of birds or bees clustering round the side-hole in the rarefied air surrounding the crucified Redeemer, or seeking shelter and rest in the wound.

As the examination of hymnody has illustrated, its most exaggerated metaphorical extravagances, found in the 1748 hymnal and its many supplements, were quickly rejected by conservative elements in the Brotherhood. One complex example of this bird imagery will suffice as illustration, here in the form of an inspirational choral praise. It is Hymn 110, 'Concerning the happy little Birds in the Cross's Air, or in the

Atmosphere of the Corpse of Jesus', a translation of no. 2251 in the German hymnal. The first verse is quoted:

> What does a Bird in Cross's Air,
> When it flies up to the Lamb near,
> When round the Lamb it moves and sings,
> And claps the Ave with its Wings?
> Dear Hearts! look, look and see,
> The little Bird finds presently
> Its Nest in the dear Cavity
> From whence the Church was dug.
> Within the hole, where Blood casts rays,
> The Bird itself entangled has;
> And round the Castle of the Side
> Are Wound-Swans in the Canal wide;
> There learns the little Piper
> In th'Hole to be a dipper.
>
> Chorus:
> My Heart with joy, with joy abounds,
> I've found the Ocean of the Wounds;
> There I'm a little Dove, a Fish,
> There is my Bed, Table and Dish, and all Things.

The verses which follow describe what the bird does when it rises in the morning, how it spends its day, responds to being melancholy, and the verse it sings when it is to go home. The conclusion describes how the birds spend eternity:

> We lie in the Side's cavity
> . . .
> There kiss the Birds each other's Lips,
> One laughs and plays, the other weeps
> . . .
> So Lamblike, bloody, happily,
> So Turtle-dove-like, prettily,
> The Lamb shall keep his Bride here,
> Till She can kiss his Side there.

Within their own convention the best hymns were dignified and moving. Meditation on the wounds was an important part of individual devotions, and some of the short single verses as well as the longer hymns were suited to this role. The central image was expressed in reverent language, with a dream-like quality and an ecstatic, emotional outpouring of love. The three examples which follow are from Part III of the 1748 hymnal:

[p. 53, no. 59]
Lovely Side-hole, take in me:
Let me ever be in Thee
O Side-hole's Wound, My Heart and Soul,
Does pant for thy so lovely Hole.
Lovely Side-hole, take in me.
Lovely Side-hole, and let me ever be in Thee.
If I once securely fit
In the bleeding Side-hole's slit,
O then I for ever dwell
In this lovely *Pleura's* Cell.

The hymn expresses the praying believer's longing for the comfort and security of belonging to Christ, but also the conditional nature of acceptance dependent on complete conformity, a requirement that the suppliant should 'fit' in order to enjoy eternal happiness.

The next extract is the first of four verses, the biblical reference being included in the text. It expresses a sense of community with other members, as well as a personal response to the wounds which Christ received as part of his redeeming sacrifice.

[p. 54, no. 61]

A Conference with the Lamb upon the dearest Side-Hole

My dearest, most beloved Lamb!
I who in tenderest Union am
To all thy Cross's Air-birds bound,
Smell to and kiss each Corpse's Wound;
Yet at the Side-Hole's Part,
There throbs and pants my Heart.
I still see how the Soldiers fierce
Did thy most lovely *Pleura* pierce,
That dearest Side-hole.
Be prais'd O God, for this Spear's Slit!
I thank thee, Soldier too for it
I've lick'd* this Rock's Salt round and round;

Where can such Relish else be found!
In this Point, at this Season,
The Side has stole my Reason.
*I John, i.I

The use of the word 'reason' is significant, since a tendency to reason was
anathema to the Brethren, leading, it was believed, to loss of a personal
response to Christ and his love. The next short meditation is a beautifully
compact expression of the writer's simultaneous awareness of community in Christ and a special personal relationship with him – the wonder
of his care for the individual:

[p. 57, no. 67]
Now rests my whole mind on [sic]
In one nook of the Side-hole,
And dreams of Blood alone:
Sometimes it as a wide Hall,
Sees that small Side-hole Slit;
Sometimes so close and Deep
As if each Heart in it
Alone did lie and sleep.

Zinzendorf was a prolific hymn-writer in this tradition[11] and was
influential in retaining some of the most exaggerated imagery of the
wounds of Christ among the Brethren even after the revision process had
begun. A copy of the 1754 hymn book in use by the Hall Moss Society
[London] in 1755[12] contains a bound-in supplement with a small selection of hymns from an earlier edition printed by James Hutton. Since
they are attributed to C.Z.,[13] they are probably some of those written by
Christian Renatus ('Christel'), when he was living in England from 1750.
Zinzendorf collected these after his son's death and published them as the
first appendix to the 1754 German *Gesangbuch*, printed in London.
Most of the hymns in the Hall Moss book are in praise of the wounds and
perpetuate the imagery of the believer as a worshipper at the side-hole.
They include an abbreviated version of 'What does a Bird in Cross's Air?'
quoted above.

Esoteric language in communal life

Partaking in the sacrament was an occasion for the singing of hymns which reflected images generated by biblical accounts of the Last Supper. The Fetter Lane Congregation Diary for 1749[15] gives an account of the Lord's Supper celebrated on 22 January: The entry is quoted in full because, like other examples recorded in the diaries, it illustrates the atmosphere of these services and shows how hymnody and the formal wounds imagery were integrated with the act of worship, creating a private ritualistic vocabulary and practice:

We had a blessed Lord's Supper. The Brethren and Sisters came together in the Chappel between 7–8 in the Morning, and as there were many communicants (near all the German Brethren and a great part of the Sisters receiving with us) therefore the Bn. except a few went into the Gallery and the Sisters staid below. First Br. Boehler sang the 1st 2nd 3rd 6th Verses of the Hymn <u>Dear Creature whom Immanuel</u>, &c and at the words <u>Arch-Petitentiary Thou!</u> all got up and kneeled down before our Husband, to whom Br. B. confessed, that we were indeed his loving poor Hearts thro' his Blood, but yet on account of many Defects must bathe his Feet with Magdalen-Tears, and beg Absolution; which he therefore should grant us with his through-pierced Hands, to make us meet to be penetrated thro' Marrow and Bone by his holy Corpse, which we should now so intimately partake of: Then was sung <u>Lord Jesus be Thou to us near</u> &c, after which, all rising, that verse was added <u>Where Agonising Blood</u> &c under which Br. J. Nitschmann and his wife bless'd those who received the first time [names follow]. Then the Ordinary, who was above in the Pulpit all the while, began singing (in German) the 1st 7th and 10th verses of the Hymn <u>Hearst Thou Elder</u> &c . . . and then the 3 first of that Hymn <u>Thou Death-Sweat mix'd with Blood</u>, &c, which was the Consecration of the Bread which Br. Boehler, J. Nitschman had in their Hands and then gave it, the latter to the Bn and the former to the Sisters. During the Distribution the Ordinary sung, <u>O that the Saviour's Faithful Bride</u> &c and some of the following Verses. Then at his singing, <u>Church Tremble</u> &c all fell down together on the Ground and there felt and took part in that Verse, <u>What does a Bird when enter in it will and dare?</u> and rose again at that, <u>Brought to the Birth dear Creature thou</u> &c. Afterwards, all being seated, he proceeded, <u>Who does the Cross-Air-Ointment mix</u> &c, <u>How is it with the Cross-Air-Eye</u> &c, which suited the case of several Eyes there present; then went on to Verse 11th and 12th of

Hear'st Thou, Elder! subjoining the Trumpet Verse, Then the Criminals Bones were broke, etc, at which all rose, and the two fore-mentioned Bn went to the Table again; then he added the thirteenth verse, whereupon they poured out the Wine, over which were also pray'd the last Verses of Thou Death-Sweat &c. While the cup was given to the Congregation, he sung several Verses, as But what does the dear Marriage-Heart, &c, Now be Glory to the Side Repeated, &c. With what heav'nly Harmony and Voices &c, Singing yea themselves out of the Body &c and the most part of the Te Pleuram. Also those two Verses, Meanwhile so Lamblike &c, To Side-ward Looking, &c. at the Close of which the Communicants kissed one another; and under the 8th Verse of Hear'st Thou Elder the following Bn and Sisters [named] coming near, received the Confirmation-Kiss. The whole transaction was liturgical, and the Lamb's Corpse and Blood were nakedly and in Stillness the near Object.

This account encapsulates the Brethren's experience in the early years of the Fetter Lane congregation, particularly when Zinzendorf and his Pilgrim Congregation were based in London. As this was a special communion service in which new members were being accepted, Zinzendorf himself took part and, in accordance with his status, he was in the pulpit, the bread and wine being dispensed by his leading colleagues. It is worth noting that the wife of the participating Bishop Nitschman took part in the blessing, in keeping with the Brethren's policy of enabling leading women to take an active role in Unity mission. Before the mixed congregation Zinzendorf sang the German version of hymns which used the characteristic imagery, emphasizing the community's special relationship with the Saviour. The liturgical nature of the occasion is remarked upon by the diarist, and the number of hymns sung reflects the Brethren's emphasis on music as integral to communal worship, the language of the hymns contributing to the spiritual content of the service. It is an interesting survival of this early tradition that congregational hymn-singing during the distribution of the sacrament has remained a feature of Moravian worship.

The same imagery appears to have been used consistently in all the offices of the church. The Fetter Lane Diary[15] contains an account of the baptism by J. Nitschman of the infant daughter of a German couple, obviously prominent members of the Brethren because those who 'stood around' were leaders of the Pilgrim Congregation or their families. They included Christian David, godfather to the baby's mother, famous among the Brethren as the man who symbolically felled the first tree for the settlement at Herrnhut. Br Nitschmann's address before the baptism described Christian emotions on such an occasion:

> . . . our Hearts . . . have an extraordinary Feeling at that Moment, when a little Heart is plunged and grafted into our Saviour's side, and declared in the Number of his Painfully produced Sweat-drops; . . . then he baptized the Child, by the name of Anna-Joanna into the Side-hole with Blood and Water, in the Name of the Father, the Son and the Holy Ghost.

Evidence that this language permeated everyday life in the settlements and among members can be found in some unexpected contexts. A document dated 10 May 1746, believed to be a copy of a speech delivered at the laying of the foundation stone of Fulneck Congregation House,[16] contains this paragraph:

> . . . and that Souls may yet be better cared for it is that we in the name of the Holy Blessed Trinity, and in the name of our bleeding Lamb and Head, for his Congregation and pilgrims' sake and for the good of his kingdom in general that we do build this house, which house is to be called the Congregation House. May the dear Lamb of God adorn and fill it with love and Unity with 1000s Lamb's blood and wounds besprinkled hearts, and may every one that goes in and out there feed and hide in the Lamb's blood and wounds, yea, may he be and abide the whole Congregations only Shepherd, High Priest and Saviour.

John Beok,[17] a brother normally serving in Greenland and shortly to return there from Herrnhaag, addressed Benjamin Ingham in similar language in a letter dated 30 March 1747 which thanked him for his charity:

> And since I know that you rejoice with us when the Wounded Lamb gets a good many for a Reward for his Smarts, for his sore Agony's-Sweat, I will with this Opportunity acquaint you that the Lamblyn has already allowed us to receive near hundred and fifty into our Congregation; and that some of 'em are very pretty little Wound-Worms.

The Brethren whose correspondence was quoted by Francis Okely[18] supported each other in the work of evangelism in a similar manner during the crucial period between 1741 and 1743.

There is no Shelter from our grand Enemy but the Wounds of *Jesus*; and whoso in his Spirit has found a Way to them, the Enemy can't touch him, but (altho' he may be ever so poor and miserable in himself) he may remain happy and secure in Time And Eternity; Jesus, the Sinner's Friend, will not be ashamed to confess him before his holy Angels in the Glory of his Father.

From extracts such as these it is evident that in the early years this esoteric language was part of everyday formal or written social intercourse as well as occurring in hymnody and official accounts. It reflected the mentality which pervaded the Unity and extended to its British province during the 1730s and 1740s. Recognisably the style of Zinzendorf's own 'Pilgrim Congregation', it remained the characteristic language of brethren and sisters nurtured in the faith at Herrnhaag after they were forced to disperse to other centres. As such, it was a strong unifying element in the most significant years of Unity expansion, contributing to the zeal and dynamic of their early missions and being adopted by their converts as a sign of acceptance into membership.

In its extreme form it did not long survive the exodus from Herrnhaag and the reassertion of temperate influences. The Fetter Lane Congregational Diary for 5 June 1750 reports a meeting of the Synod in Silesia at which Br. Johannes de Watteville had taken steps to curb the unbridled use of exaggerated language, a reflection of the disquiet which it was then causing among conservative members of the Unity, as well as their recognition that it was bringing the brotherhood into disrepute among other Christians.

He took notice of some Luxuriancies both in Doctrine and Practice which had arisen from an injudicious Pursuit of what is otherwise the present happy Path of the Congregation; and seriously reproved the Prating about the Side-hole in a light Manner, and the making of groundless Antithesis between the Doctrine of the Wounds, &c, also any crude way of treating our Marriage-Relation to our Saviour, wherein it may seem to be forgot that we are, as to our general State only humble Candidates for that great Dignity, the highest present Realizing of it being the Holy Supper. Lastly he lamented on Levities in the outward Behaviour, which was not the right kind of Chearfulness: about all which, when the Brethren concerned should have wept and repented before our Saviour.

This synod marked the beginning of the rejection process by which the

Unity gradually established the modified expression of its devotion which characterized subsequent hymnals. It is arguably the beginning of the Unity's ambivalence towards Zinzendorf himself, since so many of the hymns attributable to him published in translation in the 1740s were rich in wound imagery and other fanciful conceits. The official rejection of its excesses did not mean that this language disappeared; it lingered in the province in a modified form at least as long as British establishments were led primarily by Germans, some of whom had spent time at Herrnhaag and all of whom had been trained in Germany and regularly visited continental settlements of the Unity. The early communities' fellowship with each other and with the Saviour was so inextricably associated with their language and imagery that rejection could not be imposed, but had to come gradually from within.

The persistence and function of Unity language and imagery in the British Province

Although most entries in the house diaries recorded the mundane daily routine of the community and admissions and movements of members and leaders, some detailed accounts of Christian festivals and significant homilies continued until the diaries degenerated into scrappy notes in the early 1800s. The persistence of exaggerated language and imagery in these special accounts is particularly evident in the Fulneck Single Sisters' House Diary. After having British Labourers initially, the House was led by Germans in the earliest period from which records have survived. The familiar style was still prevalent between 1759 and 1765 when Sr Mary Vogelsang and Sr Hendringen Ohlsen were in charge as Labourer and Co-Labourer.[19]

Typically, on 2 January 1760, the morning and evening blessing were kept by Sr Mary and in the evening she sang verses. The exaggerated emotional language in which the diarist recorded choir celebrations led by these women suggests the intensity of the sisters' devotion to the Saviour and to their leaders, and illustrates the esoteric nature which still characterized the German ministry at this time.

> January 15 1760
> ... The Breezes from the dear sides shrine Brought together our house family, where our faithful heart Sisr. Mary sang many thanks and praises to our Slaughter'd Lamb, for the peacefull Slumbers on his Arms and Breast, after which she went to Gomersal Occasions to speake the Sisters in the different pl1anns, before the Sacrement, the

Evening was conclu'd here by Sisr. Hendringen, who in a simple and childlike manner sung as if her Lover's face she saw.

Sr Hendringen's discourse to the Great Girls about the 'true choir heart' on 27 January 1760 is recorded in some detail. She recommended detachment from the world and all the tendencies of fallen nature. These should be replaced by concentration on the Saviour, 'so as to attract him to make many visits . . . and create a heaven upon earth throughout our fellowship'.

The Single Brethren's records from this period suggest a regime less dominated by the claustrophobic and emotional atmosphere which Srs Mary and Hendringen generated in the Single Sisters' House. The contrast can be illustrated by the two accounts of New Year celebrations in 1760. The Sisters' diarist wrote:

Our dearly beloved Sister Mary made for herself and us a Congratulatory Opportunity for the insueing year, by seeing the Sisters in their Classes, exhorting each to love and union and to acce'd to his bleeding wounds as poor sinners, who as his purchased race are desirous to bring joy to his heart and to become one Soul and Spirit with his virgin-like nature, and that the dear Mother the Holy Ghost may not labour in vain on any one, but that each would be attentive to her teaching and assiduous to help each other, so that the Choir Spirit may be unanimously felt amongst them.

The Brethren's diarist recorded a less emotional response to the Saviour, although the characteristic relationship of brethren in the blood and wounds was essential to the message:

After closing the old Year in fellowship with the Congregation under the Blessing of the divine Family, we entered the new with the Song of Praise and Thanksgiving in the same Fellowship; and about 2 o'clock retired to rest richly comforted and blest. At 2 in the Afternoon first the Brethren then the Boys had their Doctrinal Homilies kept by Br Abraham upon the important and interesting Subject of this Day, viz the covenant Wound and Blood of our matchless Heart. Then our Choir Family held blessed new Year Agapeen together where our Friend both new and old gave us to feel his near Presence in a chearing Manner.

Part of the spiritual indoctrination of choir members was the affirmation of their gender role, again reinforced by the Brethren's accepted religious symbolism and sentiment. Both Sr Mary and Br LaTrobe emphasized to the sisters their ideal relationship to the Saviour and essential qualities as redeemed women. Warnings of the lamentable results of failure to achieve purity of heart were contrasted with the joy of conformity. The following two extracts from Sr Mary's addresses suggest the powerful effect of such repetitions on impressionable young women and older devotees alike:

13 Jan. 1760. The quarter hour of the Single Sisters kept by our dear heart Sr Mary, who in a tender and emphatical manner explain'd the blessings of being truly faithful to the Spirit's Unction, the inattention thereto might impede the Grace of our Election so that doubtful Circumstances might arise in the heart and mind so that instead of bringing joy and becoming useful to our Saviour and their Choir they would be as dark plants in the Heart Garden of their wounded friend.

10 Feb. 1760. When the Sisrs. had assembled together Our Dear Sist. Mary with a Heartfull of Love and Odoriferous Dew kept a sweet-scented and anointed quarter concerning the Wounds fragrancy. After singing Thy Oil Tinge the whole of Body and Soul she in a specifick manner beautifully delineated the consequences of being so pervaded, and that the walking in the Odour of the Bridegroom's name is not sufficient unless his Humiliation be likewise conspicuous thro' a true sense of our own sinfulness. The Heart thereby becomes so charm'd (in amour) and seeks only to ingratiate into a dear and familiar intimacy thro' the merits of his bleeding wounds.

When Br LaTrobe spoke to the sisters it was frequently to praise the superior virgin state and ensure that they understood how the natural propensity of women to succumb to fleshly temptations could be overcome by entering into a true relationship with Christ. Again the conventional language reflected the Brethren's interpretation of Christian symbols.

2. March 1760. Br Latrobe kept to our Choir an anointed quarter hour. After speaking a few words concerning our Saviour's gracious intention in the formation of man and particular of those whom he firms and constitutes in his present Church Occonomie [sic]. Especially his virgin Choir, wherein he in a decisive manner explained the

difference between a Single woman and a real virgin who is finally brought into such a connection with her Bridegroom that his dear Eyes can look thro' and thro' with delight, he having imparted from time to time so much of his dr. tormented person to the deadening and mortifying of her Soul and Limbs to his Corpses likeness that she seeks only to please his eyes and heart and to be more familiar and conversant with him who is once for all become the source of her present and future happiness, his virginlike corpses nature is of a truth become the Counterpoise to all sinfulness of her human flesh and disposition . . . therefore being only a single woman who has not attained to this point in her Choir is in a miserable situation and may of a truth say I know not the Bridegroom in his virginlike attitudes. I am not yet pervaded by that virginlike nature of his. I am yet blushing in my own sinfulness; but it is a Grace that is attainable by the desire of every faithful heart, for he has and does impress the Seal and signature of his virginlike nature upon every real heart in his virgin Choir.

Hymn 133 in their current hymnal, 'Church Hymn for the Single Sisters', taught that Christ would accept the married state as well as the single, provided that the woman was 'inclined like Mary's Mind' and obedient to Christ's will; but the virgin state was the ideal and women were to protect themselves against succumbing to fleshly temptations:

But, Single Women's Croud!
To whom the Witness Cloud
Now has undertaken
To tell their Mind avow'd:
Hast thou Lust's Filth forsaken?
Liv'st thou in the Blood,
That Lifegiving Flood
The Maid's chiefest Good?

When Br LaTrobe spoke to the Single Brethren on 25 March, celebrated as the anniversary of the Conception of Jesus, his message concerning their attitudes to the opposite sex was explicit.

Br Latrobe kept to the boys a very important and special Homily upon the Subject, by occasion of the Liturgic Text, The Son of Man, showing particularly the Necessity of their having divinely anointed Ideas of their Fraim and Make as well as that of the Srs. which would never have come to pass if our Beloved had not resolved to leave the

Throne of his divine Glory and take up his Habitation in a human Tabernacle.

At 7 he also kept that of the Brn upon the same Text, laying the Conception of Jesus in Mary's Womb as the Foundation and Basis of our whole Happiness and Choir Grace, for the Cure and Sanctification of the Soul and Members, for the regulating and bringing to Order our Thoughts and Ideas concerning the human Fraim in general and of each Body in particular according to the Mind of Jesus; also furnishes us with a Jesus-like understanding of the other Sex, gives us a Respect and Awe for their whole Make, and in the Place of Lightminded Fancies about any Part of them, we are by his aweful Conception in Mary's Womb supplyed with divine Principles of our first Formation birth and human Existence.

The psychological pressures by which men and women were encouraged to view the need for disciplined lives and appropriate behaviour in the choir houses similarly reveal a difference in their respective leaders' perception of male and female nature. There may well be some clue here as to why the sisters' communities had a longer viable life than those of the brethren. The sisters were encouraged to view passive and cheerful conformity as the ideal. Sister Mary, speaking to the choir on 23 January 1760,

declared that the propensity of every true Choir heart was to stretch forth its Soul and senses to the acquiring and fulfilling the most Minute Circumstance and rule with pleasure, and by faithfully habituating oneself thereto one entirely forgot the world, oneself and all the tendencies of our fallen nature, so that in a short process of time the fragrancy of such faithfulness would attract our dearest Bridegroom to make many particular and general visits among us.

The boys, on the other hand, were exhorted to repentance and the diligent practice of their appointed tasks, as this extract from the account of the Boys' Festival Celebration (for boys in the Single Brethren's House and Oeconomy) illustrates:

Br. Abraham . . . appealed to their own Hearts if they have made a due and good Use and Application of all his Benefits, which occasioned their kneeling before their Constituent with Sinners blush and Shame, begging his Absolution for all unfaithfulness and the misapplication of all those invaluable Favours so plentifully bestowed upon them. After the forenoon's preaching (wherein Br LaTrobe spoke as if his auditory consisted of nothing but Boys) 74 boys assembled to their Homily which Br LaTrobe kept upon his holy first Wound – his Diligence at his Lesson – His surprising Simplicity – His faithfulness in his Handicraft – the Points of the thorny Crown . . . After which the whole Assembly kneeled down and Br LaTrobe in a hearty and tender Manner laid this Choir of Boys . . . upon the faithful Heart of our dear Saviour that he might bestow upon each and all the true Spirit of the boy Jesus.

There is a marked contrast between the plainer language used here and that used by the sisters' diarist. The trace of resentment at the style of Br LaTrobe is very different from the idolizing tone of every reference to their Labourers found in the sisters' diary. These women were represented as revered and adored by the sisters: the anonymous diarist[20] wrote always as if they were paragons of virtue and their words the focus of loving attention from all their charges. For the boys, Jesus was the model by which they could understand the virtues sustaining the practice of worthy and successful craftsmanship; emotional involvement with their leaders was not evident. On the contrary, there were sometimes disciplinary problems with the younger apprentices which their masters found hard to bear. On 10 March 1760, at the Masters of Trades' Conference, they were admonished over their handling of recalcitrant youth.

> The giving of Prentices to the Journey Men and letting them make what they could of them was spoke about, and approved of by the Masters. It was also observed that the Chastisement of Boys, when necessary should be done with the greatest calmness and Presence of mind, and also effectually, but that no Brethren should strike a Boy rashly or in Anger, for by so doing he hardens the Boy, exposes himself, and prostitutes that Respect which all Boys should have for ev'ry Brother as Children of God who act in the Authority and Name of Jesus.

The language here is close to that of everyday life, but remains within the conceptual framework of the Saviour as mentor and role model and the follower as conforming to his nature.

These attitudes were entirely consistent with contemporary perceptions of the nature and role of men and women; there was nothing unique to the Brethren in regarding women as by nature a temptation and snare for men, and exhorting them to passivity and obedience, since these were the qualities which eighteenth-century society demanded of the virtuous woman and wife. The fundamental assumptions underlying the homilies were those of contemporary society; the community accepted the conventions regarding the status of women in marriage, and reflected the perceptions of a male-dominated society where women could be categorized as 'virtuous' or 'loose' and regarded as active tempters of men because of the Fall. The idiosyncrasy lies in the intimidating and guilt-making language used to justify 'appropriate' behaviour in the case of the women, and in all cases the exacting demands.

These extracts illustrate one pervasive feature of Unity imagery, namely, its representation of a marriage relationship between the redeemed soul on the one hand and God, the Church and the Saviour on the other. This was a mainstream scriptural image common to Roman Catholics and those Anglicans who encouraged separation from the world. The Single Sisters in particular were to regard Christ as their bridegroom or spouse, the virginity of Christ being a model for the pure life. The male Labourers reinforced the same message in their choir homilies, a necessary emphasis where young men and women were living in close proximity. Br Bieler, speaking to the Single Sisters in 1766 from the verse, 'Thy Oil tinge the whole of body and soul', referred to a Single Sister as,

> one whom the Holy Ghost has brought into a personal connection with our Dearest Saviour and through the lovesickness of her soul is momently seeking the familiarity of her dearest bridegroom, so that her ideas over present and future things, the Linnements of her face, the object of her eyes, the whole propensity of her mind purely and alone springs from that Lovesickness or inwardness of the heart towards her Espoused one, to the attainment of this the oil of our Saviour's blood must have operated so medicionally [*sic*] that not the least spark of fire of her own spirit can be perceived to influence the smallest fiber of her soul or body, then can such a Bee suck Honey from every flower she meets with when another who has not suffered our Saviour's blood to have this effect can suck poison from the same flower like a wasp or spider.

According to this teaching, a woman was to regard herself as committed to Christ in an emotional marriage relationship and expected to subsume her individuality totally in the attainment of such bliss. This exaggeration of traditional religious symbolism which pervaded their worship and thinking had been part of the 1740s style and continued in a modified form for some years.

The marriage symbolism was prominent, also, in hymns sung at the lovefeast and celebration of the Lord's Supper, signifying the relationship between the Unity and Christ. No. 177 in the 1746 hymnal, no. 1340 in the German original, is a hymn of fourteen verses entitled, 'Hymn for the Witnesses of Jesus, sung at the Love-Feast before the Lord's Supper'. Verse 7 describes the sharing of food before the communion service:

> Ere we to our Husband go
> In the holy Sanctuary
> And confirm the League of Blood
> With him who can't divided be;
> E'er the Lamb's beloved Wife
> Eats his Flesh, the Bread of Life
> Drinks his Blood divine and sweet:
> We here fellowshiply eat.

This hymn was retained in 1754 but rejected in 1769.

The hymns used before the 1754 revision were rich in references to the Holy Ghost as Mother and the Church as child, typified by Hymn 24 in the Zinzendorf supplement to the Hall Moss book, a hymn which placed the Unity in this relationship.

> O Holy Ghost, a Mother thou,
> Most suitably art named;
> O Spirit who, the Scriptures thro'
> Hast Jesus' Praise proclaimed
> O Spirit, whose whole Diocese
> In Jesu's Rings appeareth;
> For thy maternal Heart she prays,
> Which Heart for all Things careth.
> Thy Wounds, Lord Jesus, and the Wreath
> That pierc'd thy sacred Forehead
> And all thy sufferings unto Death,
> Shine from the <u>Moravian</u> Handmaid.

From all sources, written, sung and spoken, life in the Brethren's congregations and societies was dominated by such ways of thinking and forms of expression. These reached their most influential in the regulated and cloistered atmosphere of the settlements, where the socially constructed language and ideology fed and were sustained by their own conventions.

Since Germans were the leaders of the main British establishments during the first four decades, the diaries, intended both for Herrnhut and for local records, were probably written by them. This raises interesting but unanswerable questions as to whether such language, particularly at its most idiosyncratic, was really that of everyday life in the settlements, and how far its imagery permeated the thinking and worship of their members. Presumably the diaries give a correct record of homilies, and certainly this language is strongly represented in hymnals and other written records during the early years. It is informative, therefore, to examine changes in the language used in diaries during the late eighteenth and early nineteenth centuries.

The process of linguistic change

Changes in hymnody and the reasons for it have been described in the previous chapter, where it has been shown that the 1754 hymnal marked a turning-point in the content of hymnals used in the British Province. Even so, the modifications retained traces of earlier imagery, such as the notion of the worshipper going in and out of the side-hole in the first verse of Hymn 3, and the perception of Christ as the husband of the soul in verse 3:

[1] . . .
O let us in thy Nail-prints see,
Our Pardon and Election free;
And in the op'ning of thy pierced Side,
Freely go in and out and feed and hide.

[3] . . .
Thee, my Soul's Husband, Rock and Tower;
Whom above all Things even myself I love.

The gradual abandonment of exaggerated language is paralleled in the house diaries, coinciding with the increasing role of English Labourers in the Place Congregations and their declining membership, both of which accelerated in the early nineteenth century. Between 1772 and 1803, when Anna Rosina Anders was in charge of the Single Sisters at Fulneck, the customary phrases used to describe the choir's religious observance become increasingly formulaic. Since there are fewer lengthy accounts of homilies and expressions of adulation, these records give proportionately greater space to the comings and goings of the leaders and the practicalities of daily life, which always featured prominently. The records reveal that the emotional language, a substantial part of the recording tradition under the leadership of Sr Mary Vogelsang, peaked between 1759 and 1765 when she and Sr Hendringen Ohlsen were working together, declined after Vogelsang left in 1765, but lingered until the end of 1772 when Ohlsen left. When these two women were in charge, the language used in the diary for recording spiritual matters matched that of Herrnhaag.

The description of Easter celebrations in the Single Sisters' House in 1774, when Anna Rosina's co-Labourer was Moritz von Dohna, is a hybrid in which conceits generated by the Brethren in the 1740s are followed by a conventional expression used in other British churches:

> April 1st. The Breezes of the foregoing days had such a preparatory Effect amongst us that the direful scene which our Saviour finish'd in the Cross on this Day was of salutary Consequence to our Heart which was truly thankfully humbled before Him for the great Work of our Redemption – and the lively participation sensibly partook thereof thro' the divine operation of the Holy Spirit on the great Sabbath was closed by an Evening blessing kept by Anna Rosal in our Sleeping Chamber. The Corpses Breeze and the Holy Grave Vapours was annointedly defused with a peaceful feeling from the Holy person of our unseen friend, who blest us all together with a resting in hope to be partakers of his glorious Resurrection.

By 1780 the stylistic change is more evident, the co-Labourer then being Elizabeth Lewis:

> 22 March. We had the Holy Pedelavium with the congregation. What our hearts felt during this Transaction can't be described in words, much less are we able to describe how inly near our Savr. was to us while we satiated our hungry hearts on his Corpse and Blood in the Holy Communion on Maundy Thursday, but its sweet impression we wish may abide with us.

The abbreviation, 'can't', is very English, and the use of conventional Brethren's language, retained in the expression 'satiated our hungry hearts on his Corpse and Blood', is confined to the description of the sisters' sharing of bread and wine in the communion service.

The fiftieth anniversary of the establishment of the Single Sisters' Choir in Herrnhut was celebrated by the Fulneck community on 4 May 1780, and both the diary account and the service sheet remain in the archive.[21]

4 May. In the morning we were awoke by Musick. At 7 was our morning blessing when we presented ourselves before our Souls Bridegroom
thank'd him for the innumerable blessings already enjoy'd by this
Choir 50 years and in particular for our own happy lot to be members
of the same, when Sr Anna Rosel very feelingly laid us upon his heart
for our future course, especially that he would this day bless us in a
particular manner which we even then felt he did, after which the
Choir had a chearful breakfast. [details of admissions and homilies]
Half after 1 o'clock the Trumpets blew for the first time out of the new
building erected for that purpose, when we went over in procession to
the Congregation Hall to our Festival Love Feast, when 5 more Gt
Girls out of the Country were added to our Choir, for whom we sung
a benedictory verse. The fine Ode composed for the occasion was sung
with great liveliness and chearfulness . . . We must own with hearts full
of gratitude to our Savr that this day has been a distinguish'd day of
grace and blessing to all our hearts, the day upon which we solemnis'd
our Jubilee, which indeed has proved a day of Jubilation to us, and the
hearty share which all the Brn and Srs have taken therein has put us
much to shame.

Despite the reference to 'our Souls Bridegroom', the restrained, almost
business-like language of the account, and its English idiomatic expressions, reflect the changing nature of the organization towards the end of
the eighteenth century. Its conventional English style shows how short-
lived was the influence of the imagery and language of their German
founders on English members when the congregations had developed
their own local tradition of communal living and society participation.
From their first establishment, there were very few Germans other than
Labourers and co-Labourers in the Fulneck choir houses, and some of
the younger women living in the Single Sisters' House by the 1780s were
second-generation converts.

The 'Ode for the Choir of Virgins in the Brethren's Congregations on
Ascension-Day May 4 1780'[22] had parts for Chorus, Solo and Congregation. A brief extract from the congregation's part will suffice to illustrate its characteristic language, which retained virtually nothing of the
earlier German style, despite its conventional focus on childlike joy in the
personal relationship of the redeemed sisters with the Saviour:

That one thing needful, only good
For virgins of our Saviour,
Is that they, cleansed by his blood

Enjoy his grace and favour.
Hence, child-like minded, full of joy
At his kind approbation,
They nothing let their hearts employ
But HIM and his salvation.

Several of these printed anniversary service sheets produced for the
annual celebrations of the Single Sisters' Choir Anniversary in the early
nineteenth century remain in the archive. They provide a measure of
changes in language beyond the time when the diaries ceased to record
details of homilies and ordinary meetings. Like the hymns and litanies,
they show increasingly common ground with the British Protestant style
as it was developing in all denominations.

After 1803 the Single Sisters' Choir diary notes were gradually reduced
to a minimum, even the anniversary account being formulaic:

We celebrated this day in the usual manner. At 7 o'clock was the
morning blessing, at 10 the reception meeting [details given]. About
five o'clock we met to the enjoyment of the H. Comn. All these meetings was favoured with our dear Lord's nearness and we renewed our
Covenant with him, to live with him, and devoted ourselves with soul
and body anew to him, to be his true followers.

By 4 May 1815 their anniversary merited only a brief reference: 'We
celebrated our Festival Day in the nearness of our dear Saviour with the
usual meetings.' A list then followed, naming girls received for the first
time. In the order of service for the occasion, apart from traces of
marriage imagery, the relationship between the virgin choir and the
Saviour was expressed in sentimental generalities, as this extract illustrates:

[p. 2] <u>Liturgist</u>: Is there a Virgin seated here,
Whose eye is dimm'd by sorrow's tear,
Whose sad heart pants for peace and rest?

With confidence to Jesus haste!
He loves to cheer the mourning soul with grace,
And turn his Children's sighs to songs of praise.

[p. 4] <u>Guests</u>: Amen yea Hallelujah!
Peace and joy Your souls pervade;

Serve the Lord – Adorn his word,
Ever cleave to him Your Head;
Jesus' blood-bought righteousness
Be your spotless, snow-white dress;
Till call'd hence, You take your flight
To the blissful realms of light.

Cong: . . . Before the Father's face
Each virgin thou [i.e. the bridegroom] wilt place,
As a member – Of thy dear bride, There to reside,
While thou her portion will abide.

The Choir Anniversary order of service for 4 May 1820, when the Labourer was Elizabeth Clarke, differs completely in tone from that of the early sisterhood and, in the absence of diary material, provides a good measure of change. The language and thinking, even in this reminiscence of the origins of the Single Sisters' Choir, are close to that of contemporary worship throughout the Nonconformist denominations, a change which reflects a fundamentally indigenous community.

[pp. 1–2] Solo: In Herrnhut eighteen Virgins first united,
That by the death of God's dear Son excited,
They would obey in all things his direction,
From pure affection.
Their mind was: 'Heavenly Bridegroom, we surrender
Our all to thee, our Friend as wise as tender,
Thy will be ours, we'll follow thy kind leading
In each proceeding.'
Thus freed from care, in their allotted station,
Their aim was, to ensure salvation,
In soul and body, to be rendered holy,
And love him solely.

[p. 4] Liturgist:
O may you with the Church, Christ's spouse,
Enjoy the blessings of his house,
And with his chosen, joy and care,
Comfort and tribulations share.

The convention of the sisters and the church as brides of Christ remains, being a widely used Christian image which has survived in other denominations. One of the most significant phrases in this extract is, 'in their allotted station'. This reflects the preoccupation of contemporary English religious writers with ensuring that the lower orders knew their place in society. The fear that such people might have aspirations above their station had been strengthened among the upper and wealthy middle classes in Britain by the French Revolution, with the result that Hannah More and others inundated the market for popular texts with improving literature extolling the virtues of knowing, accepting and serving in the station in which God had placed the believer. The use of the expression here shows how far the Brethren's congregations had accepted this propaganda, and is consistent with the trend towards a more provincial way of thinking.

In 1830, when Esther Jarrett was in charge of the Single Sisters' House and they were celebrating their centenary the language of the Jubilee Ode was virtually indistinguishable from that of hymns in the mainstream tradition, as the following extract illustrates:

[p. 3] Sisters:
Borne hence to Calvary's brow,
Thy griefs and sorrows viewing,
With heart and spirit, now
Our covenant renewing,
Thy love we will record,
While we our sins bewail:
Thy blood pleads for us, Lord,
Its voice can never fail!
Guests:
Jesus, thy Virgin-choir behold,
Here met in sweet communion.
Confirm, as in the years of old,
Their sacred bond and union;
Make this a day of Pentecost,
Send down on them the Holy Ghost
The promise of the Father.

This verse shows very clearly the influence of nineteenth-century conventions. Gone is the imagery of the redeemed believer lingering in the bliss of the side-hole and adoring the wounds of Christ. Gone, also, are the birds, bees and worms. These ideas are summarized in the words, 'thy griefs and sorrows viewing' and 'thy blood pleads for us', sentiments which still persist in the language of Christian worship.

The European tradition of devotion to Christ's wounds

It is tempting to regard the Brethren's exaggerated language as a home-bred aberration within the Unity, but it can be better understood as an exotic manifestation of concepts which were part of the centuries-old meditative language of European mystics. The Brethren's preoccupation with the suffering and wounds of the Saviour and the soul's relationship with him can be seen in clearer perspective by examining the medieval tradition in which it originated, since a less intense form of such language and imagery would be familiar in Britain through Revivalist preaching and from earlier religious traditions.

The mystical tradition in Europe, which began in late antiquity with the devotions of Origen and Gregory the Great, was represented in the early twelfth century by Bernard of Clairvaux (1090–1153) among others whose works were regularly translated into the vernacular over the following centuries. Devotion to the wounds of Christ, though not a major element in his writings, was occasionally present and as explicit as in the Brethren's hymns. In *A Hive of Sacred Honiecombes*[23] he wrote,

> . . . or when (as S. Thomas) that man of desire, I covet to see and touch him: and not onely that, but also to approch to the sacred wound of his side (being the dore of the arke that was made in the side) that I may not onely put my finger, or my whole hand, but may wholy enter in, even to the verie heart of Jesus, into the holy of holyes, into the arke of the testament, to the golden potte, the soul, I meane of our humanitie, contayning within it the Mahna of the Divinitie.

The parallels with the brethren's imagery are striking. The side wound is represented here as a shelter into which the worshipper can enter, gaining access to the heart of Christ; moreover, it is a source of divine food.

Angela of Foligno (1248–1309) in her *Book of Divine Consolation*[24] described a vision of Christ:

> Firstly, He did question me; then He did say unto me, 'Put thy mouth into the wound in my side.' Then methought that I did put it there and did drink the blood which was running freshly from out of His side, and in the doing of this it was given me to know that I am cleansed.

The imagery is clearly that of the sacrament, but expressed in terms of the physical worship of the side-wound of Christ on the cross.

In medieval England one of the earliest mystics was Edmund of

Eynsham, whose first ecstatic vision was recorded in 1196.[25] Although
the adoration of the cross was a familiar part of the Easter liturgy, a
deeply emotional reaction when confronted with the suffering Redeemer
was a new phenomenon in the twelfth century, shared by celebrated
saints such as Lutgard of Tongeren and Gertrud of Helfta. Edmund
described an experience which began as a tearful adoration of the cross,
but became elevated to a higher ecstasy:

> Meanwhile, as I raised my eyes, heavy with tears, to the countenance
> of the image, I felt . . . some drops fall lightly on my forehead . . . Then
> I saw that the side of the Lord's body dripped with gore, as does the
> flesh of a living man when veined flesh is cut . . . so I caught a few of
> the falling droplets in the palm of my hand and with them I carefully
> anointed my eyes, ears and nostrils. Finally – whether I sinned thereby
> I do not know – I let one drop of that blood pass my lips and through
> excessive longing of my heart I swallowed it.

The parallel with the sacrament is again obvious in this extract, and the
whole phenomenon represents a level of mystical experience probably
peculiar to contemplatives. Nevertheless, the eighteenth-century Brethren yearned to achieve, through devoted prayer and contemplation, a
similar ecstatic experience to that recorded by generations of devout
Christians.

Julian of Norwich (c.1343–post-1416) described in *Showings*[26], a
vision of Christ in which he himself drew her attention to his wounds:

> With a joyful expression our good lord looked into his side and beheld
> it with joy, and with his sweet gaze he led forth the understanding of
> his creature through the same wound into his side; and there he
> showed a fair and delectable place, large enough for all mankind that
> shall be saved and rest in peace and in love. And therewith he brought
> to mind his dear worthy blood and his precious water which he let
> pour out for love. And with the sweet beholding he showed his blessed
> heart cloven in two, . . . strengthening the poor soul for to understand
> . . . the endless love that was without beginning and shall be for ever.

The comforting images of Zinzendorf and Christian Renatus in intimate
communion with the Saviour portrayed in the Fetter Lane Brethren's
birthday illuminations were vicarious expressions of congregational
intimacy akin to that recorded by these mystics.

The medieval tradition of the efficacy of the wounds occurred also in devotional texts and prayer manuals, where it was common to associate each wound in turn with the forgiveness of a particular associated sin, or as an antidote to vice. An undated manuscript, *Devotiones*,[27] gives instructions for using prayer as a safeguard from temptation:

> If thou be in deadly sin, go to the church and kneel before the cross and pray god that he grant you your prayer . . .
> O blissful Jesu, for the wound of your left hand keep me from the sin of envy and give me grace . . . to have this virtue of bounty . . .
> Gracious Jesu, for the wound of thy right foot keep me from the sin of covetousness that I desire no manner of thing that is contrary to thy will . . .

Examples such as these demonstrate that the imagery which for a limited time became part of regular devotional practice for the Brethren was not unique to their communities; it was an adoption and development of a form of religious expression which had a long history and was part of the mainstream European mystical tradition.

The study of hymnody has shown that there was little direct continuity between the resources for worship used by the Bohemian Brethren and those of their eighteenth-century successors, and that hymns from the old Bohemian tradition later included in the 1754 hymnal did not share this obsession with adoration of the wounds and a marriage relationship between the Saviour and redeemed members of his Church. The question is, therefore, how did it come to be such an integral part of the style of the Renewed Unity in the early years?

The act of revering the wounds of Christ was a central feature of worship among some European social elites, into whose ranks Zinzendorf was born at the turn of the eighteenth century and whose traditions he shared as a cultivated member of an aristocracy with literary and musical interests, by inclination ecumenical in outlook and familiar with Roman Catholic forms of worship.

The Imperial court of Ferdinand II of Habsburg (1619–37) was noted for its music, and Ferdinand himself revered the cross and the crucified Christ. Steven Saunders[28] describes Ferdinand's devotion to the wounds and passion, and how each day, with arms extended, he kissed the floor five times in memory of the five wounds. One of the litanies in his breviary addressed the crucified Christ and dwelt conspicuously on the wounds. Among the compositions of Valentini, who wrote sacred music for performance at Ferdinand's court, are five Christological motets, all in dialogue style, based on the events or imagery of the passion. Saunders comments that these are more explicit than any other seventeenth-century dialogues. He notes: 'These cross motets are also eloquent expressions of Habsburg spirituality, whose connotations for contemporary listeners at court can be at least partly recovered through an examination of the poetic, religious and musical traditions to which they adhere', an exercise which he undertakes. An extract from the *Salve tremendum* in translation[29] displays most of the salient textual features of this group of motets:

> Hail, honey-sweet mouth and most sweet throat of our Lord Jesus
>   Christ, for us having drunk the vinegar and gall . . .
> Hail venerable hands, very soft breast, glorious side, sacred knees,
>   entreating feet, most precious blood, most holy soul.

Saunders argues that, to the seventeenth-century mind,

> direct, quasi-sensory experience of Jesus' bodily suffering was essential to apprehending the mystery of the Passion and Crucifixion and thereby receiving their benefits. Graphic images of Christ's suffering, and in particular representations of the wounds, saturated contemporary religious thinking. Carafa's *Fascetto di Mirra* is an encyclopaedic treatment of the subject, the pages of which abound in macabre detail.[30]

Since this was the literary and musical tradition into which Zinzendorf was born, it is not surprising that he was attracted to it and that it emerges in his own hymnody.

The most direct link between mysticism and the language and ideas of the Renewed Unity, however, is through Zinzendorf's appreciation of the writings of Johann Scheffler (1624–77).[31] The son of a Polish nobleman, and brought up in a strictly Lutheran household, he abandoned its orthodoxy for the mysticism and separatism to which he was inclined. After coming under the influence of the writings of medieval mystics of the Roman Catholic tradition, he joined the church, adopting the name of Angelus Silesius, entered the order of St Francis and became an ordained priest, eventually retiring to the monastery of St Matthias in Breslau. His most important work was a five-volume cycle of hymns and poems entitled, *Heilige Seelenlust, oder geistliche Hirtenlieder . . . etc.*, the earlier volumes of which expressed a longing for mystical union with the Saviour. The Lutheran Church welcomed a judicious selection of these writings into their hymns of Jesus, and in 1727 Zinzendorf included 79 of them in his *Christ-Catholisches Singe-und-Bet-Buchlein*. Unfortunately, he admired and selected the most extreme examples from the florid writings of Scheffler's early period, and subsequently imitated their excesses in his own hymns. In this way Scheffler provided the model for a style which he himself had rejected. This depended unduly on the image of Christ as the Bridegroom of the Soul and was disfigured by those mannerisms which for a few over-enthusiastic years, encouraged by Zinzendorf, the Renewed Unity made its own.

The language and imagery adopted in the early years by the Renewed Unity, and familiarized by Zinzendorf and his immediate senior colleagues, was an expression of the devotion which powered the intense commitment to Christ and their fellow Brethren and consequent evangelistic fervour which energized their early missions. For the vital period of insecurity on the continent and expansion overseas, it characterized the thinking and communal life of the group and their converts, creating a special style which bonded together the German and indigenous elements in the communities and gave them a unique sense of identity and divine calling. Apart from its appeal to other evangelists such as Ingham and Cennick, it attracted several well-educated Englishmen such as Okely and Delamotte, who were drawn to mysticism and joined the Brethren because of these elements in their worship. As the German influence waned after the Count's death and British provincial life took on its own character and momentum, these intensely emotional forms of expression were replaced by a plainer provincial style more akin to that of other British Nonconformist denominations. The remarkable fact is that sufficient traces of the best of this legacy still survive in the hymns and litanies of the British Province to give the present Moravian Church its distinctive character.

13

The Origins and Rationale of Moravian Education

The educational establishments of the Unity in the first half of the eighteenth century were founded on the philosophy and vision of Zinzendorf, but his theories can be traced to the influence of his upbringing, education and experience of contemporary culture. For this reason the Brethren's system of education can best be understood by examining the thinking from which it evolved and the practicalities which motivated the Unity in their establishment of educational facilities for their young people.

Educational theory and practice in Europe in the sixteenth and seventeenth centuries

It is argued throughout this book that the thinking and practice of the Unity of the Brethren, though distinctive, are inseparable from long-term trends in Europe and ways in which ideas were interpreted there. From the earliest times it was regarded as desirable that men who entered the priesthood or ministry should be well educated in the classics in order to conduct the necessary offices in Latin, the international language of the Church and the law, and to understand theological writings. After the Reformation, such academic qualifications were believed to be essential, in addition to the ability to preach effectively in the vernacular. At a more elementary level, the education of children was recognized as an essential part of the churches' strategy for ensuring that the Christian heritage was passed on to the next generation along with the skills which they needed for their livelihood. With the production of cheap print came the rapid extension of literacy among artisans and the middle orders of society, and the churches recognized the value of directing this cultural development, for which task they were uniquely fitted. This view was not entirely pragmatic: many Reformation thinkers appreciated the value of schooling as a means of bringing increased harmony to society, and one important impetus to reforming zeal came from contemporary philosophical writings on the value of elementary education for a wide range of young people.

Church ordinances of the early Reformation frequently refer to the establishment of elementary schools in order to bring concord and uniformity into various institutions through the teaching of sound doctrine, which they perceived as an essential part of any reorganization. These ordinances set out the grade, syllabus, personnel and salaries of city schools and their teachers. As a result, in the most closely managed reformed states a degree of harmony and an overall increase in the number of schools was achieved.[1]

Since the adoption of an official religion was integral to the European reformed states, religion and state management went together. One objective of Luther and other reformers was to provide access to the Bible for as many people as possible through universal education. In 1524 Luther wrote his 'Letters to the Mayors and Aldermen on behalf of Church Schools', calling upon them to erect and maintain Christian schools for boys and girls, where they were to learn not only sound doctrine, but languages and history, singing, music and mathematics. In 1530 he published a sermon on 'The Duty of Sending Children to School'. In both these works he exhorted the state authorities to discharge their responsibility to provide education for children of all classes, and suggested that it should be compulsory, at least in the years of elementary schooling, so that all might have the benefit of a sound Christian education; the children of the poor could attend for one or two hours a day and spend the rest of the time learning a trade. He also saw the need to 'modernize' school teaching so that schools became cheerful places where children could enjoy learning,[2] arguing that teachers should be humane and sensitive in the treatment of their pupils.

Philip Melanchthon, Luther's close associate, wrote extensively about educational reform, urging further broadening of the curriculum to include the newly emerging sciences. These developments in liberal educational thought led in the sixteenth century to various examples of practical educational reform. Luther's principles were further developed by Sturm, in 1539 at Strasbourg. He proposed that there should be one gymnasium of liberal arts for each town, intended primarily for those who were to become men of letters, but open to some poor boys of exceptional ability. His curriculum was planned to cover nine years of education and to include mathematics, history and music, as well as teaching boys to read and speak Latin. Religious instruction was to take place on saints' days and at church festivals.

Calvin, at Geneva in 1559, took the Strasbourg school as his model, but with increased emphasis on religious discipline – each lesson was to begin with prayer. The principal was to be, as Luther suggested, a more sympathetic figure than the traditional stern and remote academic personage bringing physical retribution to those who failed to learn. The Calvinist Cordier, who taught in Geneva from 1536 until he died in 1564, regarded the encouragement of individual responsibility as the hallmark of reformed education within a scheme which fostered both learning and piety. He was a significant innovator in the teaching of Latin, using Latin conversation, an idea which was seen at the time as kindly, intelligent teaching, and which featured prominently in the prescriptions of Comenius a century later.[3]

Similar educational policies emerged in France under the Huguenots before their expulsion in 1598, and also in England, where John Brinsley, for example, discussed the process of education from the elementary to the upper secondary school, emphasizing the principle of learning through play and the need for a broader curriculum. An early advocate of reform and teacher training, he recommended that colleges be founded specifically for the training of teachers.[4]

These examples show how, as part of the gradual emergence of enlightened thinking in Europe, the appropriate education of children became of major concern to advocates of reform. While centred on the need to produce an appropriately educated professional elite, it was not exclusively so; the inculcation of piety and acceptable moral standards along with basic skills was regarded as an attainable ideal in the education of all the young, boys and girls, always in a religious framework because state organization and religious affiliation were inseparable.

By the beginning of the seventeenth century the ideas of these reformers and their successors were widely known and accepted in Europe, and it was within this established framework of educational thinking that the eighteenth-century Unity developed its educational policy. Subsequent generations of Unity leaders have cherished the church's connection with John Amos Comenius, mystic, philosopher and bishop of the old Bohemian Unity,[5] who was the link through which the first bishop of the eighteenth-century Unity was consecrated. Because of his prolific writings on education and the curriculum it has sometimes been assumed that his ideas alone inspired eighteenth-century Unity educational practice, without appropriate recognition of how far his prescriptions encapsulated the work of predecessors and contemporaries.

There was a tenuous link[6] between Comenius and the pietistic philosophy of education developed in a practical form by Francke at Halle,
and therefore brought to the attention of Zinzendorf. Francke spent
much of his childhood in Gotha, where his father served as legal adviser
to Duke Ernst the Pious, who was devoted to the promotion of popular
schooling in his small principality of Saxony-Gotha. His compulsory
school edict of 1642 was the first in Germany to introduce *Realien* –
practical subjects like natural history, geography and botany – into the
school curriculum. 'Here Ernst drew largely on the pedagogical realism
of Jan Comenius, whom he knew personally, and Wolfgang Ratke,[7] who
had once served as tutor to his mother. . . . Francke later acknowledged
the formative influence of the Duke's educational reforms on his own
pedagogy.'[8] In this indirect manner, through a connection between an
aristocrat, Ernst, and a forward-looking educationalist, Francke, the
influence of Comenius' ideas, along with those of Ratke, was assimilated
into the theoretical and practical framework on which the most
advanced Prussian educational establishments were founded.

The educational legacy of John Amos Comenius and his contemporaries

Two main strands are discernible in Comenius' writings about education. Since he believed that education was the key to the creation of
an enlightened and moral society, he advocated the reform of human
relationships by the establishment of a network of international colleges
where all knowledge could be taught from all points of view, a concept
known as pansophism. Another strand arose from his need to produce an
appropriate curriculum for children when, as an exile from his native
land, he had to earn a living by teaching in schools.

Comenius was open to the ideas of his contemporaries. His thinking
was strongly influenced by his educational background, which reflected
current theories and the tradition within which they arose. At the University of Herborn he was probably influenced by John Henry Alsted,[9] a
leading writer on Didactic, who taught there, and whose *Encyclopaedia
Scientarium Omnium* (Encyclopaedia of All Knowledge) was published
there in 1630. Their views were similar, the main difference being
that Alsted would have restricted vernacular schools to girls, and boys
destined for handicraft, a philosophy akin to that of Sturm, whereas
Comenius insisted that such primary education should be given, also, to
those who were later to enter a learned profession. Comenius' ideas were
nearer to those of Luther in this respect.

Comenius admired the work of Ratke, whose essay on the reform of schools had already been authorized and approved by the Universities of Jena and Giessen in 1612, and acknowledged that Ratke's detailed prescriptive programme inspired him to attempt similar school reform. He knew the didactic works of other near-contemporaries, including C. Vogel, headmaster of the Paedagogium at Göttingen, who had devised a scheme of daily instruction in Latin which would lead a child of moderate intelligence to master the whole language in a year by spending two hours daily. Comenius' methods also reflected the ideas of J. Cecilius Frey, a physician living in Paris, who had published a work on education in 1629 advocating that languages should be learned colloquially, and that adequate attention should be paid to arithmetic, geography, drawing and mechanics.

Comenius' *Didactic*, therefore, was an attempt to analyse and embody everything good in existing schemes and ensure that children learned lessons with less time and trouble, so enabling them to attain a more thorough grounding in morality and religion. The study of Latin became a means for learning more about nature, art and society, so that it was less arid. His *Janua* became a classic teaching text and was translated into twelve European languages including English.

The practical reason for Comenius' interest in the reform of school curricula was explained by him in *A Reformation of Schooles*, translated into English and published in London by Samuel Hartlib in 1642, in which he also pays tribute to the influence of others.

> It is now above twenty yeares since I was first touched with this desire of searching some meanes for the easing of those difficulties that are usuall in the study of learning . . . when being by God's permission banished my country with divers others, and forced for my sustenance to apply myselfe to the instruction of youth, I gave my mind to the perusall of divers Authors, and lighted upon many, which in this age have made a beginning in reforming the method of Studies, as Ratichius, Helvicus, Rhenius, Ritterus, Glaumius Coecilius, and who indeed should have had the first place, Joannes Valentinus Andreae, a man of nimble and clear brain, and also Campanella, and the Lord Verulan, those famous restorers of philosophy.[10]

Comenius revealed in a letter to an acquaintance, Montanus, that his labour had been undertaken in response to the Brethren's hope for the continuation of their schools in exile.

Having at the request of the Brethren who were grieved at the ruin of their native country, and were desirous in the first place, if God should favour the attempt, to resuscitate the schools, [I] began to compose certain books in our vernacular language, and some in the Latin and vernacular, adapted to the capacity of our youth, and having at the same time permitted myself to be carried back to scholastic labours, as a means of supporting life, it happened that the works prepared for our own private use, as they were, did not long remain unknown to others.[11]

Between 1635 and 1640 he was in charge of reorganizing the school at Lissa in Poland and, at the request of the Unity Synod in exile, drew up a Latin–Bohemian edition of his *Vestibulum* and *Janua*, and practical rules for the gymnasium there, which emphasized the need for a spirit of piety and included a code of conduct for class, street and home. His ideas became better known when Laurence de Geer's book, *All the Didactic Works of John Amos Comenius*, was published in 1657.[12]

Comenius wrote a prodigious amount about teaching in schools, but his real enthusiasm was for the other strand in his thinking – 'pansophy'. The concept was a familiar one and, having found that other British philosophers shared this vision,[13] and with the backing of Hartlib, he worked in Britain, Sweden and Holland as well as in Lissa to win further support. By the 1640s he had produced a plan for the reform of human society by, firstly, the unification of learning and its spread by an improved school system supervised by an international academy; secondly, political co-ordination through international institutions aimed at maintaining peace, and thirdly, reconciliation of the churches in a tolerant form of Christianity. Piaget regards him as a great forerunner of modern attempts at international collaboration in the field of education, science and culture,[14] pointing out that, although philosophers from Montaigne and Rabelais to Descartes and Leibniz had made profound remarks about education as corollaries to their main ideas, Comenius was the first to conceive a full-scale science of education and make it the core of an indivisible universal knowledge or general philosophic system.[15]

One attempt was made to set up a trial pansophic educational establishment. Comenius went to Hungary in 1650, where Count Rákóczy, an enthusiast for his ideas, provided him with a schoolhouse, seven classrooms and boarding accommodation. There were to be scholarships for poor students, including some Bohemians, a schoolmaster for each class, and a printing press and printers to produce the books necessary for spreading the institution's philosophy. From 1651 to 1652 Comenius wrote *Sketch of the Pansophic School*, dedicated to Rákóczy, and classes began. Since the new method involved teachers in relentless work, the school soon closed for lack of people willing to put the ideas into practice. In 1654 Comenius returned to Lissa, and in 1657 the Poles sacked the town and many of Comenius' manuscripts were destroyed.

Keatinge sums up the effect of his personality and theoretical writings on succeeding generations by suggesting that, while his school books were frequently reprinted and used all over Europe for years to come, his theoretical works remained virtually unknown. Bayle's *Dictionary*, an influential publication which circulated widely in the eighteenth century, was sceptical of Comenius, and its estimate was widely accepted, despite an attempt in 1742 by Paul Eugene Layritz, a school director at Nuremberg, to redress the balance.

There was never an opportunity for Comenius or his Bohemian successors to create vernacular schools for all in his native land and there are no indications that the small group of artisans who settled in Herrnhut brought with them any educational tradition. Education in the Zinzendorfian Unity was an eighteenth-century product, developed according to the needs of the organization and the personal experience and vision of its leader. As outlined in Part One of this book, Zinzendorf's ideas clearly derived from his schooling at Halle and the pietistic milieu. Nevertheless, it has been important to the British Province's concept of its heritage to perceive its educational tradition as following the lead of Comenius. This is less true in the Continental Province, where it is recognized that Zinzendorf's ambition was to create at Herrnhut a centre similar to Francke's theologically based pietistic establishment at Halle.[16] There is continuity in that Comenius' prescriptive school curricula were based soundly in contemporary thinking and on the wider European tradition, to which Francke subscribed through Ernst, and which Zinzendorf also absorbed from the educational institutions set up by Francke.

A pamphlet by Daniel Benham published in 1853[17] which describes the origin and history of the schools of the London Congregation illustrates how this association has been perpetuated. After a biographical sketch of Sr Martha Claggett, through whose generosity premises were provided in Broadoak, Essex, Benham added this brief note on Comenius and made an oblique association with the early educational activities of the eighteenth-century Unity:

When John Amos Comenius and his faithful companions were driven from their fatherland . . . they contemplated a vigorous and general improvement of the schools based upon Christian principles . . . but as they were not permitted to return from exile, the materials collected principally by Comenius were adopted by him in his scholastic labours, which he published in a folio volume with the expectation that future generations might be benefited thereby. His labours were truly not in vain, for they have obtained a worldwide celebrity even to the present day. The Brethren of the renewed Church also early directed their attention to the education of children in a Christian-like form, and in 1723 they began to deliberate thereon. The result was the publication of a Catechism, whose simplicity, though scoffed at by their opponents, was such, that count Zinzendorf, who wrote it, had cause afterwards to say that 'God had blessed it'.

Benham was unable to show any direct link between the work of Comenius and the educational aspirations of eighteenth-century contemporaries. He merely stated, 'The Brethren . . . also early directed their attention'. Such parallelism has been accepted as a connection throughout the history of the British Province, and Comenius, because he was a bishop of the old Bohemian Unity, has been widely regarded as the mentor on whose theories the Brethren's educational system was based.

The first educational institutions in the British Province

The close association of the Brethren with education from the early years of the Renewed Unity was the result of necessity as much as of philosophy and principle. As the earlier survey has shown, their academic educational establishments were founded on the continent because a trained ministry became essential once it was recognized that willing artisans could not provide the expertise which the mission fields required. The oeconomies which the Unity provided for the basic education of its children were needed because many Labourers and their wives were soon working in mission fields where the health of their children was at risk, and all members in responsible positions, men and women, were required to be peripatetic on demand. Their offspring were sent to establishments in suitable areas of the Brethren's activity, including Britain, where their spiritual educational and physical needs could be met. The children of German or English Labourers working in Britain were encouraged to join the Children's Oeconomies where they could be safeguarded from the world, trained in the Brethren's beliefs and experience the discipline of communal living. The children of society members, even if their parents were not always regarded as sufficiently spiritual to be accepted as full congregation members, were welcomed into the oversight of the children's Labourers. In this way the children's groups became mixed Anglo-German communities in which the sons and daughters of ministerial families and some prominent members of the English church were taught alongside those of relatively uneducated artisans.

When the Brethren decided to establish a settlement in London, one of their first priorities was to ensure that their children could be appropriately schooled. The Children's Nursery[18] was set up in two houses in Little Wild Street, London, under Maria Catherine Verding and Rebecca Moorc, and Spangenberg was made responsible for the quality of spiritual oversight maintained there. The two houses provided facilities for boys and girls separately, and teachers' salaries were funded by the Unity. On 26 November 1742 they were moved to Sr Martha Claggett's house[19] at Hatfield Broadoak, Essex, where they were directed by Br Richard Utley and his wife, Sarah. At the end of the year Revd John Gambold was sent to assist, and was joined by his wife Elizabeth after their marriage in May 1743. In the same year, Zinzendorf visited the school, renaming it Lamb's Inn.

The surviving *Diary of Lamb's Inn or Broadoaks in Essex*[20] is undated, though it probably covers the year 1745–6. The entries contain accounts of religious exhortation and warnings, given particularly to the Great Boys and Great Girls, about being 'plagued with inappropriate thoughts' and exchanging covert glances during devotional meetings, but they give no impression of the secular instruction given to the children. They help to account for the decision taken by October 1745 to remove the boys to Buttermere in Wiltshire, to a country house belonging to Mrs Stonehouse, wife of the Vicar of Islington, and in 1750 they removed once more, this time to Fulneck, where they remained. The girls, meanwhile, continued at Lamb's Inn until May 1746, when they removed to the house at Mile End which Br Hyland had rented in 1744 to provide lodging for Labourers who did not need to be in town. Twenty-two girls and five sisters moved there. This oeconomy also included some little boys, and it is clear from the brief diary that some pupils were the children of families who were not full congregation members. Br Christian Henry Müller and his wife were in charge from 1746 to February 1749, and were succeeded by Br and Sr Wurfbain. Between February and May 1754, Zinzendorf removed the Seminary, as it was now called, from Mile End to Church Lane, Chelsea; in 1755 it went to Fulneck.

The philosophy underlying these earliest institutions must be deduced from the sketchy surviving records. These rarely indicate what the children were taught, other than to conform to the Brethren's strict code of conduct and respond to pressure to accept the Lord's atonement for their sins. The accounts of the first fifteen years of provision for the young suggest an unsettled beginning, and these records of daily activities and discussion among the Labourers are biased towards issues of discipline and control. Benham[21] suggests, no doubt with both justification and prejudice, that,

> Schools were looked on as nurseries which should produce servants and handmaids to the Lord, whatever their worldly calling might be. The Brethren and Sisters took them under their peculiar care, and the children were an astonishment to all. They seemed to know nothing but the Saviour and his wounds; they thought and spake, they sang and played and dreamt of him, and in the midst they were cheerful and lively. The Labourers witness this wonder of grace with tears of joy, seeing what the blood of Christ was effecting in the hearts of the young.

This account of the ethos of the first Children's Oeconomies is probably an accurate record of the Brethren's emphasis on inculcating appropriate attitudes among the children in the Place Congregations. They evidently succeeded there and in the Societies, since the many accounts remaining in the Fulneck archive of the deaths of young converts in society families outside the oeconomies invariably suggest that they were overjoyed to be going to their Saviour and were shining witnesses to their faith.

The Lamb's Inn diary entry for 29 June 1745 describes a Prayer Day, at which first of all Sister Oxlee's young child was baptized – 'we blest this little Lamb afresh, and laid it in his Side and gave it quite anew over to him as his Right and Property' – after which,

> Br M. [John Müller] spoke to the children and told them Now their Prayer Day should begin. Then was read some letters from parents to their Children; and also many sweet Accounts from the Children's Fathers in Germany and Yorkshire concerning the Work among the Children; in which time a Love F. of tea was brought in. . . . The Losung text – Matt. 26. 49 – he that betrayed him kisses him. A good deal was said on it, and in particular how Children who were with us and did not give their whole Hearts to our Saviour (and also had Parents who did not love him) could, when taken from us into the World, become Mockers of that dear Lamb, when they had lost their

Feeling by Sin, and through the sinful World, and continued bad
example, &c. &c. They were therefore very heartily exhorted to make
a good Use of the Lamb's Grace, and Opportunity which they had
while they were with us, to see that nothing should be kept by them
which should hinder our dear Saviour's getting their whole Heart.

This extract is an illuminating example of the indoctrination to which
the children were subjected during the spiritual observances which
punctuated their lives in the oeconomy. This involved a compelling combination of emotion and intimidation, backed up on this occasion by
the observances which were part of Unity communal life. The baptism
reinforced the sacred bond with the Saviour undertaken by the parents
and congregation on behalf of their child; the accounts which were part
of the lovefeast made the children of Labourers aware of the work of
their parents in the international work of the Brethren, keeping them in
touch through the network system, and presenting them with a desirable
role model. Finally, the preacher of the homily gave dire warning of the
dangers of exclusion which faced those who did not conform.

The records of Labourers' conferences in the Fulneck archive provide
evidence of what was being taught in the Children's Oeconomy by the
1760s. These depict a caring community in which the individual's needs
were considered. A school timetable for boys, headed, 'Gracehall
Oeconomy April 29th 1761'[22] sets out the usual weekly devotional meetings, which involved the older boys in attending some adult meetings in
the Brethren's Hall. On Sundays the bigger boys attended the preachings
and all the children had meetings after the morning preaching. On week-
days all the children met for devotions at 8.30. Monday afternoon was
Children's Choir Day, and on Thursday afternoon the children had class
meetings. The timing and duration of these events is not clear, since a
timetable for afternoon school covers the time between 2 p.m. and 6
p.m., presumably on days when they were not involved in devotional
meetings. There was a fortnightly Sabbath Lovefeast and all the
children attended a monthly Congregation Day. The school timetable is
appended, with names of boys attending each subject.

From 7.30 to 8.00 a.m. the boys were divided into groups involved in
exercise on the harpsichord, copying accounts (i.e. inspiring descriptions
by missionaries of God's work in various mission fields), or spinning and
winding. These activities were available also between 11 a.m. and 12
midday. Between 9 a.m. and 10 a.m. the boys attended either writing or
cyphering (arithmetic) classes, and took the other alternative between 10
a.m. and 11 a.m. according to whether they were in the older or middle

group. Reading and spelling was taught 'in the little boys' room' between
11 a.m. and 12 midday, presumably to the youngest pupils and others
who needed it. The hours between 2 p.m. and 3 p.m. and 3 p.m. and
4 p.m. were similarly divided between, on the one hand, spelling
and reading and, on the other hand, geography and Bible history, and
between 4 p.m. and 6 p.m. the activities of harpsichord, copying
accounts and spinning and winding were again available.

This educational provision was very simple. All children attended
classes in harpsichord, copying accounts, spinning and winding, cyphering, spelling and reading, geography and Bible history. Study of the
scriptures provided a background to devotional activities; vocational and
musical skills were valued; the children's awareness of Unity missionary
work and sense of belonging to an international organization were
fostered by the copying of accounts, reinforcing knowledge acquired
from participation in congregational activities, and Geography supplemented the children's knowledge of areas where the Brethren were
active.

One account which would be of particular interest to the children was
addressed to them from Antigua and signed by Br Meder, who had
served in the Fulneck Settlement.[23] This extract shows how knowledgeable the children became about life as a missionary in the foreign
countries where Unity members, including some of their parents, were
serving. The writer called it 'an exceedingly hot country, which makes it
also very dangerous for Europeans', and described his accommodation:

> I live here in a small little house, consisting only of that room in which
> I live, it joins to our kitchen; for you must know that in this very warm
> country, one has no kitchen in the dwelling house, but a separate
> building . . . They build here in quite other manner than in Yorkshire
> or in Fulneck. Out of the window in my room I have a fine view into
> the country, into the Sugar fields and the Negro towns, and also into
> the Sea, so that I can see the Ships which come into the Harbour. Now,
> my dear children, I have oftentimes thought on your good wishes for
> me and my Voyage, which you have expressed in Words and Writing,
> and I think our Savr. has heard your and my Prayer.

The personal bond between the young people at Fulneck and Br Meder
was obviously of comfort to him, as he remembered their farewell
wishes and notes, knowing that he could expect to receive further letters
from them.

An undated document from approximately the same period shows

how demanding were the spiritual requirements of life in the Boys'
Oeconomy:

> The children in the Boys' Oeconomy, which form three rooms and are
> attended by seven Brethren, have hitherto shared in the meetings
> which are kept for all Children on Sunday, and the rest of the days in
> the week except Mondays and Saturdays on which there is none.
>   The 3rd Saturday after the Communion Day has always been the
> Children's Congregation Day, on which they pray their Litany, have
> some suitable accounts communicated to them if there are any, keep a
> Lovefeast and have a homily kept them at the close of which those
> children which are born in the congregation or have been received into
> the children's Congregation according to the prescribed manner have
> the prostration.
>   Besides the above meetings, all the Boys in the Oeconomy and the
> great Boys in the Brn's House keep the Monday before the Commu-
> nion (if nothing hinders) Liturgy.
>   They are spoken with separately the day before their Congregation
> Day, and if circumstances will not admit of it, in Classes.
>   The Great boys in the Oeconomy attend also the Weekly and
> Sunday Meetings, appointed for the Great boys in the Brn's House
>   They have no Bands yet, altho' they have several times been thought
> on, but there seemed to be not Brn enough as proper Subjects to keep
> them, till of late, they have not yet taken place.
>   Once in the month, generally before the Children's Congn Day, the
> Brn, who live with the Children, meet to a Conference in which the
> Work of Grace in the Children's Hearts and also the outward order, is
> the Subject of Conversation.

The strengthening of devotional life in the Oeconomy became a priority
as soon as qualified helpers were available, but the reference to the shortage of suitable brethren to fulfil this requirement suggests one recurrent
problem which contributed to the difficulty of maintaining the high
spiritual ideals of the community.

There were wide differences in attainment between pupils, and
Labourers ensured that boys were appropriately catered for when the
time came for them to move on, as this extract from the Minutes of the
Conferences of the Children's Oeconomy for 18 February 1765[24] shows:

> It was spoken about those boys here that are fit for study, and should
> be sent to Germany, how they could be provided for. It was thought to

be a matter for the Provinc. Synod to resolve upon. As Matters stand now, the Oeconomy is not able to pay for such Children, whose Parents cannot do it.

Syms, L. West, Horn and Cl. Nisbet were proposed as such, who might be fit for being sent in proper time to Germany into the Paedagogium, and as it was thought we would herein meet with the least Objection, Br. Steinhauer was advised to instruct them in that View, though nothing could yet be determined finally.

It was spoken about Peter Mortimer, how to employ him. It was not thought well to put him into a Shop, but rather to see if he could not get a place in Zeyst . . .

Seiffert and Willett could be proposed for Linnen Weavers in Zeyst, of which Br Johann is first to be acquainted with . . .

Evidently many facilities and career prospects were open to the boys as Unity members and great care went into placing them according to their aptitudes. Further education in Germany was a viable proposition for those whose parents could raise the money, but other deserving cases were not necessarily excluded. The German educational facilities of the Unity were available on two levels: the paedagogium was an option for the most academically able, while Zeyst provided specialist training for promising artisans. The final decision about who should be accepted for entry to the paedagogium from the British Province, a privilege for which they would be prepared by a German Labourer, was in the hands of the Anglo-German provincial synod. It was a privilege to be selected for training in Zeyst: Peter Mortimer was regarded as too able to be given a routine apprenticeship locally, the implication being that the two boys who were proposed for training in Zeyst as linen weavers would receive a specialized apprenticeship of a type unavailable in England. The thinking throughout is that of the whole Unity, with Germany as the focal point and source of the greatest opportunity for the ablest young members of British congregations.

The question of how to pay the fees of these boys was a subject of continuing argument between July and September of 1765 and reflects the financial stringency of the Unity and its English settlement at Fulneck during the early 1760s, shortly after the debt to the Zinzendorf family was shouldered by the church. Many documents in the Fulneck archive relating to the Children's Oeconomy[25] are concerned with debt and poor living conditions in the 1760s and early 1770s. Evidently, provincial and individual support for the education of Labourers' children and others was not adequate to ensure that the brightest children were certain to benefit from the facilities of the Unity as a whole.

There are indications that it became difficult from the 1760s onwards for settlement members with teaching responsibilities to make an adequate living. In February 1767 the record of the Conferences of the Children's Oeconomy expressed concern that the need of Labourers to earn money was in danger of interfering with their effective discharge of their duties: 'An Observation was made that as the Brn and Srs get no money from the Oeconomy some of them do some work by which they earn something, which may have proved the Occasion of neglecting the children.'

Despite the struggles of the British provincial administration and the individual settlements to discharge their financial obligations, there was still every sign of the centrality of German Unity organization as a source of authoritative reference in the years immediately following Zinzendorf's death. The diary of the Children's Oeconomy for 13 July 1765 recorded that, 'It was wished that some approved Children's Brethren could be got from Germany.' In October of the same year the diary reflected the Sisters' acceptance of the authority of German practice. Sr Anna Rosel had been in Germany and was referred to over a specific use of the lot: 'The question whether in Herrnhuth our Saviour was consulted when a Child was to be received into the Children's Congregation, was answered by Sr Anna Rosel in the affirmative.'

This care for the education and training of the children who were the responsibility of the settlement had little to do with contemporary educational theory, though its provisions for the teaching of reading, writing and arithmetic followed common practice. While providing a basic education, the main concern of the Brethren was that those children in their care should be taught the spiritual basis of their beliefs and provided with the means of earning a living. It still reflected perceptions of the settlements as providing potential Labourers well equipped for wider service in the Unity.

Parents who sent their children to these early schools handed over responsibility for their care to the Brethren. An undated manuscript draft application form for parents requesting a school place for their child[26] made this clear to applicants:

> And because we are well assured that the Brethren take faithful Care of the children, and our Aim with our Child can be better brought about there than in our own House or elsewhere, therefore we will give the

Care of our Child over to them, resigning our said child for ever, entirely and without any Restriction to the Man[a]gement of the Brethren, and will never remove the Child from thence without their liking.

The Brethren retained their option to send the child back without obligation to give a reason. Parents were to pay £12 a year and to provide clothes, linen and medicine.

Charles Delamotte's request for his three daughters, Christina, Elizabeth and Henrietta, to be accepted at Lamb's Hill near Pudsey, dated 22 March 1763,[27] contains this paragraph:

And as the Brethren would as far as in them lies, prevent any unhappy Consequences arising to the Children under their Care, from any Alteration in the Minds of the Parents, by taking them at an improper Time out of a recluse State, in which they are preserved as much as possible from the Knowledge of Sin and the Seductions of this World, and by bringing them into the midst of the World, I hereby make a solemn Declaration that I will at no time, nor on any account or under any pretext whatsoever take my said Children out of sd. School without the Consent of those who have the Inspection thereof.

This document goes to the heart of the philosophy behind the training of children in the oeconomies: they were in 'a recluse state', protected from the world and subject completely to the religious indoctrination and moral imperatives perceived by the Brethren as essential to the raising of children in their institutions and their faith. The carefully regulated provision of education for children, as originally conceived and practised in the British provincial settlements, contributed to the Brethren's distinctive appeal to those who accepted this philosophy during the formative years of Unity expansion.

When boarding schools were set up in the nineteenth century as providers of provincial finance they adopted the European tradition from the Brethren's paedagogium at Niesky. This establishment, being in Prussia, had developed in line with the educational system of that country which was exceptionally advanced for its time, and it is significant that, in 1835, the province was still looking to Germany for its educational model.

As the British provincial boarding school network developed, many pupils came from families of non-members, so that these institutions gradually became more akin to other denominational and secular boarding schools, providing education outside the state system for those who valued it on religious or social grounds; few of their pupils have joined the church as adults, although they may have been encouraged in Christian living. The schools have always provided an education in Britain for the children of serving ministers, including some from the American provinces, and today the two that remain attract pupils from Far-Eastern countries.

In spite of their origins in a nineteenth-century provincial educational initiative, the present Moravian boarding schools are not direct spiritual descendants of the mid-eighteenth-century institutions. The latter were products of Zinzendorf's thinking that schooling at all levels was fundamentally religious education supplemented by training in the skills appropriate to adult life in a Unity congregation.

14

Communication as a Support System

It was only in the very early days of the Unity that its activities were restricted to the immediate locality of Herrnhut. By the end of the 1740s the organization had expanded vigorously into other parts of the Holy Roman Empire and to foreign countries such as Russia, Britain, Greenland and the American continent.

Some impression of the geographical scale involved in creating and maintaining this global network can be gathered from the following statistics: on a direct line, the distance from Herrnhut to London is about 700 miles, the same as to outlying parts of the continental diaspora such as Estonia. A typical missionary posted to the West Indies would make his way from Herrnhut to London, embark there, and sail for between 3,600 and 3,800 miles. If he had been called to serve in Surinam the distance would be increased to 4,000 miles. Even for routine visits to congregations in Pennsylvania via New York or Philadelphia, a voyage of 3,100 miles was involved, and 2,000 miles for those called to serve in Greenland.

Logistically, for them as for other missionary fraternities such as the Jesuits, covering distances of this order was not a problem. The ship was the fastest form of transport in the eighteenth century, and recent work by British and American historians represents the Atlantic Ocean as a bridge rather than a barrier,[1] over which there were ample, regular well-used ocean-going shipping services available, and their focal point was London. This huge metropolis was unique, not only in the complex and mobile society of contemporary Britain, but also in Europe.[2] In 1700 its population numbered about 575,000,[3] rising to about 750,000 by mid-century, at a time when the second largest city in Britain was Norwich, with approximately 20,000 inhabitants.[4] The French historian Fernand Braudel has defined eighteenth-century London as a 'world-economy metropolis' which functioned as 'the centre of the world'[5] by 1775, because of its vast mercantile trading and shipping activity. Ships sailing to and from London had another very important role: most of them regularly carried commercial, political and personal correspondence from overseas, so that London flourished as an international postal distribution centre for the exchange of information, both printed and manuscript, and the Unity made use of this facility.

Accordingly, when Unity interest and organization radiated westward from the German heartland, spurred not only by evangelistic zeal but also by the threat of expulsion from Herrnhut, the necessary facilities for global travel were already in place. Congregations were set up in North America, and transatlantic missionary activity occurred where it did, largely because of the means provided by what David Hancock has referred to as the 'global overseas merchants'[6] of London. The West Indian islands were of immense importance to the grandeur and prosperity of the British Empire, particularly because of wealth gained from the labour of the Negro slaves employed in sugar production,[7] and it was on their behalf that these islands became the scene of the earliest and most concentrated Unity missionary activity.[8] Over the years, many of the missionaries posted from Herrnhut sailed there and to other transatlantic destinations on cargo boats which routinely provided accommodation for small groups of passengers,[9] or in the early period in the Unity's own vessel, the *Irene*.

Other brethren and sisters travelled the roads of Europe on foot or in simple carriages, directed by the leadership to work at their trades or as evangelists, sometimes in a succession of settlements, or to contribute to the establishment and running of new diaspora societies in places as far apart as Frankfurt, Berlin and St Petersburg. Among these men and women were many who worked for a while in the British Province before returning to Germany. Some of them, like Mary Vogelsang, spent the rest of their lives in Britain, far from their homeland, in Unity service. For these people, wherever they were serving, an elaborate support system involving the exchange of news, information and spiritual encouragement was created to keep them close to the caring heart of the organization.

The establishment of the Unity global information exchange

It was a permanent feature of Herrnhut as the Unity's organizational centre that people, news, doctrinal teaching and correspondence from congregations, mission stations and diaspora societies all flowed into and out of it. Personal and confidential correspondence was handled separately. In principle this information exchange was simple. The Labourers in charge of Unity institutions, predominantly a mobile, German-speaking spiritual elite, compiled diaries of their activities and posted regular summaries to Herrnhut in the form of 'open letters' intended for recirculation among congregations, who by this means could be induced to broaden their horizons, think internationally and appreciate the activity of the Unity as a whole. These Labourers were well qualified for the task, having benefited from the policy of posting them at variable and often frequent intervals to overseas stations from service in Europe among congregations or diaspora societies. In this way they gained experience of working in different environments: a period of service in Estonia could well be followed by one in the West Indies or Greenland.

The extensive distribution of Unity institutions also implied that the Labourers, like the Jesuits, faced and overcame unusual language problems, being obliged to learn to communicate with the English – not easy if the natives spoke 'broad Yorkshire' – with American Indians, Eskimos, and so on, thereby of necessity becoming bilingual or even trilingual. A typical eighteenth-century missionary Labourer was much travelled, with a wealth of experience and a perspective on the human situation which could not be acquired in any other way. They were, of course, a tiny minority; most Unity members lived much more circumscribed lives, being confined to the country of their birth or one small part of it. Since they could never have first-hand experience of Unity evangelism in the wider world, the information exchange provided them with detailed and frequently updated accounts of Unity activity throughout the network, an arrangement which was probably unique among contemporary British Protestant denominations at that time.

At Herrnhut reports and letters from Labourers were edited and sufficient manuscript copies made to ensure that one reached every principal congregation and mission station. Classified bundles of this material were allowed to accumulate for two or three months, after which they were parcelled up for dispatch. As a result, when a parcel arrived at its destination it contained a voluminous collection of material, international in character and contributed by men writing from first-hand experience. Also included were summary diaries of current activity at Unity headquarters, synonymous with Zinzendorf's residence during his lifetime, numerous sermons preached by him and his immediate entourage, and memoirs[10] (obituaries) of important individuals, all of which added a significant doctrinal element to the material selected for circulation. Delivery to congregations took place up to five or six times a year.

Since the majority of writers and congregational readers were German-speakers, most original manuscripts and copies were written in that language, arrangements being made for translation into other European languages, including English, either locally in Herrnhut or in London where bilingual Labourers were readily available. As a result, the parcels of sermons and reports which arrived at major British congregations such as Fulneck were already written in good standard English prose which could be assimilated readily by those who attended the frequent meetings for the purpose of hearing them read. These manuscripts were then circulated throughout the provincial congregational network, a leisurely and time-consuming process which aimed to deepen the ordinary members' sense of involvement in Unity objectives and activities all over the world. Ultimately they were returned and stored in the archive of the community to which they had been addressed, to be referred to from time to time on special occasions. Collectively this material constituted a developing cultural and spiritual autobiography of the Unity as a whole, recording, it was believed, the work of the Saviour among his chosen people.

The system was well established by 1747, and between then and Zinzendorf's death in 1760 his preaching and other activities were extensively reported in the information dispatched. After 1760 there was a gradual change in this practice, though frequent references to the things he had said and done were made in the discourses of others for many years; there was still a firm conviction that they were relevant. Apart from this, the arrangements as a whole remained unaltered, and the British collections of news reports of the 1780s were similar in content and style to those of the 1740s.

During the 1790s major changes began to occur. Although the Labourers throughout the Unity continued to send in regular manuscript reports as before, the copies for recirculation were printed. There was a gradual change, also, in the practice whereby all congregations in the two European provinces shared identical news items and sermons. The British Province opted to concentrate increasingly on news from the mission fields, so that the material circulating was so edited that in Britain it contained progressively less emphasis on continental congregations and diaspora societies, and from 1790 onwards the province published its own selection in the form of *Periodical Accounts relating to the Missions of the church of the United Brethren established among the Heathen*.

By the end of the eighteenth century, therefore, the system of news collection and distribution, which originally had been concerned with the Unity as a whole, tended in Europe to be divided according to provincial interests, and has remained so ever since. On the one hand, the voluminous printed Continental Provincial News Reports have continued along the original lines with contents drawn from the entire Unity and exclusively in German; on the other, the British Province's Periodical Accounts concentrated largely on foreign missions, being published entirely in English. Although there was some overlapping of content from time to time, it was far easier for continental members to sustain an international mentality of the type originally intended than it was for the British. Once the split had taken place, British congregational members soon lost any intimate sense of what was happening in the nearby Continental Province, being limited to a dramatic impression of Unity mission work thousands of miles away among natives whose traditional way of life, though colourful, was at that stage completely alien. An international mentality was maintained, but the accounts which sustained it gave undue prominence to one specialist aspect of Unity activity, introducing a different emphasis from that which the mid-eighteenth-century pioneers had in mind. For them the Continental Province, with its Europe-wide diaspora network, was the energy-centre and primary theatre of operations of the Unity; the missions to the heathen, though important, were ancillary to it. The nature of this original concept and its practice can only be fully appreciated by reference to primary sources from a British repository such as Fulneck, particularly for the 1750s when it was becoming well established, and the 1770s when the exchange was in its prime.

The information exchange in practice

On the evidence of what was received at Fulneck, it is clear that the preparation and assembly of material for circulation throughout the Unity in the early years was meticulously organized at Herrnhut. A weekly report of about ten pages was written, the weeks of each year being classified consecutively from Week 1 to Week 52 for ease of reference. The contents were heavily doctrinal, with the intention of acquainting congregational members all over the world with the spiritual concerns and practical activities of Zinzendorf and other leaders. A typical example is Week 1 (January 1–8) of 1757. Zinzendorf was in residence at Herrnhut and had an important role in the special New Year's Day celebrations, which were described in some detail. There was a transcript of his two sermons, one for the children and the other for communicant members. The next day was a Sunday, and the usual congregational meetings were briefly referred to, as was a sermon by Bishop Johannes

Nitschmann; in contrast, Zinzendorf's Sunday sermon was recorded in full. This format, in which recorded sermons had the major role, remained a feature of the weekly reports until the ethos gradually changed towards the end of the eighteenth century.

The appendices, which summarized reports sent in by Labourers stationed all over the world, were associated for ease of classification with a particular weekly report, and during 1757 there were appendices for sixteen weeks. The appendix for Week 1 illustrates their scope, though it was more than usually biased towards transatlantic sources. It contained a long report from Greenland based on congregational diaries kept there, covering the period from September 1755 to August 1756 and augmented by several letters from native converts addressed personally to Zinzendorf. Such grateful letters to Unity leaders, or messages dictated to the Labourers where the converts were illiterate, were a regular feature of the appendices, providing encouraging evidence of the success of missionary endeavour in saving souls. (The Congregation Helper at Fulneck noted in the margin that he read large parts of this report to a general meeting on 25 September 1757.)

The arrival of an appendix from Greenland tended to be an annual event, but contributions from America and the West Indies appeared more frequently and were also represented in Week 1. There were reports based on congregational diaries from the West Indian islands of St Thomas, St Croix, St John, Antigua, Jamaica, and from Rio de Barbice and Surinam on the northern fringe of South America, most of them covering the period from May to September 1756. It was noted that no diary extracts were available from Bethlehem, Pennsylvania, because the post had been seriously delayed.

The appendix to the fourth week of 1757, that is the last week of January, had a similar transatlantic bias, this time reflecting the arrival in Herrnhut of diaries from North America referring to events in the early and mid-summer of 1756. The contents were as follows:

I. Voyage Diary. An account written by Brother Schmaling, who had travelled with eleven other Single Brethren from Zeist in Holland to Bethlehem, Pennsylvania, during the months of March to June 1756.

II. A report from the congregational diary of Bethlehem for the months of June and July 1756, mentioning particularly the receipt of letters from the British and Continental Provinces and the latest arrival of the Unity ship *Irene* in New York with a party of fifteen more Single Brethren. The diarist noted on 5 June the special feeling of fellowship with 'our European Brn and Srs'.

III. An extract from the Bethlehem Children's Diary, June–July 1756.

IV. Reports from various Indian Congregations for the same months.

V, VI and VII were from centres of influence near Bethlehem, Nazareth, various Country Congregations in America, and Wachovia in Austria.

VIII. Two copies of letters which had been originally directed there from Zinzendorf, but were now considered suitable for general circulation.

IX. Memoirs (obituaries) of six congregational members of varying ages, four of them brethren in the Holy Roman Empire and two in Moravia.

From these two appendices it is clear that the readings of January 1757 provided an ample source of news from some of the farthest areas of eighteenth-century Unity activity. With the exception of Greenland, appendices for Weeks 15, 24 and 46 were equally comprehensive. During the course of the year, six appendices originated in Bethlehem, and most other transatlantic stations, particularly those in the West Indies, produced five. The flow of information was substantial and, in eighteenth-century terms, continuous: in Fulneck, for example, the local leaders were receiving detailed news of the Unity's most significant overseas work on average once every two or three months.

Other reports, the most frequent normally arriving at two-monthly intervals, originated in the Continental Province, where the bulk of the Labourers were working; for example the appendix to the eighth week of 1757 reported in detail on the activity in German congregations during the final two or three months of the previous year – Herrnhut, Gnadenfrei, Gnadenberg, Neusalz, Kleinwelke, Niesky, Berlin and Rixdorf, Barby, Ebersdorf, Marienborn, Neuwied and Zeist. They were supplemented by detailed reports classified as 'Out of the Diaspora', which referred to the widespread influence of the Brotherhood in Denmark, Switzerland and the Baltic States, where a great deal of Unity activity involved the setting-up and maintenance of religious societies for members of the Established church in those areas, in accordance with Zinzendorf's philosophy of supporting existing institutions. Further east, at least one brother was active in Transylvania, since the appendix included a copy of an informative letter to Bishop Johannes von Watteville from Br Singer, a Unity evangelist working there. From Cairo, even further afield, came an outline of Br Hocker's report to Zinzendorf on the progress of the Unity mission to the Coptic Church.

Extracts from the appendices

Appendices referring to sea voyages to America undertaken by Unity members illustrate the articulate and informative nature of these reports. They also portray a philosophical and trusting spirit and cheerfulness in the face of adversity.

Bishop Johannes von Watteville, a seasoned traveller in the service of the Unity, was in overall charge of overseas missions when he preached in London on 14 January 1755.[11] He argued that it was much easier and safer to travel by sea than overland. This was certainly the spirit of Br Joseph Waugh, who travelled from London to Antigua during the period 3 April to 20 May 1776 accompanied by his wife, Sr Margaret Waugh, and Br Samuel Watson.[12] Br Waugh compiled the voyage diary which would later be dispatched to Herrnhut for circulation throughout the Unity. He describes how he, his wife and their colleagues prepared themselves for the journey.

> After we three poor Pilgrims had on the second of April enjoyed the Holy Communion with hungry and thirsty Souls, we set out on the third, in the afternoon, in a boat from London, and reached Gravesend in the evening. The fourth of April we went on board our Ship the *Antigua Planter*, captain James King. Br and Sr Waugh got a Chamber for themselves, adjoining to which was a small Closet, which we made use of for our Meetings.[13] Br Watson also had a Chamber for himself. We were heartily thankful that our Brethren in London had cared so well for our lodgings in the Ship. . . . In the Evening we shut ourselves up in our Closet, read a part of the History of our Lord's Sufferings and recommended thereupon in a hearty manner, this Place, ourselves and our Journey and future Plan earnestly to our Saviour. In the following Days we continued to read the History of our Saviour's Passion, and his Heart was with us. On Good Friday, April fifth, our Captain came on board and we weighed Anchor. Both he and the other six Passengers, three of whom were in the Cabin and three in the Steerage, and the ship's Crew behaved friendly towards us throughout the whole Journey.

Little progress was made during the next few days because the winds were contrary, but the ship proceeded along the south coast, and on 10 April they lost sight of England. As soon as they came into the open sea and the Atlantic swell, all three suffered from sea-sickness, but they gradually recovered and by the 19th all had become fully accustomed to the motion of the ship.

Several on board the Ship who had seen Sr Watson when she was so poorly testified to their Joy at her Recovery, and the Captain made her a Present of a fresh leg of Mutton, which was an agreeable Refreshment to us all. As we read today a Chapter out of the Bible together in our Closet, the three Passengers in the Steerage listened attentively at the Door, several also of the ship's Crew took often our Books and read in them. . . . Sometimes we had also with one or the other among them some Conversation, which we hope has not been without Blessing.

Weather conditions being favourable, with a steady following wind, the ship made good progress towards the tropics. On 27 April the whole ship was washed,

and all the Things arranged otherwise on account of the Heat which we now began to feel, and in order to keep the Air as pure and healthy as possible. Today being Communion Day we had a liturgical Meeting in the Evening at which we felt the comfortable nearness of our Lord. May the seventh we passed the Tropic. Two of the other Passengers on board were dipped in the Sea, as they would not give what is customary to be given [to the crew] by Everyone who passes the Tropic for the first Time. We gave some Quarts of Brandy to the Sailors, with which they were very well satisfied. . . .

We have now [4 May] for several Days had very little Wind, and the seventh we sailed no more than twenty-seven Miles. So little Progress we have never made before; the most we have advanced in one Day was 164 miles. The eighth we at last got into the Trade Winds in the 30th degree north of Latitude. . . . Now the Water became putrefied and smelt bad, the Beer was as sour as Vinegar. In order to purify the Water they [the crew] used a hollow Stone called Bermuda Stone which is porous and like Pumice. When the Water has dropped through the Stone it is clear and cool, and the Dirt remains in the Bottom of the Hollow Stone. . . . Sr Waugh provided us with a sort of Bread, which she made of Potatoes and Meal and we liked it better than the best Biscuits.

On 13 May they met an Irish ship carrying provisions to Antigua, which sailed along with them. By 16 May they were expecting to see land, and the sails were taken in every night so that the ship would not be blown against rocks.

The nineteenth we saw with pleasure great flights of Birds, the Proof that we were near Land. The twentieth, early in the Morning before we had got up, we were saluted with the joyful News that Land could be seen. We hastened directly on Deck, that we might see with our own Eyes . . . The Land we saw was the Islands of Desirade and Guadaloupe. We soon lost sight of them, and about six o'clock we saw straight away before us at a distance of 21 miles the Hills of Antigua, in the Beginning like Clouds on the Horizon, but after an Hour quite distinctly. We were full of Joy and gave our good Lord a Thousand Thanks for bringing us so far without any Danger and without one single Storm. . . .

At noon we were so near the Island that we could distinguish everything on Land. We sailed five or six English Miles along it, and found it to be, contrary to our Expectations, full of great and small Hills, on the tops of which were the finest Sugar Plantations. About three o'clock the Pilots with three Negroes came on Board . . . and at about six o'clock we cast Anchor in the Haven of St John's. As it began to grow dark we left the Ship, on board of which we had been 48 days.

They were taken by a crew member to the house of Br and Sr Brown, who welcomed them to a hearty meal which included fruits which the Negroes had brought as a gift for the new pastor and his wife. That evening many local Negroes came to welcome them, saying how earnestly they had prayed to the Saviour to bring them there safe and well. Tears were brought to their eyes by 'the hearty Love with which our white Brethren and Sisters received us, and the noble simplicity with which the Negroes testified their love toward us'. The following day they were welcomed by their colleague Br Meder, whose letter to the children at Fulneck has already been quoted.

Another account of a voyage from London to New York from 23 September to 16 November 1754,[14] written by Nicol Gerritson, the captain of the Brethren's ship *Irene*, describes a journey undertaken in very different circumstances. Since all the passengers and the captain himself were Moravians, life on board was centred on religious practices and was recorded as a rich spiritual experience. When the passengers boarded on 22 September, Br Johannes [von Watteville] and other brethren accompanied them, and Johannes 'kept us a fine discourse of the happenings one can have at sea', and held a communion service. The following morning they began to sail round the coast, clearing the customs at Gravesend on the 24th. The captain obviously wished his readers to know that those who had dealings with them were impressed:

. . . the Inspector of the Customs came on Board, but told his People that they need not search our Ship, for he was sure that I would not cheat a Customs Office. I had no-one but good People on Board. The like he had never seen on any Vessel. . . . Our Pilot told the People in Gravesend that he never before had been on Board on such a Ship; but though it was quite full of Passengers and Sailors yet did he hear no Noise or Swearing. He said he could not comprehend how it was possible, for in other Ships People were often so noisy that he could not do his Business for the Confusion they made.

After clearing the Scilly Isles by 29 September, they settled in for the main voyage:

Now we had fine Weather for some Days, kept the Sundays as well as we could and told our Sailors how we stood affected towards our Creator and Redeemer, which they heard attentively. Br Gottlieb had a faithful and tender Care of his Brethren and one could read from all his Demeanour the Character of a Child of God. He is also a good Leader and I should wish he might always be on Board, when such a Company of Travellers go together over the Sea. The Liturgies and Meetings he kept were with Blessing. October the third we passed . . . Cape Finisterre in Portugal, a 175 Sea Miles from London Meridian. We had for some days contrary wind which sometimes drove us back, but experienced what Johannes had told us, that one could be quite happy on Sea.

We felt ourselves with the Saviour quite sequestered from the World and perceived on this Voyage particularly that he was with us. . . . Br Gottlieb took our opportunities to read out of the 'weeks' . . . and thus we passed our time very contented. At Night in stillness the Saviour owned us to be his. I often have thought that the heart of our Lamb must needs rejoice to see such a Company swimming on the Ocean, who rejoice his and the Heart of the dear Father who keeps us by his holy Angels, which we have seen in divers Circumstances.

As they approached Newfoundland on 29 October they met with stormy weather, but their lives were not endangered, and by 12 November they passed Long Island and came into shallow water. The hazards of the journey were not yet over, because the weather was wild on the following day, a dangerous situation when they were so close to land. On 16 November they came safely into harbour.

We kept a thanksgiving Lovefeast on Board and were received with joy
by the New York Brethren, who had expected us before now. We were
well cared for with a Lovefeast in our Church and rejoiced with all
sorts of good Accounts from Carolina, St Thomas and other parts of
the West Indies and then our Brethren set out in three Companies for
Bethlehem. Directly after our arrival we found fresh Cause to thank
our dear Father, that he had brought us thither at that time; for a
terrible Storm arose, which was followed by strong west Winds and
hard Frost, and thus it continued to this very Day. . . . I do nevertheless
see that the Brethren might order the Expeditions at a proper Season
that such a Company of Brethren might not come so late in the Year
into this Country.

One significant feature of Captain Gerritson's journal is that it contains
two references to the reading of 'weeks' or 'accounts' as part of the
routine of fellowship and worship. Whether on board ship or arriving for
the first time in a foreign country, the travellers, like their brethren in the
congregations, were never out of touch with the Unity communications
network.

His complaint about the danger of leaving so late in the year was obviously not heeded, because in 1757 the *Irene* made another journey in
more hazardous circumstances. On this occasion the ship left London on
22 September and did not land in New York until 12 December. It had
travelled in convoy because of the threat to shipping from American
privateers active during the Seven Years War (1756–63), and had
encountered severe storms. The three diarists were Brethren Peter
Eckesparre, William Boehler and Reuchers.
    Because of stormy weather in the English Channel they were still only
at Spithead on 18 October, in calm rainy weather. There on the 19th the
convoy came together.

We looked with Desire for the Ships which should come after us from
London and sail with us out of the Channel. Towards nine o'clock we
spied some of them and at last the whole Fleet of sixty Ships which
yielded a beautiful Sight came up one after another. Two Men of War
saluted every Ship with thirteen Guns and our Admiral returned the
Fire. Towards night a Storm arose. The second Anchor was cast and
towards Morning lifted again. Our Ship had moved from her Place a
good deal this Night and had been in Danger from fouling up a large
Holland Ship. The twentieth and twenty-first the Wind was contrary

west and south-west. During the almost perpetual Storm many Ships
arrived and Privateers have swarmed about in this Part of the Channel.
The twenty-second being the King's Coronation Day they fired the
Guns at Portsmouth at noon and the small Arms made a Train of Fire
Afterwards all the Men of War fired their Guns.

The convoy of 'about seventy Merchantmen and three Men of War',
still dogged by bad weather, eventually passed the Lizard on 25 October
and saw land for the last time. The diary of the main voyage is punctuated by regular references to the Watchwords, many of which contained references to security and protection, and to the prayer and
preaching which sustained them. From time to time they saw other ships,
always a matter for concern in case they were privateers. On 21
November, in yet another storm, they were still about 300 miles from
New York. The storm continued for several days and they had to turn
southwards. The diarist commented:

> The twenty-sixth the Storm was very hard, the Sea high and looks like
> white and blue Emeralds. Towards noon the Masts were lightened and
> the Sails let down. It was a full storm. The Captain could not remem-
> ber to have had such terrible high Waves.

These alternating storms and calmer spells continued, and the Brethren
always rejoiced and gave thanks to the Saviour when the calms enabled
them to take comfort from their liturgies and texts. Such opportunities
seemed to them to have been provided by the Saviour's grace for their
comfort and reassurance. By the beginning of December conditions were
even worse as the weather became colder, but even in these circumstances
the writer retained his eye for the beauty and grandeur of natural forces.

> The Wind was north and so strong that the Water was carried like
> Smoke and a thick Mist into the Air. It was at the same Time very cold
> and the Deck, upon which the Sailors could hardly suffer the Cold, was
> white from the Hail in the Night. The Sea yielded a Prospect like unto
> the Vogelsberg where it looked like a Valley in Winter in cold misty
> Weather. The foaming Waves looked like Mountains covered with Ice
> and Snow and some surrounded from above with a thick Cloud.

When the sea settled on the seventh they 'divided the cup of thanksgiving', partly because the ship had survived the crossing undamaged and
partly to celebrate two birthdays, Br Eckspierre's entering his twenty-

eighth year the previous day and Br Boehler his thirty-second on that very day. By this time they were in sight of land and could distinguish trees on the shore, and on 11 December the pilot came aboard. The description of their first sight of land after such a dangerous voyage would move their readers to praise and thank the Saviour for their safe arrival.

> Just when we entered at Sandy Hook an incomparable fine View of Grace presented itself, the Cloud opposite to us toward New York, part of which extended itself completely on the blue Sky which is not a common Thing and charmed us extremely at our Entrance into America. The Watchword was: now I will arise. . . . It was at two o'clock and agreeable weather. Many hundreds of birds like Ducks swam near us and flew over the Water and made a Musick. At eight o'clock at Night we cast Anchor because it grew misty, and reached New York.

They landed the following morning, heartened by the Watchword: 'Behold, now is the acceptable time.' After being welcomed at the Congregation House by the Brethren, they worshipped together, and on 13 December travelled to Bethlehem, arriving on the 16th in deep snow, but 'safe and happy'.

Some accounts were sources of spiritual inspiration and teaching, a particularly good example being those of the German mission to the Copts, probably the most arid field in which the Brethren worked. There were hardships in every foreign mission, but in most the rewards were commensurate with the sacrifice. The diaries of the Brethren who worked in Cairo and Behnesse in the 1770s record a task which needed exceptional courage, since they were living in an area troubled by plague and physical danger, and seeking to impress members of an alternative Christian persuasion. From the point of view of their readers the diaries gave insights into a difficult and dangerous way of life as they followed their crafts in order to make a living; more significantly for their inspirational and didactic role, the diaries contained details of the arguments by which these Brethren defined their own religious convictions for the benefit of those they were hoping to convert.

The mission from Herrnhut to the Coptic Church lasted only thirty years, from 1752 to 1782. After an unsuccessful attempt to establish a base in Abyssinia, another was set up in Cairo in 1769, directed by Br Friedrich Wilhelm Hocker, a physician and deacon of the church, who was by this time a specialist in Arabic. He was accompanied by Johann

Heinrich Danke, a joiner, and John Antes, a watchmaker and repairer. The latter was an American originating from Fredrickstown, near Philadelphia, and was later to work at Fulneck. Other brethren served the mission for short periods during its lifetime, but it was an unrewarding field. Ill-health and accidents took their toll and the project was closed down after Hocker's death in 1782.

Regular extracts from the diaries of the Brethren in Cairo were received in Fulneck, and are preserved in the Congregation Accounts.[15] The entry for April and May 1770 is typical of these, in this case written by Br Antes, who had been designated mission diarist:

> April 17th. . . . In outward matters our Saviour has blessed us and I particularly have till now sufficient employment, though there are above thirty watchmakers here in Cairo . . . The 30th there came two Jews to Brother Hocker to consult with him about a sick person and [he] had an opportunity to speak with them about the Messiah who shed his blood to atone for our sins and of the happiness which a soul can experience when it has felt the virtue of his atonement. As one of them was not perfect in the language the other interpreted to him what was said and they both heard with an attention which gave us much pleasure. Thus we lay hold of every opportunity to declare our Lord's death, but alas, we find in general that the hearts are as hard as nethermost millstones. Ah, could we but find one soul truly concerned about his salvation, how we should rejoice!

In 1770 an opening was found at Behnesse, a small town of Greek origin, and accommodation rented there which was used by one brother on tours of varying lengths, while the rest of the team remained in Cairo to raise funds by practising their crafts. Br Danke was the Behnesse pioneer, and his diaries are mainly concerned with the unrewarding task of trying to explain his faith to the Coptic Christians and Roman Catholics among whom he worked, who admired him as a man and befriended him, but were deaf to his message, even deriding it.

> 10 May 1771. The priests in Benesse [*sic*] showed me some of their doctrinal books which preach of the great power lodged in the Virgin Mary, who can deliver man from eternal destruction. They read me some passages out of them, which make one's hair stand on end and I am astonished more and more to see what dreadful degrees of darkness hovers over these people.

It is not surprising that the mission was short-lived, since the Brethren made scant headway with other convinced Christians and were working all the time at the margins of their capacity to maintain themselves, and in a part of the world where disease was endemic. Their experiences provided a sombre contrast to the heartening success stories which came to British congregations from other sources, but for their original hearers they provided an inspiring example of the Saviour's upholding of those who laboured to spread the gospel in distant mission fields.

The senior Labourers, like Zinzendorf himself, made a point of writing to individuals or groups of converts, letting them know that they were valued personally, and that their witness to the work of the Saviour was appreciated by Unity leaders and known to their fellow brethren and sisters in Christ. They were encouraged to reply, so that their witness could be circulated throughout the Unity, as in the example cited above. Typical of such communications are the replies to Brother Johannes[16] (von Watteville) in answer to a general letter by him to 'Negro Brethren in Antigoa, who are employed by the Missionaries as their assistants in the labour among the Negro-Slaves in their care'. The converts' replies were dictated by them to one of the missionaries. All were effusive and some were lengthy, but the following extracts show that these helpers were expressing sentiments which would rejoice the hearts of those to whom they were read in the European congregations, since they showed proper gratitude and acceptance of their humble position, as well as providing evidence of true conversion by their mastery of appropriate language.

> From Amos. I now begin to perceive that the Words of our Saviour find place in my heart, and cannot thank him enough for all the good things I enjoy of him at our meetings in Spring-garden. Blessed be the door by which I came in! Blessed be the Ship which brought me hither from Guinea. I could never have conceived such Blessings as I felt at my first entrance into this place!
>
> From John: We were extremely glad to see Master Mack and his wife when they came to Antigoa. May our Saviour keep his hand over them . . . and bring them safe and well to our Brethren in Europe . . . I greet all our dear Brethren in Europe and thank you for your loving Letter to us poor and weak people.
>
> From David: We have received your letter and our white Brethren have read it to us. It occasions always a holy joy in the whole Congn, when you inform us that such poor sinners as we are may have fellow-

ship with the Children of God. Our hearts feel our Saviour's love to us. We are not worthy of the Grace He confers upon us. We know that our white Brethren who labour among us have much trouble with us.

As a result of this extensive communication network, congregation members in the British Province would have been more familiar with the wider world than many of their contemporaries outside the gentry and rich merchant classes. A fascinating example is this description in the Congregational Accounts for the months of August 1777 to June 1778[17] of the arrival of the British forces to occupy Philadelphia during the American Revolution. Much apprehension had been felt by the inhabitants of the city, and many had left in anticipation of pillage and destruction, including some of the Brethren, though they had been exhorted to remain as a matter of faith.

About the latter end of September the whole city was in a most violent agitation. The sudden departure of the Congress, and the carrying away of the cannon and ammunition of War, put the populace into the utmost confusion. . . . We who remained were chearful and undaunted: nor did we find ourselves deceived in our hope; for the royal Army took possession of the City in the best order and in stillness; General Howe having forbidden his troops on pain of death, to molest the inhabitants, or to take from them by force the value of a penny.

During the winter which followed, some of the German troops serving with the British forces worshipped with the congregation, and departed with affectionate farewells and deep sadness when the occupation was over.

The combined weekly reports (often referred to in the British Province as either 'the weeks' or 'the weekly leaves') gave a comprehensive and continuing narrative of the distinctive activity which characterized the Unity, driven by the strong conviction that the participants were doing the will of the Saviour. The arrival of these regular bundles of 'weeks' and appendices gave pleasure. Their contents were an equivalent of the popular 'travel literature' of the time, enhanced by records of the personal endeavour of Labourers in remote areas whose names became familiar throughout the entire network, and by teaching of the Christian doctrine which was their mainstay. Many references to their receipt can be found in the Irish congregational diaries. The Dublin congregation recorded the receipt of several packets during August and September 1749:

12 August: 'We received several packs from Yorkshire and London containing some Weeks of the Congregational Journal.'

27 August: 'Rec'd letters from London and Yorkshire with some Weeks of the Pilg. Cong.'

7 September: 'Rec'd a Packet of Accounts from Yorkshire, but long to hear from Lond.'

24 September: 'We had a General Meeting of our Society which has been omitted for some Time past for want of English Accts. to read. We read some Accts. from Asia, Africa and America afterwards.'[18]

The Gracehill Congregational diaries similarly show evidence of incoming material being read and appreciated. In January 1765 it was recorded:

6 January: 'At Gloonen, the S.Srs. had a fine homily read out of the Weeks.'

13 January: 'To the Society was read some happy Courses of Lives in the Herrnhut Diary. There was likewise read a fine Homily to the Married Choir.'

20 January: 'After the Sunday Morning Service accounts of the German Congregation were read . . . anointed Homilies were read . . . weeks were communicated.'[19]

One of Okely's collection of letters expresses this pleasure, revealing in its comments the optimism with which the work of the missions was received in the congregations and the enthusiasm they generated among those who heard them read. It is a private letter to two Brethren from a third, and is headed 'N——n, Aug. 6, 1742' and signed 'Your poor unworthy Brother – '.[20]

I came from L—— on Tuesday last: The Day before was the Letter-Day, and the Accounts from abroad were very wonderful and comfortable. I cannot help thinking, but that <u>Grace</u> and <u>Blood</u> will soon be found all over the World. Amen, even so, come Lord Jesus. There was a sweet Letter from one of the Savages, and many from the Witnesses abroad, and some out of Y——; but I suppose you will have the Particulars soon.

Another letter in this collection was obviously written to Okely himself by William Delamotte, also a member of the Cambridge group attracted to the Brethren. It gives further insight into the process of dissemination, showing how letters written in German by those arriving in Philadelphia after transatlantic voyages were translated, passed round among congregations and copies made available to at least some interested individuals. It is headed 'Aug. 16, 1742, My dear Brother O.' and signed, 'Your affectionate Brother W. D——tte.'[21] The final paragraph reads:

> Inclosed is a letter from your Brother who, with all his Company is arrived safe at P——. The Particulars of their Voyage will be translated and read at the next General Meeting in L——, and, I believe, if you desire it, you may get a Copy of it.

The original global news exchange was the authentic record of the activity of a unified and supportive body which shared its experiences, secular and spiritual, as witnesses to the work of the Saviour and to reinforce the fellowship which bound them across the divides of language, race and nationality. There could have been no better way of ensuring conviction of divine leadership, and a considerable degree of sympathy, in the minds of those who could never hope to go themselves, but could participate in imagination, becoming some of the best-informed people in their locality. This state of affairs lasted only as long as the original arrangements remained intact: after the 1790s, most British provincial members were, in effect, denied the regular news of the Continental Province and its personalities, which had been available so readily to their mid-century predecessors. It is not clear why this occurred or whether it was in accordance with their wishes, but this deficiency in communication contributed to the serious lack of archival material which characterized the province during the nineteenth century and beyond.

The Watchwords

The information circulated from Herrnhut also included a separate and distinctive annual booklet which influenced the personal and devotional life of all Unity members, no matter where they were living. It preceded the circulation of information from congregational diaspora and mission sources, since it originated in the fervent revivalist period which took place in Herrnhut during the summer of 1727. At that time Count Zinzendorf regularly presided over evening worship, and introduced the practice of selecting a short scriptural sentence to read to the congregation so that each member could meditate about it overnight and during the following day. At the next evening service he used it as the text of a brief sermon. This procedure became popular, copies of his chosen texts being augmented by contributions from senior colleagues and retained for future reference. In 1728 a further development took place: at the end of every evening service, the person in charge drew out at random from the collection a text for the following day, the theory being that, as in the lot, the Saviour himself would direct the hand of the selector. Texts chosen in this way came to be regarded as the Watchword or Motto of the day.

Early in 1730 it was decided to extend this informal arrangement for the benefit of the Unity as a whole. A Watchword for each day of 1731 was extracted at random from the Herrnhut collection, and a suitable collect or line from a hymn chosen to accompany it.[22] The year's selections were translated into other languages where necessary, printed and then distributed throughout the Unity congregations, so that during 1731 members could read and meditate on the same words wherever they were living, and know that other Brethren and Sisters were doing the same. After Zinzendorf's death there were some changes: increasing use was made of Old Testament sources for the Watchword drawn by lot, and the format was enlarged by the addition of a doctrinal text from the New Testament, not drawn by lot, and its associated hymn line.

A typical example of a Watchword and hymn line from Zinzendorf's time is that for 26 September 1752: '"The Son of Man cometh in an hour when ye think not" – Luke 12:40. Shall this be the last?' After Zinzendorf's death, the Watchword, doctrinal text and hymn lines for a typical day such as 16 October 1768 were: Watchword: '"Who is there among you of all his people? His God be with him and let him go up," Ezra 1.3'; Hymn line: 'So I stretch out my hand and do that work with pleasure'; Doctrinal text: '"He openeth and no man shutteth," Revelation 3.7'; Hymn line: 'Give before us an open door'. By the end of the nineteenth century the two texts tended increasingly to be related in theme and the hymn line was often extended to a verse. This basic pattern has remained unchanged, and annual publication and worldwide distribution of the Watchwords have continued ever since.

This booklet was regarded from the beginning as far more than simply a daily devotional manual directing the prayers and meditations of individual members as they were 'reaching up' to the Saviour, vital as that was. Each Watchword was perceived as a special message 'down' from the Saviour in person to each member in person and uniquely suitable for the day. At a personal level every Watchword with its hymn line was visualized as a divine message and a human response, namely, a conversation which could be taken up at every hour of every day.[23] Great emphasis was placed on the implications of each day's message, both individually and collectively, and it was construed as having implications at congregational level in a way which was almost oracular. Watchwords also provided the basis for sermons and most other forms of devotional fellowship.[24]

As the Unity expanded, newly formed groups regularly received copies, which directed their daily devotions in such a way as to overcome the influence of physical isolation. For members in the predictable routine of a British congregation, the daily practice of meditating on the Watchwords was a discipline which enhanced their sense of belonging to a wider community. For others at the periphery of the Unity's activity they were a lifeline. A letter from Br Nathanael written to the Unity Elders' Conference at Herrnhut from Philadelphia on 12 July 1776, at the time of the Declaration of Independence,[25] was circulated to congregations.[26] In it he reported that, for the present, congregational activities were undisturbed, but,

> The most Painfull thing to us is, that we at Present are cut off from all Connexion with you, and in the Situation we are now in, being declared Independent we don't know how long it will continue so. We know nothing yet of the result of the Synod, we have no hope of getting the W.Words for next year; we know nothing concerning you but what we have learned in the letters of December last which we received this year in March.

The Brethren, like other religious groups who objected to fighting and were loyal to the British king, had many apprehensions for the future, but the question of whether they would be able to receive the Watchwords was an important aspect of their fear of isolation from the rest of the Unity. Symbolically and practically they were very significant.

On the European continent, where many small societies were set up as outposts of the Brethren's mission, the Watchwords and Accounts were routinely available, and there is evidence that travelling members made strenuous efforts to bring this spiritual sustenance to brethren and sisters in danger. One very moving account is that of Sister Anna Kriegelstein, who was given permission to accompany and sustain her husband, who had been arrested with two other brethren as part of the religious persecution in Russia. Eventually, after many years, they were allowed to leave St Petersburg where the men had been imprisoned, on condition that they travelled to Kasan, where her ailing husband soon died. The Brethren were in touch with their situation and helped them with accommodation wherever possible on their long journey via Moscow. Anna later wrote in her memoir:[27]

> Circumstances here in Casan were much easier than before, yet it was a painful consideration to me that we were now at much greater distance from the Congregation. The accounts texts and letters proved an inexpressible comfort to us, and to the end of 1759 I was very heavy at not receiving them. But on the first of January 1760 a Russian merchant brought unto us a packet with accounts and texts from Petersburg. They never proved so precious to me as at this time, and I often thought, 'Might I but use and value his precious book as it deserves.' For the rest, I spent much of my time in prayer and tears and told my Saviour often with a painful feeling, 'Thou knowest that I am resigned to suffer.'

Originally the printed Watchwords were devised to meet the particular needs of the Unity, but progressively during the nineteenth and twentieth centuries other religious bodies decided to incorporate the Unity's Watchwords as a basis for their own Daily Texts. At the present time, as the producers of the American Moravian version for the year 2000 write: 'This little book is probably the most widely read daily devotional guide in the world, next to the Bible. It forms an invisible bond between Christians of all continents, transcending barriers of confession, race, language and politics . . . in fifty languages.'[28] Yet, despite this remarkable ecumenical service with its global distribution, two-thirds of each annual print run, i.e. approximately 1 million out of 1.5 million copies, are in the German language,[29] showing that, as in the mid-eighteenth century, this book still has its greatest appeal in the European Continental Province.

Letters as a support system

The essential supportive role of letter-writing between leaders and Labourers emerges clearly from the correspondence quoted by Okely in his justification of the Brethren. In such a scattered mission, it was necessary for those working in the field to know that they could receive advice and encouragement from more experienced colleagues, and there is evidence in all eighteenth-century congregational diaries of the regular dispatch and receipt of letters independently of the 'weeks'. Here, as in the training grounds of the Place Congregations, the principles and practice of faith were inculcated. This letter to a Brother, dated 1740 and signed 'Your Fellow-Labourer in the Gospel',[30] illustrates this essential process:

Lean not in the least to your own Reason and Understanding; for, if you do, you make your Converts Faith to stand in the Wisdom of men and not of God. . . . Lay as a Worm before the Lord, that he may do as he pleases with you: Neither *dispute* nor *reason* in any Thing, but *believe* in all Things; and where you have not Faith, do not do any Thing; for whatever is not of Faith is Sin.

Another letter, signed 'Your sincere and faithful friend', written in 1741 to a Brother who had expressed doubts about the seriousness of his awakening, after admonishing him and suggesting that self-will was at the root of his problem, concluded, 'It is not good to *reason* much about *Spiritual* Things: What we *experience* we are sure of, and more we *cannot* know.'[31]

Sometimes the letters combined spiritual encouragement with the practicalities of organization and policy. The following extracts from a letter between unidentified Brethren, dated 1742,[32] suggest very clearly how the support system, operated by senior Brethren, on the one hand inspired less-experienced Labourers to service and witness, and on the other enabled them to endure irritations and difficulties with good humour and perspective. If they were discouraged, there was sound advice to hearten them, as in this case.

May our Saviour grant you a look in Spirit into his Wounds, that you may rejoice whenever you see by the Grace of the Lamb into your own sinful Heart . . . and our Saviour will give you Grace to see how his Heart burns with Love towards the poor Souls, tho' such poor sinful Creatures. This will give you Courage and Boldness to speak of the Death and Blood, and Wounds of the Lamb. . . .

My Brother, you mention the *Meeting-Place* as if you were afraid *we* should not approve of preaching in it. We can assure you, that if the People are but willing to let us speak what the Lord gives us to speak, wheresoever it may be, a Place *licensed* or *unlicensed*, we do not on our own Account mind *that*. If it was the Custom of any Place to be cloathed in a Bear-Skin, and the People desired us to do the same, we would willingly comply with it, if we could but preach the gospel to them.

This letter comes close to accounting for the fervour of the Brethren's witness at the time of rapid expansion. The symbolism of the Saviour's grace through his death and wounds provides both the dynamic and the subject matter for evangelism. The pressure from leaders to see the needy in terms of the Saviour's love for all mankind already experienced by the evangelists, was accompanied by an urgent demand that they should preach, whatever the circumstances and whenever the opportunity arose.

On a practical level the organization was closely structured. This letter, from Sp[angenberg] to an unnamed Brother, dated 1741–2, shows how the most experienced men were made available strategically where they were needed.

> We send you our Brother H——. He knows the Heart of our Saviour indeed, how kind it is to poor and lost Creatures. His Soul burns with Desire of telling it to many more, and we doubt not but there is a Hand of the Lord in his coming to you. . . . He will consult with you and Mr —— about what you shall think good. But he is but lent you, and not as one we have no Occasion for, but as one of our Hands and Feet.

An important aspect of the support system was the way in which accounts of the activities of missionaries on their way to the mission field and actively involved there were part of regular correspondence in communities of potential Labourers, to inspire them and to enable Brethren who were setting out for the first time to express their sense of belonging to Christ and to each other. A final example from the letters published by Okely was probably written by one of seven Single Brethren leaving England for service in Pennsylvania, over the New Year 1741–2, since it occurs along with other accounts of continental members who were joined for the transatlantic voyage by Brethren from the British Province. It is addressed to 'the Single Brethren at —— and signed, 'Your Fellow-Sinner in Jesus Christ'.

After having joined in a lovefeast with the Fetter Lane congregation, those who were to sail were spending several days settling in on board ship, while waiting for the contingent to be completed. There were twenty-two in the Single Choir, and other married couples, who were to undertake the dangerous wartime voyage. Much of the letter consists of an account for the Single Brethren in the writer's home congregation of the state of mind in which he was facing the future, and provides an excellent example of the spiritual pressure on those who had not yet committed themselves.

> We know and are sure we have nothing in ourselves, but are just as others, nothing differing except in this, that we know the Lamb's Atonement, and feel the Virtue of his Blood to make us happy. Therefore shall we who have tasted this Happiness, in return for his

great Love, give ourselves entirely to him Body and Soul as an Offering to the Lord, who will . . . give us this Grace to become his Witnesses to other Souls.

I wish you this, my Brethren, from the Bottom of my Heart, and wish you may gain Possession of this goodly Pearl, this Wisdom of his Children . . . May every one of you burn like Fire to advance the Glory and Knowledge of our Saviour, and bring ten thousand Souls the same Free-Grace to feel.

Something of the loneliness of those leaving close congregational fellowship for a dangerous voyage and an unknown future is expressed in the final paragraph:

It will rejoice my Heart greatly to hear of your Welfare, and I hope you will not forget to write to me by every Opportunity, though I am far from you. I salute you all in great Love and Tenderness with the Kiss of Charity.

The support system in its widest sense, including the information exchange, distribution of Watchwords, and personal communication by post, bound the missions and those who served in them at home and abroad to the congregations. Wherever they lived, ordinary members were aware of the experiences of those who lived and worked in other countries and societies, and shared their sufferings and joys, apprehensions and faith. True unity, overcoming geographical separation, depended on close personal relationships which were firmly grounded in the experience of salvation, redemption, and fellowship in Christ which all its members shared. This was the essence of Unity experience as originally conceived, and it was suited to those enthusiastic times. Later, the amount of Unity information made available year by year in the British Province, including the important doctrinal and continental congregational components, gradually declined, so that members, without fully appreciating their loss, became progressively less well-informed. By the beginning of the nineteenth century, unless they could read German, they were no longer able to share the minutiae of German congregational life, which previously had been highly regarded. No longer were they familiar with specific sermons preached in Herrnhut by Unity leaders; indeed such men appeared in Britain less frequently and for shorter visits than in Zinzendorf's time. As a result, an essential supportive aspect of Moravianism was modified or lost. Overseas missionary endeavour still retained a high profile, but even here the detailed and comprehensive chronicles of Unity activity which had characterized mid-eighteenth-century reports gradually gave way to shorter and more selective accounts, probably in response to perceived contemporary needs.

What remains for routine congregational circulation in the much-reduced *Moravian Messenger* is a limited selection of Unity news, including some information about the life and activity of the enormous and rapidly expanding congregational networks in Africa and South America. These are almost entirely self-contained and, in contrast to the eighteenth century, their leading personalities are not well known in the British Province. The most detailed information about the life and needs of other Unity congregations comes from accounts by provincial organizations of projects undertaken and money collected in aid of missions, reports of occasional visits between individuals and organizations from different provinces, and published minutes of Synodal gatherings, all of which retain something of the spirit of Moravianism.

Genuine interest in Unity as distinct from purely provincial concerns undoubtedly remains, and is one feature of present-day congregations which distinguishes them from other branches of Nonconformity and links them with their exotic past. Communication now is of its own time, and the written word is no longer of central importance. Only the Watchwords have retained their original worldwide distribution. They are published in the form handed down from the eighteenth century, though they probably fulfil a minor role compared with that in former times when they were accepted by congregations and society members everywhere as a source of divine guidance and support for the individual in everyday life.

Conclusion

Foreign Moravianism in Britain and its native counterpart, Methodism, originated from within the Pietist tradition. Both appealed preponderantly to the religious needs of artisans,[1] men and women possessing valued technical skills accompanied by a keen awareness of status, who in comparison with the greater mass of unskilled or semi-skilled labourers, willingly subscribed to a culture of work. This ethic was recommended by John Wesley, and by Zinzendorf, who famously said: 'Man does not work solely that Man shall live, but Man lives to want to work. If man has no more work he is sad or asleep.'[2] It was associated with artisan aspirations to respectability at home and integrity in business, following the traditions of their predecessors.[3] Many were drawn to religion, with its association of godliness and material progress, but for social reasons had been allowed only limited influence in established Anglican parochial organization. This was no longer the case: the Evangelical Revival and the emergent institutions of Moravianism and Methodism provided them with an unprecedented alternative extra-parochial network of religious societies, offering opportunities for personal advancement. As a result, those who felt an urge to Christian service acquired an influential and enduring role in active evangelical circles with an outlook well suited to the expansive tendencies in contemporary industrializing society.[4] In this way the Methodist movement evolved as a substantial, self-contained national institution, a strongly rooted native British plant, embodying the spiritual and secular aspirations of artisan culture, led by an educated elite, and working in a conveniently small geographical area of the country of its birth.[5]

The British Province of the Moravian Church has never been a comparable national institution, and has functioned as part of an international organization with a permanent centre of gravity in Germany. Its location on the periphery of continental Europe has helped it to retain its Anglo-German spirit, which was strong until 1914 despite superficial appearances to the contrary. It has never attracted many members. The statistics quoted at the beginning of this book are a reminder that, even at its maximum size during the First World War, the entire provincial communicant membership could have been accommodated in four or five of the largest Methodist places of worship. Yet it is worthy of comment that the province is not unique in this respect: another tiny offshoot of the eighteenth-century Evangelical Revival has survived, namely the movement associated with Selina Hastings, Countess of Huntingdon (1707–91), another of the central figures in the revival, who was a 'methodist' in style of piety, yet devoted to Anglicanism.[6] At the close of the twentieth century, 25 congregations still remained as loyal remnants of what had been her once well-known and extensive evangelical connexion.[7]

In the second half of the twentieth century the British Province has developed different perspectives. Among the older generation, particularly those with long-established family connections, there is still strong loyalty to its well-loved forms and traditions; but other interpretations of Moravian worship are becoming familiar, since easy access to Germany and America and the possibility of almost instant worldwide communication have provided opportunities to make personal links with members of congregations wherever they may live, in a manner which would have been undreamed of fifty years ago. Two other factors have hastened the process of evolution: the vigorous growth of a Caribbean-American style in some provincial congregations since the 1960s, and the amalgamation at congregational level with other denominations, particularly the United Reformed Church. The first two factors foster a sense of uniqueness in the church in that its members are very conscious of being one family with their brethren and sisters in other countries; but on the other hand, the changes necessitated by the logistics of running a small denomination compel it to decide how important to its Christian faith and worship is the Moravian name.

To account for the exotic nature of the British Province it is necessary to look back to Zinzendorf, a religious genius[8] who had access to great wealth. He was a man of the grandiose style of the Baroque, towering over his artisan followers,[9] particularly the first inhabitants of Herrnhut, who had nothing in their tradition that could have led them to invent eighteenth-century Moravianism for themselves. There appears to be no evidence that previous generations of Bohemian religious refugees who had migrated into Saxony after 1620 had attempted to re-establish the old Bohemian Unity. Left to their own devices they had found ample scope either for investing their spiritual aspirations in existing Lutheran congregations, or for emigrating to other areas of economic opportunity and religious freedom such as colonial North America, and this is what they did; but in Herrnhut, during the 1720s and 1730s, under Zinzendorf's leadership, a small, untypical group were moulded by him into an evangelistic force with a culture comprising elements of a distant and historic Christianity, which valued close communal links of the spiritually reborn, and intense devotion to beauty in music and poetry, and soon became involved in missionary activity in Europe and overseas. Its religious thinking was characterized by a new, vivid language of particular truths revealed to the membership within the context of the traditional doctrine of the atonement, and was driven inexorably towards the exotic style of Herrnhaag.

The Herrnhaag period, though lasting little more than a decade, was an inescapable feature of the evolution of Moravianism under Zinzendorf's leadership, when all that it stood for reached the pinnacle of its power and influence.[10] This had repercussions on the entire Unity because it attempted to combine aristocratic perceptions of religious practices with those of traditional artisan culture, and for a time this inherently paradoxical arrangement worked well, because both expressed the convictions of born-again Christians. The influence of Zinzendorf and his immediate family was a significant factor, since part of their philosophy was to develop a personal relationship with converts of all social origins. His son, Christian Renatus, was a charismatic figure among the young men; another leading member of his extended family, Sophia Theodora, Countess of Reuss, lived for many years in the Widows' Houses at Herrnhaag and Herrnhut, taking a special interest in the welfare of the sisters;[11] his wife worked alongside the women by taking charge of the domestic arrangements, with lasting influence on those women who came to know her personally, such as Mary Vogelsang, who led the Single Sisters at Fulneck after her years in the training-ground of Herrnhaag and later in Zinzendorf's personal entourage. Zinzendorf's approach was viewed by his critics as incomprehensible, and after a few years the fundamental incompatibility of aristocratic and artisan religious cultures, and the tension between them, became obvious. By 1749 the 'spiritual explosion' experienced at Herrnhaag was leading to schism, a 'sifting', a separation of styles in which the more aristocratic, literary religious culture receded and its artisan equivalent, as typified by the less exotic practices of Herrnhut, advanced. Finally, in 1750, after vigorous expressions of disquiet among the religious public outside the movement, the Herrnhaag era was brought to an end and its disturbing imagery gradually faded from Unity collective consciousness. In hymnals and liturgies passion was expressed less emotively; Moravianism was thought of once again as the product of Herrnhut, and great efforts were made to ensure that the Unity could present a public image that was pleasingly 'normal'. Even so, at a deeper level, the Herrnhaag influence was very much alive, remaining in an idealized form in Unity memory, strengthened by archival evidence which had accumulated at a tremendous rate, so that the surge of evangelism and missionary activity for which it was the mainspring was exceptionally well recorded. Since it was brilliant, but brief, the resulting sense of loss gradually gave rise to a mythology of Moravianism which has influenced ministers and members ever since.

This image conforms to Mircea Eliade's researches into the exemplary role of some mythologies in religious history. Theoretically the experience is repeatable, involving a controversial hero or heroine of extraordinary charisma, whose life and deeds are presented as models for posterity.[12] Zinzendorf was such a figure in his lifetime and, because there was no one of equal stature to follow him, he has retained this role in Unity mythology. Under him, Unity ideas and institutions were evolving continuously, and characterized by rapid, flexible responses to changing circumstances, with unremitting activity on the part of its members at the behest of Unity authority backed by divine guidance,[13] for another aspect of this Moravian 'myth' was the culture of obedience. The enthusiastic abrogation of free will[14] on the part of Labourers during Zinzendorf's lifetime created a disciplined missionary band whose achievements led succeeding generations to believe that the Unity's outstanding contribution to Protestantism during the 1740s and 1750s might be repeatable, the myth becoming a reality. This was a factor in the restlessness and dissatisfactions of the nineteenth century, when the British Province continually looked back to the fervour experienced during the years of enthusiasm.

Throughout the lengthy period which came to an end with the First World War, the Continental Province developed along energetic lines which were largely a continuation of what had been begun in the time of Zinzendorf, being dominant in Unity missions, boarding school provision and diaspora organization. Although in terms of communicant membership the Continental Province remained very small compared with the Lutheran and Reformed Churches, it continued to be well known because it co-operated with them, remaining influential over large parts of Protestant Europe. As the essence of conservative German Moravianism it enjoyed a worldwide reputation.

In Britain, during the same period, there was a more complex and uneasy mix of change and continuity in the evolving Anglo-German style of the church, marked by recurrent crises of identity and conflicts of loyalty, the study of which is impeded by being seriously under-recorded. The heart of the Unity was still perceived to be in Germany: at ministerial level, fraternal bonds with continental counterparts were strong, yet conflicted with an incipient desire for independence. Institutionally, the influence of the province was weakened by lack of a diaspora comparable with that on the continent, and under-representation in the staffing of the mission fields. By the middle of the nineteenth century the province had allowed itself to be propelled gradually into a form of independence from its continental parent which was more apparent than real, casting itself in the role of a separate denomination, but remaining little known in Britain as far as its domestic affairs were concerned. Among that section of the British religious public who were aware of its existence, there was a tendency to regard it as an extension of the prestigious Continental Province, particularly as a successful missionary body. The province gained strength and assurance because its members saw themselves in this light and were proud to be part of such a successful international organization.

The mythology of a 'golden age' of the 1740s and 1750s, repeatable if only the right circumstances could be recreated, was still influential at the beginning of the twentieth century. One consequence was recurrent pressure to make members more familiar with Unity history in the hope that greater knowledge might inspire this revival. The core of dedicated ministers and members made every effort to sustain the valued fraternal Anglo-German style, and were so successful that in 1914 it was still strong. Conflicting loyalties experienced during the First World War weakened the bond; by the end of the war the British Province had experienced four years during which it had become progressively more involved with the American Province as a working partner, particularly in mission, and a greater proportion of British and American ministers than ever before was needed to fill gaps created by the expulsion of German personnel. Inevitably, the Second World War renewed and probably deepened the conflicting loyalties of the First, enhancing still further the fraternal bonds of the British and American provinces.

By the late 1940s, part of the original continental congregational network had been destroyed, and a considerable proportion of the rest had become virtually isolated behind the political barriers of alien regimes. Despite this severe handicap, the imaginative approach and heroic efforts of some British ministers and members succeeded in restoring fraternal links with German church leaders, ensuring that the fragile Anglo-German mentality survived.

Cultural changes in British society since then have affected provincial development. The leadership of the church remains predominantly in the established tradition, though its ministry and synods are now beginning to reflect British multi-ethnic society, and it is probably true to say that never since its early days has the province had a more varied membership. It may need to find a new role in relation to, or as part of, another denomination, echoing the position from which it started during the Evangelical Revival when those 'destined' to become Moravians were active members of the Anglican or Presbyterian Church and were spiritually enriched in extra-parochial Moravian societies. Zinzendorf would have relished the challenge!

This concluding chapter is a summary of British provincial activity as we have outlined it throughout the book, and places it within that of the Unity as a whole. It emphasizes how the British Province has continued to express the elements in its tradition which identify it as a scion of its parent, and how it has adapted to its environment in a society with rather different religious traditions. Worldwide Moravianism continues to flourish in other adaptations, in other continents, and the British province of the church goes on into the twenty-first century in an evolving form. It is indeed an exotic plant, but one which has proved capable of survival in its foreign soil, in the face of competition and adversity. Its future is still firmly linked to that of the Unity as a whole, and as a province it is strongly committed to the ecumenical efforts of the Christian Churches as they search for a style of witness which expresses their diversity within their common heritage.

The writing of history is both a discipline and a learning process. In entitling our book 'The Exotic Plant' we come to the heart of our experience as we have studied Moravian archives and meditated on the significance of our research into worldwide Moravianism and the British Province in particular. As a result we have formulated one interpretation of the evidence which we have found, in full knowledge that it is only part, indeed a small part, of what is there. A reader would rightly be suspicious of an author who claimed to have said the last word on any subject; one of the joys of writing history is that it breaks some new ground, reinterprets what is known, and stimulates debate, at the same time bringing with it the humbling awareness that so much more could have been written, so much remains to be done, and that other emphases and other interpretations will follow. This book is an expression of the excitement and the sense of discovery with which we have perceived the emergence of patterns of significance, and the delight with which we have heard the voices of dedicated people who lived their faith and whose words and praises to their Saviour remain in their own handwriting and in the printed records.

Notes

Introduction

1. He even signed himself on at least one occasion as 'Ludovicus Moraviensis', in a letter dated 8 Dec. 1748, to Revd Mr Schmidt at Dublin. MCH, Box A3. This may not have been common, as he affected a number of different forms of signature.

2. MCH, Box A3. Letter of Zinzendorf, headed 'Marienborn Dec. 23. 46', with the salutation, 'My Revd Br'.

3. MCH, Letters of George Whitefield to James Hutton. This series of letters chronicles their professional and personal relationship, revealing Whitefield's early admiration for the Brethren and later disillusion with some aspects of their theology.

4. A typical example is David Blackbourn, *The Long Nineteenth Century: A History of Germany, 1780–1918*, Oxford: Oxford University Press, 1997.

5. This was brought into prominence by Linda Colley, in *Britons: Forging the Nation 1707–1837*, London: Pimlico edn, 1994, and her challenging study has given rise to other explorations of the concept.

6. Hans-Christoph Hahn and Hellmut Reichel (eds), *Zinzendorf und die Herrnhuter Brüder: Quellen zur Geschichte der Brüder-Unität von 1722 bis 1760*, Hamburg: Friedrich Wittig Verlag, 1977, extract from 'Anna Nitschmanns eigenhändiger Lebenslauf', pp. 454–6, p. 456.

7. Zdenek V. David, 'The Strange Fate of Czech Utraquism: The Second Century, 1517–1621', *Journal of Ecclesiastical History* 46.4 (October 1995), 641–68, pp. 647, 653 and 668. See also, Z. V. David, 'Huss and Wyclif', in Adrian Hastings, Alistair Mason and Hugh Pyper (eds), *The Oxford Companion to Christian Thought*, Oxford: Oxford University Press, 2000, p. 316; Gordon Leff, 'Wyclif and Hus: A Doctrinal Comparison', in Anthony Kenny (ed.), *Wyclif in his Times*, Oxford: Clarendon Press, 1986, pp. 105–25; and Anne Hudson, *The Premature Reformation: Wycliffite Texts and Lollard History*, Oxford: Clarendon Press, 1988, pp. 508–9, 514.

Chapter 1

1. MCH, Box A3, Letter of Zinzendorf.

2. Gerhard A. Wauer, 'The Beginnings of the Brethren's Church in England: A Chapter of the Commerce of Thought between Germany and England', Ph.D. dissertation, University of Leipzig, 1901, trans. J. Elliott, Baildon, Yorkshire: Moravian House, 1901.

3. Wauer, 'Beginnings', p. 107.

4. Wauer, 'Beginnings', pp. 7–9.

5. Gary S. Kinkel, also, has argued that the communities set up in the eighteenth century were 'the product of Zinzendorf's theological vision'. G. S. Kinkel, *Our Dear Mother the Spirit: An Investigation of Count Zinzendorf's Theology and Praxis*, Lanham, N.Y., and London: University Press of America, 1990, p. 75.

6. R. Currie, A. Gilbert and L. Horsley, *Churches and Churchgoers: Patterns of Church Growth in the British Isles since 1700*, Oxford: Clarendon Press, 1977, p. 142.

7. MCH, MPB, 39, p. 40.

8. MCH, MPB, 43, p. 222.

9. Peter Brooks (ed.), *Christian Spirituality: Essays in Honour of Gordon Rupp*, London: SCM Press, 1975, pp. 215–83. The quotations are from pp. 251–2 and 264–5 respectively.

10. Colin Podmore, *The Moravian Church in England, 1728–1760*, Oxford: Oxford University Press, 1998.

11. Podmore was a student of John Walsh at Jesus College, Oxford.

Chapter 2

1. A. J. P. Taylor, *The Course of German History: A Survey of the Development of German History since 1815*, London: Methuen, 1968, p. 5.

2. There were no fewer than 37 universities within the Holy Roman Empire, and another five in the German-speaking territories. Universities and court orchestras served as status symbols, and musicians in particular benefited from the competition for their services. Norman Hampson, *The Enlightenment: An Evaluation of its Assumptions, Attitudes and Values*, London: Penguin, 1990, p. 60.

3. Klaus J. Bade, 'From Emigration to Immigration: The German Experience in the Nineteenth and Twentieth Centuries', *Central European History* 28.4 (1995), 507–35, pp. 507, 509.

4. Bade, 'Emigration to Immigration', p. 509.

5. Bade, 'Emigration to Immigration', p. 509.

6. W. R. Ward, *The Protestant Evangelical Awakening*, Cambridge: Cambridge University Press, 1992, p. 148.

7. W. R. Ward, 'The Renewed Unity of the Brethren: Ancient Church, New Sect, or Interconfessional Movement?', *Bulletin of the John Rylands University Library of Manchester* 70.3 (Autumn 1988), 77–92, p. 77.

8. Ward, 'Renewed Unity', p. 83.

9. Matthew Spinka, *John Hus: A Biography*, Princeton: Princeton University Press, 1968, p. 321. See also M. Spinka, *John Hus' Concept of the Church*, Princeton: Princeton University Press, 1966, p. 280, where Spinka defines Peter of Chelcicky as the spiritual father of the Bohemian Brethren.

10. Josef Macek, 'The Monarchy of the Estates', in Mikulas Teich (ed.), *Bohemia in History*, Cambridge: Cambridge University Press, 1998, pp. 98–116. The information which follows is from pp. 107–10.

11. A specialist academic text concentrating on the evolution of this religious body is Peter Brock, *The Political and Social Doctrines of the Unity of the Czech Brethren in the Fifteenth and early Sixteenth Centuries*, The Hague: Mouton, 1957. During the same year Rican published a more general history in Prague. This was

later translated into English by C. D. Crews and published in America as Rudolf Rican, *The History of the Unity of the Brethren*, Bethlehem, Pa.: Dept. of Publications and Communications, Moravian Church, Northern Province, 1992.

12. Francis Dvornik, *The Slavs in European History and Civilisation*, New Brunswick: Rutgers University Press, 1962, p. 208.

13. Euan Cameron, *The European Reformation*, Oxford: Clarendon Press, 1991, pp. 76–7. The author outlines the origin and background of this obscure sect which probably began at Lyons in the late twelfth century.

14. Dvornik, *Slavs in European History*, p. 395. The existence of bishops in the Waldensian sect is unclear: there were elders, and trained and itinerant preachers who appear to have been elected. On the other hand, it seems that the Waldensians claimed that office-holders such as these constituted a true line of apostolic succession unbroken by the Constantine apostacy, via the Waldensians. Written evidence has not been found by the authors. See Gabriel Audisio, *The Waldensian Dissent: Persecution and Survival, c.1100–c.1570*, trans. Claire Davison, Cambridge: Cambridge University Press, 1999, p. 84; and Prescot Stephens, *The Waldensian Story: A Study in Faith Intolerance and Survival*, Lewes: Book Guild, 1998, pp. 66–7, 101.

15. Cameron, *European Reformation*, p. 417. 'The Reformation was not a foreseeable explosion from a discontented lay society which had long since outgrown the religious forms which the Church purveyed. On the contrary, Europe's people could choose an alternative religious form.' The one the reformers offered was based on the power of the word, that is, the power of the Scriptures. See C. Scott Dixon, 'Narratives of the German Reformation', in C. S. Dixon (ed.), *The German Reformation*, Oxford: Clarendon Press, 1999, pp. 1–32, p. 6. The strongest response for an attempt to strengthen the power of the word came from the clergy, particularly the highly educated in urban areas. R. W. Scribner, *The German Reformation*, London: Macmillan, 1989, p. 28.

16. Derek Sayer, *The Coasts of Bohemia: A Czech History*, Princeton: Princeton University Press, 1998, p. 43.

17. Josef Valka, 'Rudolfine Culture', in Mikulas Teich (ed.), *Bohemia in History*, Cambridge: Cambridge University Press, 1998, pp. 117–42, p. 120. The term 'Utraquist' covers non-Catholics of varied origins who had achieved almost true liberty of faith, a condition which had existed for more than a century.

18. Sayer, *Coasts of Bohemia*, p. 43.

19. This, the Counter-Reformation, was basically of French, Italian and Spanish inspiration, strongly influenced by German Carthusians. Its spirituality emphasized good works as essential to the attainment of salvation, and hallowed strenuous activity in the service of God. H. O. Evennett, *The Spirit of the Counter Reformation*, Cambridge: Cambridge University Press, 1968, pp. 11, 20, 24, 31, 34. See also, John C. Olin, *The Catholic Reformation: Savonarola to Ignatius Loyola*, New York: Harper & Row, 1969, p. 203, where he outlines the official foundation of the Jesuit Order, the spearhead of this movement.

20. Toynbee comments on the far-reaching consequences of this conflict on the European mentality. 'The outburst of moral indignation at the iniquity of the Wars of Religion was the explosion that blew the irreparable breach in the massive fortifications of the medieval Christian Weltanschauung. One practical expression of this moral revolt was a deliberate transference of seventeenth-century western man's spiritual treasure from an incurably polemical theology to an apparently non-

controversial Natural Science.' Arnold Toynbee, *An Historian's Approach to Religion. Based on the Gifford Lectures Delivered in the University of Edinburgh, 1952 and 1953*, Oxford: Oxford University Press, 1956, p. 169.

21. The historic national defeat of Protestant by Catholic forces, known as the Battle of White Mountain (near Prague), on 8 Nov. 1620, was the effective end of Protestantism in Bohemia. It was followed by systematic dismantling of its institutional structure and the dispersal of its congregations.

22. Orest Subtelny, *Domination of Eastern Europe: Native Notabilities and Foreign Absolutism, 1500–1715*, Gloucester: McGill-Queens University Press, 1986, pp. 99–100. Saxony was a natural magnet for refugees: it had a superb geographical location, straddling many major East–West and North–South trade routes, with high population density and extensive urbanization in eighteenth-century terms. Vast sums of money were spent on the beautification of Dresden and the court.

23. Ward, 'Renewed Unity', pp. 88–9.

24. Valka, 'Rudolfine Culture', p. 137. See also Brock, *Political and Social Doctrines*, pp. 281–2. 'The story of the Czech branch of the Unity culminates in the many-sided activities of the greatest figure in its history. The life of Comenius . . . belongs as much to the history of Western culture as to the more limited field of the annals of the Brethren.'

25. This is conveyed with beauty and sensitivity in his great allegorical work, *The Labyrinth of the World and the Paradise of the Heart*, ed. and trans. Count Lützow, London: Dent's Temple Classics, 1902, pp. 281–2, 284–5, in a dialogue between Christ and the pilgrim.

26. A recent study of his educational principles is Daniel Murphy, *Comenius: A Critical Reassessment of his Life and Work*, Dublin: Irish Academic Press, 1995, which complements an earlier publication, John Edward Sadler, *Comenius, 1592–1670*, London: Collier Macmillan, 1969. The latter text has the useful asset of a chronological list of Comenius' major works in order of publication, pp. 128–30, all dating from 1623–67, that is, after the old Bohemian Unity had been proscribed.

27. A. W. Boehm, *A Short Account of Some Persons who have been instrumental in promoting the most Substantial Points of Religion in Some Parts of Germany. Whose Proceedings some have endeavoured of late to render Odious by the newly-invented Name of Pietism*, London: SPCK, undated, c.1708, p. 18. 'Practical divinity implied being willing to lead a serious and sober life . . . to enter upon another course of life more suited to the principles and spirit of Christianity' (p. 25). The word 'pietist' was coined in 1688.

28. F. Ernest Stoeffler, *German Pietism during the Eighteenth Century*, Leiden: Numen, 1973, p. 131.

29. Henry D. Rack, *Reasonable Enthusiast: John Wesley and the Rise of Methodism*, London: Epworth Press, 1989, p. 161. He regards the English Evangelical Revival as part of this more extensive international movement.

30. Johannes Wallmann, *P. J. Spener und die Anfänge des Pietismus*, Tübingen: Tübingen University Press, 1970, p. v.

31. Trond Enger, 'Pietism', in *OCCT*, pp. 539–41, p. 540.

32. Heiko A. Oberman, 'Preface' to Arndt's *True Christianity*, trans. P. Erb, New York: Paulist Press, 1979, p. xi.

33. Thomas à Kempis, *The Imitation of Christ*, trans. L. Sherley-Price, London: Penguin Classics, 1987, intro., p. 11. 'It would be impossible to estimate the wide and

profound influence that this wonderful little book has exercised throughout Christendom for over five hundred years.' He refers to Sir Thomas More, St Ignatius Loyola, John Wesley, among other known readers.

34. Nicholas Hope, *German and Scandinavian Protestantism 1700–1918*, Oxford: Clarendon Press, 1995, p. 26.

35. Oberman, 'Preface', p. xi. This was only one aspect of a wider European phenomenon during the seventeenth and early eighteenth centuries. The analogies to be found in England are particularly noteworthy; for example, inward emotional religious experience was stressed among the Puritans, in Quakerism, and above all as far as indigenous developments were concerned, in the enthusiastic presentations of the Wesleys and George Whitefield.

36. Oberman, 'Preface', p. xii.

37. It has been argued that the 'system of thought' of the eighteenth-century Unity owed its existence to Philip Jakob Spener rather than to Amos Comenius. Ronald A. Knox, *Enthusiasm: A Chapter in the History of Religion with Special Reference to the Seventeenth and Eighteenth Centuries*, Oxford: Oxford University Press, 1950, p. 399.

38. It has been suggested that the appeal of Pietism to people such as these may also have been enhanced by contemporary perceptions of cultural inferiority compared with the French. Pietist preaching represented a 'counter-attack', stressing that it was the inner life, the life of the spirit alone, that was of supreme importance, in contrast to the wealth, arts, science and culture of the French, 'all perishable goods of corruptible flesh'. Isaiah Berlin, *The Crooked Timber of Humanity*, ed. H. Hardy, London: John Murray, 1990, pp. 35–7. Deep resentment at ruthless French military aggression in Germany during the first decades of the seventeenth century was equally important. Henry O. Wakeman, *The Ascendancy of France 1598–1715*, London: Rivington, 1921, pp. 109 and 114.

39. F. Ernest Stoeffler, *The Rise of Evangelical Pietism*, Leiden: Numen, 1965, p. 181.

40. Hope, *Protestantism*, p. 131.

41. Walter Schmithals, 'Der Pietismus in theologischer und geistgeschichtlicher Sicht', in *Pietismus und Neuzeit: Ein Jahrbuch zur Geschicht des neuen Protestantismus*, vol. 4: *Die Anfänge des Pietismus*, Göttingen: Göttingen University Press, 1979, pp. 235–301, p. 286.

42. John Gagliardo, *Germany under the Old Régime 1600–1790*, London: Longman, 1991, p. 159.

43. Jonathan Powis, *Aristocracy*, Oxford: Blackwell, 1984, pp. 31–4. Powis describes this as a characteristic strategy of the nobility to preserve their land and wealth.

44. Ulrike Witt, *Bekehrung, Bildung und Biographie: Frauen in Umkreis des Halleschen Pietismus*, Halle and Tübingen: Tübingen University Press, 1996. Review in *Central European History* 32.1, pp. 100–2. Baroness Gersdorf was reputedly the most learned woman of her day, a patroness of female Pietist education in Halle (p. 100). She and other women were influential there.

45. Hope, *Protestantism*, p. 131.

46. Hope, *Protestantism*, p. 132.

47. David J. Bosch, *Transforming Mission: Paradigm Shifts in the Theology of Mission*, New York: Orbis Books, 1995, p. 254; also, Stoeffler, *German Pietism*, p. 24.

48. Hope, *Protestantism*, p. 142.

49. Stoeffler, *German Pietism*, pp. 25–6.

50. Ward, *Protestant Evangelical Awakening*, p. 62.

51. Hope, *Protestantism*, pp. 143–4.

52. Hope, *Protestantism*, p. 145.

53. Bosch, *Transforming Mission*, p. 253.

54. Evennett, *Spirit of Counter Reformation*, pp. 122–3; also, James Brodrick, *The Origins of the Jesuits*, London: Longmans Green, 1940, p. 10.

55. Hope, *Protestantism*, p. 145.

56. Enger, 'Pietism', p. 540.

57. Kenneth S. Latourette, *A History of the Expansion of Christianity*, 7 vols., vol. 3: *Three Centuries of Advance, AD 1500–1800*, London: Eyre & Spottiswoode, 1940, pp. 26, 37 and 39. 'The Jesuit order, founded in 1540 became the chief arm of the Roman Catholic Church for carrying the gospel to the heathen . . . a Jesuit missionary training centre was set up at the University of Coimbra in Portugal in 1542. . . . Over the next two centuries it sent out about 1650 missionaries . . . Roman Catholic funds for this work came mainly from the governments of Spain and Portugal, augmented by large donations from some wealthy and devout members of the upper classes.'

58. M. Felix Bovet, *The Banished Count, or The Life of Lewis Count Zinzendorf*, trans. J. Gill, London: James Nisbet, 1865. 'Each of these men founded a powerful society, stretching over the whole earth – an order that exerted a deeper and mightier influence on the Christian World than appeared on the surface; and they both consolidated this influence by the same means – the education of the young and the establishment of missions' (p. 2).

59. Hope, *Protestantism*, p. 143.

60. Enger, 'Pietism', p. 540.

61. Ward, *Protestant Evangelical Awakening*, p. 2.

62. Bosch, *Transforming Mission*, p. 255.

63. A. Lynn Martin, *The Jesuit Mind: The Mentality of an Elite in Early Modern France*, Cornell: Cornell University Press, 1988, p. 226. The writer deals at length with the Jesuit network of communications, which made them some of the best-informed people of the world in the sixteenth century. Cicely V. Wedgwood argues that the Jesuits were in a sense the last of the military orders and the greatest; '. . . Jesuits were prepared to carry the faith by any means and at any personal cost into any corner of the globe; . . . they were a fighting force'. Cicely V. Wedgwood, *The Thirty Years War* London: Jonathan Cape, 1981, p. 21.

64. Max Weber, *The Protestant Ethic and the Spirit of Capitalism*, trans. T. Parsons, London: Routledge, 1994, p. 248, citation 138. Weber describes Zinzendorf in these terms.

65. Weber, *Protestant Ethic*, p. 136.

66. James R. Farr, *Artisans in Europe, 1300–1914*, Cambridge: Cambridge University Press, 2000, p. 145.

67. Kurt Aland, 'Philip Jakob Spener und die Anfänge des Pietismus', in *Pietismus und Neuzeit: Ein Jahrbuch zur Geschichte des neueren Protestantismus*, vol. 4: *Die Anfänge des Pietismus*, Göttingen: Göttingen University Press, 1979, pp. 155–89, p. 157.

68. Aland, 'Philip Jakob Spener', p. 136. 'The Brotherhood . . . led its members

into the paths of worldly asceticism which everywhere seeks for tasks and then carries them out carefully and systematically.'

69. Oberman, 'Preface', p. xvi.

70. Ward, *Protestant Evangelical Awakening*, p. 119, and Oberman, 'Preface', p. xiv.

71. Carl Gustav Jung, *Memories, Dreams, Reflections*, trans. R. and S. Winston, London: Collins, Fount Paperbacks, 1963, pp. 223–4.

72. Oberman, 'Preface', p. xvi.

73. Bovet, *Banished Count*, p. 45.

74. Bovet, *Banished Count*, p. 45.

75. Bovet, *Banished Count*, p. 57.

76. August G. Spangenberg, *The Life of N. L. Count Zinzendorf*, trans. L. T. Nyberg, 2 vols, Bath: printed for T. Miles and S. Hazard, 1773, vol. 1, p. 166.

77. Isser Woloch, *Eighteenth-Century Europe: Tradition and Progress 1715–1789*, New York: Norton, 1982, p. 187.

78. Gagliardo, *Germany under the Old Régime*, p. 211.

79. Woloch, *Eighteenth Century Europe*, p. 185.

80. Heiko A. Oberman, *Luther: Man between God and the Devil*, trans. E. Walliser-Schwarzbart, London: Fontana, 1993, p. 211.

81. Oberman, *Luther*, p. 211.

82. FA, MSS I, FCD, 9 April 1755.

83. Erich Bayreuther, *Zinzendorf und die Christenheit*, Marburg: Francke, 1961, p. 74.

84. The Unity as a whole, or one part of it.

85. UAH, Report of the Second London Synod of 1754, Recitative of Zinzendorf's Principles, no. 12, MS R 13 B2 2.

86. Bosch, *Transforming Mission*, p. 255.

87. Ward, *Protestant Evangelical Awakening*, pp. 128–9.

88. This is a phrase used by Braudel to define the tiny space occupied by Western Europe in relation to the world as a whole, but it effectively describes the community of Herrnhaag in relation to the whole Unity. Fernand Braudel, *The Perspective of the World*, vol. 3 of *Civilisation and Capitalism: 15th–18th Century*, trans. S. Reynolds, London: Fontana, 1984, p. 387.

89. Hans-Walther Erbe, 'Herrnhaag: Tiefpunkt oder Höhepunkt der Brüdergeschichte', *Unitas Fratrum* 26 (1989), 37–51, p. 42.

90. Thomas à Kempis, *The Imitation of Christ*, London: Penguin edn, 1987, p. 68.

91. Alexis Carrel, *Man the Unknown*, London: Pelican, 1948. He argues that mysticism is splendidly generous, bringing to man the fulfilment of his highest desires, inner strength, spiritual light, divine love, ineffable peace.

92. Oberman, *Luther*, p. 182.

93. Oberman, *Luther*, p. 198.

94. Ray C. Petry, *Late Medieval Mysticism*, Philadelphia: Westminster Press, 1957, p. 146.

95. Oberman, *Luther*, p. 273.

96. H.-W. Erbe, 'Herrnhaag, Eine Religiöse Kommunität im 18 Jahrhunderts', *Unitas Fratrum* 23–4 (1988), English summary, 196–9, p. 198. There were approximately one thousand residents.

97. Erich Beyreuther, *Studien zur Theologie Zinzendorfs*, Neukirchen-Vluyn: Neukirchener Verlag der Buchhandlung des Erziehungsvereins, 1962, p. 12.

98. Erbe, 'Herrnhaag: Tiefpunkt oder Höhepunkt', p. 42.

99. Wauer, 'Beginnings', pp. 8–9; Podmore, *Moravian Church in England*, pp. 134–5.

100. Ernst Troeltsch, *The Social Teaching of the Christian Churches*, trans. O. Wyon, 2 vols, London: Allen & Unwin, 1931. Troeltsch quotes Joseph T. Muller, *Zinzendorf als Erneuerer der alten Brüderkirche*, Leipzig: Friedrich Jansa, 1900. Of the spiritual advance made possible by life in such settlements he writes, 'Where an approximate historical realisation of the conception of an evident community of Christ is attempted, such a structure will always be more capable of realising the Christian ideal than the popular and state churches in the midst of whom it lives' (vol. 2, p. 959).

101. Paul Langford, *Public Life and the Propertied Englishman, 1689–1798*, Oxford: Clarendon Press, 1991, p. 1.

102. Powis, *Aristocracy*, p. 47.

103. Powis, *Aristocracy*, p. 47.

104. Frank E. and Fritzie P. Manuel, *Utopian Thought in the Western World*, Oxford: Blackwell, 1982, p. 18. The authors contend that medieval and monastic institutions left prototypes for an ideal Christian existence on earth, and the passion for ordering the minutiae of everyday life made its imprint on later projected Utopias. There were residual manifestations in the eighteenth century in, for example, 'the various forms of the Herrnhut communities founded by Count Zinzendorf', but the principal utopian concerns in the eighteenth and nineteenth centuries were secular, and Christian Utopias such as these were a feeble remnant.

105. T. M. Lindsay, *The Church and the Ministry in the Early Centuries*, Cunningham Lectures, London: Hodder & Stoughton, 1902, p. 35.

Chapter 3

1. Podmore, *Moravian Church in England*, p. 4.

2. The density of the German-born population was so great in Pennsylvania in the plains between the Delaware and Susquehanna that the villages were as Teutonic in style as those in 'old Germany', and there was widespread resistance to the use of English. Marcus L. Hansen, *The Atlantic Migration 1607–1860*, Harvard: Harvard University Press, 1945, p. 74. From 1727 onwards immigration shifted strongly in favour of church people, so that by 1776 they comprised 90 per cent of the German population in America. Alexander Waldenrath, 'The Pennsylvania Germans', in Gerhard K. Friesen (ed.), *The German Contribution to the Building of the Americas*, Hanover, N.H.: Clark University Press, 1977, pp. 47–74, p. 48.

3. Podmore, *Moravian Church in England*, p. 30.

4. Podmore, *Moravian Church in England*, p. 1.

5. Podmore, *Moravian Church in England*, p. 48.

6. D. Bruce Hindmarsh, *John Newton and the English Evangelical Tradition between the Conversions of Wesley and Wilberforce*, Oxford: Clarendon Press, 1996, p. 238.

7. UAH, R13 A17 9a, Letter from John Wesley to the leaders of the Church of God at Herrnhut, August 1740. In the opening section he said that the schism had led

to the Brethren's condemning him as 'a child of the Devil, a Servant of Corruption, having eyes full of Adultery, that cannot escape from Sin', etc. Later in the letter Wesley wrote, 'With regard to your Church you greatly . . . exalt yourselves and despise others . . . you receive not the Antients but the modern Mysticks as the best interpreters of Scripture.'

8. The schism is discussed in some detail by Gary S. Kinkel, 'The Big Chill', *Unitas Fratrum* 27–8 (1990), pp. 89–111.

9. It should be recognized, however, that, at this stage at least, Zinzendorf drew no distinction between Methodizing Anglican activity and Unity activity aimed at society formation. Libbey noted that, in a dispatch from Marienborn dated 21 July 1744, the Count said, 'We are not to be looked upon in England in any other light than as teachers who are in union with the English Church, whose sacred rites in all principles and essential points are the same.' He then said that Unity evangelists should be 'of all others the most acceptable seeing they spare no pains to preserve devout persons in the established discipline'. JRUL, English Manuscripts, Box 1076, Document 14, p. 3.

10. For detailed studies of the life and work of this important northern evangelist see particularly, David F. Clarke, 'Benjamin Ingham (1712–72) with Special Reference to his Relations with the Churches, Anglican, Methodist and Glassite of his Time', M.Phil. thesis, Leeds University, 1971, and the description of his early life and theological convictions in Richard P. Heitzenrater (ed.), *Diary of an Oxford Methodist: Benjamin Ingham, 1733–1734*, Durham, N.C.: Duke University Press, 1985, pp. 1–47.

11. Brian W. Young, *Religion and Enlightenment in Eighteenth-Century England*, Oxford: Clarendon Press, 1997, pp. 157–8. Okely, 'a defector from Methodising Anglicanism to Moravianism', served the Moravian community at Northampton till his death in 1794, all the time translating and editing mystical works and illustrating the fluidity of the boundary between evangelicalism and mysticism.

12. This and the following brief quotations are from MCH PHD.

13. Quoted from M. Riggall's extracts from Viney's diary, *Proceedings of the Wesley Historical Society* 14 (1924), 49–54, p. 53.

14. John Cennick's family was of Bohemian extraction. They became religious refugees from their homeland during the Thirty Years War, 1618–48. J. Taylor and Kenneth G. Hamilton, *History of the Moravian Church*, Bethlehem, Pa.: Moravian Church of America, 1967, p. 119.

15. For studies of his life and influence see Luke Tyerman, *The Life of the Rev. George Whitefield*, 2 vols, London: Hodder & Stoughton, 1877, and Harry S. Stout, *The Divine Dramatist: George Whitefield and the Rise of Modern Evangelism*, Michigan: Eerdmans, 1991. The latter emphasizes that Whitefield ensured that lengthy accounts of his activities appeared in both the London and provincial press, and that copies of his sermons were printed and distributed nationally (p. 48). Gray argues that the preaching of Whitefield took a central place in the Great Awakening. Tony Gray, 'An Anatomy of Revival', *Evangelical Quarterly* 72.3 (July 2000), 249–70, p. 250.

16. PHD, 28 August 1748.

17. Pat Hudson, *The Industrial Revolution*, London: Arnold, 1992, pp. 157–9; and D. Hay and N. Rogers, *Eighteenth-Century English Society: Shuttles and Swords*, Oxford: Oxford University Press, 1997, pp. 6–8, 10–11.

18. Geoffrey Stead, *The Moravian Settlement at Fulneck 1742–1790*, Monograph of the Thoresby Society, vol. 9 for 1998, Leeds: Thoresby Society, 1999.

19. Paul Langford, *A Polite and Commercial People: England 1727–1783*, Oxford: Oxford University Press, 1992, pp. 270–1.

20. The Established church nationally accounted for about 90 per cent of all churchgoers, and the general public associated Anglicanism with stability and continuity. David Hempton, 'Religion in British Society, 1740–90', in Jeremy Black (ed.), *British Politics and Society from Walpole to Pitt, 1742–89*, London: Macmillan, 1990, pp. 201–221, p. 202.

21. Methodism until the 1780s was largely the creation of John Wesley, who appreciated the techniques of mass communication. Langford, *Polite and Commercial People*, pp. 247–8.

22. Roy Porter, *English Society in the Eighteenth Century*, London: Penguin, 1982, 1988 reprint, pp. 187–90.

23. W. M. Jacob, *Lay People and Religion in the Early Eighteenth Century*, Cambridge: Cambridge University Press, 1996, p. 19. There is also evidence that the Church of England in the first half of the eighteenth century perhaps reached the zenith of it allegiance among the population of England and Wales.

24. Wallman J. Warner, *The Wesleyan Movement in the Industrial Revolution*, London, Longmans Green, 1930, p. 198. The rate of defection from societies was high because Methodism made exacting demands. It has been estimated that five out of six who joined did not remain permanently. See J. Cole, *Memoirs of Miss H. Ball of High-Wycomb in Buckinghamshire, with extracts from her Diary and Correspondence*, London: John Mason, 1839, p. 134. In contrast, the Brethren's much smaller congregations, which made equally exacting demands, were able to retain most of their converts.

25. Warner, *Wesleyan Movement*, p. 198.

26. His insistence on the unity of the Church meant that he would not form a separatist movement, even though he did not believe that the Anglican Church exemplified the truth of the gospel in its doctrines and practice. R. C. Monk, *John Wesley: His Puritan Heritage*, 2nd edn, London: Scarecrow Press, 1966, p. 251.

27. The name 'Labourers' applied to all ordained and lay leaders. It remained in use for ordained ministers well into the nineteenth century, and has been retained for men and women with responsibility for groups within each church who correspond to the old 'choirs'.

28. The German name for the daily 'Watchwords', mostly scriptural texts and verses from hymns, and believed to be chosen by Jesus as Elder of the Church by means of the lot.

29. The term 'Pilgrim Congregation' is used variably, to refer either to the German leaders and workers as it does here, or to the entourage which Zinzendorf took with him wherever he was in residence. Essentially it distinguishes between Germans who were part of the continental mission and their British colleagues.

30. MCH, FLCD II, p. 49.

31. PHD, 12 July 1745, 20 Oct. 1748.

32. PHD, 22 Nov. 1746, 23 Jan. 1747.

33. The information which follows, about his activities between 1736 and 1742, is from M. Riggall, 'The Diary of Richard Viney, 1744', *Proceedings of the Wesley Historical Society* 14 (1924), 13–21.

34. MCH, R. Evans and E. Cooper (compilers and eds), 'An Index of Ministers, Provincial Officials etc, serving in the British Province of the Moravian Church from 1740 to 1998'. Typescript.

35. BL, Add. MSS 44935, Diary of Richard Viney 1744.

36. Diary, 1 Jan. 1744. Despite this he had great love and respect for the Brotherhood which, in his view, had no parallel in this world.

37. PHD, 16 May 1744.

38. PHD, 27 Aug. 1744.

39. PHD, 11 Nov. 1744.

40. FLCD III, 1 Jan. 1749–31 Dec. 1749, pp. 2–3.

41. FLCD III, p. 60.

42. Podmore, *Moravian Church in England*, p. 19.

43. Podmore, *Moravian Church in England*, p. 25.

44. PHD, 8 May 1744.

45. UAH, R13 A5 119. Letter to the Archbishop of York from William Holland from Lamb's Hill (Fulneck) dated 15 Dec. 1745. 'It is with the utmost unwillingness that we at any rate call ourselves Dissenters at all from the English Church, for we love her and respect her as an episcopal Church and we willingly would be as your Lordship says in Union with her as far as possible.'

46. FA, *Jüngerhaus Diarium*, 25 June 1758.

47. FA, *Jüngerhaus Diarium*, 7 Apr. 1760.

48. John Weinlick, *The Moravian Diaspora*, Transactions of the Moravian Historical Society 17.1 (1959), p. 159. This 213-page work is an invaluable survey of society expansion and evangelism, emphasizing its great and often underestimated influence.

49. These plans are described in P. Kroyer, *The Story of Lindsey House, Chelsea*, London: Country Life, 1956, pp. 30–64.

50. Henry Rimius, *A Candid Narrative of the Rise and Progress of the Herrnhuters commonly called Moravians or Unitas Fratrum, with a short Account of their Doctrines, drawn from their own Writings*, London: Printed for A. Linde, 1753, p. 70.

51. B. S. Schlenther, *Queen of the Methodists: The Countess of Huntingdon and the Eighteenth-Century Crisis of Faith and Society*, Durham: Academic Press, 1997, p. 49.

52. Erbe, 'Herrnhaag, Tiefpunkt oder Höhepunkt', p. 50.

53. Francis Okely, *Dawnings of the Everlasting Gospel-Light, glimmering out of a Private Heart's Epistolatory Correspondence. Now made public by Francis Okely, formerly of St. John's College, Cambridge*, Northampton and London: publisher unknown, 1775. CUL 7. 77. 3.

54. Okely, *Dawnings*, p. ix. The quotations from the preface are from pp. xii and xiv respectively.

55. David C. Cranz, *The Ancient and Modern History of the Brethren*, trans. B. LaTrobe, London: W. A. Strahan, 1780, pp. 407–9.

56. Powis, *Aristocracy*. The author shows that bankruptcy was a frequent experience, because estates were often entailed, preventing their sale. They could, however, be used as security for cash loans. See also, W. R. Ward, 'Zinzendorf and Money', in *Faith and Faction*, London: Epworth Press, 1993, pp. 130–46, p. 134.

57. Powis, *Aristocracy*, p. 34.

58. Podmore, *Moravian Church in England*. This and the following information

on Zinzendorf's borrowing at this time are derived from pp. 271–2.

59. Warner, *Wesleyan Movement*, p. 248.

60. Rack, *Reasonable Enthusiast*, pp. 213, 236–7.

61. FA, MPC, 1765, MSS 336.

62. MSS 336, p. 16.

63. MSS 336, Minutes of 1765 and 1771 conferences are filed together.

64. FA, Minutes of Conference of Labourers, 1771, MSS 336, p. 3.

65. JRUL, English MSS, Box 1074, Bundle 9, p. 30.

66. FA, Minutes of Conference of Labourers, 1771, MSS 336, pp. 6 and 7.

67. Detailed summaries of the careers of most of the Labourers involved were made by John N. Libbey, and are available in JRUL, English MSS 1066, 1067 and 1068. In 1999 R. Evans and E. Cooper published 'An Index of Ministers, Provincial Officials, etc., serving in the British Province of the Moravian Church from 1740 to 1998'. Typescript copies are available from MCH (5 Muswell Hill, London N10 3TJ).

68. See Geoffrey Stead, 'The Moravian Experience on the English Mission, with reference to the Settlement at Mirfied, 1755–1800', MA dissertation, University of Leeds, School of History, 1988.

Chapter 4

1. Ward, 'Renewed Unity', p. 91, n. 3.

2. MCH, Report of Provincial Synod, 1847, Session XII, 5 July. This is the earliest precise number so far located.

3. MCH, Almanack, 1885.

4. Richard J. Helmstadter, 'The Nonconformist Conscience', in G. Parsons (ed.), *Religion in Victorian Britain*, vol. 4, Manchester: Manchester University Press, 1988, pp. 61–95, p. 77.

5. FA, MSS 54, Minutes of Elders' Conference, 14 Jan. 1792.

6. Laurence Stone, 'Literacy and Education in England, 1640–1900', *Past and Present* 42 (1969), 69–139. 'After 1780, popular education in England increased rapidly, due at first to competition between Dissenters and the Anglican establishment for control over men's minds and morals; to inculcate the people against radicalism, to suit them for industrial society' (p. 137). See also W. R. Ward, 'The Religion of the People and the Problem of Control, 1790–1830', *Studies in Church History* 8 (1972), 237–57.

7. MCH, Abstracts of Minutes of Provincial Synod, 1859, p. 11.

8. MCH, MSS, Minutes of Provincial Conference, 1824, p. 3.

9. MCH, Abstracts of Minutes of 1883 Synod, p. 26.

10. MCH, *Moravian Messenger* first issue (Jan. 1903), p. 167.

11. MCH, MS Minutes of Provincial Synod 1874, Session V.

12. MCH, Abstracts of Minutes of Provincial Synod 1883, p. 31.

13. MCH, Abstracts of Provincial Synod 1863, p. 30.

14. J. W. von Archenholz, *A Picture of England containing a Description of the Laws, Customs and Manners of England*, Dublin and London: G. G. T. and J. Robinson, 1791, pp. 101–3.

15. MCH, 1848 Synodal Report, p. 123.

16. MCH, 1848 Synodal Report, p. 123.

17. Blackbourn, *Long Nineteenth Century*, p. 286.

18. Generally estimated at about 70,000 in Unity publications. MCH, *Almanack*, 1876. German Province, list of congregations. See also, Holmes, *History*, vol. 2, pp. 353–62.

19. FA, MSS 339, MPC, 1856, p. 6.

20. FA, MSS 339, MPC, 1856, p. 10.

21. FA, MSS 357, *Diarium des Jüngerhauses*, sermon by Zinzendorf, preached at Herrnhut, 3 May 1760.

22. FA, MSS 315, Compendium of Resolutions of the 1764 General Synod at Marienborn, p. 46.

23. FA, MSS 357, *Diarium des Jüngerhauses*, sermon by Bishop Johannes von Watteville, 17 May 1760.

24. FA, MSS 338, MPC, 1824, pp. 73–4.

25. Hellmuth Erbe, *Bethlehem, Pa.: A Communistic Herrnhut Colony of the Eighteenth Century*, Stuttgart: Publications of the German Foreign Institute of Stuttgart, 1929.

26. Gillian L. Gollin, *Communal Pietism and Secular Drift*, New York: Columbia University Press, 1965, and Beverly P. Smaby, *The Transformation of Moravian Bethlehem: From Communal Pilgrims to Family Householders*, Philadelphia: University of Pennsylvania Press, 1988.

27. Smaby, *Transformation*, Preface, pp. xv and xvi.

28. Smaby, *Transformation*, p. 24.

29. Smaby, *Transformation*, Preface, p. xvi.

30. Gollin, *Communal Pietism*, p. 573.

31. Gollin, *Communal Pietism*, p. 28.

32. For the argument that such idealizations are creative, are repeatable, and serve as a model for future generations, see Mircea Eliade, *Myths, Dreams and Mysteries: The Encounter between Contemporary Faiths and Archaic Reality*, trans. P. Mairet, London: Fontana, 1977, pp. 16, 17, 23.

33. FA, MSS 337, MPC, 1795.

34. Other schools were established at Fairfield (1796), Gracehill (1798) and Ockbrook (1799). As a result, in Britain, by 1799, seven denominational boarding schools of this type, exclusively for girls, had become operational.

35. M. Marquardt, *John Wesley's Social Ethics: Praxis and Principles*, trans. J. E. Steely and W. S. Gunter, Nashville, Tenn.: Nashville University Press, 1992, p. 54.

36. W. R. Ward, *Religion and Society in England 1790–1850*, London: Batsford, 1972, p. 13.

37. J. Walvin, *The Quakers: Money and Morals*, London: John Murray, 1997, p. 151.

38. N. U. Murray, 'The Influence of the French Revolution on the Church of England and its Rivals, 1789–1802', Ph.D. thesis, Oxford University, 1975. 'For the greater glory of the established order, the religion preached by the Church of England bound the whole society together: the poor were consoled with spiritual riches to come, and in return for demonstrations of humility before God, the rich had the assurance that property was sacred, if the clergy had anything to do with it. . . . The preservation of order was a divine commandment, not a human expedient' (pp. 14 and 15).

39. Porter, *English Society*, pp. 314–15.

40. J. C. D. Clark, *English Society, 1688–1832: Ideology, Social Structure and Political Practice during the Ancien Regime*, Cambridge: Cambridge University Press, 1985, p. 377.

41. M. R. Watts, *The Dissenters*, vol. 2: *The Expansion of Evangelical Nonconformity*, Oxford: Oxford University Press, 1995, p. 536.

42. FA, MSS 337, MPC, 1795, p. 46.

43. This outburst of missionary fervour is described in principle in Bosch, *Transforming Mission*, pp. 334–9. It is also discussed at length and in detail in Latourette, *Expansion of Christianity*.

44. John Walsh, 'Methodism at the End of the Eighteenth Century', in E. Gordon Rupp and Rupert Davies (eds), *A History of the Methodist Church in Great Britain*, 4 vols, London: Epworth Press, 1965–88, vol. 1, p. 299.

45. R. Tudur Jones, *Congregationalism in England 1662–1962* London: Independent Press, 1962, p. 240.

46. Watts, *Dissenters*, vol. 2, p. 15.

47. FA, MSS 338, MPC, 1824.

48. FA, MSS 338, pp. 161–2.

49. MCH, Printed Abstracts, 1859, p. 11. Even by the middle of the nineteenth century, twelve out of the total of fifteen establishments came into this category. Of the available boarding school places, 63 per cent were in Fulneck.

50. John M. Turner, 'Methodist Religion, 1791–1849', in Rupp and Davies, *History*, vol. 2, pp. 97–112, p. 104.

51. MCH, MPC, 1847. The MSS have no defining file number.

52. John Kent, 'The Wesleyan Methodists to 1849', in Rupp and Davies, *History*, vol. 2, pp. 213–75, p. 222. One key to the history of early nineteenth-century Methodism is that both ministry and laity still found the nature of Wesleyan Methodism a problem. Wesleyan opinion was deeply divided about whether it was a new denomination or still a society which should be kept within the Anglican Church.

53. Mark Smith, *Religion in Industrial Society: Oldham and Saddleworth 1740–1865*, Oxford: Clarendon Press, 1994, pp. 273–4. See also A. D. Gilbert, *Religion and Society in Industrial England: Church, Chapel and Social Change 1740–1914*, London: Longman, 1976, pp. 51–3. He argues that, in the early industrial period, Nonconformists developed an evangelical consensus which stressed the importance of the religion of the heart. See also, Maxine Berg, *The Age of Manufactures 1700–1820*, London: Routledge, 1994. 'The age of manufactures in Britain was a complex web of improvement and decline, large and small-scale production, machine and hand processes . . . Change did not always and everywhere achieve growth' (pp. 280–2).

54. Watts, *Dissenters*, vol. 2, pp. 628–9.

55. There was a contemporary perception in European society that, 'The way of life of the worker remains simple in the countryside. If he suffers he resigns himself to God's will, because he has religion. . . . The worker in Paris covets something else beyond the work that brings in daily bread . . . [and thus] becomes dangerous to public tranquility.' Arlete Farge, 'Work-Related Diseases of Artisans in Eighteenth-Century France', in R. Forster and O. Ranum (eds), *Medicine and Society in France: Selections from the Annales, Economies, Sociétés, Civilisations*, 6, trans. E. Forster, and P. M. Ranum, Baltimore: Johns Hopkins University Press, 1980, pp. 89–103, p. 101.

56. Mark Girouard, *The English Town*, New Haven and London: Yale University Press, 1990, p. 199.

57. Kent, 'Wesleyan Methodists to 1849', in Rupp and Davies, *History*, vol. 2, p. 227.

58. Tudur Jones, *Congregationalism*, p. 240.

59. MCH. Printed Abstracts of conference proceedings have been the main source for material from this and subsequent nineteenth-century provincial conferences. These books do not have a defining file number. The 1850s conferences took place at Fulneck in 1853 and 1856, and at Bristol in 1859.

60. Fulneck Jubilee Committee, *Celebration of the Centenary Jubilee of the Congregations of the United Brethren in Wyke, Mirfield, Gomersal and Fulneck*, London: W. Mallalieu, 1855. Quotations are from pp. 35 and 53.

61. By 1851 the Methodist Church had suffered schism into nine separate segments, of which the Wesleyans, 302,209, were the largest. The next largest was the Primitive Methodists with 104,762 members; therefore the total of Methodists was very much larger than the Wesleyan figure alone would imply.

62. T. E. Jessop, 'The mid-nineteenth-century background', in Rupp and Davies, *History*, vol. 2, pp. 161–212, pp. 181–2.

63. Bound annual copies in four volumes are located in MCH and the Special Collections of the Brotherton Library, University of Leeds.

64. *Fraternal Messenger*, vol. 1, paper I, pp. 154–7, p. 155.

65. *Fraternal Messenger*, vol. 1, paper V, pp. 203–6, pp. 204 and 206.

66. *Fraternal Messenger*, vol. 2, paper XVI, 'The Diaspora', pp. 32–42, pp. 37 and 38.

67. *Fraternal Messenger*, vol. 2, paper XVII, 'The Missions', pp. 58–61, pp. 60 and 59.

68. *Fraternal Messenger*, vol. 2, paper XVIII, 'Education, the Boarding Schools', pp. 85–7.

69. *Fraternal Messenger*, vol. 2, paper XXII, 'Prospects for the Brethren's Church: Congregations, Settlements', pp. 197–201, pp. 197, 198, 199, 200.

70. *Fraternal Messenger*, vol. 2, paper XXV, pp. 282–5, pp. 282, 284.

71. *Fraternal Messenger*, vol. 1, p. 442.

72. MCH, Printed Abstract, 1856, p. 6. Subsequent decisions of the Fulneck conference are quoted from this source.

73. MCH, Printed Abstract, 1859, p. 5. Other references to this conference are from the same source.

74. MCH, *Fraternal Messenger*, vol. 4, p. 303.

75. MCH, Printed Abstract, 1863, p. 10. Subsequent references to decisions of this Synod are from the same source.

76. Helmstadter, 'Nonconformist Conscience', pp. 62 and 63.

77. MCH, Printed Abstract, 1868, p. 10. Subsequent references to this Synod are from the same source.

78. MCH, 1871 Almanack.

79. MCH, Printed Abstract, 1871, p. 28. Subsequent references to discussions during this synod are from the same source.

80. Owen Chadwick, *The Secularization of the European Mind in the Nineteenth Century*, Cambridge: Cambridge University Press, 1995, p. 94.

81. Jose Harris, *Private Lives, Public Spirit: A Social History of Britain 1870–*

1914, Oxford: Oxford University Press, 1994, pp. 170–1. Harris notes, 'Perhaps the most decisive change in the character of social thought came, however, with the great mid-century explosion of "evolutionary" ideas, an explosion of which Charles Darwin's *Origin of Species* was merely the most famous spark' (p. 225).

82. Chadwick, *Secularization of the European Mind*, p. 233.

83. MCH, 1874 Minute Book, section V.

84. This memorandum is an appended MS at the end of the 1874 MS Minute Book.

85. In 1874, as in the eighteenth century, the largest proportion of communicant members still lived in the northern triangle bounded by the Place Congregations of Fairfield, Fulneck and Ockbrook, and the dominance of this region has persisted.

86. MCH, Printed Abstracts, 1883, p. 10.

Chapter 5

1. MCH, printed Abstracts, 1888, p. 22. Further references to the 1888 Bedford Synod are from this source.

2. MCH, printed Inter-Synodal Report from PEC, 1893.

3. MCH, printed Inter-Synodal Report from PEC, 1896.

4. MCH, printed Inter-Synodal Report from PEC, 1898.

5. OCA, 'Defects of Modern Moravianism and some Proposals for Reform, 1890'. This pamphlet is attributed by J. T. and K. G. Hamilton to a concern of Maurice B. O'Connor and ministerial students with the need for the church to extend its outreach. *History of Moravian Church*, p. 385. The number of copies printed and distributed is uncertain. Another surviving copy is said to be in Church House, but this has not been verified. References and quotations are from pp. 15, 33 and 34 respectively.

6. *The Moravian Church Book*, 1891, Introduction, pp. 14–15 and pp. 180–1.

7. *Messenger*, 5 June 1897, pp. 135–8.

8. According to OCA, 'Defects of Modern Moravianism', circulation of *The Messenger* had always been small, and threatened to be smaller still. Its defects were said to be obvious and a subject of general dissatisfaction (pp. 21–2). This suggests that many church members had little interest in church affairs.

9. As the table shows, home mission stations had very few communicant members and a significant proportion of the regular congregations were small. Providing a resident minister for each one was an expensive luxury.

10. *Messenger*, 5 June 1897, pp. 135–8.

11. *Messenger*, 25 Jan. 1912. Heinrich Roy, Head of the continental theological seminary at Gnadenfeld, commented: 'In their methods of work, the British, American and German provinces have evolved along different ways; . . . in its methods of work the British Province has become more British. Each wishes to be independent, though also united . . . keeping up the spirit of the family' (p. 213).

12. Henry D. Rack, 'Wesleyan Methodism 1849–1902', in Rupp and Davies, *History*, vol. 3, pp. 119–66. 'By 1902 the pressures of half a century's developments were decisive in changing the character of Wesleyan Methodism. Its sense of a distinctive position half-way between Anglicanism and Nonconformity slowly evolved in favour of a closer alignment with the latter' (p. 119).

13. *Messenger*, 28 Nov. 1914, p. 279. This comment was made in an editorial

headed, 'The Moravian Church in Britain, a thoroughly British Church'.

14. In contrast, the continental network was thriving and continued to do so during the opening decades of the twentieth century. In 1912 it had five boys' and nine girls' boarding schools, the paedagogium at Niesky, and the theological seminary at Gnadenfeld. *Messenger*, 29 Jan. 1912, article by Heinrich Roy, p. 213.

15. Henry Cord Meyer, *Mitteleuropa in German Thought and Action, 1815–1945*, The Hague: Nijhoff, 1955, p. 9.

16. Meyer, *Mitteleuropa*, p. 9.

17. John Breuilly, 'Revolution to Unification', in Mary Fulbrook (ed.), *German History since 1800*, London: Arnold, 1997, pp. 124–41, p. 139.

18. Blackbourn, *Long Nineteenth Century*, p. 375.

19. Fritz Fischer, *Germany's Aims in the First World War*, London: Chatto & Windus, 1967, p. 3.

20. Blackbourn, *Long Nineteenth Century*, p. 374.

21. Adrian Hastings, *A History of English Christianity 1920–1990*, London: SCM Press, 1991. 'Under Bismarck's prompting her [Germany's] sheer power . . . in the spread of frontiers and colonies, her heavy industry, degree of centralization and military efficiency . . . had caught up with and then outpaced her earlier ascendancy in music, philosophy, science and theology' (p. 26).

22. Charles E. McClelland, *The German Historians and England: A Study in Nineteenth-Century Views*, Cambridge: Cambridge University Press, 1971, p. 167. The arguments which follow can be found on pp. 18, 96, 98, 63, 178–9 and 188 respectively.

23. Hartmut Pogge von Strandmann, 'Domestic Origin of Germany's Colonial Expansion under Bismarck', *Past and Present* 42 (Feb. 1969), 140–59. Germany made a sudden entry into the colonial field. Territories cited: South-west Africa, Togoland, the Cameroons, New Guinea and various Pacific islands. 'It was thought that there was internal political value in colonial expansion which would free Germans from their constant preoccupation with internal struggles and hold a great common national goal before their eyes.' Refs and quotation, pp. 140 and 147.

24. McClelland, *German Historians and England*, p. 167.

25. James Joll, 'The 1914 Debate Continues: Fritz Fischer and his Critics in the Origins of the First World War', in H. W. Koch (ed.), *The Origins of the First World War: Great Power Rivalry and German War Aims*, Basingstoke: Macmillan Education, 1984, pp. 13–29, p. 19.

26. Hans W. Gatzke, *Drive to the West: A Study of Germany's Western War Aims during the First World War*, Baltimore: Johns Hopkins University Press, 1966, p. 4.

27. Joll, 'The 1914 Debate Continues', p. 16. Joll is summarizing the main thesis of F. Fischer in *Griff nach der Weltmacht* [Grasping at World Power], Düsseldorf: Droste Verlag und Druckerei GmbH, 1961. English-language edition, *Germany's Aims in the First World War*, London: Chatto & Windus, 1967.

28. George Lichtheim, *Europe in the Twentieth Century*, New York: Weidenfeld & Nicolson, 1972, p. 9.

29. MCH, Printed Abstracts, 1888, p. 35.

30. *Messenger*, Aug. 1898, p. 195, article by A. Ward.

31. *Messenger*, Aug. 1898, p. 196. All the quotations and opinions are from this report.

32. *Messenger*, Aug. 1899, p. 202.

33. MCH, printed Inter-Synodal Report from PEC, 1901.

34. *Moravian Missions*, Jan. 1903, p. 61. Editorial comment: 'Interest in Foreign Missions is slight in several of our congregations.'

35. *Moravian Missions*, Nov. 1903, p. 172.

36. Joll, introduction to the English-language edition of Fischer, *Germany's Aims*, pp. xiii–xvi, 'The searing experience of the trenches, the mood of the belligerents – so different from that of the Second World War – and above all, the political consequences – the Russian Revolution, America's emergence as a world power, the break-up of the Hapsburg Monarchy, the establishment of the Weimar Republic – all contributed to the circumstances in which the Second World War had its origins' (p. xiii).

37. G. M. Trevelyan, *Grey of Falloden, being the life of Sir Edward Grey, afterwards Viscount Grey of Falloden*, London: Longmans Green, 1946, pp. 154–5.

38. *Messenger*, 8 Aug. 1914, pp. 242–4. 'Our Present Duty: Address at the Opening of Synod by Bishop Hasse'.

39. *Moravian Missions*, 22 Aug. 1914, pp. 263–4.

40. *Moravian Missions*, 11 July 1914, p. 211.

41. *Moravian Missions*, 25 July 1914, p. 228.

42. M. Howard, 'Europe on the Eve of the First World War', in R. J. W. Evans and H. P. von Strandmann (eds), *The Coming of the First World War*, Oxford: Clarendon Paperbacks, 1991, pp. 1–17, p. 2.

43. Keith Robbins, *History, Religion and Identity in Modern Britain*, London: Hambledon Press, 1993, p. 113.

44. *Messenger*, 28 Nov. 1914, p. 384.

45. Blackbourn, *Long Nineteenth Century*, pp. 468 and 470.

46. Cecil D. Eby, *The Road to Armageddon: The Martial Spirit in English Popular Literature 1840–1914*, Durham, N.C.: Duke University Press, 1988, p. 12.

47. Agatha Ramm, *Germany 1789–1919: A Political History*, London: Methuen, Barnes & Noble, 1967, p. 417.

48. Lichtheim, *Europe in the Twentieth Century*, p. 9.

49. *Messenger*, 11 Dec. 1915, p. 389. Article by G. W. MacLeavy.

50. *Messenger*, 10 June 1916, pp. 142–3. Letter from J. E. Pope entitled 'Future Relations with the German Moravian Church'.

51. Hastings, *History of English Christianity*, p. 46.

52. *Messenger*, 13 May 1916, p. 116.

53. *Messenger*, 22 July 1916, p.116. Article by A. H. Mumford.

54. M. Egremont, review of G. Dallas, *1918* (London: John Murray, 2000), *Financial Times*, 14–15 Oct. 2000, 'Weekend F.T', p. iv.

Chapter 6

1. *Messenger*, Feb. 1927, p. 17. Article by James Connor, in which he comments on differences between English- and German-speaking Moravianism. It was a matter of surprise to continental members that English congregations were drawn largely from the working class. The working class in Germany was commonly regarded as having no interest in religion; the socialism or communism which expressed its ideals were usually regarded as anti-religious.

2. Ward, 'Renewed Unity', p. 89.

3. Reports of this Synod are taken from accounts in *The Messenger*.

4. *Messenger*, June 1919, p. 76.

5. Robbins, *History, Religion and Identity*, p. 48.

6. *Messenger*, June 1919, p. 76.

7. *Messenger*, June 1920, pp. 51–3.

8. *Messenger*, Aug. 1921, pp. 57–9.

9. References to this Synod are from *The Messenger*, July and Aug. 1922.

10. *Messenger*, Oct. 1922, p. 87. 'Reflections', by C. S. N.

11. *Messenger*, Jan. 1925, pp. 3 and 8, article by H. Hassall, college principal, 'Something that concerns us all', and April 1925, pp. 29–30, article by A. H. M., 'A Grim Surmise'. Corroborative evidence for the Anglican Church can be found in Hastings, *History of English Christianity*, pp. 193–4.

12. *Messenger*, June 1928, pp. 63–4, article by C. H. Shawe, 'A Visit to the Continent'.

13. *Messenger*, Aug. 1930, p. 92, leading article.

14. *Messenger*, Mar. 1930, 'Ten Weeks in Germany', by G. W. MacLeavy.

15. OCD, 1919–1945, p. 103.

16. *Messenger*, Aug. 1935, p. 89.

17. References to business of the Baildon Synod are all from *The Messenger*.

18. This may have been an expression of hope rather than likelihood. OCD, 29 Sept. 1938, noted that, at the mission services, congregational support was so poor that, 'an outsider would not have realised that he was worshipping with a "missionary church" by the attendance at any of the meetings'.

19. Meyer, *Mitteleuropa*, p. 291.

20. Eric J. Hobsbawm, *Age of Extremes: The Short Twentieth Century 1914–91*, London: Abacus, 1997, p. 6.

21. Breuilly, 'The National Idea in Modern German History', in M. Fulbrook (ed.), *German History since 1800*, London: Arnold, 1997, pp. 556–84, p. 573.

22. Norman Davies, *Europe: A History*, Oxford: Oxford University Press, 1996, pp. 966–7.

23. *Messenger*, Feb. 1939, p. 18.

24. *Messenger*, Aug. 1939, pp. 85–6.

25. *Messenger*, Dec. 1939, p. 138, 'A Signalman in Training'.

26. Eric J. Hobsbawm, *The Age of Empire 1875–1914*, London: Weidenfeld & Nicolson, 1987, p. 326.

27. *Messenger*, Apr. 1940, pp. 38–9, 'As I see it', by Quaestor.

28. Joll, 'The 1914 Debate continues', p. 28. Joll notes that there was more continuity between 1914, 1940 and 1941, as far as the German High Command was concerned, than many Germans like to think.

29. Theodore S. Hamerow, *On the Road to the Wolf's Lair: German Resistance to Hitler*, Cambridge: Cambridge University Press, 1997, p. 285.

30. The reason for this is examined in detail in Trevor N. Dupuy, *A Genius for War: The German Army and Staff, 1807–1945*, London: Macdonald and Jane's, 1997, particularly pp. 303–7, where he refers to the influence of the General Staff on all German military training. They encouraged the use of initiative and imagination, and it was in this area probably more than any other that the Germans excelled in both wars.

31. The subject of German military superiority is dealt with at length in Max

Hastings, *Overlord: D-Day and the Battle for Normandy, 1944*, London: Penguin, Pan Books, 1984. He argues that, even after the Allies had been able to land vast numbers of men and equipment, they found the campaign difficult. The Germans proved superior in every field of military endeavour, except in the numbers of men and quantity of equipment which they could bring into use. In the end, the Allies overwhelmed them by vast superiority in materials and manpower. But the hard and unpalatable truth about the Normandy campaign also applied to the 1940 engagements: whenever the Allies met the Germans on anything like equal terms, the Germans always prevailed.

32. Davies, *Europe*, p. 1013.

33. *Messenger*, Jan. 1942, pp. 1 and 2, leading article, 'Preparation for Victory'.

34. Davies, *Europe*, pp. 1028 and 1030.

35. Hastings, *History of British Christianity*, p. 361. See also, Max Hastings, *Bomber Command*, London: Penguin, Pan Books, 1992, pp. 348 and 350–1.

36. Paul A. Welsby, *A History of the Church of England, 1945–1980*, Oxford: Oxford University Press, 1984, p. 7. Bell was a figure of international importance, well known for his worldwide contacts, particularly with church leaders in Germany. He had constantly pleaded for a negotiated peace, and regarded the strategic bombing of German cities, thereby deliberately attacking civilians irrespective of whether they were contributing to the war effort, as morally wrong. Bell was not alone in these views: see John Barnes, *Ahead of his Time: Bishop Barnes of Birmingham*, London: Collins, 1979, pp. 359–60.

37. Peter Alter, 'Nationalism and German Politics after 1945', in J. Breuilly (ed.), *The State of Germany: The National Idea in the Making, Unmaking and Remaking of a Modern Nation State*, London: Longman, 1992, pp. 145–76, p. 154.

38. In 1983, for example, in their preface to the new Methodist hymn book, the editors wrote, 'The Second World War . . . put an end to the idea that the 1914–18 war had been a war to end all wars, and the discovery of the concentration camps revealed a systematic and dreadful inhumanity which uncovered hitherto unimagined possibilities of evil in men and women.' *Hymns and Psalms: A Methodist and Ecumenical Hymn Book*, London: Methodist Publishing House, 1983, preface, pp. viii and ix.

39. *Messenger*, Oct. 1939, p. 121.

40. *Messenger*, Nov. 1940, p. 125. It is of interest to note that American provincial leaders were experiencing similar problems, and concluded that American congregational members did not want the church to grow. *Messenger*, Mar. 1944, pp. 17 and 18, article, 'The Little One, a Thousand'.

41. *Messenger*, Feb. 1942, pp. 15–17. See also an outstanding essay, 'The Empty Pews' by Charles Morgan, in *Reflections in a Mirror: Second Series*, London: Macmillan, 1946, pp. 141–9.

42. *Messenger*, May 1944, pp. 33–4, editorial, 'Synod 1944'.

43. *Messenger*, June 1944, p. 43, Resolutions of Synod, no. 5.

44. MPB 40 covers the period June 1940–Apr. 1946. All subsequent references to Board decisions for the wartime period are from dated entries in this book.

45. Bishop J. H. Pfohl is frequently referred to in British provincial records as 'Br Pohl'.

46. Welsby, *History of the Church of England*, p. 12.

47. Philip Longworth, *The Making of Eastern Europe*, London: Macmillan, 1994, p. 42.

48. Henry A. Turner, *The Two Germanys since 1945*, New Haven: Yale University Press, 1987, p. 10.

49. MCH Synod reports, 1947. The originals of these letters are filed with the other reports.

Chapter 7

1. This subject is handled in some detail by L. K. Stampe, 'Moravian Missions at the time of Zinzendorf: Principles and Practice,' unpublished M.Theol. thesis, Union Theological Seminary, New York, 1947, p. 99.

2. Cameron, *European Reformation*, p. 151. The importance of an educated presentation of sound doctrine is argued also by Oberman, in *Luther*, p. 57.

3. T. Grinfield, *Select Remains of the Reverend Christian Friedrich Rampftler, minister in the Church of the Moravian Brethren: with a Memoir of his Life and a Sketch of his Character and Ministry*, unclassified privately printed copy dated 1833, in Gracehill Archive, pp. 52–3.

4. FLCD XXXVII, 1 June 1860–31 May 1870, pp. 82–4.

5. 'V-n', *Fraternal Record* 1 (1858–9), 100–3.

6. MCH, Register of the Training Institution of the British Province 1860–1910.

7. J. Hurt, *Education in Evolution: Church, State, Society, and Popular Education, 1800–1870*, London: Hart Davies, 1971, p. 136.

8. Jack Simmons, *The Victorian Railway*, London: Thames & Hudson, 1991, pp. 11 and 319.

9. MCH, Printed Abstract, 1874, p. 26.

10. Edward Royle, *Modern Britain: A Social History 1750–1997*, London: Arnold, 1997, p. 383.

11. MCH, 1883 MS Minute Book, p. 88. Subsequent references to discussion during this synod are from this source, or from the Printed Abstracts, 1883.

12. MCH, 1908, Printed Inter-Synodal Report from PEC.

13. MCH, Jubilee 1910 file. This collection of MSS and printed sources includes 'An Extract from the Register of Students at the Moravian College Fairfield 1860–1910', from which the following data have been gathered.

14. *Messenger*, July 1924, pp. 51–2, article by Videns, 'As the World Goes Round'.

15. *Messenger*, Aug. 1924, pp. 68–9, article by T. H. Ellison, 'The Working of God in the Church and the Individual'.

16. *Messenger*, Sept. 1924, p. 79.

17. Hobsbawm, *Age of Empire*, ch. 3, 'Into the Economic Abyss', pp. 85–108. 'Next to war, unemployment has been the most widespread, the most corroding malady of our generation: it is the specific social disease of Western civilisation in our time' (p. 85). See also Brendan Brown, *Monetary Chaos in Europe: The End of an Era*, Beckenham: Croom Helm, 1988. Ch. 4, 'Weimar, Poincaré and the Mark's Destruction' looks in particular at the German experience and ends with a sombre reflection that it was a prelude to future political and military catastrophe.

18. Northern College selected certain books; works of Moravian interest went to Church House; some volumes in German went to the Continental Province, and the remainder were sold to a dealer. The future of the college building was under discussion.

19. For example, the *Report of the Church Service Advisory Board to Synod* in 1988 noted, 'Our students are trained in a variety of educational establishments and the Church Service Advisory Board endeavours to bring them all together for fellowship and training in things Moravian.' Of candidates for the maintained ministry, one student, having completed a BA Honours in Theology at Westminster College, Oxford, was to join a congregation for a 'Moravian year' as student/pastor. Of the three students in training for the non-maintained ministry, one was in the fourth year of study on Christian leadership at Northern College; one, after two years' full-time at Oakhill College, was to join a congregation as student/pastor whilst pursuing a 'Moravian year'; another had completed studies at Gloucester School of Ministry and was already serving a 'Moravian year'.

20. MCH, *Moravian Missions*, Feb. 1905, article by A. H. Mumford, 'An Arsenal of God, or our Mission College', pp. 29–30.

21. *Moravian Missions*, July 1913, pp. 122–3.

22. MCH, Minutes of the Sub-Committee of the College Board, Bristol, 30 Sept. 1920.

23. *Moravian Missions*, Feb. 1905, p. 30.

24. MCH, Minutes of the College Board meeting at Fairfield, 9 Mar. 1925.

25. MCH, Minutes of the Joint College Advisory Board meeting at Bristol, 24–5 Sept. 1912.

26. MCH, Minutes of Joint College Advisory Board, 22 Apr. 1913.

Chapter 8

1. *Messenger*, May 1951. Letter from Lord Calverley and others, p. 70.

2. Welsby, *History of the Church of England*, pp. 142–3.

3. This and the following information are from Patrick H. Vaughan, *Non-Stipendiary Ministry in the Church of England: A History of the Development of an Idea*, San Francisco: Mellen Research University Press, 1990.

4. Vaughan, *Non-Stipendiary Ministry*, p. 250.

5. Resolutions of Synod 1972, pp. 7–8, 'Steps to Renewal', note c.

6. Welsby, *History of the Church of England*, p. 143.

7. *Messenger*, Nov. 1991, 'The Non-Stipendiary Ministry', pp. 204–5.

8. *Messenger*, Nov. 1995, p. 214.

9. Vaughan, *Non-Stipendiary Ministry*, p. 254.

10. GA, pkt 7, item 2, *Instructions for the Members of the Unitas Fratrum who minister in the Gospel among the Heathen*, Barby: Unity Publications, 1784, p. 1.

11. FA, MSS 378, 'Memoirs of Several Ministers; Philip Heinrich Molther'.

12. FLCD IV, 1 Jan. 1750–31 Dec. 1750, p. 72.

13. FA, Congregational Diary, 1755.

14. FA, MSS 238, Single Sisters' Choir Regulations 1783.

15. GA, G2/16, Memoirs, pkt 3.

16. FA, 238, Single Sisters' Choir regulations 1738.

17. FA, 238, Single Sisters' Choir Regulations 1738.

18. Paul W. Chilcote, *John Wesley and the Women Preachers of Early Methodism*, London: Scarecrow Press, 1991, pp. 17, 48–9.

19. Library of York Minster, Census of Great Britain 1851, H. Mann, *Religious Worship in England and Wales*, abridged edition, London: Routledge, 1854, p. 26.

20. Myrtle S. Langley, 'Attitudes to Women in British Churches', in Paul Badham (ed.), *Religion, State and Society in Modern Britain*, Lewiston, New York: Lampeter Mellen, 1989, pp. 293–320.

21. The history of this institution is described below in the context of missions.

22. Langley, 'Attitudes to Women', p. 312.

23. Resolutions of Synod, June 1944, Resolution of Synod 5, p. 43.

24. *Messenger*, Mar. 1967. An article by J. Twine on the possible ordination of women referred back to the Unity Synod of 1957, pp. 62–3.

25. PB Minute Book 49, 20 Aug. 1970, pp. 150–1.

26. Programme and Agenda, Synod 1972, p. 11.

27. Resolutions of Synod, Oct. 1973, pp. 214–16.

28. Langley, 'Attitudes to Women', pp. 293–320.

29. Helen Horne, *Journey to Priesthood: An In-Depth Study of the First Women Priests in the Church of England*, Bristol: University of Bristol Press, 2000, reviewed by Tina Beattie in *The Tablet*, 14 Oct. 2000, p. 1382. These women have tended to be white, middle-class, educated and of mature years. The reviewer conveys a sense of outrage over the Church of England's treatment of women priests.

30. Grace Davie, *Religion in Britain since 1945: Believing without Belonging*, Oxford: Blackwell, 1997, p. 181.

Chapter 9

1. Royle, *Modern Britain*, p. 78.

2. Davie, *Religion in Britain*, pp. 25–7.

3. PB Minute Book 43, p. 197.

4. *Messenger*, Mar. 1957, p. 6.

5. See, for example, *Messenger* Aug. 1958, letter from P. Gubi, p. 23.

6. *Messenger*, Mar. 1961, pp. 13–14.

7. Printed Synodal Resolutions, 1961, no. 18.

8. PB Minute Book 46, 22 Sept. 1961, p. 260.

9. The stages of these negotiations are recorded in PB Minute Book 47, pp. 18, 28, 45, 49 and 60–1.

10. Printed Synodal Resolutions, 1963, no. 9.

11. Royle, *Modern Britain*, p. 78.

12. *Messenger*, June 1964, pp. 143–47. The statistical information which follows is taken from this article.

13. *Messenger*, Oct. 1964, pp. 259–60.

14. PB Minute Book 48, p. 42.

15. Davie, *Religion in Britain* pp. 25–6.

16. *Messenger*, June 1964, p. 145.

17. *Messenger*, Oct. 1966, p. 251.

18. Bruce's paper, dated c.1991, is in the possession of F. Linyard, Ockbrook. Information and notes about Kirby Spencer's ministry available from other sources are affirmed in this paper, particularly his achievement in co-ordinating the separate groups of Moravians seeking a familiar form of worship.

19. Report of PB to Synod 1978, pp. 5 and 7.

20. Davie, *Religion in Britain*, p. 63.

21. Davie, *Religion in Britain*, p. 71. Caribbean religious membership in the whole of Britain in 1990 was *c.*70,000 grouped into 965 congregations.

22. Royle, *Modern Britain*, p. 79, Table 2.1 'Population of Great Britain by Age and Ethnic Group, Spring 1996'.

23. This is now the name of the former Moravian Women's Auxiliary.

24. Statistic from Chilcote, *John Wesley and the Women Preachers*. On pp. 47 and 49, he argues that early Methodism appeared to have a particular appeal to women, a widespread contemporary view.

25. The following quotations are taken from Paper I, 'MWA – The Beginnings', Olive Linyard, Sept. 1999, for the pamphlet commemorating fifty years of the MWA in the year 2000.

26. The information which follows is based on records, notes and presidential/vice-presidential newsletters in MCH, and commemorative papers written by members. These have been collected in a pamphlet entitled *The First Fifty Years: The Story of the Moravian Women's Association, 1950–2000*.

27. Bath 1950, Resolutions of Synod, no. 8.

28. The 1997 revision sets out the present constitution of the MWA, defines its aim and organization and gives notes for the guidance of district and circle officers. Earlier versions have not been quoted.

29. Paper III, 'MWA The Circles and their Outreach', Beth Plumb, Nov. 1999.

30. PB Minute Book 45, p. 231.

31. At the 21st Anniversary Rally in 1971 this greeting was presented by Revd Ted Wilson and took the form of an ode specially written for the occasion. Paper IV, 'MWA Twenty-one Not Out', Janet Rea, Jan. 2000.

32. Paper IV, pp. 148–9.

33. Paper IV.

34. Paper V, 'MWA Forty Plus!', Janet Rea, Feb. 2000.

35. This and the following information are from Paper VI, 'MWA Retreats and Conferences', Libby Mitchell, Mar. 2000.

36. *Messenger*, May 1986, p. 90.

37. *Messenger*, Feb. 1957, p. 2.

38. *Messenger*, Sept. 1983, p. 113.

39. *Messenger*, Jan. 2000, pp. 2–3.

40. Paper VIII, 'MWA – Projects', May 2000, Jackie Morten.

41. *MWA Quarterly*, Aug. 2000.

Chapter 10

1. Geoffrey Wainwright, 'Ecumenical Movement', *OCCT*, pp. 189–91. The information which follows is taken, also, from Ans Joachim van der Bent, *Historical Dictionary of Ecumenical Christianity*, Metuchen, N.J., and London: Scarecrow Press, 1994, pp. 1–19, 155–60. For Anglican–Methodist relations see Nicholas Lossky et al., *Dictionary of the Evangelical Movement*, Geneva and London: WCC Publications, 1991, article by Geoffrey Wainwright, p. 22.

2. Martin Reardon, 'Unity', *OCCT*, pp. 732–3.

3. Wainwright, 'Ecumenical Movement', p. 191.

4. Lewis, *Ecumenical Pioneer*, Chapter 6, 'The Apostle of Unity', particularly

pp. 99–104 and p. 107. Lewis quotes freely from Zinzendorf's maxims and Fetter Lane discourses in analysing his standpoint.

5. GA, G2/12, *Diary of the Congregation of the Brethren at Plymouth and Dock for the last quarter of the year 1808; Diary of the Congregation of the Brethren at Plymouth Dock and Plymouth for the year 1809.* The diary for 1810 is also quoted.

6. GA, MIC 1/F/3/24/3, *Abstract of the Minutes of the Provincial Conference held at Fairfield from June 30th to July 16th 1847*, ch. II, 'The Doctrine and Ministry', p. 6.

7. Colin Podmore points to an increasing Anglican awareness during the 1830s of their role as part of the wider Catholic Church, fostered by the work of the Oxford Movement. *Anglican–Moravian Conversations: The Fetter Lane Common Statement, with Essays in Anglican and Moravian History by Colin Podmore*, Council for Christian Unity of the General Synod of the Church of England, Occasional Paper 5, London: Council for Christian Unity, 1996, p. 42, and 'The *Unitas Fratrum* and the Church of England', pp. 72–9, p. 79.

8. MCH, Report of the PEC to Fairfield Synod, 1914, p. 4.

9. MCH, Report of the PB to Westwood Synod, 1916, p. 4.

10. MCH, Synodal Report, Westwood Synod, 1916. Resolutions of Synod, nos. 19 and 20, the latter by Bishop Shawe, p. 41.

11. C. Podmore, 'Anglican–Moravian Dialogue since 1878', *One in Christ: A Catholic Ecumenical Review* 27.2 (1991), 150–65.

12. *Fetter Lane Common Statement*.

13. See Part Four, Chapter 13.

14. This summary of the areas covered by the *Fetter Lane Common Statement* occurs on p. 11, and the themes outlined there are covered in separate chapters.

15. *Fetter Lane Common Statement*, pp. 28–9. For the Declaration, see pp. 30–2.

16. *Priests and People* 15.1 (2001). References are to views expressed on pp. 2, 15 and 22.

Chapter 11

1. George MacDonald and Ulrich S. Leupold, 'The Hymns', in *Luther's Works*, vol. 53: *Liturgy and Hymns*, Philadelphia: Muhlenberg Press, 1965, pp. 191–309, pp. 127, 205.

2. Eamon Duffy, *The Stripping of the Altars: Traditional Religion in England, c.1400–1580*, New Haven and London: Yale University Press, 1992, pp. 217–18.

3. Friedrich Blume, 'The Period of the Reformation', trans. F. E. Peterson, in Friedrich Blume et al., *Protestant Church Music: A History*, London: Gollancz, 1975, pp. 3–123, p. 13.

4. James Robert Davidson, *A Dictionary of Protestant Church Music*, Metuchen, N.J.: Scarecrow Press, 1975, pp. 156 and 163.

5. Judith Blezzard, *Borrowings in English Church Music, 1550–1950*, London: Stainer & Bell, 1990, p. 36.

6. Blezzard, *Borrowings*, p. 98.

7. MacDonald and Leupold, 'The Hymns', pp. 201–2.

8. Walter Blankenburg, 'The Music of the Bohemian Brethren', trans. H. Heinsheimer, in Blume et al., *Protestant Church Music*, pp. 593–607, pp. 594–5.

9. Blankenburg, 'Music of the Bohemian Brethren', p. 597.

10. Blankenburg, 'Music of the Bohemian Brethren', pp. 599–600.

11. Friedrich Blume, 'The Age of Confessionalism', trans. T. Hoelty-Nickel, in Blume et al., *Protestant Church Music*, pp. 127–315, p. 258.

12. Gagliardo, *Germany under the Old Régime*, p. 211.

13. Stead, *Moravian Settlement at Fulneck*, pp. 65–6, 78, 99.

14. Blankenburg, 'Music of the Bohemian Brethren', p. 601.

15. John Julian (ed.), *A Dictionary of Hymnody*, rev. edn, London: John Murray, 1906, pp. 395–6, details Freylinghausen's influence on early eighteenth-century Pietist hymnody. For Julian, he ranks as the best of the Pietist school and the first among contemporaries.

16. The origin of the modern church trombone choir, familiar to Lutheran congregations and others, goes back to this period of Unity history.

17. William Leslie Sumner, *The Organ and its Evolution: Principles of Construction and Use*, London: Macdonald & Co., 1973, pp. 87 and 89. Snetzler (1648–1719) built at least 150 organs during his lifetime.

18. Davidson, *Dictionary*, p. 230.

19. Steven Saunders, *Cross, Sword and Lyre: Sacred Music at the Imperial Court of Ferdinand II of Habsburg, 1619–1637*, Oxford: Clarendon Press, 1995, pp. 26–7, 31, 179. Examples which follow are from p. 105 n. 44, and p. 179 respectively.

20. It was not until the 1830s that organs were allowed in Methodist churches, and it appears they were regarded with suspicion, even in the larger churches where they were introduced. N. P. Goldhawk, 'The Methodist People in the Early Victorian Age: Spirituality and Worship', in Rupp and Davies, *History*, pp. 113–42, p. 134.

21. Davidson, *Dictionary*, p. 230.

22. Alan Barnes and Martin Renshaw, *The Life and Work of John Snetzler*, Aldershot: Scolar Press, 1994. See 'The Moravians', pp. 9 and 10, and Appendix 3, 'The Fulneck Letters', pp. 284–300.

23. There is no evidence that Snetzler was a Unity member.

24. John Sharman, 'OLIM', unclassified MS in Fulneck School Archive. Further evidence occurs in Karl Kruger, 'Musical Life in the English-Moravian Settlements of Fulneck, Fairfield and Ockbrook during the Eighteenth and Nineteenth Centuries', *Unitas Fratrum* 14 (1983), pp. 95–6. 'It seems evident, from the surviving musical remains, that Fulneck, Fairfield and Ockbrook enjoyed a musical life similar in scope and variety to the Moravian communities in America and Continental Europe. Each settlement had an organ, string and wind instruments, and skilled instrumentalists to play them.'

25. Julian, *Dictionary*, p. 769. The number of English editions is derived from Henry Williams, 'The Development of the Moravian Hymnal', *Transactions of the Moravian Historical Society* 18.2 (1961–2), pp. 260–70. Lettonian was spoken by people in the Baltic region, including Lithuanians; Wendish was spoken in parts of East Saxony.

26. Blankenburg, 'Music of the Bohemian Brethren', p. 604.

27. Blankenburg, 'Music of the Bohemian Brethren', p. 604.

28. Blankenburg, 'Music of the Bohemian Brethren', p. 604.

29. G. W. MacLeavy, *Messenger*, Mar. 1930, p. 27.

30. Blezzard, *Borrowings*, p. 48.

31. It was really with Isaac Watts's recent publication of *Hymns and Spiritual*

Songs (1707) that Christian worship was liberated from the hegemony of metrical psalmody. See Hindmarsh, *John Newton*, p. 262.

32. Williams, 'Development of the Moravian Hymnal', pp. 239–65.

33. 1789 Hymnal, preface, p. iv.

34. John R. Watson, *The English Hymn: A Critical and Historical Study*, Oxford: Clarendon Press, 1997, p. 300.

35. Stephen Prickett, *Words and the Word: Language, Poetics and Biblical Inspiration*, Cambridge: Cambridge University Press, 1986, Introduction, I and II.

36. Watson, *English Hymn*, p. 303.

37. Watson, *English Hymn*, p. 304.

38. Watson, *English Hymn*, p. 326.

39. Watson, *English Hymn*, pp 320–1.

40. We have been unable to find documentary evidence to support this. *DNB* and Julian, *Dictionary*, make no mention of it.

41. MCH, Synodal Report, 1847, Session 17.

42. Watson, *English Hymn*, p. 304.

43. Watson, *English Hymn*, p. 308.

44. Watson, *English Hymn*, pp. 340 and 346.

45. Watson, *English Hymn*, pp. 413–14.

46. Watson, *English* Hymn, pp. 511–14

47. Alphonse Dupront, 'Religion and Religious Anthropology', trans. M. Thorn, in J. Le Goff and P. Nora (eds), *Constructing the Past: Essays in Historical Methodology*, Cambridge: Cambridge University Press, 1985, pp. 123–50, pp. 146–7.

48. Davidson, *Dictionary*, p. 194.

49. Paul Zeller Strodach, 'The German Litany and Latin Litany Corrected', in *Luther's Works*, vol. 53: *Liturgy and Hymns*, pp. 153–70, pp. 153 and 154.

50. *British Provincial Hymnal*, 1960 edn, p. v.

51. Davidson, *Dictionary*, p. 194.

52. 1754 Hymnal, Normal Sunday Litany, pp. 377–83; Enlarged Litany for Special Occasions, pp. 383–90.

Chapter 12

1. For the historiographical and sociological concept that any society's perception of reality is a social construct, see Peter Berger and Thomas Luckmann, *The Social Construction of Reality: A Treatise on the Sociology of Knowledge*, Harmondsworth: Doubleday, 1966. This seminal book has given rise to many subsequent studies which have explored the concept that the way a social group perceives and defines itself is as important as external events in determining the course of its development and history.

2. FLCD IV, 1749, p. 58.

3. Illuminated pictures were a popular device in eighteenth-century Britain for celebrating significant events.

4. Matthew 16.17.

5. MCH, C/1/CD/3, Congregational Diary III, 1 Jan. 1749–31 Dec. 1749.

6. UAH, Report of the Second London Synod of 1754, Recitative of Zinzendorf's Principles, no. 12, MS R13 B2 2.

7. FA, MSS 357, Diarium des Jüngerhauses, 17 May 1760.

8. FA, 210/3.

9. Moravian Hymn Book and Liturgy, 1975, no. 330; Methodist *Hymns and Psalms*, 1983, no. 273, Anglican Church Hymnary, 1927, no. 413.

10. Matthew 26.26–7; Mark 14.22–4; Luke 22.19–20.

11. During his lifetime he wrote over 2,000 hymns, the last one only four days before he died. Julian, *Dictionary*, p. 1302. The writer, James Mearns, comments that, 'if his self-restraint had been equal to his imaginative and productive powers, he would have ranked as one of the great German hymn-writers'.

12. CUL 9. 43. 5(2), *Hymns composed for the Use of the Brethren by the Right Reverend and most Illustrious CZ. Published for the Benefit of all Mankind in the Year 1749*, London: James Hutton, 1749.

13. The document is catalogued by CUL as the work of Count Zinzendorf, but this is not certain.

14. FLCD III, 1 Jan. 1749–31 Dec. 1749, p. 12.

15. FLCD III, 24 Jan. 1749.

16. FA, MSS 393, Foundation Document 1746. Ascription by R. B. Willey.

17. FA, MSS 236, Miscellaneous reports, Letters, journals &c, 1743–1747. The writer clearly signs himself 'Beok', but the anglicized version is probably 'Beck'.

18. This extract is from Okely, *Dawnings*, anonymous letter dated 1741, pp. 43–5, p. 45.

19. See also Chapter 8, the role of women in the early congregations.

20. This was probably Sr Mary, or Sr Hendringen in her absence. Since they were Germans and Sr Mary was personally familiar with the Herrnhut establishment, it would be considered appropriate to the use of diaries for Unity records and for distribution as role models, that the leaders should be represented in this way.

21. For the Diary see FA, MSS 242, and for the printed Ode and order of service see FA, pkt 241.

22. FA, pkt 241, Collection of printed sheets for the Single Sisters' Choir Anniversaries.

23. St Bernard of Clairvaux, *A Hive of Sacred Honiecombes*, translation of 1631 in D. M. Rogers (ed.), *English Recusant Literature*, vol. 194, Menston: Scolar Press, 1974, pp. 518–19.

24. Angela of Foligno, *Book of Divine Consolation*, trans. Mary G. Steegmann, New York: Cooper Square Publications, 1909, p. 8.

25. The following information and quotation are from Peter Dinzelbacher, 'The Beginnings of Mysticism experienced in Twelfth-Century England', in Marion Glasscoe (ed.), *The Medieval Mystical Tradition in England: Exeter Symposium IV*, Cambridge: Cambridge University Press, 1987, pp. 111–31, pp. 116–17.

26. Long version, *c*.1393, ch. 24, pp. 394–5. Modernized from the text quoted in Oliver Davies, 'Transformational Processes in the Work of Julian of Norwich and Mechthild of Magdeburg', in Glasscoe, *Medieval Mystical Tradition*, pp. 29–52, p. 42.

27. CUL, MS Ii. vi. 43, fos. 19–24. On the tradition of the wounds and this aspect in particular, see also Duffy, *Stripping of the Altars*, pp. 238 and 244.

28. Saunders, *Cross, Sword and Lyre*, pp. 203–4.

29. Saunders, *Cross, Sword and Lyre*, p. 204.

30. Saunders, *Cross, Sword and Lyre*, pp. 218–19.

31. Julian, *Dictionary*, pp. 1004–7.

Chapter 13

1. Cameron, *European Reformation*, pp. 257–8.

2. Daniel Murphy, *Comenius: A Critical Reassessment of his Life and Work*, Dublin: Irish Academic Press, 1995, p. 55.

3. Murphy, *Comenius*, pp. 56–8.

4. Murphy, *Comenius*, pp. 59–61.

5. J. A. Comenius, *The Labyrinth of the World and the Paradise of the Heart*, ed. and trans. Count Lützow, London: Dent, 1902, pp. 28 and 29. Lützow argues that in the second part of this book, Comenius makes a major contribution to the mystical school of thought which has been so influential in Europe, by celebrating the mystical betrothal of the pilgrim with Christ.

6. The connection described here is taken from James Van Horn Melton, *Absolutism and the Eighteenth-Century Origins of Compulsory Schooling in Prussia*, Cambridge: Cambridge University Press, 1988, p. 31.

7. Wolfgang Ratich, or Ratke (1571–1635). He was one of Comenius' forerunners in school reform. His patron was Count Ludwig of Anhalt-Köthen. He founded a school at Köthen and reorganized the schools at Augsburg, Weimar, Magdeburg and Rudolfstadt. The similarity between his methods and those subsequently advocated by Comenius are exemplified in the programme submitted by Ratke to a commission at Jena in 1629. John Amos Comenius, *The Great Didactic of John Amos Comenius, now for the First Time Englished*, ed. M. W. Keatinge, Edinburgh: A. & C. Black, 1896, pp. 455 and 136 n. 1.

8. Melton, *Absolutism*, p. 31.

9. This argument for Alsted's influence is put forward in the introduction of Comenius, *Great Didactic*, from which the information about Ratke's and Frey's influence is also taken. See particularly pp. 5–12.

10. John Amos Comenius, *A Reformation of Schooles, &c*, London: S. Hartlib, 1642, p. 46.

11. John Amos Comenius, *The School of Infancy: An essay on the Education of Youth during their first six years*, ed. Daniel Benham, London: J. Mallalieu, 1858, p. 117, fn.

12. Comenius, *School of Infancy*, p. 117, fn.

13. He was impressed by the work of Francis Bacon, particularly *Philosophical Studies*. Bacon believed that he lived in an age ordained by Providence for great advances in knowledge, because the world had been opened to navigation and commerce, and that philosophy could improve material conditions in society. See *Philosophical Studies, c.1611–1619*, ed. G. Rees, *The Oxford Francis Bacon*, 6, Oxford: Oxford University Press, 1996, p. lxv (m) and n. 125. The English educator John Brinsley had emphasized the need for a broader curriculum and the importance of play, being an advocate of colleges for teacher training. See Murphy, *Comenius*, p. 61.

14. Jean Piaget, introduction to Piaget (ed.), *John Amos Comenius, 1592–1670: Selections*, Paris: Unesco, 1957, pp. 27–8, but it must be remembered that Piaget was writing the introduction for a Unesco publication.

15. Piaget, *Comenius*, p. 12.

16. 'Eine Wesentliche Wegweisung für sein Leben hat Zinzendorf in Halle empfangen. Seine Eltern standen dem halleschen Pietismus nahe. Er selbst hätte gerne

einen Ruf als Mitarbeiter von August Hermann Francke in Halle angenommen, wenn nicht die Familie sich dagegen gestelt hätte. Später hoffte Zinzendorf aus Herrnhut ein vergleichbares Zentrum wie Halle zu machen.' ('Zinzendorf found a fundamental directive for his life in Halle. His parents were close to Hallesian Pietism in spirit. He himself would have accepted with pleasure a call from August Herrmann Francke to work with him in Halle if his parents had not been against it. Later, Zinzendorf hoped to make Herrnhut a similar centre to Halle.') German quotation from text in the Zinzendorf tricentenary exhibition in Herrnhut Museum, June 2000.

17. FA, MSS 244, Daniel Benham, *Short Sketch of the Origin and History of the Schools of the London Congregation of the Brethren, to their Removal to Fulneck*, 27 April 1853.

18. Benham, *Short Sketch*. Some information about the first schools set up in Britain is to be found in Benham's pamphlet. He does not give a date for the establishment of the Nursery.

19. Benham describes how, when she inherited the property on the death of her husband, she allowed the Brethren to establish their school there, making some expansion possible.

20. FA, MSS 244.

21. Benham, *Short Sketch*, p. 4.

22. FA, MSS 246.

23. FA, MSS 246. This may well be the man recorded as Br Meser who came to the Boys' Oeconomy from Zeist in 1759.

24. FA, MSS 245, Conferences of the Children's Oeconomy.

25. As evidenced by FA 246.

26. FA, MSS 246. Draft application form. Because of its theme and inclusion with the next item it was obviously in use at the same time, the early 1760s.

27. FA, MSS 246. Charles Delamotte's application of 22 Mar. 1763.

Chapter 14

1. David Hancock, *Citizens of the World: London Merchants and the Integration of the British Atlantic Community, 1735–1785*, Cambridge: Cambridge University Press, 1995, p. 8.

2. B. Bailyn and B. DeWolfe, *Voyagers to the West: A Passage in the Peopling of America on the Eve of the Revolution*, New York: Random House, 1988, p. 149.

3. Hay and Rogers, *Eighteenth-Century English Society*, p. 7.

4. Royle, *Modern Britain*, p. 21.

5. Braudel, *Perspective of the World*, pp. 29–31.

6. Hancock, *Citizens of the World*, p. 14.

7. E. Williams, *Capitalism and Slavery*, New York: North Carolina University Press, 1944, p. 52. Williams refers to these sugar colonies as 'the most precious colonies ever recorded in the whole annals of imperialism'.

8. During the period from 1714 to 1773, 20.5 per cent of the total value of British imports came from the West Indies. Williams, *Capitalism and Slavery*, pp. 225–6.

9. MS reports from missionaries in eighteenth-century dispatches to Herrnhut frequently refer to this mode of travel.

10. These are usually referred to as *Lebenslaufen* – Courses of Life.

11. FA, MSS 357, Diary of the Disciple's House, Week 3 (11–18 Jan.) 1755.

12. FA, MSS 357, appendix to the Weekly Accounts for the 39th week of 1776.

13. Meetings for worship.

14. FA, MSS 357, packet dated 1755, week 3.

15. Congregational Accounts 1770, Week 45. Extract of the Diary of the Brethren in Cairo from 17 Apr. to the end of July 1770. It is interesting that a diary written in July should be received in Fulneck in mid-October.

16. GA, G1/8, undated, but from their context probably *c*.1750.

17. FA, MSS 357, 'Congregational Accounts to the Unity Elders' Conference at Herrnhut, Saxony, of the Congregation in Philadelphia, from the month of August 1777 to June 1778'.

18. GA (uncatalogued), Dublin Congregation Diary, vol. I, 1749–50.

19. GA (uncatalogued), Gracehill Congregational Diary, vol. III, 1765. In 1755 the four societies of Ballymena, Dough, Gloonen and Grogan were formed into one congregation in which the principal place of meeting and administering the holy sacraments was Gloonen. This remained the headquarters of the Brethren in the North of Ireland until 1764, when land was bought between Ballymena and Gloonen in which a new settlement called Gracehill was built, and settled in 1765. Therefore the local congregational diary dates from 1755 when Gloonen was pre-eminent, the first two volumes recording events as seen from there. Subsequently, when primacy passed to Gracehill, vol. III and its successors were written there.

20. Okely, *Dawnings*, pp. 114–16, p. 115. The places mentioned in the letter were probably Northampton, London and Yorkshire.

21. Okely, *Dawnings*, pp. 116–118, p. 118.

22. J. E. Hutton, *A Short History of the Moravian Church*, London: Moravian Publication Office, 1895, p. 219, fn.

23. K. Dose, *Die Bedeutung der Schrift für Zinzendorfs Denken und Handeln*, Bonn: University of Bonn Press, 1977, p. 321.

24. A. J. Lewis, *Zinzendorf the Ecumenical Pioneer: A Study in the Moravian Contribution to Christian Mission and Unity*, London: SCM Press, 1962, p. 178.

25. The Declaration of Independence was signed on 4 July 1776. The seriousness of the coming rift with Britain and the probability of war were of great concern to members of the loyal and pacifist Unity congregations.

26. FA, MSS 357, 1776 packet.

27. FA, MSS 382, Sr Anna Kriegelstein, 1713–78.

28. *Moravian Daily Texts for the Year* 2000, American Edition, Bethlehem, Pa.: Moravian Publications, p. v.

29. Daily Texts, 2000, American.

30. Okely, *Dawnings*, pp. 46–8, pp. 46 and 48.

31. Okely, *Dawnings*, pp. 49–52, p. 52.

32. Okely, *Dawnings*, pp. 71–2.

Conclusion

1. C. Field, 'The Social Structure of English Methodism: 18th–20th Centuries', *British Journal of Sociology* 28 (1977), 199–225, p. 202. Admission to a Moravian Place Congregation was synonymous with learning or practising a craft. See Stead, *Moravian Settlement at Fulneck*, p. 91.

2. Otto Uttendörfer, *Zinzendorfs Christliches Lebensideal*, Gnadau: Unity Press, 1940, p. 142.

3. Farr, *Artisans in Europe*, pp. 4–6; also J. A. Farr, 'Cultural Analysis and Early Modern Artisans', in Geoffrey Crossick (ed.), *The Artisan and the European Town*, Brookfield, Vt.: Scolar Press, 1997, pp. 56–74, pp. 64 and 65.

4. The striking contributions of religious groups in laying the foundations of industrial society are discussed at length in W. J. Warner, *The Wesleyan Movement in the Industrial Revolution*, London: Longmans Green, 1930.

5. See, for example, Rack, *Reasonable Enthusiast*.

6. John R. Tyson, 'Lady Huntingdon and the Church of England', *Evangelical Quarterly* 72.1 (Jan. 2000), 23–34, pp. 23 and 33.

7. Boyd Stanley Schlenther, *Queen of the Methodists: The Countess of Huntingdon and the Eighteenth-Century Crisis of Faith and Society*, Durham: Academic Press, 1997, p. 184.

8. Beyreuther, *Studien*, p. 140.

9. Erich Beyreuther, *Der Junge Zinzendorf*, Marburg-an-der-Lahn: Francke, 1957, pp. 6 and 9.

10. See 'Herrnhaag', *Unitas Fratrum* 23–4 (1998), in particular 'Ruckshau', pp. 155–9.

11. For her memoir see FA, Appendices, 1777 packet.

12. Eliade, *Myths, Dreams and Mysteries*, pp. 23 and 32.

13. Even the Watchwords were formulated with this principle in mind. They were chosen at random; each one was unpredictable and unique; what had been read one day could never anticipate what was to follow on the next day.

14. This was a recurrent theme in Zinzendorf's discourses, e.g. *Sixteen Discourses on Jesus Christ our Lord. Being an Exposition of the Second Part of the Creed. Preached at Berlin by the Rt. Rev Lewis, Bishop of the antient Brethren's Churches*, anonymous translation, London: W. Bowyer, 1750, Discourse XII, pp. 69 and 132. Also, *Twenty-one Discourses or Dissertations upon the Augsburg Confession which is also the Brethren's Confession of Faith: Delivered by the Ordinary of the Brethren's Churches at Marienborn*, trans. F. Okely, London: W. Bowyer, 1753, p. 223.

Glossary

Accounts. Extracts from congregational and mission reports submitted to Herrnhut, translated where appropriate, and circulated later throughout the Unity.

Bands. Small, informal groups for discussion of personal spiritual matters.

Brethren's Church / Unity of the Brethren. Original name of what is now called the Moravian Church. Still used in the Continental Province.

Brother. Official title of a male congregational member.

Choir. Congregational subdivision according to sex, age and marital status, e.g. Single Brethren's Choir, Children's Choir.

Choir House. Communal residence for either Single Brethren or Single Sisters, occasionally for Widows.

Congregation House. Administrative centre of a Place Congregation.

Congregation Day. Once-monthly day of worship and fellowship, comprising several services.

Country Congregation. Congregation in a rural area, with its own church, manse and resident minister.

Diaspora / Diaspora Society. Scattered individuals or organized groups, not necessarily members of the church, regularly ministered to by Moravian evangelists.

Disciple. Title given to Count Zinzendorf by his followers.

Labourer. Original term for a full-time spiritual leader, man or woman, ordained or lay, in charge of the whole or part of a congregation and its associated societies, e.g. Single Sisters' Labourer.

Losung. See Watchword.

Lovefeast. Informal social gathering with refreshments.

Memoir. Written spiritual autobiography; used as testimony and obituary.

Oeconomy. General term for an institution, e.g. Children's oeconomy, a school.

Ordinary. Bishop, but in Moravian usage, Count Zinzendorf.

Pedelavium. Foot-washing. Part of the service of Holy Communion.

Pilgrim Congregation. Entourage of family members, principal colleagues and other church and domestic workers who accompanied Zinzendorf on his travels.

Pilgrim House. Zinzendorf's temporary residence when visiting an area.

Pilgrim House Diary. Record of the activities of Zinzendorf and his principal colleagues, extracts from which were circulated throughout the Unity. See Accounts.

Place Congregation. A major and exclusive residential congregation, often described by members as 'a village of Christ'.

Quarter Hour. Short devotional interlude, usually on one theme.

Settlement. A community of church members. See Place Congregation.

Singstunde. Singing Service, where the theme was explored by congregational hymn-singing from memory.

Sister. Official title of a female congregational member.

Speaking with. Confession before taking communion.

Town Congregation. Congregation in an urban area, with its own church, manse and resident minister.

Unity. Abbreviation for Brethren's Church / Moravian Church.

Watchword. Daily text chosen by lot from the Old Testament, published annually in advance. German term, Losung.

Weekly Leaves / Weeks. See Accounts.

Bibliography

Primary Sources: Manuscript

British Library

Diary of Richard Viney, 1744.

Congregational Archives

Fairfield, Manchester

Dukinfield-Fairfield Church Register: marriages, baptisms, burials 1745–1790.
Dukinfield Society Book, 1755.
Fairfield: Catalogue of the Congregation and Society, 1789.
Fairfield Congregation Diary, 1784–1792.
Fairfield: Minutes of Meetings of the Elders' Conference, 1785–1790.

Fulneck, Yorkshire

(This archive has the largest and most comprehensive collection of records.)

  Catalogues

Catalogues and notes of changes in the Single Sisters' Choir, including the Country
  Congregations, 1750–1790.
Members at Fulneck and in the other Yorkshire Congregations, 1742–1790.
Single Brethren, 1742–1772.
Single Sisters, 1752–1790.

  Diaries

Congregation Diary, 1753–1959.
Diarium des Jüngerhauses – Weekly Leaves, or German Accounts, 1757–1790.
Single Brethren's House Diary, 1753–1784.
Single Sisters' House Diary, 1755–1767.
Diary of Lamb's Inn or Broadoaks in Essex, undated, probably 1745–1746.
Pudsey Congregation Diary, 1767–1784, 1793–1811 (Pudsey united with Fulneck,
  1811).

History

J. Muller, Lists of Labourers; brief historical account of settlements in Yorkshire; document concerning laying of foundation stone at Fulneck, 1785–1786.

Account of the gathering and settling of the Moravian Congregations in Yorkshire, assumed to be an eighteenth-century manuscript.

Extract from Ranzau's Conspectus of Brethren's Congregation in Yorkshire, early nineteenth century.

History of the Brethren's Church, vol. 2 (no date).

Memoirs

Continental Brethren and Sisters, 1780–1853.
Fulneck Brethren and Sisters, 1761–1790.
Members not interred at Fulneck, 1764–1863.
Memoirs of several ministers.
Several Labourers, 1754–1849.
Yorkshire Brethren and Sisters, 1750–1784.
Yorkshire Brethren and Sisters, 1754–1787.

Minute Books: Congregational Conferences

Church Committee, 1917–1960.
College of Overseers, 1764–1829.
Congregation Council, 1764–1784.
Elders' Conference, 1750–1912.
Elders' Conference, Extracts, 1773–1774.
Helpers' Conference, 1764–1818.
Servants' Conference, 1758–1784.
Various conferences, including those with Brethren in Trade and with the Place Congregation, 1758–1764.

Minute Books: Provincial Conferences

Minutes of Synodal Committee prior to Provincial Synods, with lists of members attending the Synod and their lodgings, 1856, 1868, 1871.

Provincial Conferences of 1765 and 1771.

Provincial Conferences of the Brethren's Congregations in England, 1795, 1824, 1856.

Resolutions of General Synods before 1848

Marienborn, 1764, 1769.
Barby, 1775.
Berthelsdorf, 1782.
Herrnhut, 1789, 1801, 1818, 1825, 1836.

Sermons, Discourses

Collection of German discourses, including Zinzendorf's, 1748–1749, 1771, 1804–1815.

Discourses by Zinzendorf and Böhler, 1754 and 1756.
Packet marked 'Choir Discourses', containing discourses copied from Congregation Accounts, 1766–1790.

Gracehill, Northern Ireland

Diary Extracts: Bedford, 1808–1809.
Diary of House Congregation, Herrnhut, 1763.
Dublin: Accounts of 1746 Conference.
Dublin Congregation Diary, vol. 1, 1749–1750.
Gloonen and Ballymena Congregation Diary, vols 1 and 2, 1755–1765.
Gracehill Congregation Diary (an amalgamation of Gloonen and Ballymena), vol. 3, 1765–1766.
Plymouth and Plymouth Dock Congregation Diary, 1808–1810.
Memoirs, 1787: Sr Mary Vogelsang.
Minutes of Irish District Conferences, 1897–1926 and 1940–1949.
Mission Accounts, 1750s.
Synodal Reports of the Unitas Fratrum held at Berthelsdorf, 1782, and Herrnhut, 1825, 1836.

Ockbrook, Derbyshire

Congregation Diary, 1824–1876, 1887–1910, 1914–1938.

London, Church House Library and Archive

Fetter Lane Congregation Diary, 1742–1750, 1779, 1784–1785.
Minutes and Results of Provincial Synods before 1880.
Pilgrim House Diary, 1743–1748.

Manchester, John Rylands University Library

English MSS Collections, nos 1054–1087, History of the Moravian Church: The Revd J. N. Libbey Bequest.
A collection of notes, including transcripts from the Herrnhut archive and the archives of the British Province made by Libbey, formerly Principal of Fairfield College, Manchester.
Copies of directives from Herrnhut sent to the British Province, 1764–1805.
Index of Ministers and other Labourers of the Moravian Church in Britain, with their personal details, 1740–1790.
Historical collection described as contemporary papers by contemporary Moravians relating to concerns of the Moravian Church in Britain other than those dealt with in Benham's *Life of James Hutton*.

Unity Archive, Herrnhut, Saxony

The affairs of the English Congregations are held in Section R 13. Sources used are mostly Letters, Reports and Statutes, a selection of which appear below.

Letters

From John Wesley to Zinzendorf, dated August 1740, criticizing the arrogance of the Brethren in London.

An undated reply, probably not written by Zinzendorf.

From George Whitefield to Zinzendorf, dated 24 March 1742, criticizing the arrogant style of the Brethren.

John Gambold to James Hutton, dated 18 December 1742, about the influence of the Enlightenment at Oxford University.

Letters from Bishop August G. Spangenberg and others to Richard Viney, dated October and November 1743, condemning his insubordination.

From Benjamin Ingham to Zinzendorf, dated 15 September 1744, condemning the unscrupulous behaviour of Bishop Spangenberg before acquiring Ingham's original connexion of societies in West Yorkshire.

From William Holland to the Archbishop of York, dated 15 December 1745, opposing the idea that the Brethren were Dissenters.

From E. Clagett to Sr Anna (probably Anna Nitschmann), dated 1 October 1746, giving an account of the life and work of the Single Sisters at Lambs-Hill.

From Benjamin Ingham to Zinzendorf, dated 28 October 1747, describing a recent interview with the Archbishop of York, who said, 'he was for allowing universal Liberty of Conscience in the most ample Manner'.

Selections from various letters from Benjamin Ingham to Zinzendorf, dated 1748 and 1749, outlining his latest evangelistic outreach in West Yorkshire.

Benjamin LaTrobe to Zinzendorf, dated 28 June 1758, reporting on various English congregations.

From James Hutton to Zinzendorf, undated, about the general character of the English Brethren.

Reports and Statutes

Orders of the Fetter Lane Religious Society, 1 May 1738.

Copy of Mr Ingham's Agreement with the Brethren, dated 17 July, 1742.

Report of the Provincial Conference of the English Brethren held in London, 24 and 25 January, 1747.

Report of the Provincial Conference held in London, 13–20 May 1754.

Report of the London Synod, 10–15 November 1754.

State of the Yorkshire Congregation, written by James Hutton in 1756.

Statutes on the General Principles of Practical Christianity, derived from Zinzendorf; undated.

Primary Sources: Printed

Anon., *A Short Sketch of the Work carried out by the Ancient Protestant Episcopal Moravian Church (or Unitas Fratrum – United Brethren) in Yorkshire*, Leeds: privately printed, 1887.

Anon., *Centenary Jubilee of the Moravian Missions, August 21, 1830. Circular Address of the Bishops and Elders of the Church of the United Brethren, containing a Retrospect of the Missionary Labours of that Church during the Past Hundred Years*, trans. from German, Herrnhut: Unity Press, 1832.

Anon. (Fulneck Jubilee Committee), *Celebration of the Centenary Jubilee of the Congregations of the United Brethren in Wyke, Mirfield, Gomersal and Fulneck*, London: W. Mallalieu, 1832.

Anon., *Hymn Tunes for the Use of the Protestant Church of the United Brethren or Unitas Fratrum: A Revised and Enlarged Edition*, London: Moravian Publication Office, 1887.

Anon., *Instructions for the Members of the Unitas Fratrum who Minister in the Gospel among the Heathen*, trans. into English on Behalf of the Brethren's Society for the Furtherance of the Gospel, Barby: Unity Press, 1784.

Anon., *Journals of the United Brethren's Society for Propagating the Gospel in Ireland, 1832–1841*, printed extracts: publisher unknown.

Anon., *Sixteen Discourses on Jesus Christ our Lord, being an Exposition of the Second Part of the Creed. Preached at Berlin by the Rt. Rev. Lewis, Bishop of the Antient Brethren's Churches* (i.e. Zinzendorf), trans. from the High Dutch, London: W. Bowyer, 1750.

D. Benham, *Short Sketch of the Origin and History of the Schools of the London Congregation of the Brethren, to their Removal to Fulneck*, London: publisher unknown, 1853.

A. W. Boehm, *A Short Account of some Persons who have been instrumental in promoting the most Substantial Points of Religion in Some Parts of Germany. Whose Proceedings, some have endeavoured of late to render Odious by the newly-invented Name of Pietism*, London: SPCK, undated, c.1708.

J. W. Carey (ed.), *The Fraternal Messenger*, 4 vols, Bradford: J. Parkinson, 1850–1853.

—————— *The Fraternal Record*, 1, 1858–1859, Bradford: J. Parkinson, 1859.

St B. of Clairvaux, *A Hive of Sacred Honiecombes*, and *A Rule of the Good Life*, A. Batt (trans. of 1631), in D. M. Rogers (ed.), *English Recusant Literature*, 194, Menston: Scolar Press, 1974.

John Amos Comenius, *A Reformation of Schooles; Pansophiae Prodromus*, London: S. Hartlib, 1642.

—————— *The School of Infancy: an essay on the Education of Youth during their first six years*, ed. D. Benham, London: W. Mallalieu, 1858.

—————— *The Great Didactic of John Amos Comenius, now for the First Time Englished*, ed. M. W. Keatinge, Edinburgh: A. & C. Black, 1896.

—————— *The Labyrinth of the World and the Paradise of the Heart*, ed. and trans. Count Lützow, London: Dent, 1902.

Angela of Foligno, *Book of Divine Consolation*, trans. M. Steegmann, New York: Cooper Square Publications, 1909.

A. H. Franck(e), *Pietatis Hallensis: or an Abstract of the Marvellous Footsteps of Divine Providence, in the Building of a very large Hospital, or rather a spacious College, for Charitable, and Excellent Uses, and in the Maintaining of many Orphans and other Poor People therein at Glaucha, near Halle, etc.*, preface, Josiah Woodward, London: publisher unknown, 1707.

T. Grinfield, *Select Remains of the Reverend Christian Friedrich Ramftler, Minister of the Church of the Moravian Brethren: with a Memoir of his Life and Sketch of his Character and Ministry*, London: publisher unknown, 1833.

H. C. Hahn and H. Reichel (eds), *Zinzendorf und die Herrnhuter Brüder: Quellen zur Geschichte der Brüder-Unität von 1722 bis 1760*, Hamburg: Friedrich Wittig Verlag, 1977.

W. Law, *A Practical Treatise upon Christian Perfection*, abridged edition, London(?): publisher unknown, c.1750.
—— *A Serious Call to a Devout and Holy Life, adapted to the State and Condition of all Orders of Christians*, 6th edn, London: printed for W. Innys and J. Richardson, 1729.

F. Okely, *Dawnings of the Everlasting Gospel-Light, glimmering out of a Private Heart's Epistolatory Correspondence*, Northampton: publisher unknown, 1775.

M. Riggall, 'The Diary of Richard Viney, 1744', *Proceedings of the Wesley Historical Society* 14 (1924).

H. Rimius, *A Candid Narrative of the Rise and Progress of the Herrnhuters commonly called Moravians or Unitas Fratrum, with a short Account of their Doctrines, drawn from their own Writings*, London: printed for A. Linde, 1753.

E. de Schweinitz, *The Moravian Episcopate, reprinted from the American Edition for Private Circulation*, Bethlehem, Pa.: Moravian Publications Office, 1868.

A. G. Spangenberg, *An Exposition of Christian Doctrine as taught in the Protestant Church of the United Brethren, or, Unitas Fratrum*, trans. B. LaTrobe, London: printed by W. and H. Strahan, 1784.

N. L. von Zinzendorf, *Nine Public Lectures on Important Subjects in Religion, preached in Fetter Lane Chapel in London in 1746*, trans. G. W. Forell, Iowa: University of Iowa Press, 1973.
—— *Twenty-one Discourses or Dissertations upon the Augsburg Confession which is also the Brethren's Confession of Faith: Delivered by the Ordinary of the Brethren's Churches at Marienborn*, trans. F. Okely, London: W. Bowyer, 1753.

Printed Serial Publications

(located in the library of Moravian Church House, 5–7 Muswell Hill, London, N10 3TJ)

Almanacks:

Daily Watchwords
The Fraternal Messenger
The Fraternal Record, 1
The Messenger
The Moravian Church Book
Moravian Missions
Synodal Reports (after 1880)
Unitas Fratrum: Zeitschrift für Geschichte und Gegenwarts fragen der Brüdergemeine

Secondary Works

W. G. Addison, *The Renewed Church of the United Brethren, 1722–1930*, London: SPCK, 1932.

K. Aland, 'Philip Jacob Spener und die Anfänge des Pietismus', in *Pietismus und Neuzeit: Ein Jahrbuch zur Geschichte des neueren Protestantismus*, vol. 4: *Die Anfänge des Pietismus*, Göttingen: Göttingen University Press, 1979, pp. 155–89.

P. Alter, 'Nationalism and German Politics after 1945', in J. Breuilly (ed.), *The State of Germany: The National Idea in the Making, Unmaking and Remaking of a Modern Nation State*, London: Longman, 1992, pp. 145–76.

J. W. von Archenholz, *A Picture of England containing a Description of the Laws, Customs and Manners of England*, London and Dublin: G. G. T. and J. Robinson, 1791.

J. Arndt, *True Christianity*, trans. P. Erb, New York: Paulist Press, 1979.

G. Audisio, *The Waldensian Dissent: Persecution and Survival, c.1100–c.1570*, Cambridge: Cambridge University Press, 1999.

Francis Bacon, *Philosophical Studies, c.1611–1619*, ed. G. Rees, *The Oxford Francis Bacon*, 6, Oxford: Oxford University Press, 1996.

K. J. Bade, 'From Emigration to Immigration: The German Experience in the Nineteenth and Twentieth Centuries', *Central European History* 28.4 (1995), 507–35.

B. Bailyn and B. De Wolfe, *Voyagers to the West: A Passage in the Peopling of America on the Eve of the Revolution*, New York: Random House, 1988.

A. Barnes and M. Renshaw, *The Life and Work of John Snetzler*, Aldershot: Scolar Press, 1994.

J. Barnes, *Ahead of his Time: Bishop Barnes of Birmingham*, London: Collins, 1979.

E. Beyreuther, *Zinzendorf und die Christenheit*, Marburg an der Lahn: Francke, 1961.

—— *Studien zur Theologie Zinzendorfs*, Neukirchen-Vluyn: Neukirchener Verlag der Buchhandlung des Erziehungsvereins, 1962.

D. Benham, *Memoirs of James Hutton*, London: Hamilton, Adams & Co., 1856.

M. Berg, *The Age of Manufactures 1700–1820*, London: Routledge, 1994.

P. Berger and T. Luckmann, *The Social Construction of Reality: A Treatise on the Sociology of Knowledge*, Garden City, N.Y.: Doubleday, 1966.

I. Berlin, *The Crooked Timber of Humanity*, ed. H. Hardy, London: John Murray, 1990.

D. Blackbourn, *The Long Nineteenth Century: A History of Germany, 1780–1918*, Oxford: Oxford University Press, 1998.

W. Blankenburg, 'The Music of the Moravian Brethren', trans. H. Heinsheimer, in F. Blume et al. (eds), *Protestant Church Music: A History*, London: Gollancz, 1975, pp. 593–607.

T. C. W. Blanning (ed.), *The Eighteenth Century: Europe, 1688–1815*, Oxford: Oxford University Press, 2000.

J. Blezzard, *Borrowings in English Church Music, 1550–1950*, London: Stainer & Bell, 1990.

F. Blume et al., *Protestant Church Music: A History*, London: Gollancz, 1975.

D. J. Bosch, *Transforming Mission: Paradigm Shifts in the Theology of Mission*, New York: Orbis, 1995.

F. Bovet, *The Banished Count: The Life of N. L. Count Zinzendorf*, trans. J. Gill, London: James Nisbet, 1865.

B. Bradshaw and P. Roberts, *British Consciousness and Identity: The Making of Britain, 1533–1707*, Cambridge: Cambridge University Press, 1998.

F. Braudel, *The Perspective of the World*, vol. 3 of *Civilisation and Capitalism: Fifteenth to Eighteenth Century*, trans. S. Reynolds, London: Fontana, 1984.

J. Breuilly (ed.), *The State of Germany: The National Idea in the Making, Unmaking and Remaking of a Modern Nation State*, London: Longman, 1992.

J. Breuilly, 'Revolution to Unification', and 'The National Idea in Modern German History', in M. Fulbrook (ed.), *German History since 1800*, London: Arnold, 1997, 124–41 and 556–84 respectively.

P. Brock, *The Political and Social Doctrines of the Unity of Czech Brethren in the Fifteenth and Early Sixteenth Centuries*, The Hague: Mouton, 1957.

J. Brodrick, *The Origins of the Jesuits*, London: Longmans Green, 1940.

P. Brooks (ed.), *Christian Spirituality: Essays in Honour of Gordon Rupp*, London: SCM Press, 1975.

B. Brown, *Monetary Chaos in Europe: The End of an Era*, Beckenham: Croom Helm, 1988.

A. Carrel, *Man the Unknown*, London: Pelican, 1948.

E. Cameron, *The European Reformation*, Oxford: Clarendon Press, 1991.

O. Chadwick, *The Secularization of the European Mind in the Nineteenth Century*, Cambridge: Cambridge University Press, 1995.

P. W. Chilcote, *John Wesley and the Women Preachers of Early Methodism*, London: Scarecrow Press, 1991.

J. C. D. Clark, *English Society, 1688–1832: Ideology, Social Structure and Political Practice during the Ancien Régime*, Cambridge: Cambridge University Press, 1985.

D. F. Clarke, 'Benjamin Ingham (1712–72), with Special Reference to his Relations with the Churches, Anglican, Methodist and Glassite of his Time', M.Phil. thesis, Leeds University, 1971.

J. Cole, *Memoirs of Miss Hannah Ball of High Wycomb in Buckinghamshire, with extracts from her diary and correspondence*, London: John Mason, 1839.

P. Coleman and G. Birtill, *Anglican–Moravian Conversations: The Fetter Lane Common Statement, with Essays in Anglican and Moravian History by Colin Podmore*, Melksham: Cromwell Press, 1996.

L. Colley, *Britons: Forging the Nation 1707–1837*, New Haven: Yale University Press, 1992; London: Pimlico edn, 1994.

W. J. Couper, 'The Moravian Brethren in Scotland', *Records of the Church History Society* 35 (1935), 50–71.

D. Cranz, *The Ancient and Modern History of the Brethren*, trans. B. LaTrobe, London: W. A. Strahan, 1780.

G. Crossick (ed.), *The Artisan and the European Town*, Brookfield, Vt.: Scolar Press, 1997.

R. Currie, A. Gilbert and L. Horsley, *Churches and Churchgoers: Patterns of Church Growth in the British Isles since 1700*, Oxford: Clarendon Press, 1977.

Z. F. David, 'The Strange Fate of Czech Utraquism: The Second Century 1517–1621', *Journal of Ecclesiastical History* 46.4 (October 1995), 641–68.

J. R. Davidson, *A Dictionary of Protestant Church Music*, Metuchen, N.J.: Scarecrow Press, 1975.

C. Davie, *Religion in Britain since 1945: Believing without Belonging*, Oxford: Blackwell, 1997.

N. Davies, *Europe: A History*, Oxford: Oxford University Press, 1996.

O. Davies, 'Transformational Processes in the Work of Julian of Norwich and Mechthild of Magdeburg', in M. Glasscoe (ed.), *The Medieval Mystical Tradition in England: Exeter Symposium V*, Cambridge: Brewer, 1992, pp. 29–52.

D. E. Demaray, *The Innovations of John Newton 1725–1807: Synergism in Word and Music in Evangelicalism*, Lewiston, N.Y.: Edwin Mellen Press, 1988.

P. Dinzelbacher, 'The Beginnings of Mysticism Experienced in Twelfth-Century England', in M. Glasscoe (ed.), *The Medieval Mystical Tradition in England: Exeter Symposium IV*, Cambridge: Brewer, 1987, pp. 111–31.

C. S. Dixon (ed.), *The German Reformation*, Oxford: Clarendon Press, 1999.

K. Dose, *Die Bedeutung der Schrift für Zinzendorfs Denken und Handeln*, Bonn: University of Bonn Press, 1977.

F. Dvornik, *The Slavs in European History and Civilisation*, New Brunswick: Rutgers University Press, 1962.

E. Duffy, *The Stripping of the Altars: Traditional Religion in England, c.1400–1580*, New Haven, Conn.: Yale University Press, 1992.

A. Dupront, 'Religion and Religious Anthropology', trans. M. Thorn, in J. Le Goff and P. Nora (eds), *Constructing the Past: Essays in Historical Methodology*, Cambridge: Cambridge University Press, 1985, pp. 123–50.

T. N. Dupuy, *A Genius for War: The German Army and General Staff, 1807–1945*, London: Macdonald & Jane's, 1997.

C. D. Eby, *The Road to Armageddon: The Martial Spirit in English Popular Literature 1840–1914*, Durham, N.C.: Duke University Press, 1998.

M. Eliade, *Myths, Dreams and Mysteries: The Encounter between Contemporary Faiths and Archaic Reality*, trans. P. Mairet, London: Penguin, 1977.

T. Enger, 'Pietism', in *OCCT*, pp. 539–41.

H. Erbe, *Bethlehem, Pa.: A Communistic Herrnhut Colony of the Eighteenth Century*, Stuttgart: German Foreign Institute of Stuttgart, 1929.

H.-W. Erbe, 'Herrnhaag, Eine Religiose Kommunität im 18 Jahrhunderts', *Unitas Fratrum* 23–4 (1988), 161–4.

——— 'Herrnhaag: Tiefpunkt oder Höhepunkt der Brüdergeschichte', *Unitas Fratrum* 26 (1989), 37–50.

H. O. Evennett, *The Spirit of Counter-Reformation*, Cambridge: Cambridge University Press, 1968.

A. Farge, 'Work-Related Diseases of Artisans in Eighteenth-Century France', in R. Forster and O. Ranum (eds), *Medicine and Society in France: Selections from the Annales, Economies, Sociétés, Civilisations*, 6, trans. E. Forster, and P. M. Ranum, Baltimore and London: Johns Hopkins University Press, 1980, 89–103.

J. R. Farr, *Artisans in Europe, 1300–1914*, Cambridge: Cambridge University Press, 2000.

―――― 'Cultural Analysis and Early Modern Artisans', in G. Crossick (ed.), *The Artisan and the European Town*, Brookfield, Vt.: Scolar Press, 1997, pp. 56–74.

C. Field, 'The Social Structure of English Methodism, 18th–20th Centuries', *British Journal of Sociology* 28 (1977), 199–225.

F. Fischer, *Germany's Aims in the First World War*, London: Chatto & Windus, 1967.

J. A. Freeman, *An Ecumenical Theology of the Heart: The Theology of Count Nicholas Ludwig von Zinzendorf*, Bethlehem, Pa.: Moravian Publications, 1998.

C. R. Friedrichs, *The Early Modern City, 1450–1750*, London: Longman, 1995.

G. K. Friesen (ed.), *The German Contribution to the Building of the Americas*, Hanover, N.H.: Clark University Press, 1977.

M. Fulbrook (ed.), *German History since 1800*, London: Arnold, 1997.

J. Gagliardo, *Germany under the Old Régime 1600–1790*, London: Longman, 1991.

H. W. Gatzke, *Germany's Drive to the West: A Study of Germany's Western War Aims during the First World War*, Baltimore: Johns Hopkins University Press, 1966.

A. D. Gilbert, *Religion and Society in Industrial England: Church, Chapel and Social Change, 1740–1914*, London: Longman, 1976.

M. Girouard, *The English Town*, New Haven and London: Yale University Press, 1990.

M. Glasscoe, *The Medieval Mystical Tradition in England: Exeter Symposium IV and V*, Cambridge: Brewer, 1987, 1992.

N. P. Goldhawk, 'The Methodist People in the Early Victorian Age', in E. G. Rupp, and R. Davies (eds), *A History of the Methodist Church in Great Britain*, 4 vols, London: Epworth Press, 1965–88, pp. 113–42.

G. L. Gollin, *Communal Pietism and Secular Drift: A Comparative Study of Social Change in the Moravian Communities of Bethlehem and Herrnhut*, New York: Columbia University Press, 1965.

H. E. F. Guerke, *The Life of Augustus Herman Franke, Professor of Divinity and Founder of the Orphan-House in Halle*, trans. S. Jackson, London: R. B. Seeley and W. Burnside, 1837.

T. S. Hamerow, *On the Road to the Wolf's Lair: German Resistance to Hitler*, Cambridge: Cambridge University Press, 1997.

J. T. Hamilton and K. G. Hamilton, *History of the Moravian Church: The Renewed Unitas Fratrum 1722–1957*, Bethlehem, Pa.: Interprovincial Board of Christian Education: Moravian Church in America, 1967.

N. Hampson, *The Enlightenment: An Evaluation of its Assumptions, Attitudes and Values*, London: Penguin, 1990.

D. Hancock, *Citizens of the World: London Merchants and the Integration of the British Atlantic Community, 1735–1785*, Cambridge: Cambridge University Press, 1995.

M. L. Hansen, *The Atlantic Migration 1607–1860*, Harvard: Harvard University Press, 1945.

J. Harris, *Private Lives, Public Spirit: A Social History of Britain 1870–1914*, Oxford: Oxford University Press, 1994.

A. Hastings, *A History of English Christianity 1920–1990*, London: SCM Press, 1991.

A. Hastings with A. Mason, H. Pyper, et al. (eds), *The Oxford Companion to Christian Thought: Intellectual, Spiritual and Moral Horizons of Christianity*, Oxford: Oxford University Press, 2000.

M. Hastings, *Overlord: D-Day and the Battle for Normandy, 1944*, London: Pan, 1984.

—— *Bomber Command*, London: Pan, 1992.

D. Hay and N. Rogers, *Eighteenth-Century English Society: Shuttles and Swords*, Oxford: Oxford University Press, 1997.

R. P. Heitzenrater (ed.), *Diary of an Oxford Methodist: Benjamin Ingham, 1733–1734*, Durham, N.C.: Duke University Press, 1985.

R. J. Helmstadter, 'The Nonconformist Conscience', in G. Parsons (ed.), *Religion in Victorian Britain*, vol. 4, Manchester: Manchester University Press, 1988, pp. 61–95.

D. Hempton, 'Religion in British Society, 1740–90', in J. Black (ed.), *British Politics and Society from Walpole to Pitt, 1742–89*, London: Macmillan, 1990, pp. 201–12.

D. B. Hindmarsh, *John Newton and the English Evangelical Tradition between the Conversions of Wesley and Wilberforce*, Oxford: Clarendon Press, 1996.

E. J. Hobsbawm, *Age of Extremes: The Short Twentieth Century 1914–1991*, London: Abacus, 1997.

—— *The Age of Empire 1875–1914*, London: Weidenfeld & Nicolson, 1987.

J. Holmes, *History of the Protestant Church of the United Brethren*, 2 vols, London: privately printed for the author, 1825, 1830.

N. Hope, *German and Scandinavian Protestantism 1700–1918*, Oxford: Clarendon Press, 1995.

H. Horne, *Journey to Priesthood: An In-Depth Study of the First Women Priests in the Church of England*, Bristol: Bristol University Press, 2000.

M. Howard, 'Europe on the Eve of the First World War', in R. J. W. Evans and H. P. von Strandmann (eds), *The Coming of the First World War*, Oxford: Clarendon Press, 1991, pp. 1–17.

A. Hudson, *The Premature Reformation: Wycliffite Texts and Lollard History*, Oxford: Clarendon Press, 1988.

P. Hudson, *The Industrial Revolution*, London: Arnold, 1992.

J. Hurt, *Education in Evolution: Church, State, Society and Popular Education, 1800–1870*, London: Hart-Davis, 1971.

J. E. Hutton, *A Short History of the Moravian Church*, London: Moravian Publication Office, 1895.

—— *A History of the Moravian Church*, London: Moravian Publication Office, 1909.

W. M. Jacob, *Lay People and Religion in the Early Eighteenth Century*, Cambridge: Cambridge University Press, 1996.

T. E. Jessop, 'The Mid-Nineteenth-Century Background', in E. G. Rupp and R. Davies (eds), *A History of the Methodist Church in Great Britain*, 4 vols, London: Epworth Press, 1965–1988, vol. 2, pp. 161–212.

J. Joll, 'The 1914 Debate Continues: Fritz Fischer and his Critics', in H. W. Koch (ed.), *The Origins of the First World War: Great Power Rivalry and German War Aims*, Basingstoke: Macmillan Education, 1984, pp. 13–29.

R. T. Jones, *Congregationalism in England 1662–1962*, London: Independent Press, 1962.

J. Julian (ed.), *A Dictionary of Hymnology*, rev. edn with new supplement, London: John Murray, 1906.

C. G. Jung, *Memories, Dreams, Reflections*, trans. R. and S. Winston, London: Collins, Fount Paperbacks, 1963.

J. A. Jungmann, *Public Worship*, trans. C. Howell, London: Challoner, 1957.

Thomas à Kempis, *The Imitation of Christ*, ed. L. Sherley-Price, London: Penguin, 1987.

A. Kenny (ed.), *Wyclif in his Times*, Oxford: Clarendon Press, 1986.

J. Kent, 'The Wesleyan Methodists to 1849', in E. G. Rupp and R. Davies (eds), *A History of the Methodist Church in Great Britain*, 4 vols, London: Epworth Press, 1965–1988, vol. 2, pp. 213–75.

J. M. Keynes, *The Economic Consequences of the Peace*, London: Macmillan, 1920.

Kinkel, G. S., 'The Big Chill', *Unitas Fratrum* 27–28 (1990), 89–111.

—— *Our Dear Mother the Spirit: An Investigation of Count Zinzendorf's Theology and Praxis*, New York and London: University Press of America, 1990.

R. A. Knox, *Enthusiasm: A Chapter in the History of Religion, with Special Reference to the Seventeenth and Eighteenth Centuries*, Oxford: Oxford University Press, 1950.

H. W. Koch (ed.), *The Origins of the First World War: Great Power Rivalry and German War Aims*, Basingstoke: Macmillan Education, 1984.

P. Kroyer, *The Story of Lindsey House, Chelsea*, London: Country Life, 1956.

P. Langford, *Public Life and the Propertied Englishman, 1689–1798*, Oxford: Clarendon Press, 1991.

—— *A Polite and Commercial People: England 1727–1783*, Oxford: Oxford University Press, 1992.

M. S. Langley, 'Attitudes to Women in British Churches', in P. Badham (ed.), *Religion, State and Society in Modern Britain*, New York: Lewiston; Lampeter: Edward Mellen, 1989, pp. 293–320.

E. Langton, *History of the Moravian Church*, London: Allen & Unwin, 1956.

K. S. Latourette, *A History of the Expansion of Christianity*, vol. 3: *Three Centuries of Advance, AD 1500–1800*, London: Eyre & Spottiswoode, 1940.

A. J. Lewis, *Zinzendorf the Ecumenical Pioneer: A Study in the Moravian Contribution to Christian Mission and Unity*, London: SCM Press, 1962.

G. Lichtheim, *Europe in the Twentieth Century*, New York: Weidenfeld & Nicolson, 1972.

T. M. Lindsay, *The Church and the Ministry in the Early Centuries*, Cunningham Lectures, London: Hodder & Stoughton, 1902.

P. Longworth, *The Making of Eastern Europe*, London: Macmillan, 1994.

Martin Luther, *Luther's Works*, 55 vols, ed. J. Pelikan and H. T. Lehmann, Philadelphia: Muhlenberg Press, 1950–1965.

G. MacDonald and U. S. Leupold, 'The Hymns', in *Luther's Works*, vol. 53: *Liturgy and Hymns*, ed. U. S. Leupold, Philadelphia: Muhlenerg Press, 1955.

J. Macek, 'The Monarchy of Estates', in M. Teich (ed.), *Bohemia in History*, Cambridge: Cambridge University Press, 1998, pp. 98–116.

C. E. McClelland, *The German Historians and England: A Study in Nineteenth-Century Views*, Cambridge: Cambridge University Press, 1991.

H. Mann, *Religious Worship in England and Wales*, London: Routledge, 1854.

F. E. and F. P. Manuel, *Utopian Thought in the Western World*, Oxford: Blackwell, 1982.

M. Marquardt, *John Wesley's Social Ethics: Praxis and Principles*, trans. J. E. Steely and W. S. Gunter, Nashville, Tenn.: Nashville University Press, 1992.

A. L. Martin, *The Jesuit Mind: The Mentality of an Elite in Early Modern France*, Cornell: Cornell University Press, 1988.

J. van H. Melton, *Absolutism and the Eighteenth-Century Origins of Compulsory Schooling in Prussia*, Cambridge: Cambridge University Press, 1988.

H. C. Meyer, *Mitteleuropa in German Thought and Action, 1815–1945*, The Hague: Nijhoff, 1955.

R. C. Monk, *John Wesley: His Puritan Heritage*, 2nd edn, *Pietist and Wesleyan Studies*, 11, London: Scarecrow Press, 1999.

C. Morgan *Reflections in a Mirror*, 2nd series, London: Macmillan, 1946. `

J. T. Müller, *Zinzendorf als Erneuerer der alten Brüderkirche*, Leipzig: Friedrich Jansa, 1900.

D. Murphy, *Comenius: A Critical Reassessment of his Life and Work*, Dublin: Irish Academic Press, 1995.

N. U. Murray, 'The Influence of the French Revolution on the Church of England and its Rivals, 1789–1802', Ph.D. thesis, Oxford University, 1975.

J. D. Nelson, *Herrnhut: Friedrich Schleiermacher's Spiritual Home*, 2 vols, Chicago: Chicago University Press, 1963.

S. Nielsen, 'Die Spiritualität der Frühen Herrnhuter', *Unitas Fratrum* 27–28 (1991), 133–56.

E. R. Obbard, *'See How I Love You': Meditating on the Way of the Cross with Julian of Norwich*, Norwich: Canterbury Press, 1996.

H. A. Oberman, *Luther: Man between God and the Devil*, trans. E. Walliser-Schwarzbart, London: Fontana, 1993.

——— 'Preface' to J. Arndt, *True Christianity*, trans. P. Erb, New York: Paulist Press, 1979.

J. C. Olin, *The Catholic Reformation: Savonarola to Ignatius Loyola*, New York: Harper & Row, 1969.

R. C. Petry, *Late Medieval Mysticism*, Philadelphia: Westminster Press, 1957.

J. Piaget (ed.), *John Amos Comenius, 1592–1640, Selections*, Paris: Unesco, 1957.

C. Podmore, *The Moravian Church in England, 1728–1760*, Oxford: Oxford University Press, 1998.

——— 'Anglo-Moravian Dialogue since 1878', *One in Christ: A Catholic Ecumenical Review* 27.2 (1991), 150–65.

R. Porter, *English Society in the Eighteenth Century*, The Pelican Social History of Britain, London: Penguin, 1982; reprint 1988.

J. Powis, *Aristocracy*, Oxford: Blackwell, 1984.

S. Prickett, *Words and the Word: Language, Poetics and Biblical Inspiration*, Cambridge: Cambridge University Press, 1986.

H. D. Rack, *Reasonable Enthusiast: John Wesley and the Rise of Methodism*, London: Epworth Press, 1989.
—— 'Wesleyan Methodism 1849–1902', in E. G. Rupp and R. Davies (eds), *A History of the Methodist Church in Great Britain*, 4 vols, London: Epworth Press, 1965–88, vol. 3, pp. 119–66.
A. Ramm, *Germany 1789–1919: A Political History*, London: Methuen, 1967.
R. Rican, *The History of the Unity of Brethren*, trans. C. D. Crews, Bethlehem, Pa.: Moravian Church, Northern Province, 1992.
K. Robbins, *History, Religion and Identity in Modern Britain*, London: Hambledon Press, 1993.
E. Royle, *Modern Britain: A Social History 1750–1997*, London: Arnold, 1997.
E. G. Rupp and R. Davies (eds), *A History of the Methodist Church in Great Britain*, 4 vols, London: Epworth Press, 1965–88.

J. E. Sadler, *Comenius 1592–1670*, London: Collier-Macmillan, 1969.
S. Saunders, *Cross, Sword and Lyre: Sacred Music at the Imperial Court of Ferdinand II of Habsburg, 1619–1637*, Oxford: Clarendon Press, 1995.
D. Sayer, *The Coasts of Bohemia: A Czech History*, Princeton: Princeton University Press, 1998.
D. A. Schattschneider, 'Souls for the Lamb: A Theology for the Christian Missions according to Zinzendorf and Spangenberg', Ph.D. thesis, University of Chicago, 1975.
B. S. Schlenther, *Queen of the Methodists: The Countess of Huntingdon and the Eighteenth-Century Crisis of Faith and Society*, Durham: Academic Press, 1997.
W. Schmithals, 'Der Pietismus in theologischer und geistgeschichtlicher Sicht', in *Pietismus und Neuzeit: Ein Jahrbuch zur Geschichte des neuen Protestantismus*, vol. 4: *Die Anfänge des Pietismus*, Göttingen: Göttingen University Press, 1979, pp. 235–301.
R. W. Scribner, *The German Reformation*, London: Macmillan, 1989.
J. Simmons, *The Victorian Railway*, London: Thames & Hudson, 1991.
B. P. Smaby, *The Transformation of Moravian Bethlehem: From Communal Pilgrims to Family Householders*, Philadelphia: University of Pennsylvania Press, 1988.
M. Smith, *Religion in Industrial Society: Oldham and Saddleworth 1740–1865*, Oxford: Clarendon Press, 1994.
A. G. Spangenberg, *The Life of N. L. Count Zinzendorf*, trans. L. T. Nyberg, 2 vols, Bath: printed for T. Miles and S. Hazard, 1773.
M. Spinka, *John Hus' Concept of the Church*, Princeton: Princeton University Press, 1966.
—— *John Hus: A Biography*, Princeton: Princeton University Press, 1968.
L. K. Stampe, 'Moravian Missions at the Time of Zinzendorf: Principles and Practice', M.Theol. thesis, Union Theological Seminary, New York, 1947.
G. Stead, 'The Moravian Experience on the English Mission, with reference to the Settlement at Mirfield, 1755–1800', MA dissertation, University of Leeds, 1988.
—— *The Moravian Settlement at Fulneck 1742–1790*, Leeds: Thoresby Society, 1999.

P. Stephens, *The Waldensian Story: A Study in Faith, Intolerance and Survival*, Lewes: Book Guild, 1998.

F. E. Stoeffler, *The Rise of Evangelical Pietism*, Leiden: Numen, 1965.

────── *German Pietism during the Eighteenth Century*, Leiden: Numen, 1973.

L. Stone, 'Literacy and Education in England, 1640–1900', *Past and Present* 42 (1969), 69–139.

H. S. Stout, *The Divine Dramatist: George Whitefield and the Rise of Modern Evangelism*, Michigan: Eerdmans, 1991.

H. P. von Strandmann, 'Domestic Origin of Germany's Colonial Expansion under Bismarck', *Past and Present* 42 (1969), 140–59.

P. Z. Strodach, 'The German Litany and Latin Litany Corrected', in *Luther's Works*, vol. 53: *Liturgy and Hymns*, ed. U. S. Leupold, Philadelphia: Muhlenberg Press, 1965, pp. 153–70.

O. Subtelny, *Domination of Eastern Europe: Native Notabilities and Foreign Absolutism, 1500–1715*, Gloucester: McGill-Queens University Press, 1986.

W. L. Sumner, *The Organ and its Evolution: Principles of Construction and Use*, London: Macdonald & Co., 1973.

J. Swann, 'Politics and the State in Eighteenth-Century Europe', in T. C. W. Blanning (ed.), *The Eighteenth Century: Europe 1688–1815*, Oxford: Oxford University Press, 2000, pp. 11–51.

A. J. P. Taylor, *The Course of German History: A Survey of the Development of German History since 1815*, London: Methuen, 1968.

M. Teich (ed.), *Bohemia in History*, Cambridge: Cambridge University Press, 1998.

A. Toynbee, *An Historian's Approach to Religion. Based on the Gifford Lectures delivered in the University of Edinburgh, 1952 and 1953*, Oxford: Oxford University Press, 1956.

E. Troeltsch, *The Social Teaching of the Christian Churches*, trans. O. Wyon, 2 vols, London: Allen & Unwin, 1931.

R. Tudur Jones, *Congregationalism in England, 1662–1962*, London: Independent Press, 1962.

A. J. Turner, *The Two Germanys Since 1945*, Yale: Yale University Press, 1987.

J. M. Turner, 'Methodist Religion, 1791–1849', in E. G. Rupp and R. Davies,(eds), *History of the Methodist Church*, 4 vols, London: Epworth Press, 1965–1988, vol. 2, pp. 97–112.

L. Tyerman, *The Life of the Rev. George Whitefield*, 2 vols, London: Hodder & Stoughton, 1877.

J. R. Tyson, 'Lady Huntingdon and the Church of England', *The Evangelical Quarterly: An International Review of Bible and Theology* 72 (January 2000), pp. 23–34.

O. Uttendörfer, *Zinzendorfs Christliches Lebensideal*, Gnadau: Unity Press, 1940.

Josef Valka, 'Rudolfine Culture', in Mikulas Teich (ed.), *Bohemia in History*, Cambridge: Cambridge University Press, 1998, pp. 117–42.

P. H. Vaughan, *Non-Stipendiary Ministry in the Church of England: A History of the Development of an Idea*, San Francisco: Mellen Research University Press, 1990.

G. Wainwright, 'Ecumenical Movement', in *OCCT*, pp. 189–91.

H. O. Wakeman, *The Ascendancy of France 1598–1715*, London: Rivingtons, 1921.

A. Waldenrath, 'The Pennsylvania Germans', in G. K. Frieson (ed.), *The German Contribution to the Building of the Americas*, Hanover, N.H.: Clark University Press, 1977, pp. 47–74.

A. K. Walker, *William Law: His Life and Thought*, Church Historical Series, 94, London: SPCK, 1993.

J. Wallmann, *P. J. Spener und die Anfänge des Pietismus*, Tübingen: Tübingen University Press, 1970.

J. Walsh, 'Methodism at the End of the Eighteenth Century', in E. G. Rupp and R. Davies (eds), *A History of the Methodist Church in Great Britain*, 4 vols, London: Epworth Press, 1965–88, vol. 1.

—— 'The Cambridge Methodists', in P. Brooks (ed.), *Christian Spirituality: Essays in Honour of Gordon Rupp*, London: SCM Press, 1975, pp. 251–83.

J. Walvin, *The Quakers: Money and Morals*, London: John Murray, 1997.

W. R. Ward, *Religion and Society in England 1790–1850*, London: 1972.

—— 'Power and Piety: Origins of Religious Revival in the Early Eighteenth Century', *Bulletin of the John Rylands University Library* 63 (1981), 231–52.

—— 'The Renewed Unity of the Brethren: Ancient Church, New Sect, or Interconfessional Movement?' *Bulletin of the John Rylands University Library* 70 (1988), 77–92.

—— *The Protestant Evangelical Awakening*, Cambridge: Cambridge University Press, 1992.

—— 'Zinzendorf and Money', in *Faith and Faction*, London: Epworth Press, 1993, pp. 130–46.

—— 'The Religion of the People and the Problem of Control, 1790–1830', *Studies in Church History* 8 (1972), 237–57.

W. J. Warner, *The Wesleyan Movement in the Industrial Revolution*, London: Longmans Green, 1930.

J. R. Watson, *The English Hymn: A Critical and Historical Study*, Oxford: Clarendon Press, 1997.

M. R. Watts, *The Dissenters*, vol. 2: *The Expansion of Evangelical Nonconformity*, Oxford: Oxford University Press, 1995.

G. A. Wauer, 'The Beginnings of the Brethren's Church in England: A Chapter of the Commerce of Thought between Germany and England', Ph.D. thesis, University of Leipzig, 1901.

M. Weber, *The Protestant Ethic and the Spirit of Capitalism*, trans. T. Parsons, London: Routledge, 1994.

—— *The Sociology of Religion*, Boston: Beacon, 1993.

C. V. Wedgwood, *The Thirty Years War*, London: Jonathan Cape, 1981.

J. R. Weinlick, *The Moravian Diaspora: A Study of the Societies of the Moravian Church within the Protestant State Churches of Europe*, Columbia: Columbia University Press, 1951.

—— *The Moravian Diaspora*, Transactions of the Moravian Historical Society 17.1 (1959).

P. A. Welsby, *A History of the Church of England, 1945–1980*, Oxford: Oxford University Press, 1984.

C. Wesley and J. Wesley, *Hymns and Sacred Poems by John Wesley, M.A. & Charles Wesley, M.A.*, 5th edn, London: publisher unknown, 1756.

W. White, *A July Holiday in Saxony, Bohemia and Silesia*, London: privately printed, publisher unknown, 1858.

E. Williams, *Capitalism and Slavery*, New York: North Carolina University Press, 1944.

H. Williams, 'The Development of the Moravian Hymnal', *Transactions of the Moravian Historical Society* 18.2 (1961–2), 260–70.

U. Witt, *Bekehrung, Bildung und Biographie: Frauen in Umkreis des Halleschen Pietismus*, Halle and Tübingen: Tübingen University Press, 1996.

I. Woloch, *Eighteenth-Century Europe: Tradition and Progress, 1715–1789*, New York: Norton, 1982.

B. W. Young, *Religion and Enlightenment in Eighteenth-Century England*, Oxford: Clarendon Press, 1997.

Index

PC = Place Congregation
TC = Town Congregation